The Galilee Protocol

Christ's Method Alone!

Bill Holt

PUBLISHED BY

Advent Near Publications
123 April Ln, Hendersonville, NC 28792
www.adventnear.com

<u>Galilee Protocol Series</u>: (still under construction)
1. The Galilee Protocol –Christ's Method Alone
2. Let There Be Light –The Anatomy of a Movement (Coming Soon)
3. Almost Armageddon

<u>Galilee Protocol Core Curriculum Series</u>: (still under construction)
1. The Bible Witness
2. The History of Our Message
3. God's Eight Doctors
4. Anatomy, Physiology, and Hygiene
5. Hygienic Healthcare
6. Hydrotherapy
7. Healthful Cookery
8. Home Gardening

ISBN: 9781090893987
Amazon Edition

"Elijah's faithful soul was grieved. His indignation was aroused, and he was jealous for the glory of God... He went before God, and with his soul wrung with anguish, plead for him to save his people if it must be by judgments. He plead with God to withhold from his ungrateful people dew and rain, the treasures of heaven, that apostate Israel might look in vain to their idols of gold, wood, and stone, the sun, moon, and stars, their gods, to water the earth and enrich it, and cause it to bring forth plentifully. God told Elijah he had heard his prayer."

Ellen G. White
Review and Herald
September 16, 1873

TABLE OF CONTENTS

PREFACE

To the Trusting Ones…

"Was God punishing us?" Ellen asked this question because of the difficulty her family was having. "Did He inflict little Edson because I was holding him as an idol?"

For weeks now, disaster after disaster buffeted the White family. First, one-year-old Edson nearly died. Later, Ellen suffered from severe depression and despair that lasted for days. She thought God had left them.

After that, James got cholera. Then back to little Edson—he was sick again. This time his ailment was more like some sort of supernatural activity. He'd scream and fight the air with his fists.

"This must be Satan's work," James exclaimed. He prayed earnestly; and immediately little Edson quieted. James got cholera again.

For each disaster prayer was their best recourse. In fact, prayer proved to be the only effective remedy. Sometimes they prayed. Other times they anointed and prayed. Occasionally, results happened only when others prayed with them.

But why all this suffering and trouble? Why were they buffeted so?

The Whites were working diligently to publish a paper. This publishing effort began in June 1850 after Ellen said, "James, the Lord has shown me you must reprint the testimonies published by the leading Millerite Adventists in 1844."

"But many of them have given up their belief since the disappointment."

"That's just it." Ellen continued, "the republishing of their writings should make them ashamed for denying their faith. If the alarm had not been given by William Miller, no one would have awakened to see the true light."

"I see what you mean," agreed James. "We must continue to recognize that the *Millerite Movemen*t was directed by God!" After thinking for a few moments, he added: "Let's call the paper *The Advent Review*.

—Was God Punishing Us?

This was the paper the Whites were printing—and trying to continue to print—when the trials of sickness and discouragement pressed them down.

One day, while in vision, Ellen asked her angel about the troubles. "Was God punishing us? Did He inflict little Edson because I was holding him as an idol?"

"No Ellen. Satan did this. He wanted to sadden your hearts, and cause unbelievers to say, 'where is their God?' The purpose was to stop you and your husband from doing God's work of publishing the papers."

"Then we're to continue publishing?" she asked.

"Yes. The paper will rejoice the hearts of the trusting ones, and will help build up God's people in the faith."

The Trusting Ones, what a nice name for a scattered flock; discouraged, disappointed and struggling—yet determined to remain faithful to God.

The Advent Review was not James' first paper. He printed about a year before. In the first issue of *The Present Truth*, released in July 1849, James began with these words: "I hope this little sheet will afford you some comfort and strength. Love and duty have compelled me to send it out to you. I know you must be rooted and built up in the present truth, or you'll not be able to stand in the day of the battle of the Lord."

God directed both papers. Both papers were needed to help those who were disappointed in 1844.

—Preaching the Advent Near

Had you lived in the United States in the early 1840s you'd have heard the startling news the world was soon to come to a fiery end.

> "From the rostrum and through the printed page the awesome announcement was made that the personal second coming of Christ would take place 'about the year 1843.' A well-defined religious movement was created through this preaching of the 'advent near,' as the distinctive teaching was described.
>
> "The movement was launched by William Miller, whose name became a household term in most of America. Those who believed his views were soon known as Millerites."[1]

James White was a Millerite preacher. Feeling called to spread the news of Christ's soon return, he left his usual work as a schoolteacher to conduct preaching services. He was soon credited with over 1000 conversions.

Like so many other Millerites, he eventually fixed his hopes on a date in 1844. That year, the date of the Jewish *Day of Atonement* fell on October 22; and that night, many excited and expectant believers stayed up late. They waited until the clocks tolled midnight.

Nothing seemed to happen. Profoundly disappointed, they had to face that something was wrong. They were devastated. The great day had passed, and Jesus had not come!

> "In the days following... a tidal wave of negative emotion threatened to engulf and destroy the advent believers. Humiliation, confusion, doubt, disappointment—how could faith survive in such a maelstrom? With many of course, it did not.
>
> "Yet there were hundreds who determined to retain 'the blessed hope.'"[2]

For the faithful few the next several months and years proved to answer the bigger questions concerning the reason for their great disappointment—and the real meaning of the prophecy that came due on that date. But the faithful few still needed comfort and strength. *The trusting ones* needed something to gladden their hearts. They needed something to build them up in the faith. To this context, James White directed his papers.

The Millerite Movement was a powerful manifestation of God's Spirit. The Lord began to prepare a time-of-the-end people for His final work on earth. A fantastic development of Bible truth followed—a testing message, a warning message, and a denominated herald of righteous-

---

[1] Francis D. Nichol, *The Midnight Cry*. p. 17. (Takoma Park, Washington D.C.: *Review and Herald Publishing Association*, 1944).

[2] R. W. Schwarz, *Light Bearers to the Remnant*. Page 53. (Mountain View, California: Pacific Press Publishing Association, 1979), Prepared by the Department of Education of the General Conference of Seventh-day Adventists.

ness. All this was designed to prepare the inhabitants of this planet for the most terrible confrontation the universe will ever witness.

The forces for good and the forces for evil will eventually face off in full battle regalia. Time and providence will fully develop the issues on both sides. Two earthly armies will personify the characteristics of their respective leader. The battle will be on earth; and the battle will be for earth: and then Christ will come.

Throughout the formative years of the doctrinal, institutional, and organizational platform of the Seventh-day Adventist Church, we have ever thought that the time was near at hand. Although the understanding of the final battle has become clearer over time, we've always believed that the final movements are underway—that time is most spent.

—A Movement Grown Cold

From today's perspective, hindsight about our historical urgency becomes increasingly difficult to square. Earth is one hundred and fifty-plus years older now; and again it seems that we have to face that something has gone wrong. New generations have come, and they too are passing away. Still, Christ has not come.

The Lord led the early Adventists to believe that He was preparing their generation to make that great final stand. But they are now gone; and their precious preparation for that stand now rests with them in the grave.

We are *several* generations later. Our people are showing the fading clarity that comes from a movement grown cold; and with the passing of time, the world-context has changed beyond recognition.

Seventh-day Adventists are strangely caught up in both the then and the now. While we appreciate aspects of our Millerite roots, we also embrace many aspects of this contemporary world we now live in. It's easy to understand why. We Adventists—along with our denominated church—have found a respectable place here.

We are proud of our 28 Fundamental Beliefs for good reason. We should be enthusiastic about our unique devotion to the Bible Standard. Our doctrinal platform is solid!

The strength and quality of our institutions marvel the world. Our hospitals and the caliber of our medical personnel are very impressive indeed. Our medical institution appears strong and healthy![3]

Our schools lead the way among educational rivals. Adventist education scores an A+ when compared to every other venue![4]

ADRA, God's Closet, and our many Community Services Centers, our focused mission work, Adventist Media—all these services and programs conducted around the globe are also all at the top of the class in each of their respective fields.

We, as a church, function amazingly well in this modern setting. We are up to date. We're relevant; and according to a 2011, *USA Today* article,[5] we're the fastest growing denomination in North America. The Lord has blessed, and it shows.

But not all of us embrace this new world equally well. With some there is a gnawing—an unsettledness—that goes along with the direction the world is going... and with the way we are going with it. This restlessness stems from our deep roots; from the various movements of yesteryear.

—Nervous Agitation

Those yesteryear movements were rooted in the notion that we were situated at time's end: an investigative judgment, a close of probation, a time of trouble, and then *Parousia.*[6] So there is, deep within some Adventists, a kind of DNA subsystem that keeps all the cells agitated and alert to the dangers of being swept down the stream of time. Our genetic matter somehow knows that passing time drags us farther away from 1844 urgency; and in the murky waters—now so distant from the source—we too are losing ground and failing to hold the fort. This adds to our sense of nervous agitation.

---

[3] See Journey Films, *The ADVENTISTS 2*, a public television film about Seventh-day Adventist health work around the world. In the trailer: "Adventists also believe the body is the temple of God, something sacred to be care for. That has prompted them to build pioneering hospitals, to perform breakthrough medical procedures, and to promote a healthy lifestyle that has made them some of the longest living people on the planet, with Adventists living seven, up to ten years longer than others." The Adventist medical organization is the largest Protestant integrated network of hospitals and clinics worldwide—http://press.adventist.org/en/. Accessed 9-26-2018.

[4]See Elissa Kido, *For Real Education Reform, Take a Cue from the Adventists*, The Christian Science Monitor, November 15, 2010. An outsider discusses how Adventist schools outperform their peers. Also See Journey Films, The ADVENTIST, a public television film that profiles the second largest private education system in the word.

[5] G. Jeffrey MacDonald, *Adventists' back-to-basics faith is fastest growing U.S. church*, updated 3/17/2011, (http://usatoday30.usatoday.com/news/religion/2011-03-18-Adventists_17_ST_N.htm), Accessed 3/19/2019.

[6] *Parousia* is a Greek word meaning "presence after absence," applied in the New Testament to the Second Coming of Christ. 1 Corinthians 15:23; 1 Thessalonians 2:19; 3:13; 4:15; 5:23; 2 Thessalonians 2:1,8; James 5:7,8; 2 Peter 1:16; 3:4,12; 1 John 2:28.

The organic basis of this subsystem is our history; and integral to our historical root-system is Bible prophecy. Adventism goes far beyond a string of righteous doctrines, or a collection of impressive institutions. It's more than an assembly of fine people doing great things to improve the lives of others around them. We are a historic movement based on Bible prophecy! Our past squares with the ancient scrolls; and the seer's pen has traced our future in advance.

So why then do we feel that dull, ever-present anxiety? Why do we sometimes panic? It is because as we are watching the world charge toward Armageddon; we are seeing the church slip away from her historic identity, throw off her prophetic expectations, and become too wise for yesterday's counsels. When the world needs us the most, we are forgetting who we are.

We do a great job teaching our doctrinal system. We are marvelously evangelism minded. We support our institutions and mission fields. Most of our churches seem strong. But somehow, we do not pass along the defining sense of our Spirit-led past, and the guiding thrust of our prophetic future. Without these, we risk becoming a machine with no soul.

Ellen White emphasized the importance of our staying in touch with the movements of our past. "We have nothing to fear for the future," she warns, "except as we forget the way the Lord has led us, and His teaching, in our past history."[7]

Even as you read these pages, evidence is mounting that this old earth is in the pangs of its final moves toward Armageddon. Multitudes think it plausible that our generation, really could be the last. Has the time come to reignite the old fires? Do we need to bring the old boilers back to full steam? Are we ready to crack open the old pages of our history; and blow the dust off the faded covers of those old-fashioned red books? Let's open the sacred pages of God's precious Word, and vigorously search for light and timely instruction. This world hasn't much time left. Surely God hasn't forsaken His plan or His faithful; but the big question is, have we? What if the trumpet never gives its certain sound—only because we refuse to press it to our lips?

---

[7] Ellen G. White, *Life Sketches*. Page 196.

—History is About to Repeat

The big movements of yesteryear were like test flights. They were the trial runs of past generations trying to get off this planet and head for the better world. The stakes have always been high, but never more urgent than now. With chart and compass in hand let us aim our craft toward that small, white cloud in yonder sky! History is about to repeat itself. The midnight cry is soon to sound again.

It is to these ends I dedicate this book. Here are the goals:

- We will glean nuggets from the story of our history that clarify the nature of our mission and the prominent issues of our time.
- Jesus told His disciples He would teach them to be fishers of men. We will learn the essential characteristics of fishing His way.
- The Sabbath is intrinsically linked to the Three Angels' Messages. Its significance embraces not only worship. We will discover the Sabbath is a protocol for service, and will be a three-dimensional test.
- It is easy to paint the picture of who God is using only our favorite colors. We will see that a vital part of our work involves clearing up the mistaken identities that most of us assign to Jesus Christ.
- Prophecy tells us that a terrible storm is coming upon the church, the United States, and then the entire world. We will see how this fits into our mission and our message.
- The final presentation of truth on this decaying planet will fully polarize the last generation of people into two competing ideologies. We will probe the fundamental principles at play in this critical development.
- Our personal involvement in proclaiming the Three Angels' Messages is important to those who hear us. We will also see how it is vital to preparing our own souls for the final battle—and for the close of probation.
- We will propose a tactically spot-on approach to achieving our mission in contemporary times.

To *the trusting ones...* whoever you are, this book is for you! If you are disappointed that the Lord hasn't yet come, or discouraged because the church is less than it ought to be—this book is for you. If your DNA is in a state of nervous agitation because of how and where the world (and church) is heading, or you know little about Adventism's prophetic heritage and mission—this book is for you. Maybe you once knew more than you can now remember. If you would like a reminder, this book is for you.

I pray it will rejoice your hearts and build you up in the faith. I am no James White, but I too, can sincerely say I hope this book will afford you comfort and strength. Love and duty have compelled me to write it for you. I know you must be rooted and built up in the present truth, or you'll not be able to stand in the day of the battle of the Lord.

—Bill Holt, author

PART ONE

PERSPECTIVE

CHAPTER ONE

A Tale of Three Mountains

The year?—about 870 B.C. Ahab is king; and there is a terrible drought! The ground is cracked—the clay is baked as in a furnace. The sun's scorching rays have destroyed the vegetation. The streams are dry. Lowing herds and bleating flocks wander in distress.

Prosperous cities are places of mourning. Hunger and thirst tell upon man and beast, with fearful mortality. The horrors of famine come closer and closer. It's been a year now with no rain.

Time passes—two years. Drought and famine devastate the nation! Parents, powerless to stop their children's suffering, watch them die.

Another year and a half will pass before this drought ends. Heaven is curiously determined to make its point—as God withholds the rain these three and a half years: "*for the apostasy of Israel is more dreadful than the multiplied horrors of famine.*"[1]

So what has Israel done to deserve all this? Or what should she have done to prevent it?

---

[1] Ellen G. White, *Prophets and Kings*, p. 127.

—A Light on a Hill

Consider this from an old Adventist periodical:

> "In the days of Solomon, the kingdom of Israel extended from Hamath on the northward, to the border of Egypt on the southward, and from the Mediterranean Sea to the Euphrates River. Through this territory ran many natural highways of the world's commerce. Caravans were constantly passing to and from distant lands. Thus there was given Solomon and his people a most wonderful opportunity to reveal the character of the true God so clearly that men of all nations would be taught to reverence and obey the King of kings..."[2]

Prophets and Kings, enlarges the thought:

> "All who... turned from idolatry to the worship of the true God were to unite themselves with His chosen people. As the numbers of Israel increased, they were to enlarge their borders until their kingdom should embrace the world."[3]

Earth's only hope is for there to be a light somewhere—set high upon a hill. Zion should have been that hill; and on Zion: a city of light; and in that city: the temple of God; and in that temple: the place of God's throne. Jesus said, "I, if I be lifted up from the earth, will draw all me unto Me."[4] Israel was supposed to present Christ to the world. Lifting Christ was to be their mission, the *Galilee Protocol* was to their method, and enlarging their borders to embrace the world was to be the result.

So the psalmist sang:

> "Great is the Lord, and greatly to be praised in the city of our God, in the *mountain of His holiness*. Beautiful for situation, the joy of the whole earth, is mount Zion, on the sides of the north, the city of the great King."[5]

Can you see it?—Mount Zion was to be a holy people. Jerusalem, a bride adorned for her Husband. The temple, God's own building: with Christ being the chief cornerstone. Israel, as lively stones, was to build up a spiritual house on the foundation of Christ—a chosen generation; a royal priesthood; a holy nation; a peculiar people; showing forth the praises of Him who *called them out* of this dark world into His marvelous light![6] God's glory should have filled them; and they should have been the light of the nations.

---

[2] Ellen G. White, *The Review and Herald*, January 25, 1906.
[3] Ellen G. White, *Prophets and Kings*, p. 19.
[4] John 12:32.
[5] Psalms 48:1-2. Emphasis added.
[6] Revelation 21:2; 1 Peter 2:5-9.

> "This is the word of the Lord unto Zerubbabel, saying, not by might, nor by power, but by My Spirit, sayeth the Lord of hosts."[7]

The candlestick lamps in the temple represent God's people. From two olive trees (the old and new testament), the Holy Spirit oil flows into the candlestick—fueling the lamps and bringing the light of heaven into a dark world.

> "Who art thou, *O great mountain*? Before Zerubbabel thou shalt become a plain: and he shall bring forth the Headstone thereof with shouting, crying, Grace, grace unto it."[8]

—The Glory of God

For a better understanding of Israel's assignment, let's go back to heaven before sin. God has yet to create the earth. Perfect harmony extends throughout the universe. Fulfilling the Creator's purposes is everyone's greatest joy. They reflect His glory and sing His praises. The universe is pristine—loving God is supreme; and love for one another is confiding and unselfish.

Now let's reverently, carefully go to the heavenly throne room. God's glory manifested in this place, displays the *fullness* of His identity—impossible even for perfect beings to look at!

It is infinite energy on three scales. Its *physical* energy is pure infinite power: unlimited brightness—the force of His omnipotence. Its *intellectual* energy is pure infinite knowledge: the all-knowingness of His omniscience. Its *spiritual* energy is pure infinite goodness: the unswerving justice and mercy of God's righteousness.

God's glory is on display to the universe. It dwells here—the *standard of Deity* at full scale—infinite power, infinite knowledge, infinite righteousness. This standard *is* God—living, personal, a physical being—presented without attenuation.

> "Holy, holy, holy! Lord God Almighty, All Thy works shall praise Thy name in earth and sky and sea!"[9]

The universe depends on this three-fold energy for existence, but also for security. Individuality, diversity, liberty: these things require an arrangement for order and harmony.

---

[7] Zechariah 4:6.

[8] Zechariah 4:7. Emphasis added.

[9] Reginald Herber, *Holy, Holy, Holy*. 1826. As found in *The Seventh-day Adventist Hymnal*, (Hagerstown, Maryland: Review and Herald Publishing Association, 1985).

Every municipality recognizes the hazards of unmanaged traffic. So it is with the government of God. There's order and rank, laws and consequences. These are based in love, and essential for maintaining joy and peace within the community.

It is this *community* that needs God's infinite energy to be on display—even though finite beings can't absorb, measure, or even behold it. Still it imposes a quality of *physical*, *intellectual*, and *spiritual* authority they cannot ignore or debate. The perpetual manifestation of God's identity secures the liberty, individuality, and community of all His creatures.

—Inclusivity and Exclusivity

Two special figures stand before the throne. Michael the archangel stands on God's right hand; Lucifer, also a covering cherub, stands on his left. They occupy positions of authority above all the created hosts of heaven. They stand *between* God's infinite glory and everyone who enters there.

They stand facing each other, their heads bowed. With wings, they form a place of gentle shade from the brightness of the glory of the Almighty. With other wings they reverently cover their own faces. The glory of God is too much for even angels to behold.

> "Holy, holy, holy! Angels adore Thee, casting down their bright crowns around the glassy sea; Thousands and ten thousands worship low before Thee, Which wert, and art, and ever more shalt be."[10]

The Almighty shows His *exclusivity* in this arrangement. The magnitude of divine glory presents a barrier between Creator and created. No creature *can* cross it—the finite is no match for the Infinite.

> "Holy, holy, holy! Though darkness hide Thee, though the eye of man Thy great glory may not see; Only Thou art holy; there is none beside Thee, Perfect in power, in love, and purity."[11]

The arrangement of His throne also shows God's *inclusivity*. Notice the condescension: God put on a form that suits community comfort. Taking the form and work of angels, Michael—still fully God—freely mingles with the heavenly host. Even before sin, He veiled the brightness of His divinity. It's the *God with us* principle.[12] It's the *I want to dwell among them*, principle.[13]

---

[10] Ibid.

[11] Ibid.

[12] Matthew 1:23.

[13] Exodus 25:8.

Besides all that, God elevates Lucifer to a position close to Himself. An old issue of *The Review and Herold* says that before Lucifer's fall, "God made him good and beautiful, *as near as possible like Himself*."[14] This enabled him to better reflect God's glory. Ezekiel 28 tells us that *physically* he was "perfect in beauty;" *mentally* he was "full of wisdom," and *spiritually* he produced perfect music.[15]

Continuing in Ezekiel 28:

> "You are the anointed covering cherub; I made you so; you were on the holy mountain of God; and walked up and down among the *stones of fire*. You were perfect in your ways from the day you were created, till iniquity was found in you. By the multitude of your *merchandise* they have filled you up with violence, and you have sinned: So I will throw you out of *the mountain of God*: and I will destroy you, O covering cherub, from among the stones of fire. Your heart was lifted up because of your beauty, you have corrupted your wisdom because of your brightness... You have defiled your sanctuaries by your many sins, and by the sin of your *trafficking*."[16]

Stones of fire represent God's law, the foundation of this throne.

Lucifer is corrupted by ascribing to himself glory that is God's. He thinks the *physical*, *intellectual*, and *spiritual* energy he reflects (because of always standing in the rays of divine glory), is his own.

Notice how Lucifer seeks to *merchandise* that glory—he tries to traffic divinity. He gave his pitch to Eve when he said the *fruit of knowledge* would make her like God.[17] He claimed a tree could give *physical* power; and "she saw that it was good for food." He claimed it could give *spirituality*; and she saw "it was pleasant to the eyes."[18] He claimed it could provide *intelligence*; and she saw "a tree to be desired to make one wise".

And did you notice the *holy mountain of God*? God put Lucifer there until He found sin in him. This is mountain number *one* in a tale of three mountains. It's the mount of the congregation; and the north side is the place of God's throne. Lucifer wanted God's throne:

> "For you have said in your heart, I will ascend into heaven, I will exalt my throne above the stars of God: I will sit also upon the mount of the congregation, in the sides of the north: I will ascend above the heights of the clouds; I will be like the Most High."[19]

---

[14] Ellen G. White, *The Review and Herald*, September 24, 1901.

[15] Ezekiel 28:15, 17.

[16] Ezekiel 28:14-18. Emphasis added.

[17] See Genesis 3:1-6.

[18] Eyes symbolize spiritual vision. Matthew 6:22; 13:16; Mark 8:17, 18; Psalms 119:18; Ephesians 1:18; 2 Corinthians 4:4.

[19] Isaiah 14:13-14.

—An Infinite Glory Barrier

Lucifer wanted glory that belonged to God's Son; and he aspired to power that was the prerogative of Christ alone. So the King of the Universe summoned everyone before Him. In their presence, He would clarify the true position of His Son Michael. "The Son shared the Father's throne and the glory of the eternal, self-existent One, encircled them both."[20]

The King declared only Christ, *could* fully enter His purposes (remember there's an *infinite glory* barrier); and Christ executed the mighty counsels of the divine will. The Son created the angelic host; and homage and allegiance belong to Him too.

The vast, unnumbered throng "ten thousand times ten thousand, and thousands of thousands"—the most exalted angels, as ministers and subjects—rejoiced in this light. They joyfully acknowledged the supremacy of Christ. They bowed before Him, pouring out love and adoration.

Lucifer bowed too; but there was a strange, fierce conflict. Truth, justice, and loyalty were struggling against envy and jealousy. Christ made such efforts as only infinite love and wisdom could devise[21]—to win Lucifer back, and to show him his error. He proved his disaffection to be without cause; and Lucifer saw what his rebellion would cause.

He was convinced he was wrong. He saw the Lord is righteous—the divine statutes are just; and he ought to say so before all heaven. If willing to return, God would have reinstated his office. He nearly retuned; but pride forbade him. He felt it too great a sacrifice to confess his wrong.

Lucifer earlier left his place to diffuse discontent among the angels. With mysterious secrecy, he insinuated doubts about the laws that governed them. He suggested exalted angels need no restraint—their own wisdom sufficed to guide them: their thoughts were holy. He told them it was as impossible for them to err, even as it was impossible for God to err. He claimed that if he were so exalted, great good would come to the entire host of heaven: for he planned to secure freedom for all.[22] And so this prince of angels *merchandised* the glory and position of God.[23]

---

[20] Ellen G. White, *Patriarchs and Prophets*, p. 36.

[21] Ibid., p. 39.

[22] Ibid. p. 37.

[23] See *Appendix A – The Infinite Glory Barrier!* for an in-depth treatment of the *exclusivity* of divinity relating to the eternal divinity of Christ, the divine personhood of the Holy Spirit, and the role of pantheism in the final conflict.

—Tyre and Sidon

We know this *Ezekiel-prophecy* describes Lucifer—even though the prophet never mentions him by name. He actually names the king of Tyre;[24] and is addressing the nations of Tyre and Sidon. History helps us appreciate the *Tyre-Sidon connection.*

When the children of Israel camped at Sinai, God asked them to build a sanctuary. The portable structure would copy the heavenly throne room we've been talking about. Representing God's throne, the pure-gold mercy-seat would occupy the *most holy place*. The golden covering cherubs would stand on either side; and beneath would be two tables of stone—the stones of fire—God's holy law. The glory of God would dwell between the cherubim above the mercy-seat.

This would be a costly project for Israel. Moses asked the people to give offerings for the material; and God endowed chosen men from Judah and Dan with special skill and wisdom for the meticulous workmanship. Aholiab was one of these men. These gifted workmen passed their talent to their descendants. In time, these wanted higher wages. So they sought employment from the surrounding nations; and they applied their God-given skill in the service of heathen kings. They used their talents to build temples and idols for paganism.

Years later when Israel settled in Canaan, they drove out most of its inhabitants. Among those allowed to stay, where the people of Tyre and Sidon. Both were trading cities—seaport nations on the Mediterranean. Their costal situation made them world centers of commerce, wealthy in goods, skilled in the arts, and knowledgeable in all matters of learning around the globe.

So when Solomon needed a superintendent for building the temple on Mount Moriah, he didn't go to God for consecrated helpers and teachers. He asked the king of Tyre for someone to teach the skills to men in Judah and Jerusalem. The Phoenician king sent Huram, the son of a man from Tyre—who descended from Aholiab on his mother's side.[25] Solomon levied burdensome taxes to pay the workers' high wages.

The close relationship between Israel and Tyre continued to increase Tyre's wealth. It also helped to rend the kingdom of Israel. Solomon's son continued his father's policy of high taxation; but the northern tribes revolted and formed a separate nation. Judah to the south, continued to

---

[24] See Ezekiel 28:12.

[25] Ellen G. White, Prophets and Kings, p. 62, 63. Freemasonry claims Huram from the Bible is the same as their Hiram Abiff.

manage close ties with Tyre; and the ten tribes to the north fostered close ties with Sidon—also a wealthy Mediterranean coastal city.

—A General Movement

Why does Ezekiel now prophesy against Tyre and Sidon? Why does he link them to Lucifer's situation in heaven? Because they were exalted entities who became proud of their glory; and commercially merchandised that glory. By Ezekiel's time, Tyre and Sidon had become what Israel had been in Solomon's day: the center of *power*, *education*, and *spiritual enlightenment*. For our day, they typify a worldwide *educational, ministerial*, and *medical confederacy*:

> "I ask our people to study the twenty-eighth chapter of Ezekiel. The representation here made, while it refers primarily to Lucifer, the fallen angel, has a broader significance. Not one being, but a *general movement*, is described, and *one that we will witness*."[26]

The *Tyre-Sidon-Lucifer* connection somehow represents a last-days *general movement* that is *physically* attractive: visually pleasing, strong against her enemies, and powerful against the elements and sickness and disease. This entity also excels *intellectually*: an educational powerhouse, a wealth of scientific know-how. And it shines with *spiritual* splendor: a world leader in spirituality, a religion of religions—able to unite the entire world in common worship.

Only the *Roman Catholic Church* fits this description. Historically, Protestants have readily recognized her prophetic role. Wikipedia describes the "Reformation view" of Babylon:

> "Historicist interpreters commonly use the phrase 'Whore of Babylon' to refer to the Roman Catholic Church. Reformation writers from Martin Luther, John Calvin, and John Knox taught this association."[27]
>
> "Adventists believe that the fallen state of traditional Christianity can be seen especially in the Catholic Church, which they teach is the great whore in prophecy as seen in Revelation 17:1-[6], a false church. Her daughters are interpreted as other false churches (predominantly Protestant) which adopt false doctrines, some drawn from Catholicism itself..."[28]

Recently,[29] Christians celebrated the 500th birthday of the *Protestant Reformation; but* many denominations are reevaluating their *protest*—

---

[26] Ellen G. White, *Special Testimonies*, Series B. No. 17, p. 30. Emphasis added.

[27] Wikipedia. *Whore of Babylon*. Updated September 8, 2018. https://en.wikipdia.org/wiki/Whore_of_Babylon. Updated September 8, 2018.

[28] Ibid.

[29] October 31, 2017.

and their relationship to the Papacy. The question is being asked: *Is the reformation over?*[30]

Igniting the fires of earth's final battle, the angel of Revelation 18 repeats the second angel, saying, "Babylon is fallen, is fallen,"[31] adding, "Come out of her my people."[32] Wonderful Christians still worship within the Babylon system—but prophecy links that system to the *general movement* described in Ezekiel: and to the *mark of the beast*. It's a bad idea to call off the Reformation just now.

—Counterfeiting Glory

Revelation 18 also notices Babylon's *merchandising*—how "much she hath *glorified* herself," and how the kings of the earth will say,

> "Alas, alas that great city Babylon, that mighty city! For in one hour is thy judgment come. And the merchants of the earth shall weep and mourn over her; for no man buyeth her *merchandise* anymore."[33]

Like Lucifer and the cities of Tyre and Sidon, she is proud of her glory—and like them, she traffics in education, religion, and physical comfort. An angel takes a great millstone and casts it into the sea, saying,

> "And the voice of the harpers, and *musicians*, and of pipers, and trumpeters, shall be heard no more at all in thee; and no *craftsmen*, of whatsoever craft he be, shall be found any more in thee; and the sound of the *millstone* shall be heard no more in thee."[34]

Musicians, craftsmen, and millers correspond to the three great enterprises begun by Cain's decedents in Genesis.

> "Upon receiving the curse of God, Cain had withdrawn from his father's household... and he now founded a city... He had gone out from the presence of the Lord, cast away the promise of the restored Eden, to seek his possessions and enjoyment in the earth under the curse of sin, thus standing at the head of that great class of men who worship the god of this world. In that which pertains to mere earthly and material progress, his decedents became distinguished."[35]

Lamech's sons were the first of Cain's descendant to be so distinguished. Jabal was the father of those who dwell in tents and have cattle,[36]—providing a secular means for man's *physical* security (mill-

---

30 See *Is the Reformation Over? A Statement of Evangelical Convictions*, (http://isthereformationover.com/). 3/7/2019.

31 Revelation 18:2. See Revelation 14:8.

32 Revelation 18:4.

33 Revelation 18:7, 10-11. Emphasis added.

34 Revelation 18:22. Emphasis added.

35 Ellen G. White, *Patriarchs and Prophets*, p. 81.

36 Genesis 4:20.

stone). Tubalcain was an *instructor* of every craftsman in bronze and iron,[37]—providing a secular means for man's *intellectual* education (craftsmen). And Jubal was the father of all such as handle the harp and pipe[38]—providing a secular means for man's *spiritual* needs (musicians).[39]

Genesis also tells of the birth of a city and the laying of the foundation for her *temporal, intellectual,* and *spiritual* glory. His city was built for the same motivations that prompted him to offer his fruits and vegetables. He preferred to not trust "his salvation wholly to the atonement of the promised Savior." "He would come in his own merits." "He would express no penitence for sin."

> "He would not bring a lamb and mingle its blood with his offering, but he would present his fruits, the products of his labor. He presented his offerings as a favor to God, through which he expected to secure the divine approval."[40]

Revelation reports the judgment of "that mighty city!"—she will be destroyed in a single hour—her glory gone such that even the light of a candle shall shine no more at all in her... for her merchants were the great men of the earth; for by her medication[41] were all nations deceived.[42]

Prior to her final demise, she will receive a deadly wound; and then undergo a healing.[43] In 1798, General Berthier captured the Pope—wounding the papal power; but it was the Reformation that caused the real damage. Today the beast's power re-surges as her deadly wound quickly heals—and the world wonders after her *educational, ministerial,* and *medical* glory.

She's proud of it too. Recently she launched a media campaign called "*Catholics Come Home.*" In television commercials she boasts she invented the modern hospital, developed the scientific method—founded the college system, and compiled the Bible.[44]

---

[37]Genesis 4:22.

[38]Genesis 4:21.

[39] Music is linked to both true and false worship in the Bible. Psalms 100; Psalms 27:6; Exodus 32:1-7, 17-18; Daniel 3:4-5.

[40] Ellen G. White, *Patriarchs and Prophets*, p. 71. Emphasis is from the original.

[41] The King James uses the word "sorceries." However the Greek word for sorcery in the Bible is *mageia*, meaning "magic." The word used in this verse is *pharmakeia*, meaning "medication." It comes from *pharmakeus* and *pharmakon*, meaning "a drug" or "a druggist." See *Strong's Exhaustive Concordance of the Bible*, Greek Dictionary entries for 3095 and 5331.

[42] Revelation 18:23.

[43] Revelation 13:3.

[44] *Catholics Come Home*, (https://catholicscomehome.org/), accessed 9/25/2018. See also uCatholic.com, *Did you know? The Catholic Church Invented Hospitals*, January 13, 2017, (https://www.ucatholic.com/blog/did-you-know-the-catholic-church-invented-hospitals/), accessed 9/25/2018. See Thomas E. Woods, *The Catholic Church and the Creation of the University*. May

—Spiritual Trafficking

Daniel saw her spiritual glory in vision as a male *little horn power* that "grew as high as the host of heaven, and it cast down some of the host and some of the stars to the earth, and trampled them."[45] He elaborates:

> "It magnified itself, even to the Prince of the host; it removed His daily sacrifice and overthrew the place of His sanctuary. And on account of rebellion, the host and the daily sacrifice were given over to the horn, and it flung truth to the ground and prospered in whatever it did."[46]

Like Lucifer in Ezekiel 28, the Pope insinuates himself into the place of Christ. Setting up a counterfeit priesthood and offering counterfeit sacrifices—this false Christ derives his authority from the perpetual sinfulness (rebellion[47]) of the congregation[48] (host).[49] Seating "himself in the temple of God, proclaiming himself to be God, this power "speaks out against the Most High... intending to change times and the law."[50]

Daniel sees *the judgment* take away the power and dominion of the big-mouth *little horn*.[51] This is because *the judgment* brings an end to the perpetual sin problem in the church.[52] So long as the *little horn* perpetuates sin among the saints, (by convincing them there will always be a *daily sacrifice*[53] for them), they cannot (and will not) be sealed.[54] By changing God's *times and law*, he keeps even the "good" saints sinning. This prevents the judgment from ending the *little horn's* reign.

In "*Catholics Come Home,*" the viewer sees a large open Bible on a golden alter with six candles (not seven), and a Catholic priest waving a golden censor. This is *holy place* imagery.

Then the viewer sees a Cardinal wearing a beautiful red and gold robe while holding up the wine and host. He stands at the sanctuary[55] with

---

16, 2005. (https://www.catholiceducation.org/en/education/catholic-contributions/the-catholic-church-and-the-creation-of-the-university.htm), accessed 9/25/2018.

[45] Daniel 8:10. Berean Study Bible.

[46] Daniel 8:11-12. Berean Study Bible.

[47] Strong's Hebrew 6588: Transgression. (Preposition-b | Noun – masculine singular).

[48] Consider Ellen G. White, *Early Writings*, p. 56, Satan appears to be trying to carry on the holy place work after 1844.

[49] Strong's Hebrew 6635: A mass of organized persons. (Conjunctive waw | Noun – common singular).

[50] Daniel 7:25. Berean Study Bible.

[51] Daniel 7:9-14, 26; 8:13-14, 25-26.

[52] Ephesians 5:27; Revelation 19:7; Revelation 7:3-4, 14:1-5.

[53] Daniel 8:12, "And on account of rebellion, the host and the daily sacrifice were given over to the horn." Berean Study Bible. The *mass* does absolutely nothing to end the sin problem. "The daily sacrifice" - Strong's Hebrew 8548: 1) continuity, perpetuity, to stretch 1a) continually, continuously (as adverb).

[54] Revelation 7:3-4.

[55] In ecclesiastical architecture, the 'elevated platform that contains the main alter and associated liturgical elements that is restricted for ceremonial use by the clergy, often fenced from adjoining spaces," is called the sanctuary. See Wikipedia, Cathedral floorplan, (https://en.wikipedia.org/wiki/Cathedral_floorplan), accessed 3/21/2019.

statuary of covering cherubs on either side. This is *most holy place* imagery—the place of God's throne.

The papal system is a glorious outworking of the motives of Cain—where salvation is not entirely based on the atonement of the Savior. People can come in their own merits without repentance. As they seek to *buy* their spirituality with the fruits of their labor—the church glitters with the gold.

—Physical Trafficking

Shortly after the *Edict of Milan*[56] paved the way for the rise of a universal church, the *First Council of Nicaea* met in AD 325.

> "The council ordered a hospital to be built in every cathedral town to care for the sick, the poor, the widows, and the strangers...
>
> "In the 6th century, the Benedictines had every monastery of the order establish an infirmary to provide care for their community...
>
> "By the end of the Middle Ages, the Church had laid a foundation of healthcare all across Europe, with hundreds of hospitals dotting the map... By the advent of the Industrial Revolution, a majority of hospitals worldwide had their roots in the long-standing Catholic tradition of caring for the sick. Today the Church has over 600 hospitals and over 400 long-term care facilities in the United States alone."[57]

But modern allopathic medicine traces its roots back to well before the Roman church. It goes all the way back to ancient Egypt.

> "The medicine of the ancient Egyptians is some of the oldest documented. From the beginnings of the civilization in the late forth millennium BC until the Persian invasion of 525 BC, Egyptian medical practice went largely unchanged but was highly advanced for its time, including simple non-invasive surgery, setting of bones, dentistry, and an extensive set of pharmacopoeia. Egyptian medical thought influenced later traditions, including the Greeks."[58]
>
> "The art of healing was originally one of the secret sciences of the priestcraft, and the mystery of its source is obscured by the same veil which hides the genesis of religious belief... Candidates aspiring to membership in the religious orders underwent severe tests to prove their worthiness. These ordeals were called *initiations*. Those who passed them successfully were welcomed as brothers by the priests and were instructed in the secret teachings...
>
> "While modern physicians accredit Hippocrates with being the father of medicine, the ancient therapeutae ascribed to the immortal Hermes

---

[56] AD 313. Constantine I and Licinius met in Lilan and agreed to treat Christians benevolently within the Roman Empire.

[57] uCatholic.com, *Did you know? The Catholic Church Invented Hospitals*, January 13, 2017, (https://www.ucatholic.com/blog/did-you-know-the-catholic-church-invented-hospitals/), accessed 3/22/2019.

[58] Wikipedia, *Ancient Egyptian medicine*, (http://en.wikipedia.org/wiki/Ancient_Egyptian_medicine), accessed 3/22/2019.

the distinction of being the founder of the art of healing."[59]

Hermes (Thoth to the Egyptians) is considered to be the god of alchemy, astrology, and magic.[60] The caduceus (winged staff with two snakes wound around it) is the symbol for Hermes and has become the symbol for modern medicine.[61]

Much of the world's present knowledge of the ancient systems of medicine come from Paracelsus—a Swiss-German Renaissance physician, botanist, alchemist, astrologer, and general occultist.[62] He spent his entire life studying the exposition of Hermetic philosophy; and "pioneered the use of chemicals and minerals in medicine."[63]

> "Hippocrates, the famous Greek physician, during the fifth century before Christ, disassociated the healing art from the other science of the temple and thereby established a precedent for separateness."
>
> "During the Middle Ages the long-ignored axioms and formulae of Hermetic wisdom were assembled once more, and chronicled, and systematic attempts were made to test their accuracy.[64]

During the Exodus, the God of Heaven asserted *His* healing authority in contrast to worldly Egyptian medicine. This was His promise to the children of Israel:

> "If you will diligently hearken unto the voice of the Lord thy God, and wilt do that which is right in His sight, and wilt give ear to His commandments, and keep all His statutes, I will put none of these diseases upon thee, which I have brought upon the Egyptians: for I am the Lord that healeth thee."[65]

This contrast raises questions about worldly medicine—even the modern forms we use today. There's a chain linking it through Revelation's *Spiritual Babylon* to the secret sciences of Egyptian priest craft. Like Cain, Egypt took issue with God; and Egypt did not want health to be the result of obedience to law. They preferred to buy it.

> "Of all nations presented in Bible history, Egypt most boldly denied the existence of the living God and resisted His commands. No monarch ever ventured upon more open and highhanded rebellion against the authority of Heaven than did the king of Egypt."[66]

---

59 Manley P. Hall, *The Secret Teachings of All Ages*, p. 119. Emphasis added.

60 Wikipedia, *Hermeticism*, (https://en.wikipedia.org/wiki/Hermeticism), accessed 3/22/2019.

61 Ibid.

62 Wikipedia, *Paracelsus*, (https://en.wikipedia.org/wiki/Paracelsus), accesses 3/22/2019.

63 Ibid.

64 Hall, p. 119.

65 Exodus 15:26.

66 Ellen G. White, *The Great Controversy*, p. 269.

—Intellectual Trafficking

All able applicants were guaranteed access to a teaching license by the *Third Council of the Lateran* in 1179. Before then, the right to grant a *licentia docendi* was reserved to the church. But *able applicants* still had to be tested by the ecclesiastic scholastic until 1231—when the Pope granted that right to a university.[67]

The *scientific method* came along in the 1830s and 1850s when Baconianism was popular.[68] History credits Francis Bacon (1561-1626) with being the father of the scientific method.[69] One commentator says:

> "A worldwide state of illumination is the ancient dream and prophecy of all great sages who have ever lived on earth... Bacon's great gift to the world was his ability to see this anew and both devise and inaugurate a particular scientific method by which it might be more certainly achieved, suitable for the approaching era."[70]

It's almost impossible to overestimate Bacon's influence on our modern, scientific age. The *Royal Society* is a fellowship of many of the world's most eminent scientists and is the oldest scientific academy in continuous existence. On the foundation stones of the *Royal Society* is prose by Abraham Cowley comparing Bacon to Moses—with Bacon leading humanity to the promised land.[71] Bacon's friend, George Herbert, haled him as "the alone-only priest of nature and men's souls."[72]

In his book, *Peace Among the Willows*, Howard White warns about the purpose of Bacon's scientific method. He says it was to transform the human quest from the search for the "heavenly city," to the creation of the "well-governed country;" and to change the quest to understand God's creation (and humanity's place in it), to "a pursuit to understand what humans can make of themselves."[73]

There is true science; and there is science-so-called.[74] The scientific method bases conclusions on *observation rather than authority*. Faith

---

[67] Wikipedia, Academic degree, (https://en.wikipedia.org/wiki/Academic_degree), accessed 3/21/2019.

[68] Wikipedia, *Scientific Method*, (https://en.wikipedia.org/wiki/Scientific_method), accessed 3/21/2019.

[69] Wikipedia, *Francis Bacon*, updated September 30, 2018. (https://en.wikipedia.org/wiki/Francis_Bacon), accessed 9/25/2018.

[70] Peter Dawkins, *The Great Instauration*, (http://www.fbrt.org.uk/pages/essays/essay-gt_inst.html), accessed 12/30/2013.

[71] Abraham Crowley, *Ode to the Royal Society*, 1667, (https://www.bartleby.com/337/473.html), accessed 3/21/2019. See also Benjamin Farrington, *The Christianity of Francis Bacon*, reprinted from Baconiana, the Journal of the Francis Bacon Society (http:// www.sirbacon.org/farrington.htm). Accessed 9/26/2018.

[72] Ibid.

[73] Howard B. White, *Peace Among the Willows*, 1968.

[74] Ellen G. White, *Medical Ministry*, p, 98; See also Ellen G. White, *The Signs of the Times*, April 18, 1895.

bases conclusions on *authority rather than observation.*[75] It seems that Cain's motivation found its way in into worldly education too.

—Rebuilding Solomon's Temple

Bacon promoted what he called the *Great Restoration.*[76] He said it was *six stages of work* leading to a final stage of *rest*—the state of paradise.[77] He planned to first reform religion to restore humanity's relation to God; and second, recover the principles of natural philosophy, so that by the arts and sciences, we might restore humanity's dominion over nature.[78] Referring to this as *rebuilding* Solomon's temple, Bacon saw this as the way to overcome the ravages of sin and to rebuild humanity to is prelapsarian condition.[79]

It would also pave the way for Ezekiel's *general movement*. Bishop Sprat claimed that Bacon's scientific method will overcome narrowness of mind; and enable minds distracted by civil and religious differences to meet calmly on neutral ground; He further predicts that Bacon's scientific method will unite all the various classes, including the Presbyterian, the Papist, the Independent, and the Orthodox.[80]

Solomon's temple "is to be constructed in the human mind" as a "'Pyramid of Philosophy.' A pyramid is a 'pyre' of flame—a temple of light."[81] Sir Francis Bacon wrote: "I have held up a *light* in the obscurity of Philosophy... the establishment of good laws as an example to the world. For I am not raising a capital or pyramid to the pride of men, but laying the foundation in the human understanding for a holy temple after the *model of the World.*"[82]

—Competing Mountains

Maybe you're seeing two contrasting pictures here—two competing mountains—two plans for restoring mankind: both patterned after the original genesis.

---

[75] Hebrews 11:1.

[76] His original word was "Instauration."

[77] Dawkins.

[78] Francis Bacon, *Novum Organum*. 1620.

[79] Stephen A. McKnight, *Francis Bacon's God*, The New Atlantis, No. 10, Fall, 2005, pp.73-100. Prelapsarian mean pre-fallen.

[80] Benjamin Farrington, *The Christianity of Francis Bacon*, reprinted from Baconiana, the Journal of the Francis Bacon Society (http:// www.sirbacon.org/farrington.htm). Accessed 9-26-2018.

[81] Peter Dawkins, *The Great Instauration*. (1999, Francis Bacon Research Trust), accessed on 9-26-2018 at https://www.scribd. com/document/251893594/The-Great-Instauration-pdf

[82] Francis Bacon, *Novum Organum*, Bk I, Aph.120 (transl. Spedding & Ellis).

In the one, Christ restores by His own creative work—the atonement and the Word. In His plan there are two temples: a wilderness tabernacle made of skins, and later, a temple on Mount Moriah made of stones. Jesus Himself is the temple of skins, His humanity veiling His divinity—the incarnation, covering, but also revealing God to the world.

Christ is also the chief cornerstone[83] in the temple of stones. The last-day revelation of Himself will be that of a fully restored, fully rebuilt temple in humanity: one in which the Spirit of God dwells, like the Shekinah filled Solomon's temple.[84]

This temple (built by God, not man), is His church.[85] His bride will be without spot or wrinkle or any such thing.[86] This temple will demonstrate to the universe that our hearts of stone can become hearts of flesh[87]—the glory of His law written there by His own finger.[88] As partakers of the divine nature—as we are filled with the Holy Spirit—we will shine with the brightness of God's glory!

The other is the *second* mountain in a tale of three mountains. On it Satan attempts to restore by his *merchandise*: the *tree of knowledge*—worldly strength, worldly science, and worldly enlightenment.

His plan also has two temples. "Illuminated" individuals (*initiates*) form the temple of skins and constitute the cornerstone—the foundation of a different kind of stone temple—one built by *human* hands; a world-wide state of illumination; and a well-governed world-wide order.

Catholic Priest, Pierre Teilhard de Chardin,[89] wrote that "each of us is evolving toward the godhead,"[90] and that the only god to be worshiped is the one who will arise out of the evolving human race. He says there is to be "a general convergence of religions upon a universal Christ who satisfies them all." "I believe that the Messiah whom we await, whom we all without any doubt await, is the universal Christ; that is to say, the Christ of evolution."[91]

---

[83] 1 Peter 2:4-6.

[84] 2 Chronicles 7:1.

[85] 2 Corinthians 6:16.

[86] Ephesians 5:27.

[87] Ezekiel 11:19; 36:26.

[88] Deuteronomy 9:10; Exodus 31:18; Exodus 34:1. The first tablets were supplies by God—representing Christ who was broken for the sins of the people. The second tablets were hewed by Moses—representing the church. Both sets were written on by God.

[89] (1881-1955).

[90] Pierre Teilhard de Chardin, as quoted in Sir John Templeton, *The Humble Approach: Scientist Discover God* (Templeton Foundation Press, 1998): 92.

[91] Pierre Teilhard de Chardin, as quoted in "*Teilhard de Chardin: Christianity and Evolution*," Spiritual Conspiracies Project Journal: 56.

This temple (built by man), is the synagogue of Satan. With it, men will try to demonstrate to the universe that humanity can be its own god.

—God's Glory versus A Pyre of Flame

God is worshiped on the *first* mountain—the Father, the Son, and the Holy Ghost. On the *second* mountain, it's Lucifer-worship: it's Illuminism—it's the dragon, the beast, and the false prophet.

The Sabbath is the symbol of a finished work[92] on the *first* mountain. On the *second*: the symbol of a finished work is a human sabbath.

The work is accomplished by Christ (from heaven) on the *first* mountain. He is the true crowned and conquering Child—the Lord of heaven, and earth. On the *second* mountain the work is accomplished (from earth) by a universal Christ (anti-Christ)—a false crowned and conquering child—the lord of the aeon.

Restoration involves *coming out from among them and being separate*[93] on the *first* mountain. Touch not the unclean things: "Come out of her, my people, that ye be not partakers if her sins, and that ye receive not of her plagues."[94] Because this godly movement involves separation from the unclean, it unites Christ with His church—a *specific convergence* of faithful people presenting His balanced character of immutable law (truth and justice) and extravagant grace (mercy and long-suffering) with Holy Ghost power.

On the *second* mountain, restoration involves a general movement—a *general convergence* of all religion uniting and evolving into a singular humanity—buying and selling and drinking with all nations the wine of the wrath of her fornication; getting rich and comfortable with the kings of the earth, and the merchants of the earth; and enjoying the abundance of her delicacies.[95]

The *first* mountain represents a convergence of the human with the divine—it is *peculiar*. The *second* mountain represents the convergence of the human with the satanic—it is *ecumenical.*

—The Galilee Protocol

So Ahab ruled the northern kingdom, not one hundred years after Solomon. Israel was the jewel of the world when Solomon was king. God

[92] See Genesis 2:1-3 and Hebrews chapter 4, especially verses 4 and 10.

[93] 2 Corinthians 6:17.

[94] Revelation 18:4.

[95] Revelation 18:3.

strategically positioned her among the nations so she could light the world. Kings and queens traveled to Jerusalem to marvel at God's glory displayed by His people. They marveled at Israel's wealth and strength; wisdom and learning; her religion and her temple.

But her king and people did not improve their opportunities to enlighten those continually passing through her cities. "The missionary spirit that God had implanted in [their] hearts was supplanted by a spirit of *commercialism*.[96] Oh! Not so with Christ! When he lived there (years later), He refused to labor for selfish purposes. He took advantage of the great thoroughfares of travel to evangelize the world!

Jesus stayed at Capernaum so often it was known as 'His own city.' It was a great place to work—on the highway from Damascus to Jerusalem, and Egypt, and to the Mediterranean Sea. There, Jesus met those of all nations and all ranks; and they carried His lessons to households the world over.

He didn't follow the mold of the world. He bypassed the systems of human accomplishment—*educational*, *pastoral*, and *medical*.

> "Jesus went about all Galilee, *teaching* in the synagogues, *preaching* the gospel of the kingdom, and *healing* all manner of sickness and all manner of disease among the people."[97]

He didn't use the systems or conventions of the world. He didn't borrow techniques or procedures from the preachers, teachers, and physicians of His time. "By methods peculiarly His own, Christ helped all who were in sorrow and affliction."[98] His new *protocol* upset the entire establishment. Jesus caused a *ministerial* crisis, an *educational* crisis,

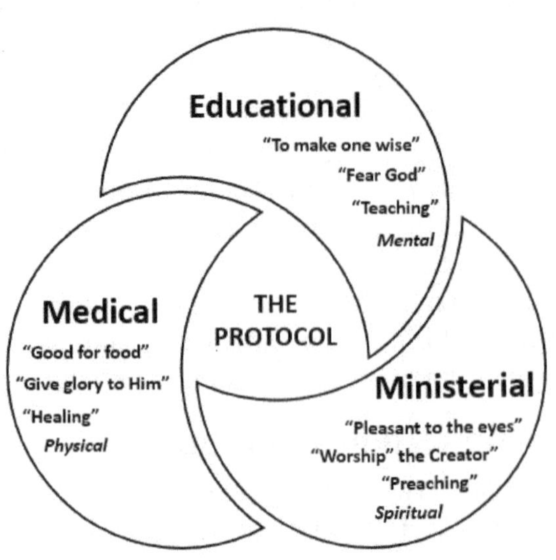

[96] Ellen G. White, *Prophets and Kings*, p. 71. Emphasis added.
[97] Matthew 4:23. Emphasis added.
[98] Ellen G. White, *The Ministry of Healing*, p. 23.

and a *medical* crisis—in the church, in the nation, and in the world.

All false religion shares this in common: it exemplifies the fundamental principle of idolatry. It is based on *human* accomplishment. This is the kingpin of Lucifer's platform. It's all about what we can make of ourselves.

Christ's *Galilee Protocol* is based on *God's* accomplishments. He invites us to enroll in the *school of Christ* for restoring our *mind*. Jesus is the only mediator between God and man; and He says to all, "Come unto Me"[99] for *spiritual* regeneration. And Jesus is the Great Physician. He offers His touch for our *physical* health and healing. Only God can heal.[100] We cannot heal ourselves.[101] "Health does not depend on chance. It is a result of obedience to law."[102] "Those who come to the great Healer must be willing to do His will, to humble their souls, and confess their sins."[103]

> "Christ came to this world and lived the law of God, that man might have perfect mastery over the natural inclinations which corrupt the soul. The physician of soul and body, He gives victory over warring lusts. He has provided every facility, that man may possess completeness of character."[104]

—Princess of the Sidonians

So, in Ahab's day there was this politically arranged marriage between Ahab and the princess daughter of the king of Sidon (of Tyre and Sidon fame). Jezebel's father, Ethbaal was king of the Sidonians, and he was Baal's priest.

By Elijah's time, this Phoenician princess—now Israel's queen—made such an impact on the nation there were four-hundred and fifty priests to Baal and four-hundred priests to Astarte.

Maybe you *were* thinking Jezebel's people were primitive, savage folks; but *now* you know that they were the cutting edge of post-modern civilization—they were powerful and educated, and wealthy and sophisticated. They were center-stage—the cultural capital of the world. Ezekiel would later epitomize them as earth's *Morning Star*—perfect in beauty, full of wisdom, as earth's *spiritual-choir-director*.

---

[99] Matthew 11:28.

[100] Ibid., p. 11.

[101] Ellen G. White, *Medical Ministry*, p. 13.

[102] Ellen G. White, *The Ministry of Healing*, p. 128.

[103] Ibid., p. 40.

[104] Ellen G. White, *The Ministry of Healing*, p. 130.

When Jezebel moved into Ahab's palace, Israel seemed like primitive savages to the Sidonian point-of-view. The new queen had to bring this backward, old-fashioned people into the "*twenty-first century*".

They didn't mind, either. It was an easy transition. Who wouldn't be attracted to Sidon's wealth, knowledge and sophistication? They liked Sidon's luxury homes and affluent lifestyle. The sensuality of Sidon's art, entertainment, and religion were tempting treats to their carnal hearts.

They completely forgot about their mission. Their loyalty to God and responsibility to the world were out of sight, out of mind. So tangled were they, they didn't realize they had fallen off God's bandwagon altogether. They still considered themselves the chosen people, they thought things were good—that they were blessed by God.

—Confronting Sidonian Science

Try not to think of Jezebel as superstitious either. Sure she was a pagan, but the Sidonians were surprisingly scientific. They claimed the good gifts of nature came from Baal—that's true. But since Baal was the sun; and the sun was Baal, they (like scientist today) knew the sun's energy enriched the earth, making it able to bring forth abundantly. So when Israel came to think the treasures of heaven, (the dew and the rain) didn't come from Jehovah—it was because they knew the science. Weather is the results of the normal forces of nature.

Elijah didn't think so! He was not impressed with post-modern civilzation. He was not caught-up in Sidonian sophistication and their trinkets and gadgets, and baubles. He was suspicious that it was the busy, comfortable, worldly lifestyles; and the secular learning and sciences; and modern worship and entertainment that was drawing Israel away from her mission and God.

Elijah was increasingly alarmed. He knew, without *a light on a hill* the entire world was without hope; and of all people—the chosen were the guiltiest. They were guilty of high treason against Jehovah!

Elijah asked God to stop sending the rain.[105] Earth's only hope was in rattling Israel back into reality. We find the *third* mountain right here. It's Mount Carmel—it's Israel's mountain. It's a high place. It's a place of worship. The groves are fruitful worship centers: where grows the grape, the olive, and the fig trees; and they are for the worship of Baal.

---

[105] Ellen G. White, *The Review and Herald*, September 16, 1873.

They are flourishing. But God's vineyard is languishing. His alter is broken down. Earth's light-on-hill has gone out!

Side-by-side with Tyre and Sidon, Israel pays homage to a pyre of flame—a temple of light built after the model of the world, a monument to what humans can make of themselves.

The people gather there between two altars—in all their Laodicean clarity—waiting for the showdown. Elijah's voice rings loud and clear: "*How long will you wait between two opinions?* If Jehovah is God, follow Him: but if Baal, then follow him."[106] The people answer not a word.

---

[106] 1 Kings 18:21. Author's paraphrase.

CHAPTER TWO

By Whose Authority?

We speak longingly of the latter rain. It's as if we tie all our hopes for successful labor to this one event. Pentecost is the historic prototype of the latter rain;[1] but it occurred only after Christ's three-and-a-half years of intensive ministry.

Since most of His followers abandoned Him at the end of His seasons of popularity,[2] we can say the real fruit of Christ's labor came *after* His earthly ministry ended. His ministry laid the groundwork for Calvary, Pentecost and beyond.

This preparation established the context needed for the *Calvary-storm* it precipitated, and was the pattern adopted (with Holy Ghost power) by the early Christians.

Let's call this pattern the *Galilee Protocol*, and let's commit to learn the pattern carefully—and to work it faithfully. Sister White wrote: "We are to work as Christ worked, in the same practical lines. Then we shall be safe. The divine commission needs no reform. Christ's way of presenting truth cannot be improved upon."[3]

---

[1] See Ellen G. White, *Last Day Events*, p. 192.

[2] See Luke 4:16-30; John 6:25-7:1; Luke 9:51-56, Ellen G. White, *The Desire of Ages*, pp. 486-487.

[3] Ellen G. White, *Evangelism*, p. 525.

—Three Theaters of Operation

Jesus worked in *three* theaters of operation. He divided the three-and-a-half years of His ministry between Judea, Galilee, and the regions beyond the Jordan.

The cities of Jerusalem, Bethlehem, and Bethany were in Judea. The Roman's allowed the spiritual and cultural center of the Jewish economy to operate there, but they gave Judea little governmental autonomy. They controlled it themselves through a Roman governor—Pontius Pilate. Jerusalem was Israel's spiritual nerve-center. They knew it as God's city. The sacred oracles were there. It was home to the fabulous temple. She was the apple of God's eye[4]—and politically boisterous because of it.

The cities of Nazareth, Cana, Bethsaida and Capernaum were in Galilee. Judaism prevailed in Galilee; but the people were an ethnic mixture. During the captivity, most of the Jews were exiled to foreign lands, and other races were brought to take their place. The resulting cultural diversity dampened political volatility. Rome allowed Galilee to have a king—Herod Antipas. As tetrarch,[5] he ruled under the authority of Rome; but having a king afforded Galilee more political autonomy.

Judea and Galilee were both part of Israel. The arrangement provided a practical separation of church and state during Christ's years of ministry. Judea was like the church—Galilee the nation. Beyond the Jordan were places like Phoenicia, Decapolis, Perea and Samaria. These were outside the boundaries of Israel; and they were not Jewish.

—Tactical Typology

This forms a useful type/antitype model for us. Adventist eschatology has end-time events unfolding in a similar three theaters arrangement—the Seventh-day Adventist Church, the United States of America, and some form of global coalition.

The original *Galilee Protocol* established a tactical sequence:

• Christ went first to Judea (the church). He did this between the first and second Passovers—A.D. 28 and A.D 29. He began with cleansing the temple and ended when the Sanhedrin rejected Him after the commotion at the pool of Bethesda. Only a few early disciples worked with Jesus in Judea.

---

[4] Zechariah 2:8

[5] Subordinate ruler. Herod was subject to Roman authority.

• Christ moved on to Galilee (the nation). He worked there between the second and third Passovers—A.D. 29 and A.D. 30. His Galilee ministry began when Herod put *John the Baptist* in prison and ended when John was executed. Most of Jesus' Galilean followers abandoned Him when He wouldn't let them make Him king. The twelve disciples were His primary crew in Galilee.

• Christ retired from His ministry to Israel after Galilee—or at least He worked underground. Between the third and fourth Passovers—A.D. 30 and A.D. 31—Jesus worked primarily in the regions beyond the Jordan. This phase of His ministry began about the time Herod killed *John-the-Baptist* and extended until His final trip to Jerusalem. During this time He had a larger crew—seventy disciples.

• The *Calvary-storm* hit at the fourth Passover—A.D. 31. "Jesus said unto them, Ye all shall be offended because of me this night: for it is written, I will smite the shepherd, and the sheep of the flock shall be scattered abroad."[6]

• Pentecost[7] marked the beginning of the *early rain*.[8] It didn't occur until after Christ's ministry—and after *Calvary-storm*. This early-rain power carried the gospel to the entire known world in one generation.[9]

—The Nature of the Conflict

Everywhere He went, Christ caused an upset. He was rejected in Judea and Galilee because His ministry challenged the status quo. The trouble boiled down to a single word: *authority*. The leaders in Judea, and the people in Galilee took issue with Christ's *authority* to work His *Galilee Protocol*.

The conflict reached a full head of steam about a week before Calvary. Jesus was at the temple.

> "Then Jesus entered the temple courts and began to drive out those who were selling there. He declared to them, 'It is written: "My house will be a house of prayer." But you have made it "a den of robbers."'... One day as Jesus was teaching the people in the temple courts and proclaiming the gospel, the chief priests and scribes, together with the elders, came up to Him. 'Tell us,' they said, 'by what *authority* are You doing these things, and who gave You this *authority*?'"[10]

---

[6] Matthew 26:31.
[7] Acts 2:1-4.
[8] Ellen G. White, *Last Day Events*, p. 192.
[9] Colossians 1:23.
[10] Luke 19:45-20:2. Berean Study Bible. Emphasis added.

—Three Fronts

Notice the large group of leaders—priests, scribes, chiefs of the people, and elders. The priests were teachers and lawyers—in addition to their ministerial duties. And even the physicians[11] were drawn from the priestly tribe of Levites. The priests cared for the sick too.

Bypassing the whole shebang, the educational system, pastoral system, and medical system: "Jesus went about all Galilee, *teaching* in the synagogues, and *preaching* the gospel of the kingdom, and *healing* all manner of sickness and all manner of disease among the people."[12] He didn't use the systems or conventions of the world. He didn't borrow techniques or procedures from the preachers, teachers, and physicians of His time. "By methods peculiarly His own, Christ helped all who were in sorrow and affliction."[13]

When Jesus taught, people "were astonished at His doctrine: for He taught them as One having *authority*, and not as the scribes."[14] *When Jesus healed*, they said, "Herein is a marvelous thing, that ye know not from whence He is, but yet He hath opened mine eyes... If this man were not of God, He could do nothing."[15] When Jesus preached, He said, "Ye have heard that it was said..." Then He'd conclude, "But *I say unto you...*"[16] He asserted His authority over the teachings and traditions of His day. His Disciples too—"He gave them power and *authority* over all devils, and to cure diseases and He sent them to preach the kingdom of God and to heal the sick."[17]

The leaders were getting frantic when Jesus cleared the temple this second time. He had just rode into Jerusalem on a colt; and the people were stirring up the old notion of making Him their king. The leaders quarreled with themselves, "Perceive ye how ye avail nothing? Behold the world is gone after Him."[18] They saw a religious revolution brewing—one beyond the sanction of their authority. They wanted it stopped and they wanted Him dead.

---

[11] See Leviticus 13:2, 14:2; Luke 17:14. See Jewish Virtual Library, *Encyclopedia Judaica: Medicine*, (https://www.jewishvirtuallibrary.org/medicine), accessed 3/22/2019.

[12] Matthew 4:23.

[13] Ellen G. White, *The Ministry of Healing*, p. 18.

[14] Mark 1:22. Emphasis added.

[15] John 9:30.

[16] Matthew 5:27-28.

[17] Luke 9:1-2. Emphasis added.

[18] John 12:19.

To stop Him, they confronted Him in the temple. "By what authority do you these things? And who gave you that authority?"[19]

> "Here you've got the Pharisees, the Sadducees, the Herodians, maybe even the Zealots and the Essenes, none of whom could agree with each other. You've got all these divergent rabbinical viewpoints coming together and everybody had their own rabbi and everybody's own rabbi had his own view. And they can't get together on much, but they can sure get together on stopping Christ."[20]

They had to declare war on the *Galilee Protocol* because the *Galilee Protocol* was not based on *their* authority! Sure Christ caused a *shaking in Jerusalem*—at the temple-church! Of course He *shook up things in Galilee*—on the national scene! He had to, this was His mission! "It was His mission to bring to men complete restoration; He came to give them health and peace and perfection of character."[21] Worldly science, religion, and medicine don't offer these things. Christ knew "that unless there was a decided change in the principles and purposes of the human race all would be lost."[22]

—The Seventh-day Adventist Mission

God led Seventh-day Adventism to develop within the framework of these same three fronts. The ministry arm is for *preaching* the gospel. The medical arm is for a *healing* work to coincide with evangelism. The education arm is to *train* disciples to be missionaries for Christ.

Let's call these the three protocols: *educational*, *ministerial*, and *medical*. They correspond to Christ's *teaching* and *preaching* and *healing* in Galilee. They are for restoration of mind, soul and body. Not only are they prominently featured in the Adventist framework; they are essential to our mission:

> "In a special sense Seventh-day Adventists have been set in the world as watchmen and light bearers. To them has been entrusted the last warning for a perishing world. On them is shining wonderful light from the Word of God. They have been given a work of the most solemn import,—the proclamation of the first, second, and third angels' messages. There is no other work of so great importance. They are to allow nothing else to absorb their attention."[23]

---

[19] Matthew 21:23.

[20] John McCarthy, *The Authority of Jesus*. December 11, 1983, (http://www.gty.org/library/Sermons/2353, accessed 3/22/2019.

[21] Ellen G. White, *The Ministry of Healing*, p. 17.

[22] Ibid. p. 18.

[23] Ellen G. White, *Evangelism*, p. 119.

Notice how the three protocols are integral to the first angel's message.

> "And I saw another angel fly in the midst of heaven... saying with a loud voice, Fear God and give glory to Him; for the hour of his judgment is come: and worship Him that made heaven, and earth, and the sea, and the fountains of water."[24]

The Psalms says, "The *fear of God* is the beginning of knowledge; fools despise wisdom and instruction."[25] This is the *educational* protocol.

Paul says: "What? Know ye not that your body is the temple of the Holy Ghost, which is in you, which ye have of God, and ye are not your own? For ye are bought with a price: therefore *glorify God* in your body."[26] "Whether therefore ye eat, or drink, or whatsoever ye do, do all for the *glory of God*."[27] This is the *medical* protocol.

The fourth commandment is about worship. It says that "in six days the Lord made heaven and earth, the sea, and all that in them is, and rested the seventh day: wherefore the Lord blessed the seventh day, and hallowed it."[28] It's the *ministerial* protocol.

—A Growing Understanding

The Adventist understanding of our mission grew as God moved us into position to warn the world using the precise pattern that Christ used in Galilee. "Christ stands before us as the *pattern Man*, the great Medical Missionary."[29]

> "We are to work the works of Christ... Isaiah says, 'Thy righteousness shall go before thee; the glory of the Lord shall be thy rereward'... This is the work that must be done before Christ shall come in power and great glory."[30]

This Isaiah passage is from chapter 58—and it turns out that Isaiah 58 is inseparably linked to the *Galilee Protocol*. It describes the very work that Seventh-day Adventists are called to do. Here is how this was plainly and forcefully presented to our pioneers:

> "The whole chapter is applicable to those who are living in this period of earth's history. Consider this chapter attentively; for it will be fulfilled... The Lord has a message for his people. This message will be borne, whether men will accept it or reject it. As in the days of Christ, there will

[24] Revelation 14:6-7.
[25] Psalms 1:7. Emphasis added.
[26] 1 Corinthians 6:19-20. Emphasis added.
[27] 1 Corinthians 10:31. Emphasis added.
[28] Exodus 20:11.
[29] Ellen G. White, *Welfare Ministry*, p. 53. Emphasis added.
[30] Ellen G. White, *The Review and Herald*, November 1, 1892.

be deep plottings of the power of darkness, but the message must not be muffled with smooth words or fair speeches, crying peace, peace, when there is no peace, to those who are turning away from God."[31] (1897).

"The fifty-eighth chapter of Isaiah contains present truth for the people of God. Here we see how medical missionary work and the gospel ministry are to be bound together as the message is given to the world. Upon those who keep the Sabbath of the Lord is laid the responsibility of doing a work of mercy and benevolence. *Medical missionary* work is to be bound up with the message, and sealed with the seal of God."[32] (1901).

"My brethren, you need to study more carefully, the fifty-eighth chapter of Isaiah. This chapter marks out the only course that we can follow with safety."[33] (1902).

"We need the clear light of the Sun of Righteousness to shine upon us. This light is given to those who keep holy the Lord's Sabbath; but *we cannot keep this day holy unless we serve the Lord in the manner brought to view in the scripture*: 'Is not this the fast that I have chosen, to loose the bands of wickedness, to undo the heavy burdens, to let the oppressed go free, and that ye break every yoke? Is it not to deal thy bread to the hungry, and that thou bring the poor that are cast out to thy house? When thou seest the naked, that thou cover him; and that thou hide not thyself from thine own flesh?' (Isaiah 58:6,7). This is the work that rests upon every soul who accepts the service of Christ."[34] (1909)

—Lest We Forget

The final several pages of this chapter contain a historical timeline of the development and progress of Adventism from its inception to the 1950's. A simple survey of the timeline makes the picture clear enough. Under the direction and authority of God, each of the three protocols were being systematically woven into our distinctive mission. We can also see our persistence in mingling them with those of the world.

This part of our history—and the long-term consequences of our past choices—presents a confusing and uncomfortable situation for us today. We don't want to spend too long dwelling on our mistakes; but it's fatal not to address and correct continuing wrongs. Avoiding them completely blocks God's ability to remedy our Laodiceanism. We need to understand our mistakes so we can apply the remedy.

Study the timeline carefully. Many important details will not make it into the narrative of this chapter and book. The timeline speaks for itself. This book will focus on understanding the solutions—what they are,

---

[31] Ellen G. White, *Manuscript 36*, 1897.
[32] Ellen G. White, *Evangelism*, p. 516. Emphasis added.
[33] Ellen G. White, *Letter* 76, 1902.
[34] Ellen G. White, *Manuscript Releases*, vol. 5, p. 33. Emphasis added.

why each part is necessary, how and why they work together, and what we should expect when we implement them. But before we can move on, we need to understand how several historic events define the problem.

—Language We Understand

The first takes us back to 1901-1903. Denominational reorganization was happening; and buildings were burning down. We needed reorganization because men in responsible positions had light poured upon them year after year but were not heeding the light God gave them.[35] Regarding the fires in Battle Creek, Ellen White wrote that she saw in the calamity, "the mercy of God... mingled with justice,"—mercy in that no workers had lost their lives: they were spared, she said, "that they might do the work which they had neglected to do and which it seemed impossible to make them see and understand."[36]

> "Notwithstanding the plain evidence of the Lord's providence in these destructive fires, some among us have not hesitated to make light of the statement that these buildings were burned because men had been swaying things in directions which the Lord could not approve.
>
> "Men have been departing from the right principles, for the promulgation of which these institutions were established, they have failed of doing the very work that God ordained should be done to prepare a people to 'build the old waste places' and to stand in the breach, as represented in the fifty-eighth chapter of Isaiah. In this scripture the work we are to do is clearly defined as being medical missionary work."[37]

The issue really is about cooperating with God's specific directions and accepting His authority. He has made it clear that His work is to be according to the Isaiah fifty-eight model. And God is serious about this:

> "The word was spoken, 'God will cleanse and purify His temple in His displeasure.' In the vision of the night, I saw a sword of fire hung over Battle Creek. Brethren, God is in earnest with us. I want to tell you that if after the warnings given in these burnings, the leaders of our people go right on, just as they have done in the past, exalting themselves, *God will take the bodies next.* Just as surely as He lives, He will speak to them in a language that they cannot fail to understand."[38]

God is long-suffering—and He has been patient. How better it will be if we cooperate with His cleansing and purifying His temple. The warning shows that we can avert the greater sword!

---

[35] Ellen G. White, *General Conference Bulletin*, April 3, 1901.

[36] Ellen G. White, *The Review and Herald*, April 14, 1903.

[37] Ellen G. White, *Testimonies for the Church*, vol. 8, p. 218.

[38] Ellen G. White, *Manuscript Releases*, vol. 4, p. 367. Emphasis added.

In 1903, Ellen White clarified that we were in danger of contaminating the peculiar protocols for commercial reasons:

> "God had given us a commission which angels might envy. The church has been charged to convey to the world, without delay, God's saving mercy. This is the trust that He has given us, and it is to be faithfully executed. Medical missionary work is to be done. Thousands upon thousands of human beings are perishing in sin. The compassion of God is moved. All heaven is looking on with intense interest to see what character medical missionary work will assume under the supervision of human beings. Will men make *merchandise* of God's ordained plan for reaching the dark parts of the earth with a manifestation of His benevolence? Will they cover mercy with selfishness, and call it medical missionary work?"[39]

—Wilderness Wandering

The second point concerns a timeline entry—also in 1901. Sister White wrote, "We may have to remain here in this world because of insubordination many more years, as did the children of Israel."[40]

> "The history of ancient Israel is a striking illustration of the past experience of the Adventist body. God led His people in the Advent Movement, even as He led the children of Israel from Egypt. In the great disappointment their faith was tested as was that of the Hebrews at the Red Sea. Had they still trusted to the guiding hand that had been with them in their past experience, they would have seen the salvation of God. If all who had labored unitedly in the work of 1844, had received the third angel's message and proclaimed it in the power of the Holy Spirit, the Lord would have wrought mightily with their efforts. A flood of light would have been shed upon the world. Years ago the inhabitants of the earth would have been warned, the closing work completed, and Christ would have come for the redemption of His people.
>
> "It was not the will of God that Israel should wander forty years in the wilderness; He desired to lead them directly to the land of Canaan and establish them there, a holy, happy people... In like manner, it was not the will of God that the coming of Christ should be so long delayed and His people should remain so many years in this world of sin and sorrow. But unbelief separated them from God."[41]

Not God's will to delay? Separated from God? We need to understand these things. During the forty-years that Israel wandered in the wilderness, they were constantly reminded that they were under divine rebuke.

---

[39] Ellen G. White, *Medical Ministry*, p. 131. Emphasis added.

[40] Ellen G. White, *Manuscript* Releases, vol. 20, p. 312-313.

[41] Ellen G. White, *The Great Controversy*, pp. 457-458.

"In the rebellion at Kadesh they had rejected God, and God had for a time rejected them."[42]

> "Since they had proved *unfaithful to His covenant*, they were not to receive the sign of the covenant, the rite of circumcision. *Their desire to return to the land of slavery* had shown them to be unworthy of freedom, and the ordinance of the Passover, instituted to commemorate the deliverance from bondage, was not to be observed."[43]

Israel's insubordination specifically concerned their *unwillingness to follow God's authority* (unfaithful to the covenant—they did not obey Him); and their *unwillingness to be separate from the world* (they wanted to go back to Egypt). These same two issues separate us from God. We refuse to obey God's directions for medical missionary work, and we follow the *educational*, *ministerial*, and *medical* models of the world—for comfort and material gain.

> "Angels of God are sent to measure the temple and the worshipers therein. The Lord looks with sadness upon those who are serving their idols, with no care for the souls perishing in darkness and error. He cannot bless a church who feels it no part of their duty to be laborers together with Him."[44]

"Yet the continuance of the tabernacle service testified that God had not utterly forsaken His people. His provenance still supplied their wants."[45] The pillar of cloud and pillar of fire still led them. His Spirit still instructed them. The manna and water continued. Their clothes did not wear out and their feet did not swell.[46]

> "During the entire forty years in the wilderness, the people were every week reminded of the sacred obligation of the Sabbath, by the miracle of the manna. Yet even this did not lead them to obedience. Though they did not venture upon... open and bold transgression... yet there was great laxness in the observance of the fourth commandment."[47]

Again, all this correlates with Laodicea. "The church is in the Laodicean state. The presence of God is not in her midst."[48] Yet He has not utterly forsaken her either. Standing outside the door, He *still* knocks. Can't we let Him in? What specifically must we do to let Him in?

---

[42] Ellen G. White, *Patriarchs and Prophets*, p. 406.
[43] Ibid. Emphasis added.
[44] Ellen G. White, *Manuscript 156*, 1898.
[45] Ibid.
[46] See Nehemiah 9:19-21.
[47] Ellen G. White, *Patriarchs and Prophets*, pp. 409-410.
[48] Ellen G. White, *Manuscript 156*, 1898.

> "The presence of the Lord is ever seen where every energy of the church is aroused to meet the spiritual responsibilities."[49]

If we humble ourselves and pray; if we seek His face; if we turn from our evil ways—then God will hear from heaven, forgive our sins, and heal our land.[50] We need to correct the two evils that have kept us in the wilderness. We must commit to following God's detailed plan of Isaiah 58 medical missionary work, and we must separate from the patterns of the world. Otherwise, God will eventually have to speak to us in a language we cannot fail to understand: *He will take the bodies next.*[51]

We can do this the easy way, or we can do it the hard way. Either way, we should expect God will soon lead us out of our wilderness detour and successfully use the church as His instrument to take the final warning message to the world. His people will (one way or the other) do this according to *God's* specific method. Isaiah 58 will be fulfilled.[52] The message will be borne whether people accept it or not.[53]

—A Fork in the Road

The timeline shows how the church continued to advance an amalgamated version of the three protocols. Today, we inherit a version that primarily resembles the pattern of the world—with some *God principles* mixed in for effect. This confuses our work, and limits the effectiveness of our mission. Later we will see how the world's methods actually short-circuit the power of the Gospel.

Still, God uses us to advance the cause of truth—as He did with Israel during the captivity in Babylon. Compared to what should have been, Israel presented a significantly muted message to the nations; but they did carry it (muted as it was) to every land where Nebuchadnezzar scattered them. The global empires from Babylon, to Medio-Persia, to Greece and then Rome—all felt the influence of the oracles that scattered with them. By the time Christ came to view, Judaism had established believers around the world. The apostolic church used this established network to conduct the gospel truth quickly everywhere.[54]

---

[49] Ibid.

[50] 2 Chronicles 7:14.

[51] Ellen G. White, *Manuscript Releases*, vol. 4, p. 367.

[52] Ellen G. White, *Manuscript 36*, 1897.

[53] Ibid.

[54] See Ellen G. White, *The Acts of the Apostles*, p. 155.

In 1874, the Lord told Seventh-day Adventists "Your house is the world."[55] "The message you bear is a world-wide message."[56] This we heard loud and clear—and so we have grown into a mighty people to the four corners of the earth. We are an evangelism-minded church, and it shows. Though not conducted strictly according to the pure principles God established for us, our educational, ministerial and medical emphases play no small role in our astonishing growth; and they form the prominent features of our world-wide identity.

Knowing the time would eventually come for the church's wilderness sojourn to end—and the Isaiah 58 pattern to revive, God took decided steps to preserve the protocols in their purity.

E. A. Sutherland and P. T. Megan realized where the educational work in Berrien Springs was going, so they took Sister White's counsel to start a new school in the south. Amid the loud protests of the denomination, the prophet directed them to keep the Madison school independent. It was 1904—and the Adventist *self-supporting work* was born. Within a few years there were as many as 47 rural units formed after the Madison model.[57] This put a fork in the Seventh-day Adventist road.

One path took the church world-wide and established her as a well-organized educational, ministerial and medical powerhouse in every nation and kindred and people and tongue. The strength of the other path has been in its *lack* of organization. Its *independent* autonomy has enabled it to preserve the pure protocols for when they will stand in their lot at the end of the days. It has also kept the self-supporting work obscure enough to survive against its formidable foes. These two paths advance side by side toward the day when they will have to join together in proper protocol evangelism—united under the authority of heaven.

—Convergence

Two paths joined when Christ reintroduced the original covenant protocols to a globally-reaching Israel—who also had long-since adopted the world's pattern. By knowing how it worked then, we will be better prepared for what is coming. The pure protocols can't be compromised forever, a convergence has to happen to save the faithful on both paths. A proper blending of God's justice and His mercy is necessary on both sides for authentic physical, mental, and spiritual redemption.

---

[55] Ellen G. White, *Christian Experience and Teachings of Ellen G. White*, p. 216.

[56] Ellen G. White, *Ellen G. White in Europe 1885-1887*, p. 31.

[57] Robert H. Pierson, *Miracles Happen Every Day*, Mountain View, California, Pacific Press Publishing Association, 1983.

The world finds it easy to downplay the differences between our muted message and contaminated protocols and their own educational, ministerial, and medical models. They all look so much alike. So, two-path convergence is needed to put *God's* authentic, unmuted educational, ministerial and medical program so squarely on the map, and in so convincing and compassionate a manner that it will clearly expose the contrast between the glory of God and Satan's worldly counterfeit. Our two-path convergence will come with a certain bang.

When He was on earth, Jesus' mission was to re-establish *His authority* through the *Galilee Protocol*. Trying to do this in Jerusalem and Judea agitated such a commotion that it developed widespread interest in Galilee. The commotion in Galilee piqued the interest of the world. This same progression occurred again after Pentecost.[58]

—Starting the Ball to Roll

John the Baptist was the one that set the ball rolling. This is important to know because his special situation and upbringing placed him on the *self-supporting* side of things. "John was to stand as a reformer." "He must impress [men] with the holiness of God's requirements, and their need for His perfect righteousness."[59] By His abstemious life and plain dress he was to rebuke the excesses of his time."[60]

> "In order to fulfill his mission he must have a sound *physical* constitution, and *mental* and *spiritual* strength. Therefore it would be necessary for him to control all his powers that he could stand among men as unmoved by surrounding circumstances as the rocks and mountains of the wilderness."[61]

John was no city-boy. As the son of Zacharias, he would have been educated for the priesthood in the rabbinical schools. But God "called him to the desert, that he might learn of nature and nature's God. It was a lonely region where he found his home, in the midst of barren hills, wild ravines, and rocky caves."[62] He wore simple clothes; he ate the simple food found in the wilderness. He drank the pure water from the hills. He bore a prophetic message—"repent ye, for the kingdom of heaven is at hand."[63] He bore a message of judgment—"the axe is laid unto the root

---

[58] See Acts 13:14-52.
[59] Ellen G. White, *The Desire of Ages*, p. 100.
[60] Ibid.
[61] Ibid. Emphasis added.
[62] Ibid., p. 101.
[63] Matthew 3:1-2.

of the trees: therefore every tree which bringeth not forth good fruit is hewn down, and cast in to the fire."[64]

John's work was compared to the spiritual power of Elijah.[65] He drew average people as well as Priests, Pharisees, Sadducees, Herod Antipas, and others.[66] Jesus Himself responded to the preaching of John. Some of Jesus' early disciples were disciples of John.[67]

A two-path contrast is apparent between the disciples of Jesus and the disciples of John. Jesus and His disciples came mingling with the people, eating and drinking at their tables. They were accused of being gluttons and winebibbers.[68] "John's disciples observed many of the rules prescribed by the rabbis, and even hoped to be justified by the works of the law."[69] They fasted often and complained when Christ's disciples didn't.[70] John's disciples tended toward the law and justice, Christ's toward acceptance and mercy. Jesus blended them both—He lived righteousness, preached judgment, and practiced mercy.

The proper presentation of Christ to a dying world requires this perfect blending of divine justice and divine mercy. This is the power of the *Galilee Protocol*. But since our pioneering brethren refused to blend these two vital components properly in medical missionary work—God's permissive will provided two paths so both will be carried to the final work.

The final movement will blend the faithful souls of both paths into one unified work of *protocol evangelism*. Because of our *self-supporting* brothers and sisters, the movement will properly present the immutable law and divine justice. And because of our *organized* brothers and sisters, the movement will have a worldwide framework and properly present divine mercy with wide-open arms. United and led by the power of the Holy Spirit: the character of Christ will be perfectly reproduced in His people.[71]

—A Terrible Storm

All this does not happen easily or suddenly. When divine power and the mighty principles of the *Galilee Protocol* finally and fully clash with

---

64 Matthew 3:10.
65 Matthew 17:10-13.
66 John 1:19, 24; Matthew 3:7, Mark 6:16-19.
67 John 1:35-39.
68 See Ellen G. White, *The Desire of Ages*, p. 276. Jesus ate with publicans and sinners to bring them the light of heaven.
69 Ibid.
70 Matthew 9:14.
71 See Ellen G. White, *Christ's Object Lessons*, p. 69.

Satan and his counterfeit, there will be trouble beyond imagination. The *Galilee Protocol* will bring a great crisis on three fronts and in three theaters: it will cause a ministerial crisis, an educational crisis, and a medical crisis—in the church, in the nation, and in world. On each level of the battle—the contenders will simply be those who unite under the banner of our Prince Emmanuel and those who unite under the banner of the prince of this world. We need not put any finer point on it than that. There will only be two sides—and everyone gets to pick their side.

Before we will ever see the full power and glory of the latter rain, we will have to endure this terrible storm. Before that storm, we need to prepare the church, the nation, and the world for its strange developments. This is a task we will have to do without the permission and sanction of established authorities: because mostly, they won't approve of our protocol. Yet we should be undaunted in our resolve because our *authority* does not come from man—nor from man's system of things.

> "Following [Christ's] example in our medical missionary work, we shall reveal to the world that our credentials are from above... United with Christ in God, we shall reveal to the world that as God chose His Son to be His representative on the earth, even so has Christ chosen us to represent His character."[72]
>
> "The storm is coming, the storm that will try every man's faith of what sort it is. Believers must now be firmly rooted in Christ or else they will be led astray by some phase of error."[73]

—The Adventist Historical Timeline

The outline of our history tells the story of God's plan and our response to His authority. "We have nothing to fear for the future, except we forget the way the Lord has led us, and His teaching in our past history."[74]

1830-1844 •*Millerite Movement*. God separates a distinctive people for ministry.

•(1840-1844) *First Angel Sounds*.[75]

[72] Ellen G. White, *Medical Ministry*, p. 10.

[73] Ellen G. White, *Evangelism*, p. 361.

[74] Ellen G. White, *Last Day Events*, p. 72.

[75] Ellen G. White, *The Great Controversy*, p. 355, 1884 ed.

1844 •(Spring) Fredrick Wheeler Accepts the Sabbath. Millerite preacher, Fredrick Wheeler is influenced by Rachel Oaks to keep the Seventh-day Sabbath, He is joined by William and Cyrus Farnsworth.

•(Summer) *Second Angel Sounds*. Consistent with most protestants, Millerites identified Babylon in the book of Revelation as the Papacy. "The proclamation. 'Babylon is fallen,' was given in the summer of 1844, and as a result, about fifty thousand withdrew from the churches."[76]

•(Summer) *T. M. Preble Accepts the Sabbath*. Preble, who traveled with Miller, accepts the Sabbath a few days before the Great Disappointment.

•(October 22) The Great Disappointment.

•(October 23) *Cornfield Vision*. Hiram Edson sees the heavenly sanctuary application to Danial 8:14 while crossing through a cornfield.

•(December) *Midnight Cry Vision*. Ellen Harmon receives her first vision identifying the Midnight Cry with the Millerite Movement, and showing Adventists on the narrow path to heaven.

•*The Third Angel Begins to Sound*. "When Christ entered the most holy place of the heavenly sanctuary to perform the closing work of the atonement, He committed to His servants the last message of mercy to be given to the world. Such is the warning of the third angel of Revelation 14."[77] The third angel's message has to do with the *seal of God* (the Sabbath of the decalogue), and the *mark of the beast* (the opposite, keeping Sunday as the Sabbath); and that those who "keep the commandments of God," can only do so if their righteousness comes through faith in Jesus.[78]

1845 •(February 28) *Sabbath View Published*. T. M. Preble began publishing a column and tract about the Sabbath question.

•(April) *Sanctuary View Published*. Edson, Crosier, and Hahn publish their view of the sanctuary in a few issues of the Millerite periodical: *The Day Dawn*.

•(May) *Joseph Bates Accepts the Sabbath*, after reading Preble's tract. He travels to New Hampshire to meet with Fredrick Wheeler.

1846 •(February 7) *The Day Dawn Extra*. Enoch Jacobs, editor of *The Day Dawn*, publishes an *Extra* with an expanded and refined version of the sanctuary view.

---

[76] Ibid. p. 380.
[77] Ibid, p. 432.
[78] Revelation 14:12.

•*Sanctuary Vision*. A few weeks after Jacob prints *The Day Dawn Extra*, Ellen Harmon receives a vision confirming the correctness of Crosier's view of the sanctuary as published by Jacobs.

•*Joseph Bates Accepts Crosier's Sanctuary View*.

•*J. N. Andrews Accepts the Sabbath*, after reading Preble's tract. He would later be the first to write a book-length defense of the Sabbath.

•(August) *Marriage of James White and Ellen Harmon*.

•(Autumn) *The Whites Accept the Sabbath*. After studying a tract on the subject written by Joseph Bates.

1847 •(April) *Sabbath Vision*. Ellen White receives a vision confirming the Sabbath, its connection to the three angels' messages, and that it would play a key role in final events.

1848 •(April) *First Sabbath Conference*. Conference called for in Rocky Hill, Connecticut. Leaders begin hammering out Bible-based doctrines.

•(August) *Second and Third Sabbath Conferences*. Held in Volney, New York and Port Gibson, New York.

•(September) *Fourth Sabbath Conference*. Rocky Hill again. The Sabbath Conferences brought general agreement (with confirming visions) on eight specific points of doctrine:

1. *the imminent, personal, premillennial second advent;*
2. *the two-fold ministry of Christ in the heavenly sanctuary, whose cleansing began in 1844;*
3. *the seventh-day Sabbath;*
4. *God's special supernatural enlightenment through Ellen White;*
5. *the duty to proclaim the three angels' messages;*
6. *conditional immortality and death as a dreamless sleep;*
7. *the timing of the seven last plagues;*
8. *the final, complete extinction of the wicked after the millennium.*

•(November) *Streams of Light*. Ellen White receives a vision showing an expanding message going like "streams of light clear around the world."[79]

1849 •(March) *Sabbath a Special Test*. Ellen White receives a vision connecting the *open and shut doors* of Revelation 3, to the transfer of ministry in the heavenly sanctuary; showing light shining from the sanctuary on the Sabbath; and that the Sabbath had not been a test before the new light, but that from then on it would be a special test of loyalty.

---

[79] Ellen G. White, *Life Sketches*, p. 125.

1853 •*First School*. Martha Byington began the first church school in Buck Bridge, New York.[80]

1858 •*Final Atonement*. Ellen White's third book is published, *Spiritual Gifts*, volume I. In it she makes this statement:

> "As the priest entered the most holy once a year to cleanse the earthly sanctuary, so Jesus entered the most holy of the heavenly, at the end of the 2300 days of Daniel 8, in 1844, to make *a final atonement* for all who could be benefited by His mediation, and thus to cleanse the sanctuary... "This atonement is made for the righteous dead as well as for the righteous living."[81]

1862 •Civil War Begins.

1863 •*Health Vision*. God gave Ellen White the famous health vision.

•(May 21) *Organization*. Official organization of 3500 members with the name *Seventh-day Adventist Church*.

1865 •*Civil War Ends*.

•*Health Institute Vision*. Ellen White is told that Adventist were to start a health institute for the care of the sick and to educate about health.

1866 •*Western Health Reform Institute Established*, in Battle Creek, Michigan.

1868 •*Care for the Needy*. Ellen White calls for Sabbathkeepers to bear genuine "fruits that are manifested in good works, in caring for the needy, the fatherless, and widows."[82]

•*Goodloe Bell*. Bell opens a "select school" in Battle Creek.[83]

> "Bell was solid for Spirit of Prophecy principles and a strong advocate of vocational training, which he also highly recommended. Not once did he ever deviate from them. Not only were the students to learn book knowledge, but also how to work at various skills and trades. However it bothered some people that Goodloe Bell tended to be strict, and, worse, that he had no degrees. Bell had studied in Oberlin College... was well-educated, and firmly believed that vocational work should be included in the curriculum. But Bell had not graduated from any school."[84]

1870 •*Time Check*. Ellen White writes, "We are... on the borders of the eternal world."

1872 •*First Denominational School*. The General Conference adopts Bell's school as a denominational school.

1873-1874 •*Battle Creek College*. General Conference voted to form an Educational Society, purchase 12 acres in the city of Battle

[80] Vance Ferrell, *The Broken Blueprint*, p. 16.
[81] Ellen G. White, *Early Writings*, pp. 253-254. Emphasis added.
[82] Ellen G. White, *Testimonies for the Church*, vol. 2, p. 24-25.
[83] Ferrell, p. 17.
[84] Ibid, p. 19.

Creek (near the Sanitarium) and construct a three-story building for a new *Battle Creek College*.

•(1874) *State Sunday Laws*. The *National Reform Association* begins pressing for the enforcement of state Sunday laws.

1875 •*Sidney Brownsburger*. Fresh from the University of Michigan, Brownsburger was elected president of *Battle Creek College*, Bell was placed in charge of the English department, and Uriah Smith became Bible teacher. "Brownsburger believed in a classical (liberal arts) curriculum; he demanded that only that be taught."[85]

> "Brownsburger... taught a curriculum little different from that of other educational institutions. This was largely because Brownsburger, according to his own testimony, knew nothing about operating a program that included industries and farming."[86]
>
> "It was a difficult problem for the new school to adjust itself to the plan of education outlined by Mrs. White in 1872. The education of the day was classical, the main emphasis being placed on a knowledge of the classics, mathematics, ancient languages, philosophy, and certain science. Her message called for an education that would include practical training and character training. Just how to accomplish this baffled many of the early educators of the Seventh-day Adventist Church."[87]

1878 •*Time Check*. "Our feet are on the borders of the eternal world, and every probationary moment is more precious than gold."[88]

1879 •*Time Check*. "We are standing upon the very borders of the eternal world. We have no time to lose."[89]

1880 •*Growth Check*. Church Membership at about 16,000 due to revival and missionary efforts of the 1870's.

1881-1883 •*Brownsburger Resigns*. *Battle Creek College* closes for a year because of disagreement about whether the college should provide a classical or practical education.

•(1881) *Time Check*. "I have been shown that we are standing upon the threshold of the eternal world."[90]

1882 •*South Lancaster Academy Established*. S.N. Haskell urges the brethren in New England to start a college in Massachusetts. *South Lancaster Academy* (college-level) began under the direction of Goodloe Bell. The curriculum that Bell provided did not include classical studies:

> "The course of study will embrace English Language; Mathematics;

---

[85] Ferrell, p. 20.

[86] Emmett K. Vande Vere, *Adventism in America*, Gary Land, ed., p. 70.

[87] General Conference Department of Education, *Lessons in Denominational History*, p. 181. 1942.

[88] Ellen G. White, *The Review and Herald*, August 8, 1878.

[89] Ellen G. White, *The* Review and Herald, January 2, 1879.

[90] Ellen G. White, *Testimonies for the Church*, vol. 5, p. 18.

Geography; Human Physiology and Hygiene; and Bible History; together with practical instruction in Tract and Missionary Work, and in the most useful of the Agricultural, Domestic and Mechanic Arts... But of all studies, the Bible ranks highest... a practical knowledge of the laws of health is all-important... Pupils will be expected to take but a few studies at a time, thereby mastering them the more rapidly."[91]

•*Healdsburg College Established*. California. Under the leadership of Brownsburger.

"After leaving the headship of Battle Creek College in the spring of 1881, [Brownsburger] became sick. While convalescing that summer, he declared that he recognized his error... Arriving at Healdsburg that fall, he fully endorsed the blueprint program his associates arranged, even though he himself was still learning more about it."[92]

During the first year, Brownsburger wrote,

"The commencement of this year has been one of unusual anxiety to many friends of the college. An untried field of responsibility was entered upon in uniting physical employment with mental labor, and every step in the development of the system was watched with intense interest... Almost from the very first there has been a steady increasing interest on the part of the students, in the practical workings of this new system, and I doubt there is one of our number who would willingly return to the old method... The students are hard at work at their various employments, and they are happy because they are faithful."[93]

1884 •*Final Atonement and the Investigative Judgment*. The 1884 edition of *The Great Controversy* is released, with this statement linking a final atonement with the investigative judgment:

"In the typical service, only those who had come before God with confession and repentance, and whose sins, through the blood of the sin-offering, were transferred to the sanctuary, had a part in the service of the day of atonement. So in the great day of *final atonement* and investigative Judgment, the only cases considered are those of the professed people of God.

1885 •*Adventists Arrested*. Five Adventists, (one a minister) were arrested for working on Sunday.

•*Time Check*. Ellen White writes: "We are on the very verge of the eternal world."[94] "Eternity stretches before us. The curtain is about to be lifted."[95]

•*J.O. Corliss in Australia*. He and some helpers arrive in Australia to start a mission there.

---

[91] Ellen G. White, *The Review and Herald*, March 7, 1882.

[92] Ferrell, p. 26.

[93] Sidney Brownsburger, *Review and Herald*, January 15, 1884.

[94] Ibid. p. 460.

[95] Ibid. p. 464.

1888 •(1888) The Blair Bill. Introduced in Congress for a national Sunday law.

•*Righteousness by Faith*. Jones and Waggoner present *Righteousness by Faith* at the General Conference. Despite Sister Whites strong endorsements, the leading brethren resisted the new emphasis on *righteousness by faith*. But even before the 1888 General Conference in Minneapolis, we were tampering with God's plan. On nearly every front, we were conducting the work according to human wisdom, and following our own human counsel.

•*Latter Rain "kept away from the world."* Our actions at the Minneapolis conference actually *prevented* us from obtaining the Holy Spirit Pentecostal power needed to lighten the whole earth with glory.

> "An unwillingness to yield up preconceived opinions, and to accept this truth, lay at the foundation of a large share of the opposition manifested at Minneapolis against the Lord's message through brethren Waggoner and Jones. By exciting that opposition, Satan succeeded in shutting away from the people, in a great measure, the special power of the Holy Spirit that God longed to impart to them. The enemy prevented them from obtaining that efficiency which might have been theirs in carrying the truth to the world, as the apostles proclaimed it after the day of Pentecost. The light that was to lighten the whole earth with its glory was resisted, and by actions of our own brethren has been in a great degree kept away from the world."[96]

1889 •*Benevolence*. Dr. Kellogg was impressed with some benevolence work he observed while on a trip to New York City. This was later reinforced through his familiarity with the well-known city mission work of Dr. Dowkonnt.[97]

1890 •*Time Check*. "We are upon the very borders of the eternal world."[98]

•*Christ's Blood Didn't Cancel Sin*. Patriarch and Prophets first published. In it, Ellen White states:

> "The blood of Christ, while it was to release the repentant sinner from the condemnation of the law, *was not to cancel the sin*; it would stand on record in the sanctuary until the final atonement; so in the type the blood of the sin offering removed the sin from the penitent, but it rested in the sanctuary until the Day of Atonement."[99]

1891 •*Ellen White sent to Australia*. She was sent there by the General Conference.

•*Union College Founded*, in Lincoln, Nebraska.

---

[96] Ellen G. White, *Manuscript Releases*, vol. 1, p. 130.
[97] Dave Fiedler, *D'Sozo, Reversing the Worst Evil*, p. 55.
[98] Ellen G. White, *Manuscript 7*, 1890.
[99] Ellen G. White, *Patriarchs and Prophets*, p. 357.

1892-1900 •*Australian Mission*. This mission has been endorsed as being according to the inspired blueprint.

1892 •*Walla Walla College Established*. Washington State, E. A Sutherland is principal.

> "Sutherland set to work to educate the new facility into Spirit of Prophecy principles; and... the entire faculty took hold of them."[100]
>
> "Sutherland convened his faculty for a week or more prior to opening day in order that its members might jointly study Ellen White's counsels on education. From the start, Walla Walla College demonstrated its commitment to health reform by serving only a lacto-ovo-vegetarian diet; it was the first Seventh-day Adventist school to take this step."[101]

•(November) *Loud Cry Already Begun*. The *Review and Herald* contains the following statement from Ellen White:

> "The time of test is just upon us, for the loud cry of the third angel has already begun in the revelation of the righteousness of Christ, the sin-pardoning Redeemer. This is the beginning of the light of the angel whose glory shall fill the whole earth."[102]

1893 •*Christian Help Bands*. In six lectures, Dr. Kellogg presents a strong case for Christian Help Bands from the Bible and the Spirit of Prophecy at the General Conference.[103] The concept was endorsed by Ellen White.

•*The True Basis of Marking and Credits*. At the 1893 General Conference Session, W.W. Prescott stated:

> "The basis on which students should be encouraged to earnest work in securing an education is an important matter. You know to what extent it is coming to be a practice in educational institutions in almost every line. The marking system very generally encourages a feeling of rivalry. The basis of the work is thus made to be personal ambition. It is not so much to personal excellence, nor to reach any certain ideal, but to be above a neighbor. Of two students, with different capacities, one may by much less hard work take the higher rank, and yet his fellow student may do better work and be a better student. The True basis seems to me to be this: Everyone is endowed with certain capabilities and faculties. God has given him a certain ideal which he can reach by proper use of time and opportunities. He is not to be satisfied with the fact that he outstrips his neighbor. His effort should be to get what God would have him, and success is to meet the ideal the Lord has for him in view of his capacity and opportunity... The true basis of credit is not by comparing one with another to see if one secures better standing or more prizes than his neighbor, but to compare the actual standing of every student with the ideal which God intends he should gain."[104]

---

100 Ferrell, p. 49.

101 Schwarz. p. 201.

102 Ellen G. White, *The Review and Herald*, November 22, 1892.

103 See Fiedler, chapters 5-8.

104 W.W. Prescott, *1893 General Conference Bulletin*, pp. 357-358.

1897 •*Avondale Opens in Australia.* "Avondale was to be the model school of higher grades for all the Adventist world. It was to be marked with simplicity, industry, devotion, adherence to the pattern."[105]

•*John Corliss in Canada*. John returns to America and conducts evangelism in Ottowa, Canada according to the Australian model.[106]

•*Sutherland at Battle Creek College*. The delegates at the 1897 General Conference are so pleased with what Sutherland accomplished in four years at *Walla Walla*, they voted to call him to *Battle Creek College*. He joined his old friend Percy Magan there. The *Review* carried an announcement that the school was offering short courses for mature students, missionary workers, teachers, bookkeepers, and canvassers. Those short courses were only 12 weeks in length.[107] The August issue of the school journal included a quotation from a Roman Catholic pamphlet: "The conferring of degrees was originated by a pope." The announcement was made:

> "The College, under its new organization, ceases, with this year to grant degrees. Preparation for usefulness in the cause of Christ will be the subject constantly held before students, replacing the courses and diplomas of the past."[108]

1899 •*Medical Fraternity*. Ellen White warns Dr. Kellogg that the medical fraternity had been represented to her as of the spirit of Freemasonry, and that they would call the Lord's prescription for Hezekiah quackery; and that the students in his institution are to be educated to leave drugs alone.[109]

•*San Francisco Mission*. John Corliss sent to San Francisco to play "a key role in perhaps the most fully developed program of Gospel-Medical Missionary Evangelism ever carried out in modern times."[110] After visiting that mission, Sister White said:

> "We have every reason to believe that the work carried on in San Francisco by brother Corliss and his brethren is the work that needs to be done. San Francisco is a center, and must be thoroughly worked. A much more extensive work should be done in this great and wicked city."[111]

---

[105] Arthur Spalding, *Captain of the Host*, p. 651.

[106] See *General Conference Daily Bulletin*, February 22, 1899.

[107] E.A. Sutherland, *The Review and Herald*, November 1, 1897.

[108] Advocate, August, 1898.

[109] Ellen G. White, *Letter 67*, 1899. (April 6, 1899).

[110] Fiedler, 161.

[111] Ellen G. White, *Manuscript Releases*, vol. 17, p. 41.

1901 •*Reorganization*. Ellen White began calling for reorganization, saying that "God calls for a decided change,"[112] where there would be "no kings"[113] in the Seventh-day Adventist church, and no "entrusting responsibilities to men who have had light poured upon them year after year for the last ten or fifteen years, and yet have not heeded the light God has given them."[114] The Church was reorganized. Ellen White endorsed the new plan saying, "God has brought it about."

•*Timeline Reset*. By the time of the 1901 reorganization, our unfaithfulness had already seriously jeopardized the mission:

> "God's people have been far behind. Human agencies under the divine planning, may recover something of what has been lost because God's people who have had great light did not have the corresponding piety, sanctification, and zeal, in working out God's specified plans. They have lost to their own disadvantage what they might have gained to the advancement of truth if they had carried out the plans and will of God.... Man cannot possibly stretch over the gulf that has been made by workers who have not followed the divine Leader. We may have to remain here in this world because of insubordination many more years, as did the children of Israel, but for Christ's sake His people should not add sin to sin by charging God with the consequences of their own wrong course of action."[115]

•*Growth Check*. Rapid growth continued through the 1880's and 1890's. Membership at 75,000.

1902 •*San Francisco Warning*. Ellen White warned with urgency that "not long hence these cities will suffer under the judgment of God. San Francisco and Oakland are becoming like Sodom and Gomorrah, and the Lord will visit them in wrath."[116]

•(February 18) *The Battle Creek Sanitarium burns down*.

•(Spring) *GC & The Living Temple*. The General Conference Committee approved a plan to print and sell ½ million copies of Dr. Kellogg's book, *The Living Temple*, to fund the rebuilding of the Battle Creek Sanitarium. Later they change their mind because Prescott was concerned about its pantheistic leanings.

•(December) *Kellogg & The Living Temple*. Kellogg orders an initial printing of *The Living Temple* from the Review and Herald. They were never printed because the Review burned down.

---

[112] Ellen G. White, *Manuscript Releases*, vol. 13, p. 195. (1901).
[113] Ellen G. White, *Manuscript Releases*, vol. 13, p. 201 (1901).
[114] Ellen G. White, *General Conference Bulletin*, April 3, 1901.
[115] Ellen G. White, *Manuscript* Releases, vol. 20, p. 312-313.
[116] Ellen G. White, *Manuscript 114*, 1902.

•(December 30) _The Review and Herald burns_.

1903 •_Reorganized (Again)_. The Church is reorganized again, effectively undoing some important changes made in 1901.

1904 •_Sutherland and Magan Head South_. They realized opposition to their efforts at Emmanuel Missionary College in in Berrien Springs, would eventually push them out, they head south. Ellen White had counseled them to start a new school in the southern states. They buy a 414-acre farm about fifteen miles from Nashville, Tennessee. Ellen White tells them that if they incorporate Madison as an independent organization, she will serve on the board.[117] This was the beginning of the *self-supporting* work.

1905 •_College of Medical Evangelists Established_. Loma Linda, California.

> "The work at Battle Creek is going down. God will reestablish His medical work in this place. We are farther from the true picture of medical missionary work then when we first began. God never designed that our work should blossom out in the great professional and commercial way in which it stands before the world. We have educated bedside nurses. He intended that we should educate missionary nurses to go into the homes of the people of the villages, towns, and cities, ministering to the people, singing gospel songs, and giving Bible readings. We must have men here who have had an experience in the early development of the work, such men as Elder Haskell, to help us build this on the right foundation."[118]

1906 •(October) _Ellen White & The Living Temple_. Ellen White sends letters to a group of leaders who were reconsidering *The Living Temple*. She clearly condemns the ideas in the book.

•(April 16) _San Francisco Vision_. Ellen White awakes from a vision at 1:00 a.m. and pens scenes of destruction she saw in San Francisco.

•(April 18) _San Francisco Earthquake_. At 5:12 a.m. San Francisco is hit with a major earthquake.

•(April 20) _Warning to Cities_. Ellen White warned, "I am bidden to declare the message that cities full of transgression, and sinful to the extreme, will be destroyed by earthquake, by fire, by flood. All the world will be warned that there is a God who will display His authority."[119]

•(July) _Pacific Press Burns_. The Pacific Press—freshly repaired after the earthquake—burns to a total loss. They abandoned all commercial printing after the fire.

•(November 10) _Dr. Kellogg Disfellowshipped_.

---

[117] Ferrell, pp. 59-61.

[118] J. A. Burden, *The Story of Loma Linda*, p. 91.

[119] Ellen G. White, *Manuscript 35*, 1906.

1907 •(June 18) *Madison Approved of God*. Sister White writes:

"The Lord does not set limits about His workers in some lines as men are wont to set. In their work, brethren Magan and Southerland have been hindered unnecessarily. Means have been withheld from them because in the organization and management of the Madison school it was not placed under the control of the Conference. But the reasons why this school was not owned and controlled by the Conference has not been duly considered... The work that has been done there is approved of God, and He forbids that this line of work should be broken up."[120]

1908 •*Healdsburg College Closed*. This was because of too-little land, and later management that did not understand the blueprint of how to manage the finances.

•*Burden to Ruble*:

"Our understanding of the testimonies is, that while thousands are to be quickly qualified for thorough medical-evangelistic work, some must qualify to labor as physicians. We have been instructed again and again to make the school as strong as possible for the qualification of nurses and physicians."[121]

1909 •*Pacific Union College Established*.

•*Clarification on Charter*. Elder Burden asked Sister White for some clarifications:

[Mr. Burden:] "Would the securing of a charter for a medical school, where our students might obtain a medical education, militate against our depending upon God?"

[Mrs. White:] "No, I do not see that it would if a charter were secured on the right terms. Only be sure you do not exalt men above God. If you can gain force and influence that will make your work more effective without tying yourselves to worldly men, that would be right."

[Mr. Burden:] "In planning our course of study, we have tried to follow the light in the Testimonies; and in doing so, it has led us away from the requirements of the world. The world will not recognize us as standing with them. We shall have to stand distinct, by ourselves."

[Mrs. White:] "You may unite with them in certain points that will not have a misleading influence., but let no sacrifice be made to endanger our principles. We shall always have to stand distinct. God desires us to be separate; and yet, it is our privilege to avail ourselves of certain rights. But rather than to confuse our medical work, you had better stand aloof and labor with the advantages that you yourselves can offer... You must arrange this matter as best you can, but the principle that is presented to me is that you are not to acknowledge any power as greater than that of God. Our influence is to be acknowledged by God because be keep His commandments."[122]

---

[120] Ellen G. White, *Special Testimonies*, Series B, no. 11, p. 32. June 18, 1907.

[121] John Burden, *Letter to W. A. Ruble*, April 13, 1908.

[122] John Burden Interview with Ellen White, September 20, 1909.

•*Constant Danger*. Speaking to 30 teachers at *Union College*, Ellen White says,

> "There is the constant danger among our people that those who engage in labor in our schools and sanitariums will entertain the idea that they must get in line with the world, study the things which the world studies, and become familiar with the things the world becomes familiar with. This is one of the greatest mistakes that could be made."[123]

•*No Compromise*. The same year she wrote,

> "I am instructed to say that in our educational work there is to be no compromise in order to meet the world's standards. God's commandment-keeping people are not to unite with the world to carry various lines of work according to worldly plans and worldly wisdom. Our people are now being tested as to whether they will obtain their wisdom from the greatest Teacher the world ever knew or seek the god of Ekron. Let us determine that we shall not be tied by so much as a thread to the educational policies of those who do not discern the voice of God and who will not harken to His commandments... Shall we represent before the world that our physicians must follow the pattern of the world before they are qualified to act as successful physicians? This is the question that is now testing the faith of some of our brethren. Let not any of our brethren displease the Lord by advocating in their assemblies the idea that we need to obtain from unbelievers a higher education than that specified by the Lord."[124]

•(December 9) *State Charter Obtained*. California requirements for a full, accredited medical school, required that it conform to the requirements of the *Association of American Medical Colleges*—an AMA subsidiary. AMA-approved accreditation was impossible; but partial approval sufficient to meet Loma Linda's needs was available. Osteopaths had fought for recognition, and the State Legislature—instead of only approving osteopaths, "threw the gate wide open for any school whose requirements for entrance to the medical course were equal to a high school preparation on the ten fundamental branches that underlie medical education."[125] Under this accommodation, on December 9, the College obtained a charter from the State of California, signed and recorded in Los Angeles.

> "[The College of Evangelists] is authorized to grant such literary, scientific, and professional honors and degrees as are usually granted by literary, scientific, medical, dental, or pharmaceutical colleges, and particularly the honors and degrees of Bachelor of Arts, Bachelor of Science, Doctor of Medicine [M.D.] Doctor of Surgery, and Doctor of Dental Surgery [D.D.S.], and in testimony thereof to give suitable

---

[123] Ellen G. White, *Fundamentals of Christian Education*, p. 534.
[124] Ellen G. White, *Letter 132*, 1909, *Medical Ministry*, pp. 61-12.
[125] Burden Letter to W.A. Ruble, April 3, 1908.

diplomas under the corporate seal."[126]

1910 •*Asheville Agricultural School Established*. The Asheville Agricultural School and Mountain Sanitarium later became Fletcher Academy, Inc., Fletcher, North Carolina. [*Self-Supporting*].

•(April) *Must Not Confederate*. Ellen White wrote an urgent letter to Elder Burden, warning him that our medical work, including Loma Linda, must not confederate with worldly organizations and should not seek to meet their standards.

> "It is not necessary that our medical missionaries follow the precise track marked out by the medical men of the world. They do not need to administer drugs to the sick. They do not need to follow drug medication in order to have influence in their work... Some of our medical missionaries have supposed that a medical training according to the plans of the worldly schools is essential to their success. To those who have been taught that the only way to success is by being taught of worldly men and pursuing a course that is sanctioned by worldly men, I would now say, put away such ideas. This is a mistake that should be corrected."[127]

•(July) *Company Evangelism*. John Tindall pioneers the concept of Company Evangelism in response to Ellen White's call for a "decided change from past methods of working."[128]

1911 •(Fall) AMA Visits Loma Linda. Dr. Nathan P. Colwell, Inspector of Medical Colleges of the AMA, visited Loma Linda. "No request had been made for accreditation, and Colwell had not come to ask them to apply for it. He just wanted to see what the place looked like."[129] Dr. Colwell asked Burden why they were "starting a new school when there are already a hundred and fifty medical schools in the United State?" Burden said it was for three reasons: to prepare medical missionaries, to educate our own young people for our own work, to give them training in the special line of treatments we use in our institutions. His "reply was that he was in full sympathy with such a movement and that he saw the need for such a school."[130] Burden told him that, "Wherever we go we build our gospel plan on a threefold foundation. The spiritual, the mental, and the physical... 'Will you tell me, Doctor, to what school can we send our young people to equip them for this World mission work with this threefold preparation?' He replied that there was no such school in existence."[131] Colwell said, "Mr. Burden, when I took my

---

[126] Charter of the College of Evangelists, 1909.

[127] Ellen G. White, Letter 61, 1910. April 27, 1910.

[128] Fiedler, chapter 18.

[129] Ferrell, 261-262.

[130] W.A. Ruble, in *The Medical Evangelist*, January 1912. Pp. 17-18.

[131] John Burden, letter to Dr. E.H. Risley, June 3, 1929.

medical course it was to become a medical missionary... the medical got me, and the mission lost out."[132] He never did go to the mission field. "From that day Dr. Colwell became a friend of the College of Medical Evangelists."[133] Before leaving, Dr. Colwell told the leaders at Loma Linda that in view of the type of work they were doing, "they did not need AMA approval."[134]

1915 •(February) *College of Medical Evangelists Accredited*. The Council on Education of the AMA granted CME a "C" rating. The decision and process to obtain accreditation began around 1910. God had arranged it so that the State had already granted Loma Linda a charter to train physicians. He arranged our special friendship with Colwell at the AMA, who had already told Loma Linda that AMA approval was not needed. In fact, when Colwell eventually learned that Loma Linda was trying to seek an approval rating from the AMA, he was astonished. He penned a memo in which he said, "They have gone and done what I told them not to do."[135]

•(July) *Ellen White Dies*. She was 87 years old. Shortly before her death, she spoke with John Burden.

> "In talking with Elder John Burden before his death, he told me that, during his last visit with Sister White, she made the statement that God was going to lay her to rest in order to save her the heartbreaking experience of seeing her message to the church rejected."[136]

1917 •(April) *Madison Accredited*. The Southern Accrediting Association accepted the Madison High School into its Association.

1924 •*Little Creek Sanitarium and Academy*. The Layman Foundation purchased a 185-acre farm on Little Creek. From this rural outpost, medical missionary work began in Knoxville, Tennessee. [*Self-Supporting*].

1926 •(January) *P.T. Megan to Warren Howell*:

> "If our people had wholeheartedly set themselves at the time to carry out God's simple plan of education, we might now be in a very different position than we are today. But our leaders, to a very great extent, urged the selling of land attached to the schools and doing away with a large amount of our physical work. This has been true of Walla Walla, Union College, and Washington Missionary College at Takoma Park. It has also been true in other places in a smaller degree. You have felt pained and saddened at all of this, and my personal belief is that you have honestly done your best to stem the tide. But as I see it, you have not been able to put your ideas across

---

[132] Ibid.

[133] Ibid.

[134] Ferrell, p. 264.

[135] W. Fredrick Norwood, M.D., *The Vision Bold*, p. 193.

[136] S.A. Nagel, Newsletter, July 1961.

with our educators generally anymore than E.A. Sutherland and I in earlier days."[137]

1928 •*Madison, a Junior College*. The *Southern Association of Colleges and Schools* accredits Madison as a junior college.

1931 •*Survey Commission on Education*. The General Conference authorizes a survey to look into the issue of accreditation for our colleges.

•*Walla Walla and PUC*. The way was opened up for these two senior colleges to seek accreditation—with some restrictions.

1933 •*Madison, a Senior College*. The *Tennessee College Association* accepts Madison as a four-year college, so they could do a premedical course.

1935 •*Branson Report*. The *Survey Commission* shares their findings on accreditation at the General Conference Autumn Counsel. Elder C. H. Watson (president) presided at the Autumn Council. Other leading men in those days included J. L. McElhany, W. H. Branson, and N. C. Wilson—all three of these men would become future GC presidents:

> [Brother Rice is speaking] "Mr. Chairman, I do not wish to appear opposed to the resolution, But I remember 4 years ago, when I was talking to Elder McElhaney about this matter when the vote was taken. He said, we will see the day when we will rue what we have done. Now we have accredited two senior colleges. Now we propose to recommend that another college be accredited, and that all junior colleges proceed with caution. If this is wrong, then how can it be right to recommend to accredit another? If we should not be tied by so much as a thread, why not cut loose?"
>
> [Elder Watson] "...We recognize that very much of the urge for accreditation for educational work is come from the medical college, for it can only carry on its work on that basis, the basis allowed by the *American Medical Association...* Unless we decide to wholly discontinue that medical college, there has to be accreditation of the schools that prepare the students for entrance to the courses in the college. There is no other way..."
>
> [Elder Watson also said] "The facts involve us in the consideration of whether or not we will continue with an educational program that has become more and more worldly or whether we will start an educational plan that is in harmony with the instruction we have received from God. The plan of accrediting our schools, adopted four years ago, has been a very strong contributing factor during these four years to our educational program becoming more and more worldly in its character, in its aim, in its determination to meet the requirements of outside accreditation bodies. These accreditation bodies have not only shown their determination, they are determined to control the program of our educational work and also the methods by which that program shall be carried out. There is no

[137] Percy T. Magan, *Letter to Warren Howell*, January 13, 1926.

doubt about it."

[Elder Piper (Union College board chairman)] "The policy provided in 1931, that we only select teachers with definite Christian experience to enter upon graduate training in the universities of the world. Experience has taught us this is impossible, for the moment we set the standards for teaching efficiency, with a university training, that moment every young man and woman who seeks to reach the highest in teaching, feels forced to enter upon training that will bring him to the highest place. And we have not been able to control it. We have such a situation here. As a result of this action, within the last four years, forty of our young people were in one university at the same time seeking training to help them reach their objective in education. If you can continue this program which destroyed our own denominational ideals of true education, then we are wasting our time by discussing the report of this commission. It gives some of us a burden, for it has shown itself to be beyond the control of the policy adopted in 1931. The medical college was at one time the chief urge for accreditation. It is a large part of the urge today; and, if it comes to a choice between whether we continue the medical college or go worldly, my vote shall be that we shall not continue our medical work; and as a leader in the denomination I am calling upon you, in the fear of God, to take this step to keep our principles of true education from being lost to us. That is my appeal. It is silly and useless for us to go to the world with any statement that God has given us the principles of true education and then take steps that will lead us to ignorance of those principles in the very near future..."

[Elder H.H. Votaw (Religious Liberty)] I think that Brother Watson's talk just now has risen to the height of his Tuesday morning talk, yet we are preparing to send boys to hell in three of our schools. If this is the plan, we have no right to set up two colleges—already set up, going to set up a third one (EMC), and do the very thing that we ought not to do... If this accreditation is wrong, it is wrong altogether... Let us face the thing... If it is wrong, let us quit it."

[Elder E.K. Slade (Walla Walla board chairman)] "Mr. Chairman, I do not intend to take the position that accreditation can be abandoned now... It would be unfortunate to have a vote here on which we are divided so seriously... We don't want to make another mistake now by hastily voting something here that we feel is not agreeable to all. I think of Walla Walla College. Last year its enrollment was the largest. I suppose it will be larger this year... We, of the northwest, have visited our own people, and the educational people of the state up there. I don't know what they will think of us, or what they will say if we go back and say we have changed our minds. Really, Mr. Chairman, we are placed in an embarrassing place..."

The question was tabled. Within a few years, all our colleges in America were accredited. Before long, nearly all our academies and elementary schools followed suit.

1941 •*Wildwood*. Neil Martin begin plans to create a rural sanitarium and medical missionary institute using Hayward's 500-acre farm outside Chattanooga, Tennessee. W.D. Frazee and George McClure joined them in establishing Wildwood Sanitarium and Hospital. [*Self-Supporting*].

1945 •*Growth Check*. 210,000 members in the U.S. and Canada; 360,000 members elsewhere. 140,000 in church schools.

1947 •*ASI-Adventist Laymen's Services and Industries*. At the recommendation of the 1945 General Conference Fall Council, an association to promote the interests of self-supporting institutions was organization.

1950 •*Stonecave Institute*. Archie and Ruth Peek form a non-profit corporation and began developing a new training facility near Dunlap, Tennessee. [*Self-Supporting*].

1955-1956 •Evangelical Conferences. Barnhouse, an evangelical scholar, gave his evaluation of present-day Adventism in an article printed in *Eternity* magazine He based his evaluation on extensive meetings with prominent Adventist theologians concerning what we really believe. He wrote:

> "Immediately it was perceived that the Adventists were strenuously denying certain doctrinal positions which had been previously attributed to them."
>
> "On the morning after the 'Great Disappointment' two men were going through a corn field in order to avoid the pitiless gaze of their mocking neighbors to whom they had said an eternal Good-bye the day before. To put it in the words of Hiram Edson (the man in the corn field who first conceived this peculiar idea), he was overwhelmed with the conviction 'that instead of our High Priest coming out of the most holy of the heavenly sanctuary to come to this earth on the tenth day of the seventh month at the end of 2,300 days, He for the first time entered, on that day the second apartment of that sanctuary, and that He had work to perform in the most holy before coming to this earth. It is to my mind, therefore, nothing more than a human, face-saving idea! It should also be realized that some uninformed Seventh-day Adventists took this idea and carried it to fantastic, literalistic extremes. Mr. Martin and I heard the Adventist leaders say, flatly, that they repudiate all such extremes. This they have said in no uncertain terms. Further, they do not believe, as some of their earlier teachers taught, that Jesus' atoning work was not completed on Calvary, but instead that He was still carrying on a second ministering work since 1844. This idea is also totally repudiated. They believe that since His ascension Christ has been ministering the benefits of the atonement which He completed on Calvary."[138]

[138] Donald Barnhouse, "*Are Seventh-day Adventists Christians?*" Eternity, September 1956.

CHAPTER THREE

Sabbath—The Protocol for Service

It was Sabbath in Galilee. The year was A.D. 29. Jesus was visiting the synagogue in His hometown—Nazareth. Every Sabbath an elder would read something from the scriptures and exhort the people to still hope for the coming Messiah.[1] Since Jesus was visiting home, someone invited Him to read something from Isaiah.

He found chapter 61; and He read: "The Spirit of the Lord is on Me, because He has anointed Me to preach good news to the poor. He has sent Me to proclaim deliverance to the captives and recovery of sight to the blind, to release the oppressed, to proclaim the year of the Lord's favor."[2]

They knew the passage well. They recognized it was about the Messiah.[3] Closing the scroll, Jesus gave it back to the attendant. Every eye fastened upon Him.[4] Word of His mighty works and teachings in Judea arrived ahead of Him. Everyone was curious to hear what He would say. They wondered, what would He do?

---

[1] Ellen G. White, *The Desire of Ages*, p. 236.
[2] Luke 4:18-19.
[3] Ellen G. White, *The Desire of Ages*, p. 236.
[4] Luke 4:20.

They liked what He said!—for Luke says that everybody bore witness and wondered at the words of grace which proceeded out of His mouth.[5]

—The Desire of Ages

"Jesus stood before the people as a living expositor of the prophecies concerning Himself. Explaining the words He had read, He spoke of the Messiah as a reliever of the oppressed, a liberator of captives, a healer of the afflicted, restoring sight to the blind, and revealing to the world the light of truth. His impressive manner and the wonderful import of His words thrilled the hearers with a power they had never felt before. The tide of divine influence broke every barrier down; like Moses, they beheld the Invisible. As their hearts were moved upon by the Holy Spirit, they responded with fervent amens and praises to the Lord."[6]

But as soon as Jesus announced: "This day is this scripture fulfilled in your ears," they suddenly realized He was talking about them. Jesus represented them—Israelites, children of Abraham—as being in bondage. He said they were prisoners needing deliverance from evil; in darkness, without the light of truth. Their pride was offended. Their fears were aroused. "The words of Jesus indicated that His work for them was to be altogether different from what they desired."[7]

The people of Nazareth understood the context of Isaiah 61. "Little Jesus" (that's how the folks remembered Him); "Little Jesus" had stumbled into *already fulfilled* prophecy. These words were just a few verses away:

"And they shall build the old wastes, [Jerusalem] they shall rise up the former desolations, [the temple] and they shall repair the waste cities, the desolations of many generations."[8]

Verse 6 says: "Ye shall be named the *Priests of the Lord*: men shall call you the *Ministers of our God*." They were also acquainted with its sister passage, Isaiah 58:

"And they that shall be of thee shall build the old waste places: thou shalt raise up the foundations of many generations; and thou shalt be called, The repairer of the breach, The restorer of paths to dwell in."[9]

The seer expounds the Sabbath in this regard:

---

[5] Luke 4:22.
[6] Ellen G. White, *The Desire of Ages*, p. 237.
[7] Ibid.
[8] Isaiah 61:4. Bracketed contents added.
[9] Isaiah 58:12.

> "If thou turn away thy foot from the sabbath, from doing thy pleasure on my holy day; and call the sabbath a delight, the holy of the LORD, honorable; and shalt honor him, not doing thine own ways, nor finding thine own pleasure, nor speaking thine own words: Then shalt thou delight thyself in the LORD; and I will cause thee to ride upon the high places of the earth, and feed thee with the heritage of Jacob thy father: —for the mouth of the LORD hath spoken it."[10]

This stuff already happened! They already rebuilt Jerusalem. The temple was already restored. They had a fully functional priesthood. The sacrificial system was a well-oiled machine.

There were strict guards around the Sabbath. They *had* turned their feet away from doing their own pleasure on that day. They couldn't even take an afternoon walk. It was unlawful to spit on the ground or rub the ground with the foot, because that might plow[11]—or the spit might mix with the dirt to make clay[12] or brick.

So what was Jesus talking about? Why did He say He was sent to proclaim liberty to the captives? What captives? Why did He think they needed the light of truth?

—House of Mercy

The Nazareth folks knew that Jesus was in trouble with the Sanhedrin at Jerusalem. They knew He had just come from there. It started with a skirmish with the Pharisees at Bethesda. It was Sabbath that day too—a high Sabbath—it was *Passover Sabbath*. Passover was a big deal in Jerusalem.

Bethesda was a pool near the sheep market. Its name means *House of Mercy*.[13] It had five porticoes with roof structures supported by columns or enclosed walls. Archeologists have uncovered this facility. It was really two pools surrounded with four porticoes—with a fifth between them. Water filled the upper pool, piped from a spring. The upper pool fed the lower pool.[14]

---

[10] Isaiah 58:13-14.

[11] Alfred Edersheim, *Law of the Sabbath*, from *Life and Times of Jesus the Messiah*, Appendix XVII, 1886, (http://mb-soft.com/believe/txo/lawsabba.htm), accessed 3/24/2019.

[12] Daniel Giron, *What is the Significance of Jesus' Spitting on the Ground in the Book of John?*, January 19, 2015, (https://christianity.stackexchange.com/questions/36538/what-is-the-significance-of-jesus-spitting-on-the-ground-in-the-book-of-john), accessed 3/24/2019.

[13] Wikipedia, *Pool of Bethesda*, (https://en.wikipedia.org/wiki/Pool_of_Bethesda), accessed 10-6-2018.

[14] Dr. Lizorkin-Eyzenberg, The Pool of Bethesda As Greek Asclepion. July 7, 2016, (https://israelstudycenter.com/the-pool-of-bethesda-as-greek-asclepion/), accesses 10-6-2018.

John describes a great multitude of impotent folk, of blind, halt, withered—laying in these porticoes, waiting around for the moving of the water.

Scholars think Bethesda was part of the Hellenization of Jerusalem—that it was really built according to the pattern of the Greco-Roman hospitals.[15] Over four hundred of these healing temples existed in the First-Century Roman Empire. They were sacred to the god *Asclepius*. The hospitals were known as *asclepeion*.[16] The priests that did the healing were part of an exclusive order. Their symbol was a serpent wrapped around a staff.[17] The water in the *asclepeion* pools were sacred and believed to have curative powers.

These hospitals were state-of-the art, for their day. They offered curative potions and minor surgical cures. They had a primitive form of anesthesia. "Hippocrates is said to have received his medical training at an *asclepeion;*"[18] and gained the knowledge of many cures from what he found inscribed on their walls.

Evidently the Jews tried to make Bethesda compatible with Judaism. They changed the superstition of the curative waters to include an angel's part: coming from time-to-time to stir it. This coincided—no doubt—with open valves and fresh water being added to the pools.

Visiting the sick on Sabbath must be an old practice because on that Sabbath Jesus went to the hospital at Jerusalem to visit the sick. He saw a hopeless old man—who had been there some 38 years. Moved with compassion, He healed the invalid. He didn't do it secretly. Jesus specifically wanted people to know about it. He wanted people to know *Jesus healed on the Sabbath day!*

Once, Jesus healed a man born blind—also on a Sabbath. He spat on the ground. He made clay on the Sabbath—clay packs to put on the man's eyes; and He sent him to the *Pool of Siloam* to wash. Referring to this act, the Spirit of Prophecy tells us that while Jesus "did not give countenance to drug medication, He sanctioned the use of simple and natural remedies."[19]

---

[15] Ibid.

[16] Randy Niles, *Pool of Bethesda*, September 19, 2016. (https://www.drivethruhistory.com/pool-of-bethesda/), accessed 10-6-2018.

[17] Wikipedia, *Rod of Asclepius*, (https://en.wikipedia.org/wiki/Rod_of_Asclepius), accessed 10-6-2018.

[18] Wikipedia, *Asclepeion*, (https://en.wikipedia.org/wiki/Asclepeion), accessed 10-6-2018.

[19] Ellen G. White, *The Ministry of Healing*, p. 233.

The priests drew water for the sanctuary services from the *Pool of Siloam*—it wasn't a healthcare facility; it was a religious institution. But Bethesda *was* a healthcare facility. Jesus didn't use the waters, cures, or healing rituals *there*. He simply said: "Rise, take up thy bed and walk."

—People Needed to Know

The invalid had been there 38 years. The establishment knew of him. His healing would attract a lot of attention. Carrying a bed on the Sabbath would cause an uproar. *But the people needed to know!* They needed to know the normal healthcare of the day had not healed him—it was a divine work! They needed to know the Spirit of the Lord was upon Jesus—anointed to preach the gospel to the poor, relieve the oppressed, liberate the captives, heal the afflicted, restore sight to the blind, and reveal the light of truth to the world.

They needed to know the Sabbath is not about counting footsteps; strife and debate; afflicting your soul; bowing down your head like a bulrush—with sackcloth and ashes. It's about loosening the bands of wickedness; undoing heavy burdens; freeing the oppressed; breaking every yoke. It's about giving food to the hungry. It's about bringing poor people home; and putting your own clothes on the naked.

They needed to know these things make the Sabbath a delight—not doing your own stuff; going your own way; saying your own words. The Lord's servant admonishes us that Isaiah 58 "marks out the only course that we can follow with safety." Quoting it, she says,

> "'Cry aloud, spare not, lift up thy voice like a trumpet, and show my people their transgression, and the house of Jacob their sins.' Though they are called the people of God, the house of Jacob, though they profess to be linked with God in obedience and fellowship, they are far from Him. Wonderful privileges and promises have been given to them, but they have betrayed their trust. With no words of flattery must the message be given them. 'Show my people their transgression, and the house of Jacob their sins.' Show them where they are making a mistake. Set their danger before them. Tell them of the sins they are committing, while at the same time they pride themselves on their righteousness. Apparently seeking God, they are forgetting Him, forgetting that He is a God of love and compassion, long suffering and goodness, dealing justly and loving mercy. *Worldly policy has come into their business and religious life.* Their hearts are not purified through the truth. God looks on their outward ceremonies of humility as a solemn mockery. He regards all religious sham as an insult to Himself."[20]

---

[20] Ellen G. White, *Seventh-day Adventist Bible Commentary*, vol. 4, p. 1149. Emphasis added.

—Back at the Nazareth Church

Isaiah pretty-well described what was going on in Israel; and Jesus knew He had to deal with it. But the Nazareth church was now suspicious. They could see the bricks and mortar establishment at Jerusalem didn't impress Jesus much. Their preaching and watered-down *Isaiah seminars* didn't satisfy Him. He didn't subscribe to the teachings of the rabbis. He was an embarrassment and insult to the medical work. Worst of all, He said the most arrogant things. He was from their town, so they were sensitive to this. He seemed to think *He* was the only answer to folk's *physical*, *intellectual*, and *spiritual* needs—and that the organization was selling out to the world.

"Little Jesus" was right there in Nazareth—implying that they (His family and friends), were in bondage: were prisoners needing Him to deliver them from the power of evil; were in darkness: needing Him to give them the light of truth! Who did He think He was, anyway? They'll not be so gullible. They'll not buy His claim to be the Messiah—not without some amazing proof.

—The Protocol for Service

Jesus knew their thoughts. They wanted Him to perform miracles to substantiate His claims; but they already knew the truth. The evidence had been mounting for years. They were acquainted with His spotless life. Reports of His public ministry in Judea had been filtering back for more than a year now. Man never taught like this man! Never a man preached as He does! His healing surpasses everything on earth! They know the truth; but they refused to believe the truth.

Sadly, Jesus changes the tone of His Sabbath message. He says,

> "I tell you truthfully that there were many widows in Israel in the time of Elijah, when the sky was shut for three and a half years and great famine swept over all the land. Yet Elijah was not sent to any of them, but to the widow of Zarephath in Sidon."[21]

And then He said:

> "And there were many lepers in Israel in the time of Elisha the prophet. Yet not one of them was cleansed—only Naaman the Syrian."[22]

Yes, the Sabbath is about going to church and refraining from secular life. It's about spiritual refreshing and spiritual renewal. The Sabbath *is*

---

[21] Luke 4:25-26. Berean Study Bible.
[22] Luke 4:27.

a holy day—guard it as sacred and special. Don't treat it as common—to please yourself or for your entertainment. It's the heart of His moral law. It's the seal of God. Yes, worship God on the Sabbath—put Him first. But selflessly serve others, too. The Sabbath is the *protocol for service!*

Jesus instigated Sabbath reform in Judea and in Galilee. We need to instigate it here, today. Even Seventh-day Adventists are wrong about the Sabbath.

> "The fifty-eighth chapter of Isaiah contains present truth for the people of God. Here we see how medical missionary work and the gospel ministry are to be bound together as the message is given to the world. Upon those who keep the Sabbath of the Lord is laid the responsibility of doing a work of mercy and benevolence. *Medical missionary work is bound up with the message, and sealed with the seal of God.*"[23]
>
> "We need the clear light of the Sun of Righteousness to shine upon us. This light is given to those who keep holy the Lord's Sabbath; *but we cannot keep this day holy unless we serve the Lord in the manner brought to view in the scripture*: 'Is not this the fast that I have chosen, to loose the bands of wickedness, to undo every burden, to let the oppressed go free. And that ye break every yoke? Is it not to deal thy bread to the hungry, and that thou bring the poor that are cast out to thy house? When thou seest the naked, that thou cover him; and that thou hide not thyself from thine own flesh?' (Isaiah 58:6, 7) This is the work that rests upon *every soul* who accepts the service of Christ."[24]

"We are to work the works of Christ... Isaiah says, 'Thy righteousness shall go before thee; the glory of the Lord shall be thy rereward.' This is the work that must be done before Christ shall come in power and great glory."[25]

What is Sabbath—*Protocol for Service*? It's the *Galilee Protocol.* It's what Jesus came to do. It's Isaiah 61. It's Isaiah 58. It's what we should be doing. It is medical missionary work bound up with the gospel ministry and sealed with the seal of God!

What is the *Galilee Protocol?* It's a specific method of work whereby we bring relief to the oppressed, liberty to the captives, healing to the afflicted, sight to the blind, and the light of truth to the world. It is working as Christ worked. It's Christ's character radiating through the activity of His church.

---

[23] Ellen G. White, *Evangelism*, p. 516. Emphasis added.

[24] Ellen G. White, *Manuscript Releases*, vol. 5, p. 33. Emphasis added.

[25] Ellen G. White, *The Review and Herald*, November 1, 1892.

—How It Looked Back Then

What would that look like today? Probably much like it looked when Jesus did it! This is how He did it. He went to the cities. Once there, He attended the synagogue on Sabbath; and shared His plan for that city with the Sabbath-keepers there. He showed the details of His mission from the inspired record. Those who liked what He said, joined Him.

Then He went to the streets. He knocked on doors. He looked for lost sheep. He specialized in people who knew they needed Him. He found the sick, the poor, the discouraged, and the downcast. Jesus loves everyone—the rich and the poor, the educated and the ignorant, the healthy and the sickly. But He looked for those desperate enough to respond to His gestures of love and mercy—who would accept His peculiar ways and non-establishment methods. They needed His help. They wanted His help. And His success with them attracted the attention of many high society folks who otherwise would have had no use for Him.

So Jesus often worked with the lowly—He didn't care they were lowly. To Jesus they could be kings and queens. Jesus mingled with them—

> "as one who desired their good. He sought them in the public streets, in private houses, on the boat, in the synagogue, by the shores of the lake, and at the marriage feast. He met them in their daily vocations, and manifested an interest in their secular affairs. He carried His instructions into the household, bringing families in their own homes under the influence of His divine presence."[26]

Jesus feed the poor, and gave them clothes to wear. He touched the infirm, and He healed their sickness. Jesus showed the guilty how to find forgiveness; He showed the discouraged the way to victory.

Then He took them from the cities to some country retreat—to a mountainside, or a seashore, or to some desert place. The sick, the lame, the simple folk, and everyday people flocked to the countryside to hear and see Jesus. He taught with simple stories. He described the coming kingdom of God.

Soon, Titus and his Roman legionnaires would come and destroy their cities. Millions would be killed, or scattered around the globe. Jesus preached—*Fear God and give glory to Him; for the hour of His judgment was come.*[27]

---

[26] Ellen G. White, *The Desire of Ages*, p. 151.

[27] See Revelation 14:7; See Ellen G. White, *Maranatha*, p. 341.

After a while, He would tell them He needed to go to other cities—for that is what God *sent* Him to do.[28]

—How It Should Look Today

What should the *Galilee Protocol* look like in these last days? Well, the best we can tell from inspiration: it should start out like a small, grass-roots movement. Maybe just a few people, somewhere—folks who conclude they cannot wait any longer for some "compelling power to take hold of them." They decide "they must act, they must take hold of the work themselves." They conclude that the "scenes which are passing before them are of sufficient magnitude to cause them to arouse and to urge the truth home to the hearts of all who will listen."[29] They take to heart these words: "The presence of the Lord is ever seen where every energy of the church is aroused to meet the spiritual responsibilities."[30] They make the *Galilee Protocol* their top priority.

From there, it will grow.

> "When our churches will fulfill the duty resting upon them, they will be living, working agencies for the Master. The manifestation of Christian love will fill the soul with deeper, more earnest fervor to work for Him who gave His life to save the world... We shall see the medical missionary work broadening and deepening at every point of its progress, because of the inflowing of hundreds and thousands of streams, until the whole earth is covered as the waters cover the sea."[31]

How does the *Galilee Protocol* look in these last days? It looks like companies of disciples going to large cities. Finding Adventist churches there, they share their mission from the inspired record. They recruit disciples to the Master's work. Then they go to the streets. They knock on doors. They look for lost sheep. They look for people who know they need help. They look for the sick. They look for the poor. They look for the discouraged and the downcast. They look for those searching for truth.

They tell the stories of the Bible that teach present truth. They set up Bible readings in peoples' homes and in public places. They pray for the sick and teach them to care for their bodies. They share lessons about the laws of health—practical lessons for better cooking, and the therapeutic use of water to promote circulation and healing. They help the

---

28 Luke 4:43.

29 Ellen G. White, *Testimonies for the Church*, vol. 1, p. 261.

30 Ellen G. White, *Notebook Leaflets*, vol. 1, p. 99.

31 Ibid. p.18.

poor with food and clothing. They show the guilty the way to Jesus and forgiveness. They lead the discouraged to victory.

After a while, they invite people from the cities to some country retreat—to a mountainside, a seashore, or some desert place. The prophecies are unfolded; and warning given of judgments soon to fall on the cities and the world. They describe Christ's eminent return in the clouds of glory; they unmask the counterfeit works of the antichrist. They talk of the mark of the beast. They tell of the time of trouble; and the seven last plagues. They clearly present the seventh-day Sabbath, and the binding, uncompromising nature of God's law—in both health and moral matters.

They boldly present Jesus, the only mediator between God and man—our only answer for *physical*, *mental*, and *spiritual* restoration. They present Jesus, the sin bearer—who chose Calvary's cross so they might choose life. They present Jesus, a personal, loving Savior—who wants to be the closest friend of every child of humanity. They present Jesus—the fullness of divine power offering Himself freely to everyone desiring freedom from the chains of sin.

After a while, they go to other cities—for that is what God *sent* them to do.[32] The work advances with 'voices of thanksgiving and praise," as there is "a reformation such as we witnessed in 1844.[33]

> "In visions of the night, representations passed before me of a great reformatory movement among God's people. Many were praising God. The sick were healed, and other miracles were wrought. A spirit of intercession was seen, even as was manifested before the great Day of Pentecost. Hundreds and thousands were seen visiting families and opening before them the word of God. Hearts were convicted by the power of the Holy Spirit, and a spirit of genuine conversion was manifest. On every side doors were thrown open to the proclamation of the truth."[34]

What does the *Galilee Protocol* look like in these last days? It's not rocket science, really. It's good old-fashioned Adventism—an old-fashioned Adventism that has yet to ever really catch on. But it will. What does the *Galilee Protocol* look like in these last days? Well—if only we would *reactivate* the *Galilee Protocol* in these last days—I think it would look a lot like Jesus. Don't you?

---

[32] Matthew 10:5-13.

[33] Ellen G. White, *Testimonies for the Church*, vol. 9, p. 127.

[34] Ibid.

CHAPTER FOUR

Mistaken Identity

A carriage makes its way through the city streets. Towers and chimneys are toppled. Rows of wood-framed houses crumpled—cornices and walls crashed into the streets. Buildings sunk into the ground. Steel rails, and bridges, and pipelines are twisted and broken.

In just seventeen minutes there were explosions, and fifteen fires were reported in the downtown area. Fire engines rushed in to answer the calls, only to find broken water mains.

The firemen could only stare at empty hoses as the resulting conflagration burned down much of the city. Sometimes the flames achieved the intensity of a blast furnace—with heat raging upwards to 2000 degrees.

Riding in the carriage—making her way through a city just ravaged by earthquake and fire—is a little lady with tears in her eyes. She now views firsthand what she herself warned about.

Four hundred and ninety city blocks were destroyed; two hundred and fifty-six thousand people were left homeless. Four hundred and ninety-eight died. Property was destroyed at the rate of one million 1906 dollars every ten minutes.[1]

---

[1] Story adapted from "*Lightning from the Earth*", Prophet of the End (chapter 1), Harvestime Books, Altamont, TN 37301.

—The Great San Francisco Earthquake

On Wednesday, April 18, 1906, the great San Francisco earthquake struck at 5:12 a.m. Four years earlier—in 1902—the little lady predicted this devastation of San Francisco. Just two days before the quake—at 1:00 a.m. on Monday—she awoke from a nighttime vision, turned on the light, and wrote a description of the very scenes that are now the reality before her.

Disasters happen. We can think of Katrina in 2005—killing over eighteen hundred people and displacing a million more.[2] Think of the earthquake with the twenty-three-foot tsunami that in 2011 damaged the Fukushima Nuclear Facility in Japan—leaving over twenty-one thousand people dead or missing.[3] And Haiti—in 2010, that earthquake killed over three-hundred thousand people.[4]

San Francisco's 1906 earthquake is not the worst disaster to hit our planet. But it is noteworthy in one respect: Why did God let a seventy-eight-year-old lady know about it ahead of time?

—Establishing a Context

None of us were in San Francisco in 1906. That earthquake happened long ago. We will reconstruct the context so we can better understand the historical significance of the event. We'll do this from a peculiarly Adventist point-of-view—dripping with the stuff of 1844, the *Great-Disappointment*, and the *Investigative Judgment*. So don't be surprised or put off if it rings with the sound of *Three Angels* declaring the "hour of judgment had come," and "Babylon had fallen." If it sounds urgent, it is because it was about raising the alarm of God's last warning of love to a dying world: "Come out of her My people;"—receive not of her plagues.[5]

God moved the hearts of the Millerites—testing them with *great disappointment*. He entrusted the faithful with the *Galilee Protocol*. He bade them go from city to city "saying with a loud voice, "Fear God, and give glory to Him; for the hour of His judgment is come: and worship Him who made heaven, and earth, and sea, and the fountains of water."[6]

---

[2] Borgna Brunner, *Hurricane Katrina, A disaster and its catastrophic aftermath,* Fact Monster, (http://www.factmonster.com/hurricane-katrina/), accessed 3/25/2019.

[3] Armand Vervaeck and Dr, James Daniell, *Japan Tohoku tsunami and earthquake: The death toll is climbing again!,* Earthquake_Report.com. updated 8-15-2011, (https://earthquake-report.com/2011/08/04/japan-tsunami-following-up-the-aftermath-part-16-june/), accessed 3/25/2019.

[4] Alisha Davis, *Haiti Earthquake: 5 Years Later, Country Still Feeling Aftershocks*, ABC News, January 12, 2015, (https://www.yahoo.com/news/haiti-earthquake-5-years-later-country-still-feeling-180634477--abc-news-topstories.html), accessed 3/25/2019.

[5] See Revelation 14:7-14.

[6] Revelation 14:7.

God commissioned *Seventh-day Adventist* to herald the imminent second *advent* of Jesus; and to shine a light on the Bible Sabbath for proper worship of the Creator of heaven and earth.[7]

It was a reformation message—telling people that God wanted them to be temples of the Holy Ghost; to *glorify God* in their bodies.[8] It was a reformation message—about *fearing God*: for the fear of the Lord is about "bringing into captivity every thought to the obedience of Christ."[9] "Let this mind be in you which was also in Christ Jesus."[10] Paul asks, "Where is the wise? Where is the scribe? Where is the disputer of this world? Hath not God made foolish the wisdom of this world?" And then he says, "We preach Christ crucified, unto the Jews a stumbling block, and unto the Greeks foolishness; but unto them that are called, both Jews and Greeks, Christ the power of God, and the *wisdom of God*."[11]

To *"Fear God"* called for a *reformation of mind*. To *"Give glory to Him"* called for a *reformation of body*. And to "*Worship Him that made heaven and earth"* called for a *reformation of spirit*. Together, these were "the everlasting gospel"[12] in a global context—for we were to preach it "unto them that dwell on the earth, and to every nation, and kindred, and tongue and people."[13] These were "the everlasting gospel," in a judgment context—"for the hour of His judgment is come."[14]

The San Francisco earthquake occurs in this peculiarly Seventh-day Adventist context. Our job was to warn the world of God's terrible wrath in a way calculated to show His tremendous love. We could only accomplish this by carefully using the *protocols* He supplied for that purpose. As agents of Christ—living as He lived, working as He worked, going from city to city as He did—Adventists were to preach the everlasting gospel in the context of advent *and* judgment—the same as when He ministered on earth.

The first century Christians warned that the kingdom of God was at hand. The last century Christians are to warn that the hour of judgment is come. They preached the gospel. We're to preach the everlasting gospel. They taught people to pull down "every high thing that exalteth itself

---

[7] Revelation 14:7; Exodus 20:8-11; Genesis 2:1-3.

[8] Revelation 14:7, 1 Corinthians 6:19-20. Emphasis added.

[9] Revelation 14:7; Proverbs 1:7; Proverbs 1:7; 2 Corinthians 10:5. Emphasis added.

[10] Philippians 2:5.

[11] 1 Corinthians 1:20-24. Emphasis added.

[12] Revelation 14:6.

[13] Revelation 14.6.

[14] Revelation 14:7.

against the knowledge of God."[15] We're to teach people to *fear God* through the renewing of their minds in obedience to Christ—the wisdom of God. They healed the sick. We're to show people how to give glory to God in what they eat and drink—teaching wellness comes from living in harmony with the laws of health. They cast out demons. We're to bring people to spiritual wellness through worship to the Creator—teaching them to live in harmony with all the moral law of ten commandments.

—Justice and Mercy

The *Galilee Protocol* shows the crucial symbiotic relationship between justice and mercy in the righteousness of God's character. Christ preached a judgment-hour message—a message of justice. As He went from city to city[16] He declared, "Repent, for the kingdom of heaven is at hand."[17] *John the Baptist* also preached this message. He identified it with judgment, saying, "O, generation of vipers, who hath warned you to flee from the wrath to come?... and now also the axe is laid to the root of the trees: therefore every tree that bringeth not forth good fruit is hewn down, and cast into the fire."[18]

> *"In His teachings, Christ sought to impress men with the certainty of the coming judgment,* and with its publicity. This is not the judgment of a few individuals, or even of a nation, but of a whole world of human intelligences, of accountable beings. It is to be held in the presence of other worlds, that the love, the integrity, the service, of man for God, may be honored to the highest degree. There will be no lack of glory and honor.... The law of God will be revealed in its majesty; and those who have stood in defiant rebellion against its holy precepts will understand that the law that they have discarded, and despised, and trampled underfoot is God's standard of character."[19]

The coming judgment of their day—while having global implications—had to do primarily with Jerusalem and Israel. Divine judgment enforced their fate that ultimately played out in death, dispersion, and the fires that consumed Jerusalem in A.D. 70.

While the *spoken message* of Christ was of judgment, the *demonstrated message* of Christ was a message of undeniable love—a message of mercy. As Jesus moved from city to city, He tenderly healed the sick and the lame. He gave sight to the blind. He cast out demons. When

---

[15] 2 Corinthians 10:5.
[16] See Luke 4:16, 31, 42-43; Mark 1:35-39; Matthew 4:23; Luke 8:1.
[17] Matthew 4:17.
[18] Matthew 3:7, 10.
[19] Ellen G. White, *Maranatha*, p. 341. Emphasis added.

leaving one city for the next, He often left only after healing every sick person.[20] Everything He had, and everything He was—He devoted to the work of saving people who were facing certain doom. "Foxes have holes, and the birds of the air have nests, but the Son of Man has nowhere to lay His head."[21]

He sent twelve disciples as missionaries to the cities. He instructed them saying,

> "Provide neither gold, nor silver, nor brass in your purses, nor script for your journey, neither two coats, neither shoes, nor yet staves: for the workman is worthy of his meat."[22]

His message was of judgment and fire—yes, but in love, He left no stone unturned as He reached out to save sinners. Justice combined with mercy. Judgment: the "wine of the wrath of God, poured out without mixture into the cup of His indignation,"[23] combined with healing—the gentle touch of the *great Galilean Physician*. Justice and mercy bundled together in the ignominious life and death of cheerful poverty, servitude, and ransom. It declares the selfless, loving nature of divine righteousness—*and* the uncompromising rectitude of God's moral law.

Recall Christ's summary of that law in just two words: faithful love and worship to God; and faithful love and service to man. The Master not only *spoke* these two words—He *showed* them as He lived and worked the *Galilee Protocol*.

—Dress Rehearsal

The local Jewish battle in Christ's day will soon be global—to every kindred and people. The famine, pestilence, sword, and fire that were then about to plague and destroy Jerusalem, are now gathering for a time of global trouble too horrific to picture.

The earthquake of 1906 was a kind of dress rehearsal. It happened in San Francisco because that was the one U. S. city that Seventh-day Adventists had properly worked. We diligently applied the principles of the *Galilee Protocol* there as in no other place in modern times.[24] The message of mercy and warning sounded in San Francisco; but with little response. The little-old-lady's urgent warning rings down through the

[20] Ellen G. White, *From Heaven with Love*, p. 153.
[21] Matthew 8:20.
[22] Matthew 10:9-11.
[23] Revelation 14:10.
[24] Dave Fiedler, *D'Sozo, Reversing the Worst Evil*, p. 161.

pages of history—to our day, "Not long hence, these cities will suffer under the judgment of God. San Francisco and Oakland are becoming as Sodom and Gomorrah, and the Lord will visit them in wrath."[25]

Here is the story from her biography:[26]

> "Monday night, April 16, while still at Loma Linda, a solemnizing vision was given to her. 'A most wonderful representation,' she said, 'passed before me.' Describing it in an article appearing in Testimonies for the Church, volume 9, she wrote:
>
> "'During a vision of the night, I stood on an eminence, from which I could see houses shaken like a reed in the wind. Buildings, great and small, were falling to the ground. Pleasure resorts, theaters, hotels, and the homes of the wealthy were shaken and shattered. Many lives were blotted out of existence, and the air was filled with the shrieks of the injured and the terrified.... The awfulness of the scenes that passed before me I cannot find words to describe. It seemed that the forbearance of God was exhausted, and that the judgment day had come....
>
> "'Terrible as was the representation that passed before me, *that which impressed itself most vividly upon my mind was the instruction given in connection with it.* The angel that stood by my side declared that God's supreme rulership and the sacredness of His law must be revealed to those who persistently refuse to render obedience to the King of kings. Those who choose to remain disloyal must be visited in mercy with judgments, in order that, if possible, they may be aroused to a realization of the sinfulness of their course.'[27] (Italics supplied.)
>
> "She woke up and switched on the lamp by her bed. It was 1:00 A.M. Tuesday morning. She was relieved to discover that she was safe in her room at Loma Linda Sanitarium.
>
> "During the hours of Tuesday morning she seemed dazed.[28] In the afternoon she and her helpers took the train for Los Angeles and went on to Glendale.
>
> "That night Ellen White was given another vision:
>
> "'I was again instructed regarding the holiness and binding claims of the Ten Commandments, and the supremacy of God above all earthly rulers. It seemed as if I were before many people, and presenting scripture after scripture in support of the precepts spoken by the Lord from Sinai's height.'[29]
>
> "On Wednesday as she neared the Carr Street church to fill her speaking appointment, she heard the newsboys crying: 'San Francisco destroyed by an earthquake!'
>
> "A paper was purchased, and she and those with her in the carriage quickly scanned the 'first hastily printed news'.[30]

---

[25] Ellen G. White, *Manuscript 114*, 1902.

[26] Arthur L. White, *Ellen G. White: The Later Elmshaven Years: 1905-1915*, p. 79.

[27] Ellen G. White, *Testimonies for the Church*, vol. 9, pp. 92, 93.

[28] Ellen G. White, *Letter 137*, 1906.

[29] Ellen G. White, *The Review and Herald*, July 5, 1906.

[30] Ellen G. White, *Testimonies for the Church*, vol. 9, pp. 94.

"As to the visions on Monday and Tuesday nights, she later commented, 'It has taken me many days to write out a portion of that which was revealed those two nights at Loma Linda and Glendale. I have not finished yet.'[31] She expected yet to write several articles on the binding claims of God's law and the blessings promised the obedient."

Eleven days after the earthquake she wrote:

"I am bidden to declare the message that cities full of transgression, and sinful in the extreme, will be destroyed by earthquakes, by fire, by flood. All the world will be warned that there is a God who will display His authority as God. His unseen agencies will cause destruction, devastation, and death. All the accumulated riches will be as nothingness.

"Notwithstanding the scientific care with which men safeguard buildings from destruction, one touch of the great and rightful Ruler will bring to nothingness the idolatrous possessions that have been laid up in a sightly and magnificent display. The devices of men will come to naught."[32]

Ellen White rode a carriage amid the stifling stench of destruction. The terrible scenes of judgment shocked her—even though she saw visons of them just two days before:

"During the vision of the night, I stood on an eminence from which I could see houses shaken like a reed in the wind. Buildings, great and small, were falling to the ground. Pleasure resorts, theaters, hotels, and the homes of the wealthy were shaken and shattered. Many lives were blotted out of existence, and the air was filled with the shrieks of the injured and the terrified.

"The destroying angels of God were at work. One touch, and buildings so thoroughly constructed that men regarded them as secure against every danger quickly became heaps of rubbish. There was no assurance of safety in any place. I did not feel in any special peril, but the awfulness of the scenes that passed before me I cannot find words to describe. It seemed the forbearance of God was exhausted, and that the judgment day had come.

"The angel that stood by my side then instructed me that but few have any conception of the wickedness existing in our world today, and especially the wickedness in the large cities. He declared that the Lord has appointed a time when He will visit transgressors in wrath for persistent disregard of His law.

"At about one o'clock I awoke, and was impressed to write out some things regarding the supreme rulership of God and the sacredness of His law. When I met my secretary early in the morning, I told her that wonderful representations had been passing before me in the night season. After breakfast, we received a message asking us to go to Los Angeles by the afternoon train; but I was unable to take any part in preparing for

[31] Ellen G. White, *The Review and Herald*, July 5, 1906.

[32] Ellen G. White, *Manuscript Releases*, vol. 4, p. 91, April 27, 1906.

> the journey. I was as one dazed by the awful scenes that had passed before me."[33]

And then after the quake she added,

> "These things make me feel very solemn, because I know that the judgment day is right upon us. The judgments that have already come are a warning, but not the finishing, of the punishment that will come on wicked cities...
>
> "San Francisco in ruins is the most complete, thorough, awful calamity I have ever looked upon. In the night season I have had many presentations of the judgments of God coming upon our cities; and now I can understand better the real meaning of these scenes that I have witnessed."[34]
>
> "The Lord will not suddenly cast off all transgressors or destroy entire nations; but He will punish cities and places where men have given themselves up to the passion of Satanic agencies. Strictly will the cities of the nations be dealt with."[35]

—The Divine Rationale

We can observe some things of the intent, the sequence, the method, and the rationale concerning this event.

The Intent: "God's supreme rulership, and the sacredness of His law must be revealed." God must preserve His authority as a "judge, the avenger of justice."[36] He will maintain and validate "the rectitude, justice, and moral excellence of the law... before the heavenly universe and the unfallen worlds"[37]—and "to those who persistently refuse to render obedience to the King of kings."[38]

The Sequence: First, we must warn the cities "of their impending doom."[39] And then, the warning will intensify into calamity. Once warned, "those who choose to remain disloyal, must be visited in mercy with judgments, in order, that, if possible, they may be aroused to a realization of the sinfulness of their course."[40] God "will punish cities and places where men have given themselves up to the possession of Satanic agencies."[41] These judgments "are a warning."[42] "The time is near when

---

[33] Ellen G. White, *Manuscript 47*, 1906.
[34] Ellen G. White, *Manuscript 154*, 1906.
[35] Ellen G. White, *Evangelism*, p. 27.
[36] Ellen G. White, *Manuscript 145*, December 30, 1897.
[37] Ibid.
[38] Ellen G. White, *Testimonies for the Church*, vol. 9, p. 92.
[39] Ellen G. White, *Evangelism*, p. 30.
[40] Ellen G. White, *Letter 137*, 1906.
[41] Ellen G. White, *Evangelism*, p. 27.
[42] Ellen G. White, *Letter 157*, 1906.

the large cities will be swept away, and all should be warned of these coming judgments."[43]

The Method: The method God's messengers use to give the warning is important. Only the *Galilee Protocol* (medical missionary work) properly balances divine justice and mercy. We show the character of Christ by faithfully working the plan of the *Pattern-Man*. We emphasize living in harmony with God's laws.

"We are to work the works of Christ. This is a work that must be done before Christ shall come in power and great glory."[44]

"If you do not encourage medical missionary work... it will be done without your consent; for it is the work of God, and it must be done."[45]

"The work that is done for God in our large cities must not be according to man's devising.[46]

"There are many ways of practicing the healing art, but there is only one way that heaven approves. God's remedies are the simple agencies of nature that will not tax or debilitate the system through their powerful properties."[47]

"It is the Lord's purpose that His method of healing without drugs shall be brought into prominence in every large city."[48]

"Let little companies go forth to do the work which Christ appointed His disciples. Let them labor as evangelists, scattering publications, and talking of the truth to those they meet. Let them pray for the sick, ministering to their necessities, not with drugs, but with nature's remedies, and teaching them how to regain health and avoid disease."[49]

The Rationale: God always warns first. "The wrath of God is not declared against unrepentant sinners merely because of the sins they have committed, but because, *when called to repent*, they choose to continue in resistance, repeating the sins of the past in defiance of the light given them."[50]

"God's judgment on the cities will not be visited in the extreme of God's indignation, because some souls will yet break away from the delusions of the enemy, and will repent and be converted."[51]

---

43 Ellen G. White, *Evangelism*, p. 29.
44 Ellen G. White, *The Review and Herald*, November 1, 1892.
45 Ellen G. White, *Testimonies for the Church*, vol. 8, p. 75.
46 Ellen G. White, *Manuscript Releases*, vol. 7, p. 393.
47 Ellen G. White, *Counsels on Health*, p. 323.
48 Ellen G. White, *Counsels on Health*, pp. 393-394.
49 Ellen G. White, *Counsels on Health*, p. 397.
50 Ellen G. White, The *Acts of the Apostles*, p. 62.
51 Ellen G. White, *Evangelism*, p. 27.

—Mercy's Most Precious Gesture

In light of the urgent situation at the end, mercy's most precious and delicate gesture comes in the form of startling warnings followed by calamity—and in opportunities of grace before it is forever too late. Mercy cannot survive in a vacuum. When evil presses mercy beyond the limits of justice, mercy ceases to be merciful. Lawless mercy is an oxymoron—for it has no mechanism to stop unimaginable terror.

Because we are born in a sinful world, we are acquainted with sin's dark side. Still, we cannot begin to comprehend its enormity. God can. He does comprehend. He weighs the combined effects of sin. His divine reach has an infinite grasp of the *horror of darkness.* So God's mercy sets its limits. When a sinner passes the limit in guilt, Christ stops pleading in his behalf. Without a mediator, the sinner has no shield against the unmitigated power of Divine Righteousness.

In the *physical realm,* God's righteousness is manifest as intense glory—glory that is like a consuming fire[52] to a sinner. In the *intellectual realm,* His righteousness is manifest in His Word—it is "quick, and powerful, and sharper than any two-edged sword, piercing even to the dividing asunder of soul and spirit, and of the joints and marrow, and is the discerner of the thoughts and intents of the heart."[53] The *spiritual realm* is emotion. God's mercy and His justice are manifested through emotional expressions of His all-encompassing experience. This includes the realities of His experience with all the horrors and injustices of sin.

—Securing the Universe

God's anger and fury against sin is His righteous emotional reaction to an evil whose darkness is beyond our ability to comprehend. His wrath is His emotional outcry against the atrocities of sin. It is rational, appropriate, and righteous; and it is necessary to preserve His authority, vindicate His law, and ultimately secure the universe. It is intense!

> "It was [this] expression of justice against sin that crushed out the life of the Son of God... In dying upon the cross, Christ did not lessen in the slightest particular the vital claims of the law of Jehovah. He endured the punishment in the sinner's stead... But in His death, He gave evidence to the heavenly universe that God will punish for the sins of a guilty world."[54]

---

[52] Hebrews 12:29.

[53] Hebrews 4:12.

[54] Ellen G. White, *Bible Echo*, May 30, 1898.

"It is a fearful thing for the unrepenting sinner to fall into the hands of the living God... This was proved... in the agony of Christ, the Son of the infinite God, when He bore the wrath of God for the sinful world."[55]

"The transgression of God's law in a single instance, in the smallest particular, is sin. And the non-execution of the penalty of that sin would be a crime in the divine administration. God is a judge, the Avenger of justice, which is the habitation of His throne. He cannot dispense with His law; He cannot do away with its smallest item in order to meet and pardon sin. The rectitude, justice, and moral excellence of the law must be maintained and vindicated before the heavenly universe and the worlds unfallen."[56]

"But it was not merely to accomplish the redemption of man that Christ came to the earth to suffer and to die. He came to "magnify the law" and to "make it honorable." Not alone that the inhabitants of this world might regard the law as it should be regarded; but it was to demonstrate to all the worlds of the universe that God's law is unchangeable. Could its claims have been set aside, then the Son of God need not have yielded up His life to atone for its transgression. The death of Christ proves it immutable. And the sacrifice to which infinite love impelled the Father and the Son, that sinners might be redeemed, demonstrates to all the universe—what nothing less than this plan of atonement could have sufficed to do—that justice and mercy are the foundation of the law and government of God.[57]

The beauty of Christ's love is His willingness to stand as a *Living Veil*—shielding us from the fullness of divine displeasure with sin. The door still stands open for His great mercy to do its gracious work for you and for me. But "oh, that God's people had a sense of the impending destruction of thousands of cities, now almost given to idolatry."[58] "Who is giving to the accomplishment of this work the wholehearted service that God requires?"[59]

—Fracturing Divinity

The Psalmist says, "Mercy and truth are met together; righteousness and peace have kissed each other."[60] Micah tells how the Lord expects the same from us: "He hath shewed thee, O man, what is good; and what doth the LORD require of thee, but to do justly, and to love mercy, and to walk humbly with thy God."[61] Ellen White wrote of Christ: "His

---

[55] Ellen G. White, *Manuscript 35*, 1895.
[56] Ellen G. White, *Manuscript 145*, December 30, 1897.
[57] Ellen G. White, *The Great Controversy*, p. 503.
[58] Ellen G. White, *The Review and Herald*, Sept. 10, 1903.
[59] Ellen G. White, *Manuscript 53*, 1910.
[60] Psalms 85:10
[61] Micah 6:8.

teaching made plain the ennobling, sanctifying principles that govern [His] kingdom. He showed that justice and mercy and love are the controlling powers in Jehovah's kingdom."[62] God said to Moses,

> "I will make all My goodness pass before thee, and I will proclaim the name of the LORD before thee... And the LORD passed by before him, and proclaimed, The LORD, The LORD God, merciful and gracious, longsuffering, and abundant in goodness and truth, Keeping mercy for thousands, forgiving iniquity and transgression and sin, and that will by no means clear the guilty; visiting the iniquity of the fathers upon the children, and upon the children's children, unto the third and fourth generation"[63]

God gave Moses a perfect verbal representation of Himself—His own expression of His *identity*. He blended descriptions of mercy and justice. If we try to represent the character of Christ without the justice component or without the mercy component, we fracture the divine identity—we fashion an idol made of our own imagination. This cannot be.

> "Through Jesus, God's mercy was manifested to men; but mercy does not set aside justice. The law reveals the attributes of God's Character, and not a jot or tittle of it could be changed to meet man in his fallen condition. God did not change His law, but He sacrificed Himself, in Christ, for man's redemption. 'God was in Christ, reconciling the world unto Himself.'[64]"[65]

Lucifer tried to fracture the divine identity—and he broke the universe.

> "The inhabitants of heaven and of the worlds, being unprepared to comprehend the nature or consequences of sin, could not then have seen the justice of God in the destruction of Satan."[66]
>
> "God permits the wicked to prosper and to reveal their enmity against Him, that when they shall have filled up the measure of their iniquity all may see His justice and mercy in their utter destruction. The day of His vengeance hastens, when all who have transgressed His law and oppressed His people will meet the just recompense of their deeds; when every act of cruelty or injustice toward God's faithful ones *will be punished* as though done to Christ Himself."[67]

Calvary shows the wonderful mercy of God, tears away Satan's disguise, and breaks the last link of sympathy between him and the

---

[62] Ellen G. White, *Gospel Workers*, p. 396.

[63] Exodus 33:18-20, 34:6-7.

[64] 2 Corinthians 5:19.

[65] Ellen G. White, *The Desire of Ages*, p. 762.

[66] Ellen G. White, *Patriarchs and Prophets*, p. 42.

[67] Ellen G. White, *The Great Controversy*, p. 48. Emphasis added.

heavenly worlds. Still, God did not destroy Satan. "Angels did not even then understand all that was involved in the great controversy."[68]

> "In the opening of the great controversy, Satan had declared that the law of God could not be obeyed, *that justice was inconsistent with mercy*, and that, should the law be broken, it would be impossible for the sinner to be pardoned. Every sin must meet its punishment, urged Satan; and if God should remit the punishment of sin, He would not be a God of truth and justice. When men broke the law of God, and defied His will, Satan exulted... Satan claimed that the human race must be forever shut out from God's favor. God could not be just, he urged, and yet show mercy to the sinner.
>
> "But even as a sinner, man was in a different position from that of Satan. Lucifer in heaven had sinned in the light of God's glory. To him as to no other created being was given a revelation of God's love. Understanding the character of God, knowing His goodness, Satan chose to follow his own selfish, independent will. This choice was final. There was no more that God could do to save him. But man was deceived; his mind was darkened by Satan's sophistry. The height and depth of the love of God he did not know. *For him there was hope in a knowledge of God's love*. By beholding His character he might be drawn back to God.[69]

By His life and death, Jesus showed God's mercy in a way everyone can understand. His love is vibrant and personal to a hopeless sinner. But His life and death also proved mercy does not set aside justice. His life perfectly revealed the living attributes of the law; and His death, that God does not ignore the wages of sin.

Satan loves to confuse. He tries to deceive us about God's character. He fractures the divine identity saying God has no mercy. When the gospel of Jesus Christ exposes the lie, Satan manipulates the gospel to fracture the divine identity again: He says God is not just—that Jesus destroyed the law at the cross.

> "Another deception was now to be brought forward. Satan declared that *mercy destroyed justice*, that the death of Christ abrogated the Father's law... *It was because the law was changeless*, because man could be saved only through obedience to its precepts, *that Jesus was lifted up on the cross*. Yet the very means by which Christ established the law Satan represented as destroying it. *Here will come the last conflict of the great controversy between Christ and Satan*."[70]

This brings us to now—the crisis at the end. Those who do not know the love of God easily fall for a mistaken identity—*God without mercy*.

---

[68] Ellen G. White, *The Desire of Ages*, p. 761.

[69] Ibid. Emphasis added.

[70] Ellen G. White, *The Desire of Ages*, p. 762. Emphasis added.

Satan still paints Him as a tyrant. Those who know the love of God easily fall for a different mistaken identity—*God without justice*. Satan paints Him as accommodating sin and evil behavior. Many contemporary Christians change the clear teaching of the Bible to suggest God is just too good and too loving to destroy the wicked; and they play right into Satan's strategy for the final conflict.[71]

—Runaway Mercy-Loop

The earthquake shook San Francisco over 100 years ago. Now the world plunges deeper into iniquity and spiritualism than 1906-people could have even imagined. So what of the limits of wickedness? and the fullness of iniquity's cup? What of the destruction of the cities? and the end of the world? What of the judgment? the close of probation? and the seven last plagues? And what about those three angels' messages? the loud cry of Revelation 18? and the latter rain?

It seems we veered off course and entered an alternate reality—a world somehow beyond the judicial reach of Daniel's court.[72] Something has neutralized the prophetic expectations of yesteryear. It is true. We are stuck in some sort of *probationary anomaly*—a runaway mercy-loop; and the result is a world gone mad in sin and rebellion. Sin is on a frantic up-tick—one that seems destined to bring about planetary self-annihilation. There is no stop button. We have no exit strategy.

It's all because of a *mistaken identity*. The *Man from Galilee* is the world's *only* hope! But somehow the masses have hijacked his true character by declaring Him to be *all mercy with no justice*, or *all justice with no mercy*. Our crisis is a matter of *mistaken identity*—an identity that we are commissioned to repair. We must share Christ's true identity and break the anomaly! We have to *warn* the cities that justice is coming! We need to *show* the cities God's love. This is the *Galilee Protocol!*

"Christ is waiting with longing desire for the manifestation of Himself in His church. When the character of Christ shall be perfectly reproduced in His people, then He will come."

—Christ's Object Lessons, p. 69

---

[71] See *Appendix B – God's Righteous Cry!* for an in-depth treatment of this issue.
[72] Daniel 7:10. See also Revelation 4 & 5.

CHAPTER FIVE

The Sign of Jonah

One day the Pharisees and the Sadducees came to Jesus, wanting Him to show them a sign from heaven. He said to them: "When there is a red sky in the evening, you know the weather is going to be good. And when there is a red sky in the morning, you know the weather is going to be bad. How is it that you can discern the face of the sky, but you cannot discern the signs of the times?"

Then Jesus said, "A wicked and adulterous generation seeketh after a sign; and there shall no sign be given unto it, but the sign of the prophet Jonah. And He left them, and departed."[1]

You already know the story of Jonah and the great fish. This well-known Old Testament Bible story is a favorite with children. But here Jesus suggests it had special significance for people in His day; and we will find out it has special significance for us too.

God commissioned Jonah to warn the city of Nineveh that it would soon suffer the judgment of God. Jonah preferred not to do this work. Instead, he boarded a ship bound for Tarshish.

Tarshish was renowned for its wealth of gold and silver. Jonah thought he'd like it better there than being a Nineveh-missionary.

---

[1] Matthew 16:4; see verses 1-4.

In Nineveh (where God wanted him), life would be difficult. The work would be hard; and money would be scarce. His message would be unpopular; and the people wouldn't like him very much.

So Jonah preferred Tarshish. Things promised to be good there. That's where he was going—and he was going there by ship.

—Solomon's Fleet

It was King Solomon who first established Israel's naval fleet. He established it for the purpose of sailing this same route—from Joppa to Tarshish. That was many years before—back in Israel's glory-days. But in Jonah's time things weren't so good. It was a time of national distress for Israel. Israel was doing evil in the sight of the Lord; and national judgment was fast approaching for them too.

Actually, the cause of Israel's current problems (current to Jonah's day) began way back in Solomon's time—back then Israel was the wealthiest nation on earth, the wonder of the world. Even when Israel was wealthy and strong, God made it clear that He wanted her to rely wholly upon Him. He wanted her to obey His voice.

God told Israel's kings not to multiply horses to themselves—for He would be their defense. But Solomon built a strong military force anyway. He went to Egypt for horses; and eventually he had fourteen-hundred chariots, and twelve-hundred horsemen—just in case.

Solomon also built ships. But his ships weren't for war or national defense. In those days, all the nation respected Israel. She had a lot to offer. She had the oracles of God. She had the sanctuary truth; the Sabbath; the Spirit of Prophecy; present truth about a soon-coming Messiah. With a fleet of ships Solomon could easily evangelize the nations.

But Israel's fleet wasn't for spreading truth—not really. Solomon was more interested in *business and commerce*. He used his ships to go to Tarshish for gold and silver. The Bible says, "The king made silver and gold in Jerusalem as plenteous as stones."[2]

When Jonah was alive,[3] gold and silver were not plenteous anymore; but still Israel neglected her responsibility to evangelize the surrounding nations. There was a prophet in Israel, though—one that predicted Israel would return to national strength.[4] Unfortunately, he was in the bowels of a ship heading for Tarshish.

---

[2] 2 Chronicles 1:15.

[3] Sometime between Elijah and Isaiah.

[4] 2 Kings 14:25.

In mercy, God sent a storm. God sent it square into Jonah's path; and when the storm hit, Jonah was asleep... in the ship!

—Nineveh's God

Nineveh was an ancient city. Its founder was Nimrod—Ham's grandson; Noah's great grandson. By Jonah's day, it had become a great city. It was the capital of the Assyrian Empire; and it was very wicked.

It was wicked, but not necessarily irreligious. The people worshiped a pagan god named Dagon. Dagon was the second-person, Mesopotamian trinity-god. He was said to be part man and part fish.

According to an ancient legion, Nimrod became so wicked some surrounding judges (probably from Shem and Japheth's lines), had him executed and thrown in pieces into the sea. One day when his widow-wife was fishing, she caught Dagon—half man and half fish—Nimrod, reincarnated.

In the hands of pagan priests, this legion eventually became the basis for a whole religion. It was now (in Jonah's time), the principal religion of Nineveh; and even of all the Assyrian Empire.

Dagon was a fertility god. In Nineveh, religion was licentious. Immorality, self-indulgence, and wickedness prevailed. If Jonah was obedient, his work would be to call people out of this false system of religion—inviting them to "fear God and give Him glory, because the hour of His judgment has come."[5]

—Jonah's Storm

Instead, Jonah was in the water. The storm caught up to the ship. It was so severe it appeared the ship wouldn't make it through. And since the storm was Jonah's fault, the rest of the men on board threw him overboard; and a great fish swallowed him. For three days and three nights he stayed in the belly of that fish; and then God caused the fish to spit him out upon the shore.

God can really fix a hopeless situation. Jonah—hopelessly unwilling to minister to the city of Nineveh—became willing to do it God's chosen way. Nineveh—presumably hopelessly disinterested in anything Jonah might have to say—was now very attentive to this missionary, coughed up by a fish.

---

[5] Revelation 14:7. Berean Study Bible.

This is really the point of the story: God sent a storm to convince His own unfaithful servant to do the city work He assigned him to do—and in so doing, God also set up the circumstances for an effective presentation of gospel truth to a very wicked city.

—Christ's Mission to the Cities

Fast-forwarding now, let's go to when Israel's long-awaited Messiah came onto the scene. It was heaven's purpose to turn the chosen people into missionary bands and teach them to take the judgment-hour message to the cities of the world.

Christ's message was a judgment-hour message. *John the Baptist* made this clear when he said Christ would baptize "with the Holy Ghost and with fire: Whose fan is in His hand, and (that He would) thoroughly purge His floor, and (that He would) gather the wheat into His garner; but the chaff He would burn with fire unquenchable."[6]

That Christ's mission was specifically to the cities, He Himself testified, for when some people ask Him to stay in their city, He answered, and said: "I must preach the kingdom of God to other cities also: for therefore am I sent."[7] Luke says that Jesus "went throughout *every city*... preaching and shewing the glad tidings of the kingdom of God."[8]

That Jesus intended for Israel to form missionary bands is clear by the expanding nature of His recruiting and training activity. When working in *Judea* (from the *first to the second* Passover), He recruited a band of just a few early disciples.

When working in *Galilee* (between the *second and third* Passovers), He chose twelve disciples; and later sent them out throughout all Galilee to teach and preach and to heal the sick.

Eventually His work expanded to regions beyond the Jordan—to Phoenicia, Peraea, and Samaria. This was after the third Passover. He trained and sent out seventy missionaries.

Jesus' work in Galilee followed a peculiar pattern—a pattern we could call the *Galilee Protocol*. He focused on the cities: warning them about the judgment. Think about all of Jesus' parables—how so many of them ended with "and there shall be wailing and gnashing of teeth."

Sure, we know Jesus was all about love and mercy:

---

[6] John 3:16-17.

[7] Luke 4:43.

[8] Luke 8:1. Emphasis added.

> "He sympathized with the weary, the heavy-laden, the oppressed. He fed the hungry and healed the sick. Constantly He went about doing good. By the good He accomplished, by His loving words and kindly deeds, He interpreted the gospel to men."[9]

Because we know this about Him, we sometimes don't notice His firm commitment to justice. But His character is the perfect blending of justice and mercy; and when we look at what He *said,* most of it was about judgment. When we look at what He did we can't help but see His marvelous love.

So this was Christ's peculiar method;[10] and this is His divine commission (to us) that needs no reform.[11] Christ's way of presenting the truth cannot be improved upon.[12] He warned of judgment while living His gospel of love!

—From Artificial to Natural

When Christ would first enter a city, He'd go to a synagogue there to read and teach the people. He would show them from the scriptures and the prophecies, the details of His mission and work. Then He would work the city streets, or city centers—central places like the crowded home where some friends lowered a paralytic through the roof. He healed people. He cast out demons. He befriended people and ate with them. He taught them to pray; and show them how to keep the Sabbath.

Before long, Jesus led the people away from the city. It's true! The Bible says, "Jesus went about *all* the cities and villages, teaching in their synagogues, and preaching the gospel of the kingdom, and healing every sickness and every disease among the people."[13] Then He'd head out to the seashore, "and when much people were gathered together, and were come to Him *out of every city,* He spake by a parable."[14]

Often Christ took them to some *outpost*—a mountain, a lake, some grassy plain, or even a desert place. Leading them away from the cities, He took them to the country—a place better suited for preaching, and teaching, and healing.

---

[9] Ellen G. White, *Counsels on Health*, p. 498.
[10] Ellen G. White, *The Ministry of Healing*, p. 23.
[11] Ellen G. White, *Evangelism*, p. 525.
[12] Ellen G. White, *Counsels on Health*, p. 498.
[13] Matthew 9:35.
[14] Luke 8:4. Emphasis added.

"During His ministry Jesus lived to a great degree an outdoor life. His journeys from place to place were made on foot, and much of His teaching was given in the open air. In training His disciples He often withdrew from the confusion of the city to the quiet of the fields, as more in harmony with the lessons of simplicity, faith, and self-abnegation He desired to teach them...

"Christ loved to gather the people about Him under the blue heavens, on some grassy hillside, or on the beach beside the lake. Here, surrounded by the works of His own creation, He could turn their thoughts *from the artificial to the natural.* In the growth and development of nature were revealed the principles of His kingdom."[15]

—Show Us a Sign

It was in this context that the Pharisees and the Sadducees came asking for a sign. It was not the first time they came on such an errand; nor was this the first time Christ spoke of the sign of Jonah.

We're in Matthew 16, but Matthew 12 tells of an earlier occasion when Christ had just healed the demoniac—and how the Pharisees accused Him of casting out devils by Beelzebub, the prince of devils.[16]

Jesus responded by explaining a house divided against itself cannot stand;[17] a good tree is known by its fruit;[18] and then He told them about the unpardonable sin against the Holy Spirit.[19]

That's when a certain scribe of the Pharisees asked for a sign. Jesus said to them,

"An evil and adulterous generation seeketh after a sign; and there shall no sign be given it, but the sign of the prophet Jonah: for as Jonah was three days and three nights in the whale's belly, so shall the Son of man be three days and three nights in the heart of the earth."[20]

He continues,

"The men of Nineveh shall rise in judgment with this generation, and shall condemn it: because they repented at the preaching of Jonah; and, behold, a greater than Jonah is here."[21]

Jesus clinches His point by referring to the incident with the demoniac. He says:

---

[15] Ellen G. White, *Counsels on Health*, pp. 162,163. Emphasis added.
[16] Matthew 12:24.
[17] Matthew 12:25.
[18] Matthew 12:33.
[19] Matthew 12:31.
[20] Matthew 12:39-40.
[21] Matthew 12:41.

> "When the unclean spirit is gone out of a man, he walketh through dry places, seeking rest and findeth none. Then he saith, I will return unto my house from whence I came out; and when he is come, he findeth it empty, swept, and garnished. Then goeth he and taketh seven other spirits more wicked than himself, and they enter in and dwell there: and the last state of that man is worse than the first. Even so shall it be also unto this generation."[22]

So is Jesus talking about a demoniac or a people?

He's talking about His people in His generation. He is focused on the plight of a nation in the very throws of committing the unpardonable sin. In verse 28, He just claimed He cast out devils by the Spirit of God—thereby proving the "Kingdom of God was come" unto them." Empowered by the Holy Spirit, Christ was acting out the principles of His *Galilee Protocol*; but the church leaders were blaspheming the Spirit by attributing His works to Satan.

The situation was dire. It's dire enough for anyone to commit the unpardonable sin: but here it's an entire generation—a whole people whose swept and garnished house (devoid of the glory of God's presence) was about to be re-infested with demons.

—Israel's Storm

Israel was fast approaching her own judgment hour; and history would show that when it came, she would indeed be under satanic control. The situation was urgent: two-and-a-half years of Christ's three-and-a-half-year ministry was used up. Still Israel—like Jonah—was refusing to make good on her commission to warn the world.

The *Ministry of Healing* says Jesus "knew that unless there was a decided change in the principles and purposes of the human race, all would be lost."[23] God assigned Israel the work of warning the world of judgment. For generations she refused her vital mission. Now time was running out. While she was bantering around about signs, and who's who—Christ was warning that the morning skies where getting red. A storm of judgment was coming; and it was aimed directly at *her*.

Like Jonah's storm, Israel's was calculated to get them to do their job. Notwithstanding that the whole people (the disciples apparently included) where stubbornly persisting in rebellion and insubordination—a storm was coming that would aggressively boot them (as many as

---

22 Matthew 12:43-45.

23 Ellen G. White, *The Ministry of Healing*, p. 18.

would) into the very position they had been running away from. And in the calm after that storm (on the day of Pentecost), a purified group of people would emerge upon whom the Spirit of God could fall in abundant rain.

The storm was to cleanse and purify the living temple—one built without hands—so the presence and glory of God could fill His house. With faces lighted up, the people of God went from city to city doing the work the nation had refused to do. In that day, the early Christian Church closely followed the prototype established by the *Master Evangelist* and *Great Physician*. Using the techniques of the *Galilee Protocol* these missionary bands reached the entire world in a single generation.

—Our Storm

Of all this, the sign of Jonah *spoke*. It would be one final sign to that unfaithful generation. And of all this, the sign of Jonah *speaks*. For, "in a special sense Seventh-day Adventists have been set in this world as watchmen and light bearers. To them have been entrusted the last warning message to a perishing world. They have been given a work of the most solemn import—the proclamation of the first, second, and third angels' messages. There is no other work of so great importance."[24]

> "The work in the cities is the essential work for this time. When the cities are worked as God would have them, the result will be the setting in operation of a mighty movement such as we have not yet witnessed."[25]

Let's go over several statements from the Spirit of Prophecy to get a quick overview of what God has intended for us to be doing...

> "The inhabitants of the ungodly cities so soon to be visited by calamities have been cruelly neglected. The time is near when the large cities will be swept away, and all should be warned of these coming judgments. But who is giving to the accomplishment of this work the wholehearted service that God requires?"[26]
>
> "I am bidden to declare the message that cities full of transgression, and sinful in the extreme, will be destroyed by earthquake, by fire, by flood. All the world will be warned that there is a God who will display His authority as God. His unseen agencies will cause destruction, devastation, and death. All the accumulated riches will be as nothingness...
>
> "The Lord will not suddenly cast off all transgressors or destroy entire nations; but He will punish cities and places where men have given themselves up to the passions of Satanic agencies. Strictly will the cities of the

[24] Ellen G. White, *Testimonies for the Church*, vol. 9, p. 19.
[25] Ellen G. White, *Medical Ministry*, p. 304.
[26] Ellen G. White, *Evangelism*, p. 29.

nations be dealt with."[27]

"O that God's people had a sense of the impending destruction of thousands of cities, now almost given entirely to idolatry."[28]

"As a people we need to hasten the work in the cities, which has been hindered for a lack of workers and means and a spirit of consecration. At this time, the people of God need to turn their hearts fully to Him; for the end of all things is at hand. They need to humble their minds, and be attentive to the will of the Lord, working with earnest desire to do *that which God has shown must be done* to warn the cities of their impending doom."[29]

"There is to be no wavering. The trumpet is to give a certain sound. The attention of the people is to be called to the third angel's message. Let not God's servants act like men *walking in their sleep*, but like men preparing for the coming of Christ."[30]

"Most startling messages will be borne by men of God's appointment, messages of a character to warn the people, to arouse them. And while some will be provoked by the warning, and led to resist the light and evidence, we are to see from this that we are giving the testing message for this time... We must also have, in our cities, consecrated evangelists through whom a message is to be borne so decidedly *as to startle the hearers.*"[31]

"We are living in the close of this earth's history... Prophecy is fulfilling. Soon Christ will come with power and great glory. We have no time to lose. Let the message sound forth in earnest words of warning... We must persuade men everywhere to repent and flee from the wrath to come. They have souls to save or to lose. Let there be no indifference in this matter. The Lord calls for workers who are filled with an earnest, decided purpose."[32]

—Insubordination

So we see that just as it was for Israel in the days of Christ—and just as it was for Jonah—it is for us today. For generations now, we have been unfaithful to our work; and a storm of judgment is coming. Just as the storm prepared Jonah for his work—and just as the storm prepared the disciples for the outpouring of the Spirit at Pentecost—our storm *will prepare Adventists to do the work they should have done* when things were better. Of this storm, Sister White says: "This is a terrible ordeal, but nevertheless it must take place."[33]

---

27 Ibid., p. 27.

28 Ibid., p. 29.

29 Ibid., p. 30. Emphasis added.

30 Ellen G. White, *The Review and Herald*, March 2, 1905. Emphasis added.

31 Ellen G. White, *Evangelism*, p. 168. Emphasis added.

32 Ibid., p. 217.

33 Ellen G. White, *Selected Messages*, book. 2, p. 380.

In chapter two of this book, the timeline of the early years of Adventism, shows how our understanding of the nature of our mission grew as God moved us into position to warn the world using the pattern Christ used in Galilee.

We were also told that "Christ stands before us as the pattern Man, the great Medical Missionary."[34] This next statement quotes from the 58th chapter of Isaiah:

"We are to work the works of Christ... Isaiah says, 'Thy righteousness shall go before thee; the glory of the Lord shall be thy reareward.'...This is the work that must be done before Christ shall come in power and great glory."[35]

In fact Isaiah 58 is inseparably linked to the *Galilee Protocol*—it describes the very work that *Seventh-day Adventists* were called to do. This was made known to our pioneers. Notice these statements:

> "The fifty-eighth chapter of Isaiah contains present truth for the people of God. Here we see how medical missionary work and the gospel ministry are to be bound together as the message is given to the world. Upon those who keep the Sabbath of the Lord is laid the responsibility of doing a work of mercy and benevolence. Medical missionary work is to be bound up with the message, and sealed with the seal of God."[36]
>
> "Consider this chapter attentively; for it will be fulfilled... The Lord has a message for his people. This message will be borne, whether men will accept it or reject it. As in the days of Christ, there will be deep plottings of the power of darkness, but the message must not be muffled with smooth words or fair speeches, crying peace, peace, when there is no peace, to those who are turning away from God."[37]
>
> "This light is given to those who keep holy the Lord's Sabbath; but we cannot keep this day holy unless we serve the Lord in the manner brought to view in the scripture: 'Is not this the fast that I have chosen, to loose the bands of wickedness, to undo the heavy burdens, to let the oppressed go free, and that ye break every yoke?...' This is the work that rests upon every soul who accepts the service of Christ."[38]

—A Crisis in the Government of God

So we see that all three storms—Jonah's, Israel's and ours—had (or have) to do with God's people not doing their appointed work of mercy to warn the cities of coming judgment. In our case, "The Lord calls for us to render back to Him the endowments He has given to men, whereby

---

[34] Ellen G. White, *Welfare Ministry*, p. 53.
[35] Ellen G. White, *The Review and Herald*, November 1, 1892.
[36] Ellen G. White, *Evangelism*, p. 516.
[37] Ellen G. White, *Manuscript 36*, 1897.
[38] Ellen G. White, *Manuscript Releases*, vol. 5, p. 33.

they can use all their powers of intellect, and all their strength, physically and morally, in His service to do good and bless others. *A crisis has arrived in the government of God on earth.* Divine compassion has been flowing to the people, notwithstanding that the heavenly current has been beaten back by stubborn hearts."[39]

In 1901, the early pioneers received the word. Because of *insubordination*, they, like the children of Israel would be turned back into the wilderness.[40] What was their "wrong course of action"? What was the test? It was whether or not they would use the *Galilee Protocol!*

> "God had given us a commission which angels might envy. The church has been charged to convey to the world, without delay, God's saving mercy. This is the trust that He has given us, and it is to be faithfully executed. Medical missionary work is to be done. Thousands upon thousands of human beings are perishing in sin. The compassion of God is moved. All heaven is looking on with intense interest to see what character medical missionary work will assume under the supervision of human beings. Will men make merchandise of God's ordained plan for reaching the dark parts of the earth with a manifestation of His benevolence? Will they cover mercy with selfishness, and call it medical missionary work?"[41]

Remember how after Christ spoke of the sign of Jonah, He spoke again of the demoniac: how after his house was swept and garnished, if it was still empty—the devils would move back in and the condition of the man would be worse than at first. Is our house still empty? It was, in 1898:

> "The church is in the Laodicean state. *The presence of God is not in her midst.* Angels of God are sent to measure the temple and the worshipers therein. The Lord looks with sadness upon those who are worshiping their idols, with no care for the souls perishing in darkness and error. He cannot bless a church who feels it no part of their duty to be laborers together with God. *What a terrible thing to exclude Christ from His own Temple.*"[42]

—Serious Medicine

This is something to wrestle with. It seems clear enough that our church—a church we love dearly—stands today in even worse shape than back then. Our history is one of steady retreat toward Egypt. If the Church was in no shape to receive the latter rain then—how can it ever hope to receive it now?

---

39 Ellen G. White, *The Upward Look*, p. 354. Emphasis added.

40 Ellen G. White, *Manuscript* Releases, vol. 20, p. 312-313.

41 Ellen G. White, *Medical Ministry*, p. 131.

42 Ellen G. White, *Last Day Events*, p. 49. Emphasis added.

Is it even possible to reform a church that thinks she needs no reform in the first place? How do you ask a church proud of her "magnificent buildings" and "great marble stones" to tear away those aspects of her structure that are most admired by both her and the world around her?

When we see our people lay aside counsel after counsel concerning entertainment, worship styles, dress, adornments, sexual orientation; when we see our hospitals wholly devoted to worldly medicine, serve flesh foods in our cafeterias, and perform elective abortions; when many of our ministers and educators are teaching spiritual formation, creative forms of pantheism, and embracing a concept of God's character that makes a mockery of the atonement; when our worldly careers come first, and we relegate missionary work to an occasional ten-day field-trip—then asking the church to embrace the *Galilee Protocol* seems laughable—or it would if one could laugh under these dire circumstances.

No. It's not plausible to think time will heal our problems. The denomination is in serious trouble. Apostasy is growing faster than our ability to meet it. We need serious medicine—the strongest heaven has to offer *even if God has to speak to us in a language we cannot fail to understand.*[43]

Elijah went before God to plead for Him to save His people, even if it must be by judgments. Seeing no other way to turn them from their idolatry, he pled with God to withhold the rain and dew. God told Elijah that He heard his prayer.[44]

Oh, brothers and sisters, a calamity is coming. Time has run long. Our merciful Savior has given every moment to us that we might turn and make good on our assignment—but now time has run its course. Ready or not we approach the end of all things. We cannot put it off this time—and neither can God. The sands have passed through the hourglass with but a few precious grains remaining. God must now intervene, or all will be lost. The gathering clouds are about to burst upon an unsuspecting church. We are told:

> "All heaven is represented to me as watching the unfolding of events. A crisis is to be revealed in the great and prolonged controversy in the government of God on earth. Something great and decisive is to take place, and that right early. If any delay, the character of God and His throne will be compromised. The armory of heaven is open; all the universe of God and its equipment is ready. One word has justice to speak, and there will be terrific representations upon the earth, of the wrath of

[43] See Ellen G. White, *Manuscript Releases*, vol. 4, p. 367.
[44] Ellen G. White, *The Review and Herald*, September 16, 1873.

God. There will be voices and thunderings and earthquakes and universal desolation. Every movement in the universe of heaven is to prepare the world for the great crisis."[45]

"Angels are now restraining the winds of strife, until the world shall be warned of its coming doom; but the storm is gathering, ready to burst upon the earth, and when God shall bid his angels loose the winds, there shall be such a scene of strife as no pen can picture... A moment of respite has been graciously given us of God. Every power lent us from heaven is to be used in doing the work assigned us by the Lord for those who are perishing in ignorance... God's people should make mighty intercession to Him for help now. And they must put their whole energies into the effort to proclaim the truth during the respite that has been granted."[46]

—A Storm to Try Every Man's Faith

We cannot wait for the denomination or the leaders to join us in this. *There is much work to do before the storm.* The mission depends upon us! If God is convicting your heart right now—the mission depends upon you! Many will oppose the peculiar nature of our mission—many opposed it in Christ's day. Many of our pioneers opposed it too.

Many will wait for the organized church to lead the way; and many will wait for a *sign from heaven*. But Jesus said, there will be no sign given to this wicked and adulterous generation*, except the sign of Jonah!*

A man by the name of W. E. Ross, a friend of Ellen White, often repeated a story until his death in 1945. The story was about something Sister White said to a small group he was part of. It happened around the year 1908.

It goes like this: he, and brother D. E. Robinson, sister McInterfer, and Ellen White were all at Loma Linda—at the depot—waiting for a train. Sister White told of a terrible storm of persecution that was coming, like a windstorm that would blow down every standing object. Not one Seventh-day Adventist was to be seen. They, like the disciples, all forsook Christ and fled. All who had sought positions were never seen anymore.

After the storm there was a great calm. Then the Seventh-day Adventists arose like a flock of sheep, but without shepherds. They all united in earnest prayer to God who answered by helping them to choose leaders of their number who had never sought positions. They prayed most earnestly again for the Holy Spirit, which was poured out upon them,

[45] Ellen G. White, *Manuscript 27*, 1892.
[46] Ellen G. White, *Evangelism*, p. 704.

making them fully ready for service. They then went forth 'as an army with banners' fearlessly and fully to give the message to the world.

When the storm was breaking in AD 31, Christ quoted Zechariah, "Smite the shepherd and the sheep will be scattered." But the context of Zechariah actually puts this prophecy in our day—because Zechariah is describing the shaking to take place before the *latter rain* can fall.

> "And it shall come to pass, that in all the land, saith the Lord, two parts therein shall be cut off and die, but the third shall be left therein. And I will bring the third part through the fire, and will refine them as silver is refined, and will try them as gold is tried: They shall call upon My name, and I will hear them: I will say, it is my people: and they will say, The Lord is my God."[47]

Inspiration is consistent. Like in the days of Jonah, a storm is coming.

"The storm is coming, the storm that will try every man's faith, of what sort it is."

—The Review and Herald, August 31,1905.

[47] Zechariah 13:8, 9.

CHAPTER SIX

Protocol Physiology

Modern advances in technology make it possible to observe brain activity. Scientists can see the physiology facilitating the *physical*, *mental*, and *spiritual* natures in the human organism. So it is not surprising when they say our brain is really *three brains* in one.[1]

> "We have three brains that allow us to go from thinking to doing to being. Each brain is its own individual bio-computer with its own anatomy and its own circuitry, its own physiology and chemistry. They even have their own history as well as their own sense of time and space."[2]

When we picture a brain, we usually picture the neocortex. It's the big walnut-looking outer layer. It's the thinking, analytical, logical part of the brain. It's responsible for sensory perception, spatial reasoning, generation of motor commands, conscious thought, and intellectual memory. It's the home of our determination and will: and is the seat of our *mental* nature.

The center of the brain is called the limbic system. About the size of a lemon, it releases chemicals into the body; and the body "feels" the

[1] PsychEducation.org, *"3-Brains-in-One Brain"*, Updated 12/2014, Accessed 10/29/2019 at https://psycheducation.org/brain-tours/3-brains-in-one-brain/.

[2] Dr. Joe Dispenza, *Transformation*, TED Talks with Dr. Joe Dispenza, Posted February 8, 2013, accessed 10/29/2019 at https://www.youtube.com/watch?v=W81CHn4l4AM&feature=youtu.be.

changes caused by the chemicals. It's responsible for emotions, learning, emotional memory, and spirituality. It is vital to social relationships; and is the seat of our *spiritual* nature.

The Cerebellum is the brainstem at the top of the spinal cord. This is the instinctive brain wired to all the parts and systems of the body. It controls the physical mechanism and basic life support functions. To affect the physical body, the neocortex and the limbic brain have to influence the cerebellum. It is the seat of our *physical* nature.

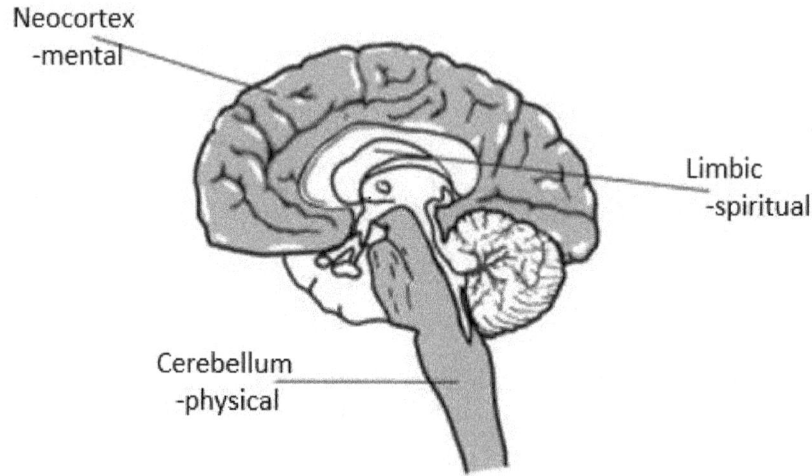

—Ideas, Concepts, Philosophies, and Theories

Scientists estimate there are 100 billion neurons in the human brain. Neurons are brain cells that store information and communicate among themselves. When we experience new events—sense something new about our environment through our senses, or think about things already learned—information about what is happening is being stored in these neurons. The neurons involved in gathering and storing this new information are all firing at the same time. It is a principle in neuroscience that cells that fire together wire together.[3] So this information is being biologically wired into our cerebral architecture.

While they are storing new information, the cells are communicating with each other about the new information. The brain sorts and organizes all the information and compares it to old information. Through this process the brain is constantly forming new synaptic connections. As the

[3] Hebbian theory, Psychology Wiki, accessed 12/1/2019 at https://psychology.wikia.org/wiki/Hebbian_theory.

neurons are firing and wiring together, the brain sorts them and wires them into gangs of neurons called neural networks. We call them "ideas" and "concepts." These are wired together into larger networks forming more complex groups of ideas we call "philosophies" and "theories." The brain also forms groupings of data into memories, skills, and behaviors.

—Experiences

Once we understand something intellectually, we apply that new understanding to the way we live. We personalize it. We demonstrate it. We change our behavior or some action. We do things a little different—and so we have *new* experiences.

The brain processes the new experiences. This causes new information to rush into the brain and the jungle of neurons organize into new patterns. At the moment those patterns string into place, the limbic brain releases chemicals. We feel them as emotions. Experiences reinforce the electrical connections of the neocortex. They trigger chemical responses from the limbic brain to help us remember.

—Gigantic Models

These chemicals alter feelings inside us; so we perk up and pay more attention to whatever caused them. The limbic brain tags our memories with emotional data both to help us recall our reaction later, and to associate our reaction to what we are experiencing. In this way our minds form complex structures that somehow factor in all the dimensions of our personal experiences—our thoughts, ideas, lessons learned, books read, mistakes made, emotions felt, and a myriad of sensory data. Our brains build gigantic models of our personal views of reality—views based on our own experiences with the world.

The brain does more than just gather, organize and record information and emotional responses to ideas and events. It is more than a database. It is the seat of who we are—our being. To define who we are, it uses processes of thinking and learning and feeling. But then it goes deep by involving the cerebellum—our subconscious being.

—Genetic Changes

When our thinking brain uses ideas repeatedly in such a way as to cause an experience to happen repeatedly, our thinking brain is teaching our body to understand emotionally what our thinking brain understands intellectually. Knowledge is for the mind what experience is for the body.[4] So when our emotional brain agrees with our thinking brain concerning an idea—at that moment our limbic brain mixes a batch of peptides that signal the body to change genetically—encoding this idea into our new being. We change because the brain instructs the body chemically to become genetically what it understands electrically.

Arlene R. Taylor, PhD, is a leading speaker on brain function and is sometimes referred to as the *brain guru.* In a lecture at a Carolina Conference campmeeting, she referred to a phenomenon she called *cellular memory*. Scientists have observed that sometimes organ transplant patients come out of surgery with new habits—those formed by the donor.[5] This is because the cerebellum encodes memories and behaviors into the cellular structure of the whole body. These cellular memories can even be passed on genetically to three or four generations.[6]

Repeating the same thoughts and actions over and over cause them to become part of who we are on a subconscious and then physical level. They become automatic, second nature, easy— habits. When we get to this level of memorizing an internal chemical order surrounding certain thoughts, feelings, and actions, we have caused them to become part of who we are. When we get to where no person, or thing, or experience can remove them from us—it is because we have sustained this level of coherence intellectually (electrically) and emotionally (chemically) to the point that it has become part of our state of being physically (genetically).[7] Notice how the steps are progressive: intellectual, emotional, and then physical encoding.

—Truth

Ideas and memories form into a giant model of "truth." But the "truth" of these models is relative. It varies from one mind to another because individual brains build their own models based on their own experiences—and their experiences are not necessarily absolute fact. *Truth is absolute*; and brains *can* incorporate ideas that are *absolute truth*—but since their access to information is limited to their experiences—

---

[4] Dr. Joe Dispenza, *Transformation*, TED Talks with Dr. Joe Dispenza, Posted February 8, 2013, accessed 10/29/2019 at https://www.youtube.com/watch?v=W81CHn4I4AM&feature=youtu.be.

[5] Gianna Absi, Is the Brain the Only Place that Stores Our Memories, November 11, 2014. Accessed 10/29/2019 at https://sites.bu.edu/ombs/2014/11/11/is-the-brain-the-only-place-that-stores-our-memories/.

[6] See Arlene R. Taylor, PhD., *Cellular Memory*—Déjà vu to the third and fourth generation, (DVD, amazon.com 2010); and see Exodus 20:5.

[7] Dr. Joe Dispenza, *Transformation*, TED Talks with Dr. Joe Dispenza, Posted February 8, 2013, accessed 10/29/2019 at https://www.youtube.com/watch?v=W81CHn4I4AM&feature=youtu.be.

absolute truth is hard for any brain to determine. It is the brain's job to keep its model of truth as accurate as possible.

God alone is infinite in knowledge and truth. Only God has the whole truth—and nothing but the truth. We incorporate nuggets of truth into our incomplete models. We incorporate theology and religion into our models. We alter our models when we learn truth. We change things when we realize we've been wrong. So we adjust our models—but we never really completely fix them. Without infinite knowledge and experience our models cannot fully mirror reality.

—Authorities

Our models are not strictly limited to *our own* experiences. When we learn from others' experiences, they become part of our own experience model. Trusted people become our authorities—people like authors, teachers, preachers, educational institutions, professionals, respected family and friends. We often evaluate information from our authorities with less scrutiny; but this can be dangerous because their models are usually subject to the same limitations; and it is important to remember that experience is not necessarily the same thing as truth.

God is to be our ultimate authority—only He is complete. And "the holy scriptures," too, for they come from God and are able to make us "wise unto salvation through faith" in Christ Jesus.[8]

> "All scripture is given by inspiration of God, and is profitable for doctrine, for reproof, for correction, for instruction in righteousness: that the man of God may be perfect, thoroughly furnished unto good works."[9]

Scripture needs to mold and shape our models—even to the point of changing them and correcting errors. Peter says, "the word of God" "lives and abides forever."[10] It's the Word of God that speaks worlds into existence[11] and is able to make real changes to the human mechanism.

> "For the word of God is quick and powerful, and sharper than any two-edged sword, piercing even to the dividing asunder of the soul and spirit, and the joints and marrow, and is the discerner of the thoughts and intents of the heart."[12]
>
> "*The word destroys the natural, earthly nature,* and imparts a new life in Christ Jesus. The Holy Spirit comes to the soul as the Comforter. By the

---

[8] 2 Timothy 3:15.
[9] 2 Timothy 3:16-17.
[10] 1 Peter 1:23, New King James Version.
[11] John 1:1.
[12] Hebrews 4:12.

transforming agency of His grace, the image of God is reproduced in the disciple; he becomes a new creature."[13]

Adventists should also take note: "Believe the LORD your God, so shall ye be established; *believe His prophets*, so shall ye prosper."[14]

—Downshifting

Dr. Taylor also describes *downshifting*. She compares the three brains to gears in a vehicle with an automatic transmission. When engaged in normal comfortable activity, your mind is in third gear. It likes to be in the neocortex where your thoughts are—thinking, questioning, planning, relating, learning, remembering, managing emotions, and choosing things: this or that. But when you "encounter something fearful, uncomfortable, traumatic, or stressful, your brain's tendency will be to downshift. Automatically."[15]

Downshifting is "an unexpected jerk, a sudden process of slowing down or halting cognitive abilities—a focusing of attention and energy toward one of the two lower layers as the brain perceives a lack of safety."[16]

Second gear places the limbic brain in the driver's seat. The highly developed limbic system processes and monitors emotions essential for remembering. It processes information 80,000 times faster than the neocortex—and searches the brain to collect pieces of information to recall memory. It expresses a collective *sense* of all the stored information the slower neocortex cannot handle at the moment.

Antonio Damasio studied people with damaged limbic systems. He made a groundbreaking discovery: they seemed normal except they could not feel emotions—*and they were not able to make decisions*.[17] According to an article in *Psychology Today*, "It is said that emotion drives 80 percent of the choices Americans make, while practicality and objectivity only represents about 20 percent of decision-making."[18]

This downshifting to second gear in times of stress or fear is more conservative than going all the way down to first gear. The limbic is used to

---

[13] Ellen G. White, *The Desire of Ages*, p. 391. Emphasis added.

[14] 2 Chronicles 20:20. Emphasis added.

[15] Arlene R. Taylor, PhD., W. Eugene Brewer, EdD., *Your Brain Has a Bent (Not a Dent!)*, p. 172. (Success Resources International, Napa, California. 2009).

[16] Ibid., p. 173.

[17] Jim Camp, *Decisions are largely emotional, not logical: the neuroscience behind decision-making*, June 11, 2012. Accessed 11/4/2019 at https://bigthink.com/experts-corner/decisions-are-emotional-not-logical-the-neuroscience-behind-decision-making.

[18] Michael Levine, *Logic and Emotion—Delving into the logical and emotional sides of the human brain*, July 12, 2012, accessed on 11/4/2019 at https://www.psychologytoday.com/us/blog/the-divided-mind/201207/logic-and-emotion.

split-second decision-making based on its *sense* of experiences—and with its many direct connections to the right hemisphere of the neocortex—it benefits from some continued input from the thinking brain. Emotions maintain a balance between the thinking brain and the action brain (the cerebellum). It translates thinking-brain information into language the action brain understands.

The action brain is first gear—and it dominates when survival is top priority. Called the *sensory/motor* brain, it consists of the brain stem, portions of the spinal cord, and the cerebellum.[19] It provides awareness of the outer sensory world, and it reacts to "look out for me." It initiates fast protective reflexes and survival strategies; houses automatic and ritualistic behaviors; reacts instinctively to stress with fight/flight, tend/befriend, and conserve/withdraw. It alerts the thinking brain in an emergency; maintains critical life functions; learns and performs rapid, highly skilled movements; and uses sensory information to start corrective action.

—Moral Character

All three brains combine to make up character; and "it is character alone that God values."[20] "A character formed according to the divine likeness is the only treasure that we can take from this world to the next."[21] "In the word of God [we] learn that all who enter heaven must have a perfect character; for then they will meet their Lord in peace."[22]

There is confusion about what it means to have a perfect character. The idea sometimes becomes controversial within the church. It is not necessarily the same thing as being flawless in every way. It's not the same as being sinless—but neither does it allow for carelessness, selfishness,[23] or laxness toward resisting temptation.[24] Recall that Jesus was already sinless—still "learned He obedience by the things which He suffered"—"being made perfect."[25] And realize we continue in these fallen, sinful bodies until changed in a moment—in the twinkling of an eye.

Sanctification is the process by which character is perfected. It deals with known sin—and those things we have the opportunity to know and

[19] Taylor & Brewer, p. 174.

[20] Ellen G. White, *Testimonies to Ministers*, p. 362.

[21] Ellen G. White, *Christ's Object Lessons*, p. 332.

[22] Ellen G. White, *Counsels on Sabbath School Work*, p. 112.

[23] Ellen G. White, *Testimonies for the Church*, vol. 3, p. 531.

[24] Ellen G. White, *Testimonies for the Church*, vol. 2, p. 638.

[25] Hebrews 5:7-9. See also Ellen G. White, *The Desire of Ages*, p. 762.

improve upon.[26] "Every transgressor of God's law is a sinner, and none can be sanctified while living in known sin."[27] "The only ones who will be found faithful" are "those who would rather die than perform a wrong act."[28] So what is character; how is it perfected; and what does it mean to have a perfect character?

> "Actions repeated form habits, habits form character, and by the character our destiny for time and for eternity is decided."[29]
>
> "If the thoughts are wrong, the feelings will be wrong; and the thoughts and feelings combined make up the moral character."[30]
>
> "Both thought and action will be necessary if you would attain to perfection of character."[31]

So we see "the body is a most important medium through which the mind and soul are developed for the upbuilding of character"[32]—we see the physiology of the three brains is fundamental to reformation.

> "The Holy Spirit has been prevented from coming in to mold and fashion heart and mind, because men suppose that they understand best how to form their own characters. And they think that they may safely *form their characters after their own model*. But there is only one model after which human character is to be formed—the character of Christ.[33]
>
> "Divine wisdom has appointed in the plan of salvation the law of action and reaction, making the work of beneficence, in all its branches, twice blessed. He that gives to the needy blesses others, and is blessed himself in a still greater degree...
>
> *It is in doing the works of Christ*, ministering as He did to the suffering and afflicted, *that we are to develop Christian character*. It is for our good that God has called us to practice self-denial for Christ's sake, to bear the cross, to labor and sacrifice in seeking to save that which is lost. This is the Lord's process of refining, purging away the baser material, that the precious traits of character which were in Christ Jesus, may appear in the believer.[34]
>
> "But Christ has given us no assurance that to attain perfection of character is an easy matter. A noble, all-round character is not inherited. It does not come to us by accident. A noble character is earned by individual effort through the merits and grace of Christ. God gives the talents, the powers of the mind; we form the character. It is formed by hard, stern battles with self. Conflict after conflict must be waged against

---

[26] See Ellen G. White, *The Review and Herald*, April 29, 1884.

[27] Ellen G. White, *Faith and Works*, p. 30.

[28] Ellen G. White, *Testimonies for the Church*, vol. 5, p. 53.

[29] Ellen G. White, *Christ's Object Lessons*, p. 356.

[30] Ellen G. White, *The Review and Herald*, April 21, 1885.

[31] Ellen G. White, *Testimonies for the Church*, vol. 4, p. 568.

[32] Ellen G. White, *Prophets and Kings*, p. 488.

[33] Ellen G. White, *Seventh-day Adventist Bible Commentary*, vol. 6, p. 1098. Emphasis added.

[34] Ellen G. White, *Welfare Ministry*, p. 301. Emphasis added.

hereditary tendencies. We shall have to criticize ourselves closely, and allow not one unfavorable trait to remain uncorrected."[35]

"The people are asleep in their sins, and need to be alarmed before they can shake off this lethargy. Their ministers have preached smooth things. God's servants, who bear sacred, vital truths should cry aloud and spare not, that the truth may tear off the garment of security, and find its way to the heart...God's servants must bear a pointed testimony. It will cut the natural heart, and develop character."[36]

—Collective Character

As *personal* as character perfection is, the Bible does not treat it as a strictly individual matter. When the Lord talked to Jeremiah[37] about two covenants with Israel, He was not talking about Israel—the man; He was talking about Israel—the people.

The old covenant was ratified at Sinai; the new covenant would be ratified at Calvary. The new covenant would restore *the people's* physical, mental, and spiritual natures. When, in the early Christian church, this did not happen to Paul's satisfaction,[38] he referred back to what the Lord said to Jeremiah:

> "This is the covenant that I will make with the house of Israel after those days, saith the Lord; I will put my laws into their mind, and write them in their hearts: and I will be to them a God, and they shall be to me *a people*: And they shall not teach every man his neighbor, and every man his brother, saying, Know the Lord: for all shall know me, from the least to the greatest."[39]

While God's work is the same at all times, He has been gradually unfolding His purposes in the plan of redemption.[40] There are different degrees of development and different manifestations of the power of God to meet people in the different ages. The Savior typified in the old covenant rites and ceremonies is the same revealed in the gospel. The old covenant best suited Israel's needs at that time.

> "In their bondage the people had to a great extent lost the knowledge of God... Living in the midst of idolatry and corruption, they had no true conception of the holiness of God, of the exceeding sinfulness of their own hearts, their utter inability, in themselves, to render obedience to

---

[35] Ellen G. White, *Christ's Object Lessons*, p. 331.
[36] Ellen G. White, *Spiritual Gifts*, vol. 2, p. 300.
[37] Jeremiah 31:31-34.
[38] Hebrews 5:11-14.
[39] Hebrews 8:10-11. Emphasis added.
[40] Ellen G. White, *Patriarchs and Prophets*, p. 373.

God's law, and their need of a Savior. All this they must be taught."[41]

The terms of the old covenant were, obey and live.[42] "Cursed be he that confirmeth not all the words of this law to do them."[43] The children of Israel felt that they could establish their own righteousness—so they quickly accepted its terms. [44]

> "Yet only a few weeks passed before they broke their covenant with God, and bowed down to worship a graven image. They could not hope for the favor of God through a covenant which they had broken; and now, seeing their sinfulness and their need of pardon, they were brought to feel their need of the Savoir... shadowed forth in the sacrificial offerings. Now by faith and love they were bound to God as their deliverer from the bondage of sin. Now they were prepared to appreciate the blessing of the new covenant."[45]

God said the new covenant will *not* be "according to the covenant that I made with their fathers in the day that I took them by the hand to bring them out of the land of Egypt; which my covenant they brake."[46] That old covenant wasn't perfect. It could not make the "comer thereunto perfect"—it couldn't bring a permanent end to sin.[47] But the new covenant is a *better* covenant established upon better promises.[48] It has the power to change human DNA—actually writing the law in our hearts and minds.

—A Pattern

The book of Hebrews deals extensively with the covenants. It links the old covenant with the tabernacle's holy place and the new covenant with the most holy. The temple is a fitting analogy; and it too has a personal and corporate aspect.

> "*Each worker* is to become just what God designs him to be, building his life with pure, noble deeds, that in the end his character may be a symmetrical structure, *a fair temple*, honored by God and man."[49]
>
> "*His church* on earth is to assume divine proportions before the world *as a temple built of living stones*, each one reflecting light. It is to be the

---

[41] Ibid.
[42] Ezekiel 20:11; Leviticus 18:5.
[43] Deuteronomy 27:26.
[44] Exodus 24:7.
[45] Ellen G. White, *Patriarchs and Prophets*, p. 372.
[46] Jeremiah 31:31.
[47] Hebrews 10:1-4.
[48] Hebrews 8:6.
[49] Ellen G. White, *Testimonies for the Church*, vol. 8, p. 173. Emphasis added.

light of the world as a city set on a hill, which cannot be hid."[50]

The sanctuary is also a fitting illustration of restoring man *physically*, *mentally*, and *spiritually*. It begins in the courtyard even before we enter a formal covenant with God. For Israel, this took place while they were still in Egypt. The Passover, like the altar of burnt offering, symbolizes the cross. The Red Sea corresponds to the laver (also called the great sea[51])—they symbolize baptism.[52]

—The Courtyard

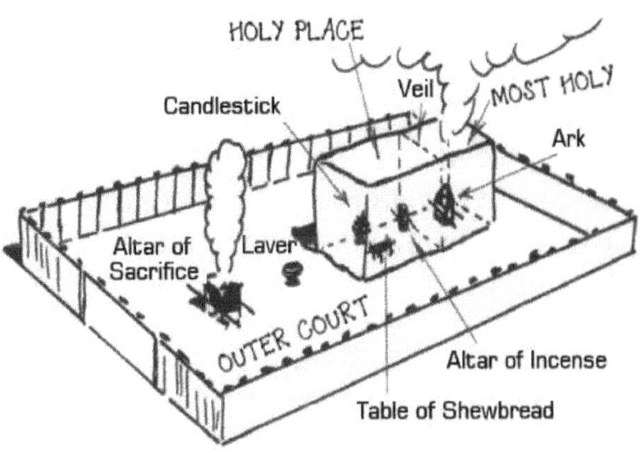

The *courtyard* is about physical obedience. Israel understood very little of the plan of salvation or the nature of true religion at the time of the Exodus. Enticed by the prospects of freedom, they cooperated with God's instructions; and God honored their simple obedience. Even baptism is a physical, courtyard event; it's a *physical enactment* that represents the entering a formal covenant relationship with God—preparing the believer for transfer into the first apartment, the holy place.

Wilderness testing follows baptism. This was true of Israel after crossing the Red Sea,[53] and it was true of Christ going into the wilderness to be tested by the devil.[54] These tests measure the believer's determination for *physical* obedience to the word of God in matters pertaining to their physical, mental and spiritual natures. Christ was tempted three times—once for each of the three natures. In each case, Christ determined to conform His physical behavior to the written word.

It starts in the courtyard. We understand we are sinners—that we need a Savior. We come to know something of His love—that He died to save

---

[50] Ibid. Emphasis added.

[51] The laver is called the "Sea" in 2 Kings 16:17, and the "molten sea" in 1 Kings 7:23.

[52] "All were baptized unto Moses in the cloud and in the Sea." 1 Corinthians 10:2.

[53] See Exodus 15:22-17:16.

[54] See Matthew 4:1-11; Mark 1:12, 13; Luke 4:1-13.

us. We confess our sins; we turn away from them. We are baptized and determine to apply what we know about God's plan to the way we live. We personalize it. We demonstrate it. We change our behavior and our actions. We do things differently—and so we have *new* experiences.

—The Holy Place

The *holy place* is about *mental* obedience—it's about understanding and believing the things the old covenant symbols point to. Here we turn the obedience of "thus saith the Lord," into the obedience of *personal experiences* with the things of God.

The holy place contains the table of shewbread, the altar of incense, and the golden candlesticks. These represent the educational tools used in the *school of Christ*[55] to restore our minds. The table of shewbread contains bread and drink—representing the word of God.[56] The Altar of incense is about our prayer mingled with the merits and intercessions of Christ.[57] The light of the candles represents the illumination of the Holy Spirit through the activity of the church.[58] Bible study, prayer, and ministry are the essentials to Christian growth.

The brain processes all this new information and these new experiences—and as it all rushes into the brain, the jungle of neurons organizes into patterns. When the patterns string into place, the limbic brain chemically reinforces the electrical connections of the neocortex; and the chemical responses they trigger help us remember it all.

When this all happens repeatedly our thinking brain is teaching our body to understand spiritually what our brain understands intellectually. And when our experiences agree with what we understand about the truths of God, the limbic brain signals the body to change genetically—encoding truth right into our new being.

Just as there were tests before entering the holy place; there are tests before entering the most holy. These later tests measure the believer's determination to yield *mentally* in obedience to the word of God in

---

[55] Ellen G. White, *Testimonies for the Church*, vol 5, p.578. "The trial of faith is more precious than gold. All should learn that this is a part of the discipline in the school of Christ, which is essential to purify and refine them from the dross of earthliness. They must endure with fortitude the taunts and attacks of enemies, and overcome all obstacles that Satan may place in their path to hedge up the way. He will try to lead them to neglect prayer and to discourage them in the study of the Scriptures, and he will throw his hateful shadow athwart their path to hide Christ and the heavenly attractions from their view."

[56] "Man shall not live by bread alone, but by every word that proceededth out of the mouth of God." Matthew 4:4. "Christ also loved the church, and gave Himself for it; That He might sanctify and cleanse it with the washing of the word.." Ephesians 5:26.

[57] :And there was given unto Him much incense, that He should offer it with the prayers of the saints upon the golden alter which was before the throne." Revelation 8:3.

[58] See Zechariah 4; Revelation 1-3.

matters pertaining to their physical, mental and spiritual natures. Christ's struggles in Gethsemane illustrate this—and again, a struggle for each of the three natures. Christ asked that the cup might pass from Him three times. He *learned* what it would involve, and His mind recoiled from the thought of it. His body so keenly felt the intellectual struggle that He "sweat as it were great drops of blood."[59] And He said how He was "*exceedingly sorrowful*,[60] even unto death."[61] Christ was determined to submit to the will of His Father in each case, saying: "Nevertheless not as I will but as Thou wilt."[62]

—The Most Holy

The *most holy place* is about *spiritual* obedience. It's about obedience written into our very being—where Christ has so blended "our hearts and minds into conformity to His will, that when obeying Him we shall be but carrying out our own impulses."[63]

> "What? know ye not that your body is the temple of the Holy Ghost *which is* in you, which ye have of God, and ye are not your own?"[64]
>
> "And I will give them one heart, and I will put a new spirit within them; and I will take the stony heart out of their flesh, and will give them an heart of flesh."[65]

When Christ died, He ratified the new covenant[66]—and passing through the veil Himself—He "consecrated for us" "a new and living way" into the "holiest."[67] Hebrews speaks of this in connection with the new covenant and admonishes us to boldly enter into the holiest by the blood of Jesus[68]—after "having our hearts sprinkled from an evil conscience (altar of incense—*holy place*), and our bodies washed with pure water (laver-*courtyard*)."[69]

Covenants are agreements—promises. They pertain to future things. God made the promise to Abraham,[70] and later He confirmed it with an

---

[59] Luke 22:44.

[60] Sorrow – *an emotion of great sadness*; The Free Dictionary by Farlex. Accessed 12/1/2019 at https://www.thefreedictionary.com/sorrow.

[61] Matthew 26:38. Emphasis added.

[62] Ibid., verses 39, 42, 44.

[63] Ellen G. White, *The Desire of Ages*, p. 668.

[64] 1 Corinthians 6:19.

[65] Ezekiel 11:19.

[66] See Ellen G. White, *Patriarchs and Prophets*, p. 370-371; and Hebrews 10:29.

[67] Hebrews 10:19-20.

[68] Hebrews 10:16-19.

[69] Hebrews 10:22. Parentheses added.

[70] Genesis 15:4.

oath.[71] Hebrews tells us that this hope is sure and steadfast—the anchor of the soul—especially now the *Forerunner* (Christ) is entered within the veil. Christ ratified the agreement by His own blood and experience; but to all still in the first apartment, it is still a promise of something *future*.

So what *does* it promise? The answer: He who began a good work in *us* "will continue to perfect it until the day of Jesus Christ."[72] It is that *we* will leave "the elementary teachings about Christ"[73] going "on unto perfection."[74] It is that *we* will enter "into God's rest," resting from *our* "own work just as God did from His."[75] It is that *we* will be "made perfect" by following and obeying the "author of our salvation"—who, "although He was a Son, He learned obedience from what He suffered."[76] It is "our Lord Jesus, that great shepherd of the sheep, through the blood of the everlasting covenant," making *us* "perfect in every good work to do His will, working in you that which is well pleasing in His sight."[77] It literally is that He will put His laws *in our minds* and inscribe them *on our hearts*; and He will remember our sins no more—because there will no longer need to be "an annual reminder of sins."[78]

—The Promised Rest

Sure, all this has to do with people individually; but the bigger picture shows that it is really about the church corporately. That's the point of Hebrews 11—Abel, Enoch, Noah, Abraham, Isaac, Jacob, Joseph, Moses, Mary, Rahab, Gideon, Barak, Sampson, Jephthah, David, Samuel, the prophets, etc., "these all, having obtained a good report through faith, received not the promise: God having provided some better thing for us, that they without us should not be made perfect."[79]

> "Christ also loved the church, and gave himself for it; That he might sanctify and cleanse it with the washing of water by the word, That he might present it to himself a glorious church, not having spot, or wrinkle, or any such thing; but that it should be holy and without blemish."[80]

[71] Genesis 22:16-17.
[72] Philippians 1:6. Berean Study Bible.
[73] Hebrews 6:1 Berean Study Bible.
[74] Hebrews 6:1.
[75] Hebrews 4:10.
[76] Hebrews 5:8-9. Berean Study Bible.
[77] Hebrews 13:20-21.
[78] See Hebrews 8:10; Hebrews 10:16; and Hebrews 10:1-3. Day of atonement, cleansing of the sanctuary, blotting out of sins.
[79] Hebrews 11:39-40. Berean Study Bible.
[80] Ephesians 5:25-27. Berean Study Bible.

It is in this *whole-church* context that the discussion about *today* and the *promised rest* takes place in Hebrews 3 and 4. Quoting Psalms 95, Paul[81] argues that even though Joshua led Israel into Canaan, they did not enter the promised rest. This is because the promise still needed fulfilling when the Psalms were written—that's why the psalmist was still offering it in his day, saying, "Today, if ye will hear his voice..."[82]

> "For if Joshua[83] had given them rest, God would not have spoken later about another day. There remains, then, a Sabbath rest for the people of God. For whoever enters God's rest also rests from his own work, just as God did from His. Let us, therefore, make every effort to enter that rest, so that no one will fall by following the same pattern of disobedience."[84]

This all ties into the *most holy place* new covenant theme of Hebrews. Once the *church* really follows Christ into the *most holy* (experientially), she will be holy and without blemish—ready to receive the seal of the living God.[85] Probation will close, and the Lord will return.

> "'When the fruit is brought forth, immediately He putteth in the sickle, because the harvest is come.' Christ is waiting with longing desire for the manifestation of Himself in His church. When the character of Christ shall be perfectly reproduced in His people, then He will come to claim them as His own."[86]

—All Your Heart, Soul, and Mind

Jesus promises total restoration to the believer so He can say, "Love the Lord your God with all your *heart* and with all your *soul*, and with all your *mind*."[87] He refers here to the protocol physiology of the three brains—the three natures. He calls the spiritual nature the heart,[88] the mental nature the mind,[89] and here the physical nature is the soul (body+ breath).[90] So the new covenant promises a thorough-going renovation of the whole being. Isaiah refers to the righteous this way too:

> "He who walks righteously and speaks with sincerity, who refuses gain

---

[81] Paul is the author of Hebrews. See Ellen G. White, *The Great Controversy*, p. 347; *Patriarchs and Prophets*, p. 352.

[82] Psalms 95:7.

[83] Some translations say Jesus, some say Joshua. Both are ok. "Jesus" is Greek for the Hebrew "Joshua." Joshua was the boots on the ground, but God was the real Leader—and ultimately it is Jesus who gives rest.

[84] Hebrews 4:8-11. Berean Study Bible.

[85] Revelation 7:2.

[86] Ellen G. White, *Christ's Object Lessons*, p. 69.

[87] Matthew 22:37. Berean Study Bible. Emphasis added.

[88] Greek καρδίας (kardias) the heart i.e. feelings.

[89] Greek διανοίας (dianoias) deep thought, properly, the faculty, by implication, its exercise.

[90] Greek ψυχῆς (psychēs) breath, life. Same as Hebrew לְנֶפֶשׁ (lə·ne·p̄eš) living being, life,—used in Genesis 2:7 where body+breath=a living soul.

> from extortion, whose hand never takes a bribe, who stops his ears against murderous plots and shuts his eyes tightly against evil—he will dwell on the heights; the mountain fortress will be his refuge; his food will be provided and his water assured."[91]

In this context, *walking* is spiritual,[92] *speaking* is mental,[93] and *taking* is physical. Likewise: *hands* are physical, *ears* are mental, and *eyes* are spiritual. This person is reflecting the image of God in each of the three natures—and is prepared to flee to the mountains where his food and water is assured.

Physical, mental, and spiritual restoration involves a process. Since human depravity goes to the core—written in the DNA—the decision to change has to go deep too. It has to be more than a single choice—it has to be a *series of choices* that continue to cooperate with divine power to transform the body, mind, and soul. We have to *continue to choose* because it is the process of changing that really tests our resolve to leave our darling sins behind. It easy to once say, "Make me like you, Lord." But when facing the many details of life, it's harder to always say, "Don't let me be like me."

—Sealed unto the Day of Redemption

We get special help when we are converted. The *three great powers of heaven* pledge themselves to get us through the reformation process.

> "Those who submit to the solemn rite of baptism pledge themselves to devote their lives to God's service; and the three great powers of heaven, the Father, the Son, and the Holy Spirit, pledge themselves to cooperate with them, to work in and through them."[94] "As they accept Christ as their Savior, they receive power to become the sons of God."[95]

Specifically, "having heard and believed the word of truth—the gospel of your salvation—you were sealed with the promised Holy Spirit, who is the pledge of our inheritance until the redemption of those who are God's possession, to the praise of His glory.[96]

> "The gift of the Spirit is not only a seal, but an earnest, firstfruit, or installment, a pledge that the rest shall follow. The seal of the Spirit not only assures us of the full inheritance to come, but gives us a right conception of its nature. It shows us the kind of provision God makes for

91 Isaiah 33:15-16.

92 Galatians 5:16-17, 25; Ephesians 5:8; 2 Corinthians 5:7; Psalms 119:105; 1 John 2:6;

93 Proverbs 2:6, 1:5, 4:5, 15:2; Psalms 49:3:

94 Ellen G. White, *The Signs of the Times*, March 11, 1903.

95 Ellen G. White, *Manuscript Releases*, vol. 21, p. 150.

96 Ephesians 1:13-14.

> those whom He takes as His heritage, His peculiar people... The full inheritance will consist in a heart in full sympathy with God, and in those occupations and joys, intellectual and moral, which are most congenial to such a heart... The *until* [in the translation] does not give the force of [original], which implies that the earnest of the Spirit is a contribution toward the result described; it tends to realize it.[97]

In other words, the Godhead gives us special help and consideration (mediation) while we're in the holy place *school of Christ*—continually learning what's right and wrong under the Holy Spirit's tutelage. There we continually apply what we are learning to the way we live; personalizing it and demonstrating it.

But more than this, the special help *tends to realize* the ultimate goal. The same Holy Spirit who *pledges that the rest will follow* is also (right now) bringing the heart into *full sympathy with God* today—even before the ultimate goal is realized. He enables us to remedy the defects of our characters. He makes it possible for us (even now) to rather die than to choose to do wrong. He *is doing* this for us even *before* we reach the ultimate goal that comes at the corporate "time of refreshing"—when our sins are blotted out in the books of heaven; and before they are entirely erased on the cellular level—from our own individual DNA.

—A New Creation

This *school-of-Christ* behavior modification causes us to have new experiences. As the brain processes these new experiences, information rushes into the brain and the jungle of neurons organizes into new patterns and the limbic brain releases emotions. Thus the experiences reinforce the electrical connections of the neocortex; and the emotions help us remember them.

For the Christian, this is more than mere human biology. The "Spirit of truth" influences the thinking brain, guiding "into all truth."[98] The *providences* of God also ensure that there are appropriate experiences to reinforce what our thinking brain is learning. When our thinking brain repeatedly uses what the Spirit teaches in ways that cause divinely appointed experiences to happen repeatedly, our thinking brain is teaching our body *spiritually* to understand what our thinking brain understands *mentally*.

---

[97] *The Pulpit Commentary*, on Ephesian 1:14. Electronic Database by BibleSoft, inc., 2001, 2003, 2005, 2006, 2010.
[98] John 16:13.

Jesus said, "I will not leave you comfortless," "I shall give you another Comforter... even the Spirit of truth."[99] Comfort is emotion—and so, essentially, should be the *fruits of the Spirit*:[100] love, joy, peace, patience, kindness, goodness, faithfulness, gentleness, and self-control. These should be spontaneous and genuine *spiritual* graces of all those who are influenced by the Comforter.

When our emotional brain agrees with our thinking brain concerning Bible truth—the limbic brain signals our body to change genetically—literally encoding truth into our new being.[101] When we get to this level of memorizing an internal chemical order around truth, spirituality, and actions *(mental, spiritual, and physical)*, it becomes part of who we are. When we get to where no person, thing, or experience can remove it from us—it is because we have sustained this level of physical, mental, and spiritual coherence until it has become part of our genetic makeup.

This time the gigantic model is built after the similitude of Christ. The Holy Spirit comes to the believer "with no modified energy, but in the fulness of divine power. It is the Spirit that makes effectual what has been wrought out by the world's Redeemer. It is by the Spirit that the heart is made pure. Through the Spirit, the believer becomes a partaker of the divine nature. Christ has given His Spirit as a divine power to overcome all hereditary and cultivated tendencies to evil, and to impress His own character upon His church."[102]

While our temple still falls very short of infinite knowledge, power and righteousness—this no longer matters. Indwelt by the Spirit of God, it radiates with His glory because it is constantly connected with *the unsearchable riches of Christ*.[103]

Christ told His disciples that they already knew the Holy Spirit, saying, "for He dwelleth with you"—"and He *shall be* in you."[104] This is the difference between the *holy place* and the *most holy place*. In the *holy place*, the Spirit is *with* us (teaching and comforting) as the *earnest*—the contribution of *what will be* that tends to realize it. In the *most holy*, it is realized—He *is* in us.

---

[99] John 24:15-18.

[100] Galatians 5:22-23.

[101] 2 Corinthians 5:17. "Therefore if any man *be* in Christ, *he is* a new creature: old things are passed away; behold, all things are become new."

[102] Ellen G. White, *The Desire of Ages*, p. 671.

[103] Ephesians 3:8.

[104] John 14:17.

—The Mystery of God

This is the mystery of God—"Christ in you, the hope of glory."[105] It has been hidden "from ages and from generations—but now is made manifest in His saints." This "mystery will be finished" ("the character of Christ" "perfectly reproduced in His people"[106]) at some future moment in time—"in the days of the voice of the seventh angel,"[107] when the church is sealed ("not having spot or wrinkle, or any such thing"[108]). That will be when the "servants of God, with faces lighted up and shining with holy consecration, will hasten from place to place to proclaim the message from heaven."[109] It will be the "outpouring of the Holy Spirit" as "the 'latter rain'... for the ripening of the harvest."[110]

> "[God's] love is past all language to describe. It is the mystery of God in the flesh, God in Christ, and divinity in humanity. Christ bowed down in unparalleled humanity, that in His exaltation to the throne of God, He might also exalt those who believe in Him, to a seat with Him upon His throne."[111]

—Defective Constructs and Their Tug of War

The disciples were fighting among themselves during the last supper. James and John sparked this particular round of quarreling.

> "They said unto Him, Grant unto us that we may sit, one on Thy right hand, and the other on Thy left hand, in Thy glory. But Jesus said unto them, Ye know not what ye ask: can ye drink of the cup that I drink of? And be baptized with the baptism that I am baptized with?... To sit on My right hand and on My left is not Mine to give; but it shall be for them for whom it is prepared."[112]

Two things prevent Christ from effectively working through His church to prepare the world for the end—our striving for supremacy and our not understanding the nature of His kingdom. Both problems exist when we rely on fleshly models—worldly models of "reality." We have our own ideas about religion. We have our own ideas of godliness. We have our own ideas about how the work should go—who should be the greatest, what should happen—and when. We live according to our

---

[105] Colossians 1:27.

[106] Ellen G. White, *Christ's Object Lessons*, p. 69. Once this happens, "Christ will come to claim His own." "Quickly the last great harvest would be ripened, and Christ would come to gather the precious grain."

[107] Revelation 10:7.

[108] Ephesians 5:27.

[109] Ellen G. White, *The Great Controversy*, p. 612.

[110] Ibid., p. 611.

[111] Ellen G. White, *Christian Education*, p. 77.

[112] Mark 10:37-40.

ideas; and we constantly need to validate and promote our reality against others. But the scriptures say, "There is a way that seemeth right unto a man, but the end thereof are the ways of death."[113]

We cannot (all at once) abandon our own models of reality. They are literally who we are and all we know. The only solution is to remodel them (bit by bit) after the similitude of Christ. And since our models are too defective to know how to do this—the only solution is to continually *choose* to be under the control of Christ.

> "Everything depends on the right action of the will. Desires for goodness and purity are right, so far as they go; but if we stop here, they avail nothing. Many will go down to ruin while hoping and desiring to overcome their evil propensities. They do not yield the will to God. They do not *choose* to serve Him.
>
> "God has given us the power of choice; it is ours to exercise. We cannot change our hearts, we cannot control our thoughts, our impulses, our affections. We cannot make ourselves pure, fit for God's service. But we can *choose* to serve God, we can give Him our will; then He will work in us to will and to do according to His good pleasure. Thus our whole nature will be brought under the control of Christ.
>
> "Through the right exercise of the will, an entire change may be made in the life. By yielding up the will to Christ, we ally ourselves with divine power. We receive strength from above to hold us steadfast. A pure and noble life, a life of victory over appetite and lust, is possible to everyone who will unite his weak, wavering human will to the omnipotent, unwavering will of God."[114]

It's not about trying harder to know or do what is right. It's not about fixing our defective models. It's about submitting to Christ. He knows what is right; and He knows how to do what is right. "He has divine power to demolish strongholds," and "tear down arguments and every presumption set up against the knowledge of God." He can "take captive every thought to make it obedient to Christ."[115]

By not understanding the nature of God's government, and by selfishly fighting to be right or to be number one—and on the throne—we show that we are wholly unfit to sit with Him on His throne. Religious people are not immune to this tug-of-war. The constructs of conservatives verses liberals are generally *human models* built on defective understandings of Christ's identity. *Unity in Christ* requires us all to submit to Christ—the *real* Jesus of Nazareth (not our fragmented pictures of

---

[113] Proverbs 14:12; 16:15.

[114] Ellen G. White, *Temperance*, p. 112.

[115] 2 Corinthians 10:3-5.

Him). The church still has to demonstrate that the whole idea of placing human beings on the throne of the universe is reasonable and plausible.

So who will sit on Christ's right hand? John describes the 144,000—as the first fruits unto God. They have no guile and are without fault—singing a new song only they can sing—singing before the throne.[116] John sees them going everywhere the Lamb goes.[117] They have "an experience no other company has ever had."[118] They've "been translated from the earth, from among the living."[119] "They have endured the anguish of the time of Jacob's trouble; they have stood without an intercessor through the final outpouring of God's judgments."[120] "Therefore are they before the throne of God, and serve Him day and night in His temple;"[121]—for only the 144,000 are able to enter there.[122]

—Jacob's Trouble

So there are courtyard tests, and holy place tests, and most holy tests. The *time of Jacob's trouble* will be the ultimate *most holy place* test—and through downshifting this test will go deep to prove what our innermost being (character) has become in the *school of Christ.*

> "Those who live in the last days must pass through an experience similar to that of Jacob. Foes will be all around them, ready to condemn and destroy. Alarm and despair will seize them, for it appears to them as to Jacob in his distress, that *God himself has become an avenging enemy*."[123]

Notice how Dave Feidler describes this in his excellent book *D'Sozo—Reversing the worst evil*:

> "This is why this is the time of *Jacob's* trouble. This is not the same test that the martyrs faced. Despite their suffering, they had the sense of God's acceptance and approval. Not so at the time of the end, and for a shockingly simple reason. This test, in order to guarantee that the righteous are safe to save, must be the hardest of all possible tests of faith.
>
> "Since the basic issue in sin has always been 'will God take care of me?' there can be no harder test than for God to '*obviously*' be seeking my harm. Do I trust Him *now*?
>
> "There have been foreshadowing's of this test. Job is a standout example from the Old Testament. 'Though He slay me, yet will I trust in Him,'

116 Revelation 14:1-5.
117 Ibid., verse 4. See a literal translation.
118 Ellen G. White, *The Great Controversy*, p. 649.
119 Ibid.
120 Ibid.
121 Revelation 7:15.
122 Ellen G. White, *Testimonies for the Church*, vol. 1, p 69.
123 Ellen G. White, *The Signs of the Times*, November 27, 1879. Emphasis added.

he said. And, of course, in the New Testament we have Christ Himself crying out, 'My God, My God, why have You forsaken Me?'

"It is the path that the 144,000 are called to walk. When every sensory input is screaming 'God has abandoned you!' faith in His promise of love will alone prevail."[124]

—Jesus' Trouble

Jacob took hold of the angel. With almost superhuman strength refused to let him go. Job held onto God, "though He slay me." And when,

> "Satan with his fierce temptations wrung the heart of Jesus, The Savior could not see through the portals of the tomb. Hope did not present to Him His coming forth from the grave a conqueror, or tell Him of the Father's acceptance of the sacrifice. He feared that sin was so offensive to God that their separation was to be eternal. Christ felt the anguish which the sinner will feel when mercy shall no longer plead for the guilty race. It was the sense of sin, bringing the Father's wrath upon Him as man's substitute, that made the cup He drank so bitter, and broke the heart of the Son of God."[125]

This is the cup that Christ spoke of when answering James and John. It's the baptism He was about to be baptized with. Hebrews speaks of it:

> "Consider Him that endured such contradiction of sinners against Himself, lest ye be wearied and faint of minds. Ye have not yet resisted unto blood, striving against sin."[126]

This experience will show how God is just while saving sinners. Ultimately, He does not set aside the demands of the law. Rather, even the redeemed will stand before the awful majesty of Infinite Justice; but they can say, "we are persuaded that nothing shall be able to separate us from the love of God;"[127] and "Satan has nothing in us."[128]

> "Satan had overcome a large proportion of the human race, and his success had made him feel that the control of this fallen planet was in his hands. But in Christ he found one who was able to resist him, and he left the field of battle a conquered foe. Jesus says, "He hath nothing in Me." His victory is an assurance that we too may come off victors in our conflicts with the enemy. But it is not our heavenly Father's purpose to save us without an effort on our part to cooperate with Christ. We must act our part, and divine power, uniting with our effort, will bring victory.[129]

---

[124] Dave Feidler, D'Sozo *Reversing the worst evil*, pp. 37-38.
[125] Ellen G. White, *The Desire of Ages*, p. 753.
[126] Hebrews 12:3-4.
[127] Romans 8:38-39.
[128] John 14:30.
[129] Ellen G. White, *Counsels on Diets and Foods*, p. 153.

—The Ultimate Test

The final test is principally a *spiritual* test—it was Calvary for Christ. The wilderness temptation was principally *physical*; Gethsemane was principally *mental*. Still, each one involved all three natures. The final test is the ultimate test; and downshifting takes it to the core.

How can we be sure to pass such a test? Here is what inspiration tells us about how Christ gained the ultimate victory:

> "Amid the awful darkness, apparently forsaken of God, Christ had drained the last dregs in the cup of human woe. In those dreadful hours He had relied upon the evidence of His Father's acceptance heretofore given Him. He was acquainted with the character of His Father; He understood His justice, His mercy, and His great love. By faith He rested in Him whom it had ever been His joy to obey. And as in submission He committed Himself to God, the sense of the loss of His Father's favor was withdrawn. By faith, Christ was victor."[130]

His knowledge of His Father, reinforced by His experience with His Father, made *faith in His Father* part of His DNA—no person or thing, or experience could remove it from Him.

—The Three Protocols

From Lucifer to Laodicea, the test is always three-fold. It involves all three natures. The choice is between God's plan for us and Lucifer's counterfeit merchandise. The choice is between God's accomplishments and our own accomplishments. The choice is between the *Galilee Protocol* and the way of the world. While some of us may never be tested to the extent the 144,000 will—the principles of preparation, restoration, and testing are the same for all of us.

We cannot say it loud enough or often enough—Christ's method is radical and incompatible with our own ideas and the world's standards. His peculiar *teaching*, and *preaching*, and *healing* caused an *educational* crisis, a *ministerial* crisis, and a *medical* crisis in the church, and in the nation, and in the world. They will cause these crises in your life as well. His model of reality is incompatible with your individual model of "reality;" just as it is incompatible with the collective model of the church, the national collective, and the global. It's a big deal. The *Galilee Protocol* was so incompatible in Christ's day the established authorities felt they actually needed to crucify Him.

---

[130] Ibid., p. 756.

This crisis is not incidental. It is *necessary* to develop character (personal and corporate). Meanwhile, our own personal model-building seeks to insulate us from the very wilderness experiences we need to prepare for the storm. A whole-hearted change is needed in our approach to molding and fashioning our hearts and minds. We need to accept that we do not *understand best how to form our own characters—after our own models.* "There is only one model after which human character is to be formed—the character of Christ."[131]

> "The Lord permits His people to be subjected to the fiery ordeal of temptation, not because He takes pleasure in their distress and affliction, but because this process is essential to their final victory. He could not, consistently with His own glory, shield them from temptation; for the very object of the trial is to prepare them to resist all the allurements of evil."[132]

The world has changed a lot since the *Galilee Protocol* principles were given to the pioneers. Our personal models (and those of the church and the world) have become very sophisticated—and very appealing. Abandoning them for the *Galilee Protocol* will be a fiery test for sure—but this has always been. It was a struggle for Jacob. It was a struggle for Christ in the wilderness. But despite the modern sophistication of the world—and the struggle ahead of us—Jesus still says: "*I am* the way, the truth, and the life. No one can come to the Father except through me."[133] And Peter still says: "Neither is there salvation in any other: for there is none other name under heaven given among men, whereby we must be saved."[134] We still have to do this thing God's way—using *Christ's method alone!*

"The weapons of our warfare are not the weapons of the world. Instead, they have divine power to demolish strongholds. We tear down arguments, and every presumption set up against the knowledge of God; and we take captive every thought to make it obedient to Christ."

—2 Corinthians 10:4-5, Berean Study Bible.

---

[131] Ellen G. White, *Seventh-day Adventist Bible Commentary*, vol. 6, p. 1098.
[132] Ellen G. White, *The Great Controversy*, p. 528.
[133] John 14:6. Emphasis added.
[134] Acts 4:12.

CHAPTER SEVEN

Cellular Mechanisms

There are trillions of cells in our bodies. There are different cells designed for specific purposes. There are bone cells, liver cells, skin cells, muscle cells, brain cells, and many more. These cells group together to form bones, skin, muscles, the brain, and other organs.

"How do our bodies accomplish the various functions that keep us alive and allow us to engage in our everyday activities?... How do certain cells of the pancreas produce insulin? Why do muscles contract? How do liver cells make bile? How does the mucous membrane of the stomach manufacture hydrochloric acid and not be dissolved by it? And how is a molecule of hemoglobin fabricated? In a living organism all this happens because of millions upon millions of complex biochemical activities proceeding at incredible speeds within the cells that make up the tissue and organs of our bodies."[1]

Dr. Mervyn Harding describes a cell as a tiny chemical factory. Each cell has a very particular work to do; and each cell faithfully performs its task. The work is actually done by specifically designed protein molecules called enzymes. Since it takes several steps to manufacture a

---

[1] Mervyn G. Hardinge, *A Physician Explains Ellen White's Counsel on Drugs, Herbs, & Natural Remedies*, p. 60. 2001, Review and Herald Publishing Association.

product such as insulin or hemoglobin, the cell has the various enzymes arranged in a well-organized assembly line.

Each enzyme performs its single operation and then passes what it has produced on to the next stage until the substance is complete. Every individual factory (each cell) has an outside covering called a cell membrane. In these walls there are ports, through which substances can enter the cell. Outside the ports there are other specialized enzymes that are port keepers to control the gates, opening and closing them.

—Locks and Keys

There are receptors on the surface of the cell that act like locks, requiring the correct keys, or regulators, to activate them. So from outside, a regulator can influence the operations inside a cell, by attaching to a receptor on the surface of the cell wall.[2] These keys (or regulators) are chemical molecules. Chemicals have shapes; and each lock requires a specific shape for the chemical to influence the cell. Chemicals properly shaped for a specific receptor are called regulators (keys) because they regulate the activity inside the cells.

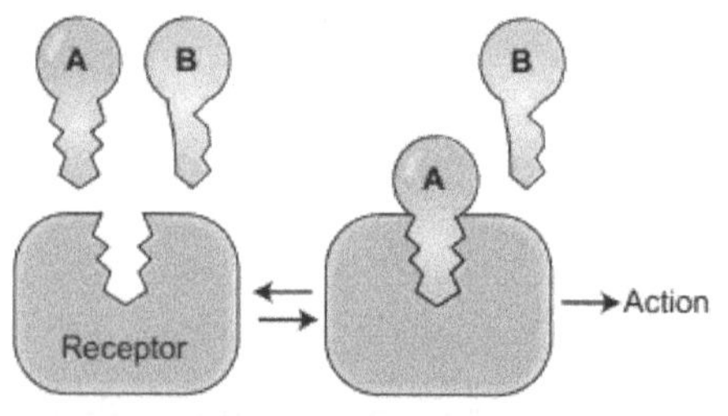

Drug **A** binds to receptor
Drug **B** cannot bind to receptor

Our bodies are biochemical machines and if properly nourished, our cells manufacture all the proper chemicals and automatically regulate all the biochemical activity necessary for life and health. Complex chemical substances drive all the functions of the body; and the production and release of these complex chemical substances is accomplished and regulated by the tiny chemical factories, their ports, locks, and keys.

The chemical keys are important—so important in fact, that the body produces them itself. This is because each key must precisely match each lock or problems arise.

> "Molecules of different chemicals have different shapes. Some are relatively simple; others are highly complex. All the chemicals naturally present in our bodies are so shaped that they interact only with receptors [locks] for which they are designed. This prevents unwanted responses."[3]

---

[2] Ibid., pp. 60-61.
[3] Ibid., pp. 66-67.

Regulating cells is a highly complex process, and scientists do not understand all the mechanisms involved."[4]

—Substitute Keys

But scientists attempt to introduce into the body chemicals that approximate the shape of natural keys to speed up, slow down, or stop the process of certain cells. In a nutshell, this is the objective of modern medicine. Drugs regulate the activity in certain target cells. Dr. Elliott Ross, of the University of Texas, states it this way:

> "A drug potentially is capable of altering the rate at which any bodily function proceeds... Drugs do not create effects, but they modulate functions."[5]

Cells are factories where the body's work is done. Enzymes *do* the work. So the chemicals that make up medicine have to influence the enzymes. Each biochemical regulator in the body has part of its molecule shaped like a 'key' to fit its special receptor for certain cells. Similarly, drugs can act as regulators of cell function.

> "A number of factors determine how well a drug works: its chemical shape, how well its shape fits the shape of the receptor, the number of receptors present in the tissues, and how many receptors are actually available for the drug molecules to attach to."[6]

The effectiveness of a drug depends primarily on two things: the fit of its shape in the receptors (how well the key fits the lock), and its dosage (are there enough keys to open enough gates). The drug must reach a minimum concentration, called the threshold level, before the drug will have the desired effect. The drug will not work below minimum dose.[7] On the other hand—the higher the dose, the more toxic it is.

—Oops, Wrong Door!

> "At any moment, within and around the cells of our bodies, a bewildering array of complex chemical processes are taking place at incredible speeds. They give us life and allow us to function. Both regular and botanic drugs influence them. Their chemical shapes allow them to behave as regulators influencing either the cell's external or internal chemistry. Usually they effect an organ or system in a way we consider beneficial. Other parts of the drug molecule, though, can interfere with cell

---

[4] Ibid., p. 61.

[5] Elliott M. Ross, *Mechanisms of Drug Action and the relationship Between Drug Concentration and Effect*, in The Pharmacological Basis of Therapeutics, 9th ed. (New York: McGraw-Hill, 1995), p. 29.

[6] Hardinge, pp. 63-64.

[7] Ibid., p. 64.

> processes elsewhere in the body, resulting in an adverse or toxic response."[8]

The things we use for medicine (be they vitamins, minerals, hormones, or some other chemical compounds—from plant, or animal, naturally occurring or synthesized by man), function as regulators to turn up, turn down, or turn off cell activity in specific cells. They use the same mechanisms used by the natural chemical regulator produced inside our bodies.

There is a difference though. All the keys that are naturally present in our bodies contains shapes that are exact fits for the locks they are designed to operate. The substitute keys we use for medicine are not exact fits; and this causes problems. The molecules of these keys have additional shapes that fit the locks of other receptors—inadvertently effecting the operation of other parts of the body.

> "When a substance not normally a constituent of the body [such as a drug] enters the bloodstream and passes into the tissue fluids, its shape resembles only in part the natural [regulator molecule]. The conforming part attaches to the target [receptor] and accomplishes the purpose the patient intended. However, another part of the drug molecule interacts with other unwanted receptors, for example, on the cells of the salivary glands and on certain neurons in the brain causing dryness of mouth and drowsiness, producing what we call side effects... A drug's molecular shape may be such that it may jam certain cell receptors, inactivate enzymes on the cell membrane, or, passing through a port in the cell wall, raise havoc from within the cell. Such adverse responses can seem minor or they can be extremely severe."[9]

—Moving Targets

Side effects are not the only issues associated with using outside chemicals to regulate internal processes. Another is the matter of dosage. As already noted, it takes a certain amount of any medicine to produce the desired effect; but as the amount increases, so does toxicity. Unfortunately, the body's mechanisms for determining the precise needed dose do not communicate to the outside world. A person's weight, race, gender, age, etc.,—these are all factors that influence dosage requirements. But these are just a few. Some people are hypersensitive to some chemicals. Chemicals interact with foods, other drugs, the ever-changing biochemistry inside and outside the body. All these things affect how

---

[8] Ibid., p. 68.
[9] Ibid., p. 67.

well a drug will fit the shape of the receptors, the number of receptors present in the tissues, and how many receptors are actually available for the drug molecules to attach to. These things all affect the dose requirement.

Since the precise dosing target is unknown and always moving, doctors have to administer medicines at doses that are higher than the true minimum effective dose. To overcome the uncertainty of the true minimum requirement, a doctor's aim is to find a dose that is high enough to be effective under most circumstances, while minimizing the undesirable side-effects.

So far, we have looked at the pharmacological mechanisms that influence cells when we use drug medications; and we have looked at the issues of side-effects and dosing. But we also need to consider the impact that drug medications have on other factors.

In any factory setting there are always three important subsystems: the environment, the supply chain, and waste management. These are also vital to our bodies' tiny biochemical factories.

—Environmental Protection

The body naturally produces the perfect chemical shapes to manage its own biochemistry. But site contamination can interfere with the manufacturing process and damage the final product. So it's necessary to prevent unwanted and harmful substances from entering the system. Several environmental safeties are built into the human organism.

Skin is one of these. It is an important barrier against dirt, viruses, and bacteria. The saltiness of sweat and tears provide further protection. Mucus guards the openings. Mechanisms such as coughing, sneezing, vomiting and diarrhea also prevent contamination from getting into the blood system and finding its way to the cellular level. These are the body's environmental defenses.

Because drug medications are not normal constituents of the body, they have to overcome the body's environmental defenses.

—Supply-Side

A proper supply chain is also important to the body. The cells need certain raw materials before they can manufacture the right chemicals for optimum health and function. These raw materials are supplied through eating, drinking, breathing, and some are absorbed through the skin. The body's digestive system breaks down food into the components (nutrients) needed so that the bloodstream can supply them to all the areas of the body.

Nutrient-rich plasma passes out through the walls of the blood vessels and in through the walls of the cells. In fact, this clear watery spa of oxygen and nutrition bathe the cells inside and out.

The lungs process the air we breathe, passing necessary air-borne components to the blood. The body's lymph system picks up things absorbed through the skin and helps them find their way into the bloodstream.

Our bodies' supply-side systems know what our bodies need; and God designed them to select specifically what is good and necessary, and dump the rest. But these systems have their limits. We must properly care for them. The digesting organs are designed for real food in manageable quantities and in simple configurations. They need clean water. The lungs need pure, fresh air. When we abuse these systems, they become confused and overwhelmed.

—Waste Management

Even under ideal circumstances the body must deal with waste. The biochemistry within the cells themselves produce waste products that are toxic. Food, water, and air all bring components into the body that it must remove. The body has built-in mechanisms to process and remove waste products.

The kidneys filter out waste products into the urine. The liver filters out waste products through the bile duct into the feces. The lungs expel wastes into the air we exhale. And skin disposes of waste products through sweating.

Blood plasma not only bathes the cells with oxygen and nutrients, it also carries away waste. In this capacity it is called lymphatic fluid. The lymph system has a complex system of vessels similar to blood vessels. Lymphatic fluid passes in through the vessels' walls to be carried off for elimination. Lymphatic vessels have valves to keep the fluid moving in one direction, but there is no pump. The lymph depends on muscle action throughout the body to push the fluid along to the lymph nodes where the fluid is filtered and then pushed on to be reabsorbed into the bloodstream.

All organic waste material eventually becomes toxic. In the warm, moist environment of the body it quickly breaks down and putrefies creating toxins. God designed human digestion to work quickly and then dump wastes before they load the system with toxins.

We deal with two types of toxins: endogenous toxins and exogenous toxins. Endogenous toxins are produced inside the body. Some of these are waste products from normal metabolic activities—carbon dioxide, urea, and lactic acid are examples of endogenous toxins that the body churns out by the second. Healthy bodies easily eliminate endogenous toxins from the system.

Exogenous toxins are chemicals made outside the body; and they can harm the cells if they are ingested, inhaled, or absorbed into the bloodstream through some other channel. It's not possible to avoid exogenous toxins completely; but we should strive to minimize our exposure to them. From the body's perspective, drug medications are exogenous toxins.

—Elimination Overload

Since the body always works within the framework of trying to preserve health, its first defense against toxins is to eliminate them through one of the normal elimination channels. Overloaded channels trigger more drastic measures. Diarrhea, coughs, rashes, fever, mucus discharge—these are examples of the body's more drastic arsenal.

But what happens if something interrupts these attempts to purge the system? What if these processes are already too overwhelmed to be effective? What if the body is too fatigued or is dealing with some other crisis and cannot spare the resources to fight toxins right now? Under these circumstances, the body stores them away until another time.

Knowing better than to keep excess toxins around the production areas of the body's most important biochemistry labs, the body tries to store toxins in less sensitive areas. It stores excess toxins in fat tissue. It stores excess toxins in myelin (the fatty sheath of insulation that lines the nerves). It stores excess toxins in connective tissue (ligaments, bone, blood, etc.), It stores excess toxins in muscle tissue, and in nerve tissue.[10]

As toxins accumulate in fat tissue, things like cysts, lipomas, and other benign tumors can develop. As toxins accumulate around the nerves, they can cause irritation and headaches. As toxins accumulate in connective tissue, generalized joint pain or aches and pains in the various bones can occur.

---

[10] Dr. Ben Kim, *A No-Nonsense Look at Toxins and How Your Body Deal with Them*, September 13, 1012, http://drben-kim.com/toxins-cleansing-detoxing.htm.

If they are exposed to toxins long enough, even the cells can accumulate them in their inner membranes and inner lumen areas. If enough cells of one organ or gland become dysfunctional because of a buildup of toxins, organ or glandular dysfunction can occur. Thyroid disease, impaired vision, congestive heart failure, chronic obstructive pulmonary disease, kidney failure, and any stage of liver degeneration (fatty liver, cirrhosis, etc.)—these are some examples of what can occur.[11]

If the innermost part (nucleoli) of enough cells in one area accumulate enough toxins, the DNA that controls those cells can become affected. This can lead to a lack of control over cellular reproduction—the hallmark of malignant growth (cancer).[12]

—Never Give Up!

It's important to note that as our body accumulates toxins and develops dysfunction and disease, it's constantly doing the best it can with the resources it has to cleanse and repair itself. It is well designed to do the work of recognizing and eliminating toxins. But it is our responsibility to minimize our exposure to exogenous and endogenous toxins and to provide our bodies with the support they need to clear out those that make their way into the system. We call this cleansing activity hygienic healthcare—and it is a fundamentally different approach to healthcare than what the world prescribes.

—What About Herbs?

We need to say something about herbs. Many herbal formulas are drugs made from chemicals derived from medicinal foods and medicinal herbs. These have the same pharmacological effect and use the same cellular mechanisms as any other drug.

So how are they different?

Actually, when the chemicals are extracted or concentrated, there is little difference. But medicinal foods and medicinal herbs themselves *are* different—even if their active ingredients activate the same desirable cellular mechanisms and produce the same pharmacological effects.

It's a matter of design. With food, the whole is greater than the sum of its parts.[13] Food and herbs are designed to be food. To this our Creator gives witness in Genesis—"Behold, I have given you every herb bearing

---

[11] Ibid.

[12] Ibid.

[13] T. Colin Campbell, PhD and Thomas M. Campbell II, MD, *The China Study*, p. 226.

seed, which is upon the face of all the earth, and every tree, in the which is the fruit of a tree yielding seed; to you it shall be for [food]."[14] Satan had not yet introduced poisonous plants.

Dr. Colin Campbell, in his book, *The China Study*, tells us to "take a small look at the biochemistry of a meal."

> "Let's say you prepare sautéed spinach with ginger and whole grain ravioli shells stuffed with butternut squash and spices, topped with tomato sauce.
>
> "The spinach alone is a cornucopia of various chemical compounds... [so] you've just introduced a bundle of nutrients into your body. In addition to this extremely complex mix, when you take a bite of that ravioli with its tomato sauce and squash filling, you get thousands and thousands of additional chemicals, all connected in ways in each different food—truly a biochemical bonanza.
>
> "As soon as this food hits your saliva, your body begins working its magic, and the process of digestion starts. Each of these food chemicals interacts with the other food chemicals and your body's chemicals in very specific ways. It is an infinitely complex process, and it is literally impossible to understand precisely how each chemical interacts with every other chemical. We will never understand how it all fits together...
>
> "The chemicals we get from the foods we eat are engaged in a series of reactions that work in concert to produce good health. These chemicals are carefully orchestrated by intricate controls within our cells and all through our bodies, and these controls decide what nutrition goes where, how much of each nutrient is needed and when each reaction takes place."[15]

The makeup of food—the compounding of different chemicals for specific purposes, the concentrations, factors involving interactivity and reactivity, additives to promote absorption, improve effectiveness, and provide for safe function—these things a wise and loving Creator has engineered right into the genetic code of fruits and vegetables and grains and nuts. Even the unbeliever accepts that fruits, nuts, grains and vegetables contain amazing food properties for health and healing.

Maybe pharmacologists would design their products that way too—if they could. But they can't. They do not know how. The complexity of it all boggles the mind. The best human scientists can produce are fairly blind stabs at it. We have no way of measuring or understanding or controlling all the mechanisms and activities involved. Neither can we measure or control all the effects that any one chemical manipulation will have upon the complex biochemistry of the human organism.

---

[14] Genesis 1:29.

[15] Campbell, pp. 226-228.

—Why Do We Try?

So why do we try? Isn't that the bigger question, really? We could similarly ask, "why do we break whole foods into various components and reassemble them into 'refined foods?" If whole foods perfectly meet the nutritional needs of the body, why should we change them? If our bodies are designed for health and contain all the mechanisms for health-maintenance and health-restoration, then why do we reach for those magic pills?

Maybe it is a question we shouldn't ask out loud. The only plausible answer is an uncomfortable one. Fallen man is no more content with obeying God's physical laws than we are with obeying His moral laws. We change the food-chain to cater to our sinful appetites and then we turn to the *Tree-of-Knowledge* to engineer a fix for our ruined health.

How is pharmacology unlike a modern *Tower-of-Babel?* It seeks no faith; it requires no confession or repentance. It is not selective or judgmental—it promises to serve all persons equally without regard for religion or lifestyle choices. It tries to restore health to the lawless; and to lift people high above the flood waters of consequence.

—Recap

1. At any moment, within and around the cells of our bodies, a bewildering array of complex chemical processes are taking place at incredible speeds. Our Creator knows every atom of our being.
→*Scientists are incapable of understanding, measuring, and safely managing the chemical environment of the human body.*
2. God created our body to be chemically self-regulating. The regulating of cells is a highly complex process.
→ *Scientists do not understand all the mechanisms involved in cell regulation.*
3. God created the body's natural regulators to be exact fits for the cells they regulate so they cause no side effects.
→ *Scientists cannot provide regulators that fit precisely. Drugs are only approximate fits—causing unintended, unknown, and unwanted side-effects.*
4. God designed into our body's natural biochemistry the mechanisms needed to provide precise control over the manufacture and application (dosing) of the chemicals needed for life and health.

→ *Scientists are incapable of factoring in all the variables in a single body at any given time. They cannot determine or administer ideal and safe artificial dosing.*
5. "God has made the provision that nature shall work to restore the exhausted powers. The work is of God. He is the great Healer."[16]
→ *Scientists use drugs that do not create effect, they only modulate function. They also introduce toxins into the system that cause difficulty at some other time or in some other place.*

—Revelation

So far, we've discussed the science. Now let's look to revelation.

> "Nothing should be put into the human system that will leave a baleful influence behind. And to carry out the light on this subject, to practice hygienic treatment, is the reason which has been given me for establishing sanitariums in various localities."[17]

> "Christ's remedies cleanse the system. But Satan has tempted man to introduce into the system that which weakens the machinery, clogging and destroying the fine beautiful arrangements of God. The drugs administered to the sick do not restore, but destroy... [They are] seeds that bear a very bitter harvest."[18]

> "We must leave drugs entirely alone, for in using them we introduce an enemy into the system. I write this because we have to meet this drug medication in the physicians in this country, and we do not want this practice to... steal into our midst."[19]

> "Drugs never cure disease. They only change the form and location. Nature alone is the effectual restorer, and how much better could she perform her task if left to herself... When drugs are introduced into the system, for a time they seem to have a beneficial effect. A change may take place, but the disease is not cured. It will manifest itself in some other form... And the disease, which the drug was given to cure, may disappear, but only to re-appear in a new form, such as skin diseases, ulcers, painful diseased joints, and sometimes in a more dangerous and deadly form. The liver, heart and brain are frequently affected by drugs, and often all these organs are burdened with disease."[20]

---

[16] Ellen G. White, *Medical Ministry*, p. 11.
[17] Ellen G. White, *Medical Ministry*, p. 228.
[18] Ellen G. White, *Selected Messages*, book 2, p. 289.
[19] Ellen G. White, *Letter 67*, 1899.
[20] Ellen G. White, *Spiritual Gifts*, vol. 4a, p. 135.

"Administering drugs to the sick is the precise track marked out by the medical men of the world—we do not need this."[21]

"The sufferers, in such cases, can do for themselves that which others cannot do as well for them. They should commence to relieve nature of the load they have forced upon her. They should remove the cause. Fast a short time, and give the stomach chance for rest. Reduce the feverish state of the system by a careful and understanding application of water. These efforts will help nature in her struggles to free the system of impurities. But generally, the persons who suffer pain become impatient. They are not willing to use self-denial, and suffer a little from hunger. Neither are they willing to wait for the slow process of nature to build up the overtaxed energies of the system. But they are determined to obtain relief at once, and take powerful drugs, prescribed by physicians. Nature was doing her work well, and would have triumphed, but while accomplishing her task, a foreign substance of a poisonous nature was introduced. What a mistake! Abused nature has now two evils to war against instead of one. She leaves the work in which she was engaged, and resolutely takes hold to expel the intruder newly introduced into the system. Nature feels this double draft upon her resources, and she becomes enfeebled."[22]

"Nature will want some assistance to bring things to their proper condition, which may be found in the simplest remedies, especially in the use of nature's own furnished remedies —pure air, and with a precious knowledge of how to breathe; —pure water, with a knowledge of how to apply it;—plenty of sunlight in every room in the house, if possible, and with an intelligent knowledge of what advantages are to be gained by its use. All these are powerful in their efficiency, and the patient who has obtained a knowledge of how to eat and dress healthfully, may live for comfort, for peace, for health, and will not be prevailed upon to put to his lips, drugs, which, in the place of helping nature, paralyze her powers. If the sick and suffering will do only as well as they know in regard to living out the principles of health reform perseveringly, then they will in nine cases out of ten, recover from their ailments."[23]

"Nature's simple remedies will aid in recovery without leaving the deadly aftereffects so often felt by those who use poisonous drugs."[24]

"This is God's method. The herbs that grow for the benefit of man, and the little handful of herbs kept and steeped and used for sudden ailments, have served tenfold, yes, one hundred-fold better purposes, than all the drugs hidden under mysterious names and dealt out to the sick."[25]

---

[21] Ellen G. White, *Letter to Elder J. A. Burden*, April 27, 1910.
[22] Ellen G. White, *Selected Messages*, book 2, p. 450.
[23] Ellen G. White, *Manuscript Releases*, vol. 15, p. 277.
[24] Ellen G. White, *Loma Linda Messages*, p. 355.
[25] Ellen G. White, *Letter 69*, 1898.

> "It would have been better if, from the first, all drugs had been kept out of our sanitariums, and use had been made of such simple remedies as are found in pure water, pure air, sunlight, and some of the simple herbs growing in the field. These would be just as efficacious as the drugs used under mysterious names, and concocted by human science. And they would leave no injurious effects in the system."[26]

> "The Lord has provided antidotes for diseases in simple plants, and these can be used by faith, with no denial of faith; for by using the blessings provided by God for our benefit we are cooperating with Him. He can use water and sunshine and the herbs which He has caused to grow, in healing maladies brought on by indiscretion or accident. We do not manifest a lack of faith when we ask God to bless His remedies."[27]

—The Big Question

On August 15, 1893, a third-year medical student wrote to Ellen White, to find out what she considered a drug to be. He, with some of his fellow med students, had read her comments on the nonuse of drugs in the *Testimonies* and in her book *How to Live*.

There had been some improvements made in the practice of medicine since she first began to speak against drugs. So even in the late 1800s there was the temptation to think that her animus against drugs was limited to the early potions that contained things like arsenic, strychnine, and mercury. But these medical students genuinely wanted to know if it also included the newer, "simpler remedies" such as potassium and iodine.

Now apparently, Sister White thought her contrasting descriptions of drug medications verses God's hygienic methods where already clear. Her response pointed out that their questions were "answered largely, if not definitely, in *How to Live*."

But to accommodate them, she made it as concise and as simple as she could. She explained that the "simpler remedies are less harmful in proportion to their simplicity; but in very many cases these are used when not at all necessary." Continuing, she adds, "There are simple herbs and roots that every family may use for themselves and need not call a physician any sooner than they would call a lawyer. *I do not think that I can give any definite line of medicines compounded and dealt out by doctors, that are perfectly harmless.*"[28]

---

[26] Ellen G. White, *Selected Messages*, book 2, p. 291.
[27] Ellen G. White, *Selected Messages*, book 2, p. 289.
[28] Ellen G. White, *Selected Messages*, book 2, p. 279, emphasis added.

PART TWO

DEFINITION

CHAPTER EIGHT

A Mission with Protocols

God's end-time church has a specialized mission articulated by three angels in the Bible's last book. When the great time prophecies of Daniel neared their fulfillment in the late 1700's[1] and early 1800's,[2] many of the faithful recognized their responsibility to proclaim these important messages.

Though these Bible scholars did not yet realize the full day-of-atonement significance of "then shall the sanctuary be cleansed," and "the hour of His judgment is come," they sounded the message of the first angel from 1840 to 1844.[3] They sounded the second angel's message

---

[1] 1798 A.D. marked the end of the *time, times, and the dividing of times* (3 ½ years, or 1260 days equaling 1260 years) and the beginning of the time of the end (both in Daniel 12:7-9. We understand that the 1260 began in 538 A.D. when Ostrogoths abandoned their siege of Rome, and this left the Bishop of Rome to exercise the prerogatives of Justinian's decree of 533 A.D.—the power and authority of the Papacy grew and grew until 1798, when because of the spectacular victories of the armies of Napoleon in Italy placed the Pope at the mercy of the French Revolutionary Government. The French general Berthier, with a French army, marched into Rome and proclaimed the political rule of the Papacy at an end and took the Pope prisoner. The Pope died in exile.

[2] Daniel 8:14 places the cleaning of the sanctuary in the year of 1844, exactly 2300 years from 457 B.C., when Darius gave Ezra authority over the Jews—to teach them the law of his God, a territory, and authorization to withdraw from the treasury to restore and rebuild Jerusalem. See Ezra 7:12-26.

[3] Ellen G. White, *The Great Controversy*, p. 194, 1884 edition. This was the first edition, and the first sentence of chapter 14 says, "The prophecies of the first angel's message, brought to view in Revelation 14, found its fulfillment in the Advent movement of 1840-1844." This chapter was expanded a couple years later when the whole book was revised to include more historical references. This sentence does not appear in the later editions. It also appears in "*The Story of Redemption*, p. 356.

(proclaiming the fall of Babylon) in the summer of 1844.[4] "Since 1844, in the fulfillment of the prophecy of the third angel's message, the attention of the world has been called to the true Sabbath, and a constantly increasing number are returning to the observance of God's holy day."[5]

—Lacking the Protocols

In those early days, the mission was pure and Spirit-led in its youthful exuberance. Beginning in simplicity, it was destined to mature as greater understanding of those prophetic events were revealed by God. That this happened is clearly borne out in the timeline in chapter two of this book. October 22, 1844 was not *the end of the world* as the Millerites first thought it would be—it was rather, *the beginning of the end.* It was the birth of a vital mission—the birth of an essential movement needed to prepare the world for earth's final moments.

The Millerites had the date; and they had the proper sense of urgency. They were led by the Holy Spirit.[6] But they lacked the protocols for a complete work. The great disappointment revealed that for so many, the preparation had been surface preparation—not a deep, thorough-going work of reform. When their faith was tried, it did not hold up to the test.

> "The time of expectation passed, and Christ did not appear for the deliverance of His people. Those who with sincere faith and love had looked for their Savior, experienced a bitter disappointment. Yet the purposes of God were being accomplished; He was testing the hearts of those who professed to be waiting for His appearing. There were among them many who had been actuated by no higher motive than fear. Their profession of faith had not affected their hearts or their lives."[7]

In the several years to follow, God worked with the *still faithful* to develop an organization with the proper mission-specific protocols—protocols that will prepare a people to be faithful under even greater trial. A deeper reading of the first angel's message of Revelation 14:7 reveals the three fundamental protocols of our mission.

Dr. Russell Burrill is Professor Emeritus of Andrew University Seminary, and retired director of the North American Division Institute of Evangelism. He sums it up this way:

> "Jesus does not wish simply to save us in our sins, He envisions complete victory over sin for His people through His victorious power.

---

[4] Ibid., p. 202. This sentence is also not found in the later editions. It does appear in *The Story of Redemption*, p. 364.
[5] Ibid., p. 254. This sentence is also not found in the later editions. It does appear in *The Spirit of Prophecy*, vol 4, p. 286.
[6] Ellen G. White, *The Great Controversy*, p. 369. Later editions.
[7] Ibid., p. 374.

Revelation 14:7 hints at this restoration as a result of the proclamation of the eternal gospel of verse 6: 'He said with a loud voice, Fear God and give him glory, because the hour of his judgment is come. Worship him who made the heavens, the earth, the sea and the springs of water. (Rev. 14:7 NIV).'

"The three injunctions of this verse—'fear God,' 'give him glory,' and 'worship him'—convey a message of restoration preached in the setting of the eternal gospel in preparation for the *parousia*. The call to fear God in this passage is reminiscent of the definition given by Solomon, the wise man, that 'the fear of the Lord is the beginning of knowledge' (Prov. 1:7). The call to fear God envisions the mental restoration of redeemed people to the image of God...

"The second injunction of Revelation 14:7 calls upon people to give glory to Him. While there are many ways for Christians to glorify God, the apostle Paul enumerates one that should not be neglected: 'What? Know ye not that your body is the temple of the Holy Ghost which is in you, and which ye have of God, and ye are not your own? For ye are bought with a price: therefore glorify God in your body, and in your spirit, which are God's (1 Cor. 6:19-20).'

"This call to glorify God is clearly identified with the physical restoration of humankind, with the understanding that the body is the temple of God... It is in this setting that Adventists developed their health philosophy of caring for the body temple through abstaining from that which is harmful and using in moderation that which is good. This is seen as a part of physical restoration to the image of God...

The third injunction of Revelation 14:7 is to 'worship Him.' Obviously, this call deals with spiritual restoration to the image of God. Those redeemed through the eternal gospel are not called simply to worship, but to 'worship Him that made heaven and earth.' It is calling a redeemed people back into a relationship with their Creator...

The call of the first angel, then, declares that the eternal gospel redeems people to Christ and begins the work of restoration. It calls for a three-fold restoration to the image of God by cleaning up the mind, keeping the body in good health and free from sexual immorality, and taking time for the development of a deep relationship with Christ through Sabbath keeping.

"One final aspect of Revelation 14:7 needs to be addressed: the reason for the call to restorative discipleship, which is that 'the hour of His judgment is come' (Rev. 14:7 NIV). The judgment spoken of here has already commenced. Adventist understanding of this pre-advent judgment is that it commenced in 1844 at the conclusion of the 2300-day prophecy of Daniel 8:14."[8]

In this context we can see the divine purpose in building the Seventh-day Adventist movement with an educational emphasis (*mental*

[8] Dr. Russell C. Burrill, *Recovering an Adventist Approach to The Life & Mission of the Local Church*, pp. 57-59. 1998, Hart Books, Fallbrook, California.

restoration), evangelistic-ministerial emphasis (*spiritual* restoration) and health-medical emphasis (*physical* restoration). These three pillars have formed the foundation of our work. They are the three fundamental protocols of our mission.

—Some Bible Examples

Revelation 14 is not the only Bible occurrence of this three-protocol emphasis. As Burrell also points out, they go all the way back to the first chapters of Genesis.

> "Sin originated in the mind of Eve before she performed the outward act. Eating the fruit was the natural result of her fallen nature. Thus humankind, who had been created in God's image, fell away from that image: physically, Eve saw that the tree was good for food; spiritually, she saw that the tree was pleasant to the eyes (eyes are symbolic of the spiritual nature—see Revelation 3:18); and mentally, she saw that the tree was desirable for gaining wisdom. The fall of our first parents was complete; physically, mentally, and spiritually they had departed from the divine image."[9]

From there we see Cain build the first earthly city,[10] and his descendants formulate a worldly *alternative* to meet the needs of the three-fold nature of humanity.[11] Tubalcain became the father of education: "the *instructor* of every artificer in brass and iron." Jubal became the father of worldly spirituality: "of all such as handle the harp and organ." Jabal became the father of physical security—food and shelter: "of such as dwell in tents and all such as have cattle.

We see the world's *alternative* greatly developed by the time of Babylonian captivity. The great monuments to Nebuchadnezzar's kingdom were his fortress (physical might and security), the Ziggurat[12] (wisdom and learning), and Esagila[13] (spirituality). In contrast to the world's *alternative*, we see Daniel and the three worthies validating the superiority of God's great original. They were ten-times wiser. Faithful in their diet they proved fairer than the rest; and with their *witness under fire*, they proved that their God was the *real* deal.

---

[9] Ibid., p. 56.

[10] Genesis 4:17.

[11] Genesis 4:20-22.

[12] The name of the Ziggurat was Etemananki. It *was* built on the remains of the old tower of Babel, refurbished by Nebuchadnezzar himself.

[13] Esagila means "the temple that raises its head." It was the temple of Marduk—the chief of all the Babylonian gods.

We see the three protocols under attack in the wilderness temptation of Christ. Satan tried to get Jesus to break away from His *physical* dependence on His Father by turning stones to bread. He tries to get Jesus to exercise *intellectual* independence in how He interprets the Bible promise concerning angel-protection. And he encourages Jesus to be spiritually independent by worshiping a god of His own choosing.

In the several verses proceeding the three angels' messages—we find a description of those still remaining faithful at the very end—those finally sealed with the Father's name written in their foreheads.[14] Their words show they are *intellectually* without guile. The nature of their new song shows they are *spiritually* unique among men—for no man could learn their song. Because of their *physical* purity they are called virgins, following the Lamb wherever He goes—they are the first fruits to God.

These are contrasted yet again with the world's alternative, which, at the very end will be under the complete control of spiritual Babylon. When the plagues fall, the kings of the earth will lament for her. "Standing afar off for the fear of her torment, saying, Alas, alas, that great city Babylon, that mighty city! For in one hour is thy judgment come."[15] Then it will be said of her: "The voice of harpers, and *musicians*, and of pipers, and trumpeters, shall be heard no more at all in thee; and no *craftsman*, of whatsoever craft he be, shall be found any more in thee; and the sound of a *millstone* shall be heard no more at all in thee."[16] In the final analysis, the three great enterprises of Jubal, Tubalcain, and Jabal are seen as perfect failures.

Most important to our purposes here, we see that Christ's method of work and ministry sets the pattern for our work in these last days. He is the Author of the *Galilee Protocol*—and as Author He demonstrated His vital technique. "Jesus went about all Galilee, *teaching* in their synagogues, and *preaching* the gospel of the kingdom, and *healing* all manner of sickness and all manner of disease among the people."[17]

The *Galilee Protocol* is a grassroots movement within the Seventh-day Adventist Church community. It is our purpose to reach this generation with the *Three Angels' Messages* using Christ's own peculiar method.

---

[14] Revelation 14:1.

[15] Revelation 18:10.

[16] Revelation 18:22. Emphasis added.

[17] Matthew 4:23. Emphasis added.

—The Mission

The *Galilee Protocol* mission is to work using *Christ's Method Alone*: presenting a balanced demonstration of His character to the largest cities in America—through self-sacrificing service and clear, bold warnings from the *fourth angel.*[18]

When at Capernaum, Jesus said to them, "I must preach the kingdom of God to other cities also: for therefore am I sent."[19]

In Christ's day the situation was urgent. "He knew that unless there was a decided change in the principles and purposes of the human race, all would be lost." [20] This urgency was intensified by the fact that He had so short a time to accomplish so much. So He did not use the systems or conventions of the world. He did not borrow techniques or procedures from the teachers, preachers, or physicians of His time. "By methods peculiarly His own, Christ helped all who were in sorrow and affliction."[21] He began such a movement as the world has never seen. Within the space of a single generation the world had been reached with His life-changing gospel.

We believe that the situation is urgent today too. The world is on a rapid course to destruction, and unless God's people work diligently to bring about a decided change in this generation—it might be forever too late. "We are to work as Christ worked, in the same practical lines. Then we shall be safe. The divine commission needs no reform. Christ's way of presenting truth cannot be improved upon."[22] "*Christ's method alone* will give true success in reaching the people."[23] We must reactivate the *Galilee Protocol!*

—The Vision

The *Galilee Protocol* vision is to use the cities of America as a stage upon which to ignite a glorious display of Christ's righteousness to set the global context for the last conflict in the great controversy between Christ and Satan.

Scripture promises that this last conflict will be a *time of trouble* such as the world has never seen. Earth's great apostate power will place

[18] The angel of Revelation 18.
[19] Luke 4:43.
[20] Ellen G. White, *The Ministry of Healing*, p. 18.
[21] Ibid. p. 23.
[22] Ellen G. White, *Evangelism*, p. 525.
[23] Ellen G. White, *Ministry of Healing*, p. 143.

every energy into warfare against God's law. In this battle there will be but two classes of people. Every character will be fully developed; and all will show whether they have chosen the side of loyalty or rebellion.

God's law is the transcript of His Character: it is the perfect blending of His justice and mercy. In preparation for the soon-coming righteous judgments of God, His people unite together fully surrendered to His Spirit. Reactivating the *Galilee Protocol* they begin forming a living *Master*piece of self-sacrificing love and service in a way that vindicates the rectitude, justice, and moral excellence, of God's holy law. When the forces of the enemy are at their strongest, at a time when every possible inducement to evil is arrayed against them, God's faithful stand strong and pure. They keep the commandments of God, and the faith of Jesus.[24]

Just as when Christ Himself walked the earth, divinity is clothed with humanity: this time in the person of a purified church. They are His temple, filled with the Shekinah glory—His character!

—The Protocols

The current condition of humanity, the ecumenical moving of faith groups, the general tendency of political activity, and the lateness of the hour, all present an unprecedented urgency. This urgent situation requires the principles of the *great controversy* be brought into bold focus. The *Galilee Protocol* strictly follows Christ's city-centric missionary approach to build a highly visible, deliberate contrast between the principles of this world, and those of God's government.

Through a decidedly missionarial process, the *Galilee Protocol* asserts the two great principles of God's law—worship to God and service to man.[25] This plan *tactically* combines works of kindness and mercy with a tough-love judgment-hour warning to present the character of Christ: "The Lord, The Lord God, merciful and gracious, long-suffering, and abundant in goodness and truth, Keeping mercy for thousands, forgiving iniquity and transgression and sin, and that will by no means clear the guilty."[26]

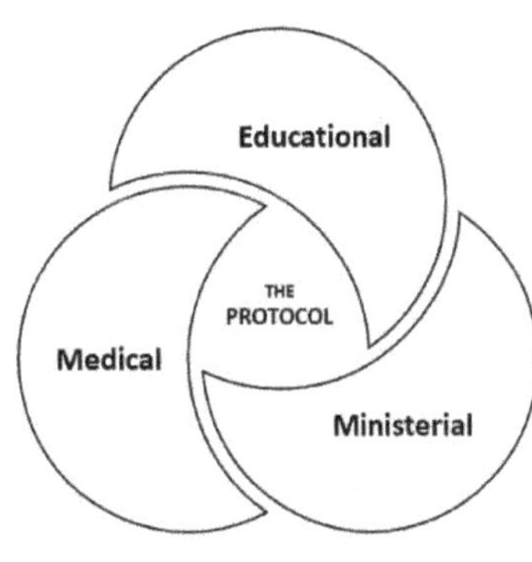

[24] Revelation 14:12.

[25] John 13:35; Matthew 22:37-40; Ellen G. White, Education, p. 16.

[26] Exodus 34:6-7.

The *Galilee Protocol* is an urgent intervention plan. It sounds the alarm to the people of this world: that unless they turn to the Great Physician for physical healing; enroll in the School of Christ for restoration of their mind; and come to Christ (the only Mediator between God and man)[27] for spiritual regeneration; the judgments of God are soon to fall upon *them*. In these final moments of reprieve, the offer of salvation is free to all. To *whosoever will*,[28] God promises to "restore in man the image of his Maker, to bring him back to the perfection in which he was created, to promote the development of body, mind, and soul, that the divine purpose in his creation might be realized."[29]

"Jesus went about all Galilee, *teaching* in the synagogues, and *preaching* the gospel of the kingdom, and *healing* all manner of sickness and all manner of disease among the people."[30] The *Galilee Protocol* operates as three primary elements: educational, ministerial, and medical; it uses specific activity to present Jesus as man's only hope for mental, spiritual, and physical restoration.

—The Directives

The *Directives* are program absolutes. While some things are negotiable, others are not. We cannot negotiate the *directives*. They come from clear instructions from God and if neglected, altered or changed constitute insubordination and disobedience. To maintain the integrity of the *Galilee Protocol*, we must carefully and completely follow the directives of *The Galilean*.

- City-centric: Christ said that He was sent to preach to the cities. We will see that this is our work too.
- Missionarial: Christ worked as a missionary, sacrificing everything for the benefit of humanity. We will see why this is how we must work too.
- Provocative: Christ did not work quietly behind the scenes. His work and message demanded attention. Today the world's focus must be captured by Christ's disciples.

---

[27] 1 Timothy 2:5.

[28] John 6:37.

[29] Ellen G. White, *Education*, p. 15.

[30] Matthew 4:23.

- Advocative: Though provocative, Christ made it very clear that He was an advocate for man. We must present Christ as the sinner's best friend and only hope.
- Representative: "Christ is waiting with longing desire for the manifestation of Himself in His church. When the character of Christ shall be perfectly reproduced in His people, then He will come to claim them as His own."[31] There must be a revival of primitive godliness[32] in the lives of His messengers. In our lives, we need to reverse the popular war against Christian standards.
- Organized: "Diligent work is now called for. In this crisis, no halfhearted efforts will prove successful. In all our city work, we are to hunt for souls. Wise plans are to be laid, in order that such a work may be done to the best possible advantage."[33]

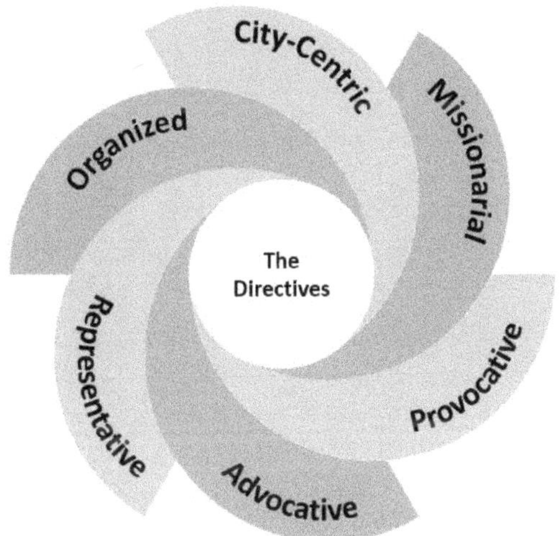

"The power which stirred the people so mightily in the 1844 movement will again be revealed. The third angel's message will go forth, not in whispered tones, but with a loud voice."

—Evangelism p. 693.

[31] Ellen G. White, *Christ's Object Lessons*, p. 69.
[32] Ellen G. White, *The Great Controversy*, p. 478.
[33] Ellen G. White, *Evangelism*, p. 59.

CHAPTER NINE

First Protocol—Educational

Being twelve years old was special for a Hebrew boy. New opportunities opened up to him for religious instruction; and from then on, he was expected to attend the annual feasts.[1]

When He was twelve Jesus went with His parents to celebrate the Passover for the first time. The Passover was immediately following the seven days' feast of unleavened bread. This gave Jesus the marvelous opportunities to observe all the workings of the temple. "Every act seemed to be bound up with His own life. New impulses were awakening within Him. Silent and absorbed, He seemed to be studying the great problem. The mystery of His mission was opening to the Savior."[2]

The temple had a school connected with it. Leading rabbis assembled there with their students. Jesus discovered them and sat down at the feet of the grave, learned men. He listened and asked questions about the prophecies and great events then taking place that pointed to the Messiah. "With the humility of a child He repeated the words of Scripture, giving them a depth of meaning that the wise men had not conceived of."[3]

---

[1] Ellen G. White, *The Desire of Ages*, p. 75.

[2] Ibid., p. 78.

[3] Ibid., pp. 78-79.

> "The rabbis knew that Jesus had not been instructed in their schools yet, His understanding of the prophecies far exceeded theirs... The youthful modesty and grace of Jesus disarmed their prejudices. Unconsciously their minds were opened to the word of God and the Holy Spirit spoke to their hearts. They could not but see that their expectations in regard to the Messiah were not sustained by prophecy; but they would not renounce the theories that had flattered their ambition. They would not admit that they had misapprehended the Scriptures they claimed to teach."[4]

When Jesus was a boy, the towns and cities educated the young. But the teaching was formal, and they cherished traditions above Scripture. They crowded minds with material that was worthless and not recognized in the higher school above.

> "The experience which is obtained through a personal acceptance of God's word was out of place in the educational system. Absorbed in the rounds of externals, the students found no quiet hours to spend with God. They did not hear His voice speaking to the heart. In their search for knowledge they turned away from the Source of wisdom. The great essentials of the service of God were neglected. The principles of the law were obscured. That which was regarded as superior education was the greatest hinderance to real development. Under the training of the rabbis the powers of the youth were repressed. Their minds were cramped and narrow."[5]

Jesus did not go to the synagogue schools. His mother taught Him of heavenly things and the prophetic scrolls. "As He advanced from childhood to youth, He did not seek the schools of the rabbis. He needed not the education to be obtained from such sources; for God was His instructor."[6]

Every child today can learn as Jesus did; and if they would, the angels would draw near to them to teach them.[7] The Reformers, Luther and Melanchthon, understood the importance of education. So they set up protestant schools.[8] Their system of education was so powerful that one historian wrote:

> "The nobility... studies at Wittenberg—all the colleges of the land were filled with Protestants... Not more than the thirtieth part of the population remained Catholic... The Protestant nations extended their vivifying

[4] Ibid., p. 80.
[5] Ibid. p. 69.
[6] Ibid. p. 70.
[7] Ibid.
[8] Dr. E. A. Sutherland, *Studies in Christian Education*, p. 5.

energies to the most remote and most forgotten corners of Europe. What an immense domain had they conquered within the space of forty years."[9]

But education also became the kingpin of the *Counter-Reformation.* The history is clear; the papacy developed our modern system to combat the work of the reformers.[10] Like the Jewish rabbis, they used methods that repressed the minds of their students. "The memory was cultivated as a means of keeping down free activity of thought and clearness of judgment."[11] "The conferring of degrees was originated by a pope."[12]

The "course of study was impractical; its methods of instruction mechanical; memory work was exalted; its government was arbitrary and empirical."[13] "A dead knowledge of words took the place of a living knowledge of things... The pupils were obliged to learn, but were not educated to see and hear, to think and prove, and were not led to true independence and personal perfection. The teachers found their function in teaching the prescribed text, not in harmoniously developing the young human being according to the laws of nature."[14]

Thomas Macaulay, speaking of this system adds: "They promised what was impractical; they despised what was practical. They filled the world with long words and long beards, and they left it as ignorant and as wicked as they found it."[15]

> "[Teachers] made much of emulation... Nothing will be more honorable than to outstrip a fellow student, and nothing more dishonorable than to be outstripped. Prizes will be distributed to the best pupils with the greatest solemnity... It sought showy results with which to dazzle the world: a well-rounded development was nothing...
>
> "When a student could make a brilliant display from the resources of a well-stored memory, he had reached the highest points to which the [teachers] sought to lead him. Originality and independence of mind, love of truth for its own sake, the power of reflecting and forming correct judgments were not merely neglected, they were suppressed in the [school] system."[16]

This Catholic system of education was remarkably successful, and for nearly a century all the foremost men in Christendom came from their

---

[9] Leopold von Ranke, *The History of the Popes*, p. 135. 1901. P. F. Collier & Son.

[10] Sutherland, pp. 7-15.

[11] Karl Rosencranz, *The Philosophy of Education*, p. 270. 1886. D. Appleton and Company, New York.

[12] B. Hartmann, *Religion or No Religion in Education*, p. 43. 1894. Melling & Gaskins; 2d edition.

[13] Sutherland, p. 8.

[14] Franklin Verzelius Newton Painter, *A History of Education*, p. 156. 1886. D. Appleton and Company, New York.

[15] David Salmon, *Macaulay's Essay on Bacon*, p. 379. 1904. Longmans, Green and Co.

[16] Painter, pp. 172-173.

schools.[17] As soon as possible, this system of education was planted upon the shores of the new world "and in every one of their Christian schools. They ignorantly fostered it and scattered it, and their successors, like the successors of Luther and Melanchthon, became so infected with the spirit of Rome that by 1844 the Protestant churches were morally like their mother."[18]

—Comparing Methods

These are the methods and principles used by the rabbis and papists:

1. Memory was used to repress the mind and cloud the judgment.
2. Courses were impractical—a dead knowledge of words.
3. Emulation was encouraged.
4. They taught the prescribed text.
5. They encouraged competition and personal ambition.
6. Absorbed in rounds of externals, no quiet hours with God.

The methods and principles of the Reformers and of Blueprint Adventism were just the opposite:

1. Taught to be thinkers, not mere reflectors of other men's thoughts.[19]
2. Knowledge and experience to be gained by practical work.[20]
3. Develop individuality, the power to think and to do.[21]
4. Harmonious development according to the laws of nature.[22]
5. Personal excellence, pursuit of ideals, well-rounded development.[23]
6. Instructed by God, and "angels will draw near to teach them.[24]

—A Message From Elder Prescott

Elder W.W. Prescott's parents were part of the Millerite movement. From 1885-1894, he served as president at Battle Creek College. He helped found Union College served as president there in 1891. In 1892, he assumed the presidency of the newly founded Walla Walla College. We will see from statements below, that in the early years, Adventist educators understood the principles of blueprint education.

---

[17] Rosencranz, p. 272.
[18] Sutherland, p. 13.
[19] Ellen G. White, *Education*, p. 17.
[20] Ellen G. White, *Welfare Ministry*, p. 125.
[21] Ibid.
[22] Franklin Verzelius Newton Painter, *A History of Education*, p. 156. 1886. D. Appleton and Company, New York.
[23] W.W. Prescott, General Conference Director of Education, February 23, 1893, *1893 General Conference Bulletin*, pp. 357-358.
[24] Ellen G. White, *The Desire of Ages*, p. 70.

"The real purpose of our educational work is to restore the image of God in the soul... The basis on which students should be encouraged to earnest work in securing an education is an important matter. You know to what extent it is coming to be a practice in educational institutions to stimulate efforts by prize competitions in almost every line. The marking system[25] very generally encourages a feeling of rivalry. The basis of the work is thus made to be personal ambition. It is not so much to personal excellence, not to reach an ideal, but to be above a neighbor. Of two students with differing capabilities, one may by much less hard work take a higher rank, and yet his fellow student may do better work and be a better student.

"The true basis seems to me to be this: Everyone is endowed with certain capabilities and faculties. God has for him a certain ideal which he can reach by the proper use of time and opportunities. He is not to be satisfied with the fact that he outstrips his neighbor. His effort should be to get what God would have him, and success is to meet the ideal the Lord has for him in view of his capacity and opportunity. His neighbor, who may have only half the capacity will reach the same degree of success and will be worthy of the same commendations if he reached the ideal that God has for him in view of his capacity and his opportunity.

"The true basis of credit is not to be comparing one with another to see if one secures a better standing or more prizes than his neighbor, but to compare the actual standing of every student with the ideal God intends he should gain in view of the capacities with which he was endowed and the opportunities God's providence has given him.

"This is a very different basis than simply the idea of personal ambition to excel another. It is very much easier for a teacher to impel one to earnest work by appealing to personal ambition, because it is a trait of human nature easily cultivated. So many teachers, as being the easier method to get work (as they say) out of students, appeal to them on the basis of their standing, as compared with another. (2 Cor 10:12-13).

"But that trait of human nature needs no cultivation. It is the same old self. When the mind of Christ is brought into our plans of education, the purpose will not be to draw out and strengthen elements of self, but it will be, as in all other parts of the work, to empty self, to take a humble position, and yet by that very means to attain to an exaltation impossible any other way."[26]

"And the test should not be, 'Have you studied this?' 'Have you studied that?' 'Have you passed an examination, with certain percent in such subjects?' 'Have you a diploma in such a course?' But, 'What are you?' That should be the constant test. The examination should be the application of God's ideal for the individual, to him personally."[27]

---

[25] Credits and grading.

[26] W.W. Prescott, General Conference Director of Education, February 23, 1893, *1893 General Conference Bulletin*, pp. 357-358.

[27] W.W. Prescott, *General Conference Bulletin*, 1897.

Notice what Sister White has written:

> "True education does not ignore the value of scientific knowledge or literary requirements; but above information it values power; above power, goodness; above intellectual acquirements, character. The world does not so much need men of great intellect as of noble character. It needs men on whom ability is controlled by steadfast principle... True education imparts wisdom. It teaches the best use not only of one but all our powers and acquirements. Thus it covers the whole circle of obligation—to ourselves, to the world, and to God... At such a time as this, what is the trend of the education given? To what motive is appeal most often made? To self-seeking."[28]

—Educational

The protocol's *Educational Element* involves the training of Christ's disciples for their work of ministry using the *Galilee Protocol*. When we think of education, we usually think of reading, writing, and arithmetic. We think of training children to be productive members of society. We think of preparing people for a career. When we think of *Christian* education, we consider all these things from a Christian context. But this *Educational Element* prepares God's people to do the special work for our time. "God's purpose in giving the third angel's message to the world is to prepare a people to stand true to Him during the investigative judgment. This is the purpose for which we establish and maintain our publishing houses, our schools, our sanitariums, hygienic restaurants, treatment rooms, and food factories. This is our purpose in carrying forward every line of work in the cause."[29]

It is true of each of the protocol's three elements: that the fundamental thing that distinguishes them from the way of the world, is their basis in divine command rather than worldly wisdom. "We want none of that kind of 'higher education' that will put us in a position where the credit must be given, not to the Lord God of Israel, but to the god of Ekron.[30] The Lord designs that we shall stand as a distinct people, *so connected with Him that He can work with us*."[31] "Our people are now being tested as to whether they will obtain their wisdom from the greatest Teacher the world ever knew or seek to the god of Ekron. Let us determine that we shall not be tied by so much as a thread to the educational policies of

---

[28] Ellen G. White, *Education*, p. 225.

[29] Ellen White, *Manuscript Releases*, vol. 1, p. 228; 1902.

[30] Ekron was one of the principle cities of the Philistines. The god of Ekron was also known as Baalzebub (actually Satan, himself) and the people inquired of him about the future. He was considered to be the god of knowledge.

[31] Ellen G. White, *Manuscript 71*, 1909. Emphasis added.

those who do not discern the voice of God and who will not hearken to His commandments."[32] "The so-called higher education of the present day is a misnamed deception... All this higher education that is being planned will be extinguished; for it is spurious. The more simple the education of our workers, the less connection they have with the men whom God is not leading, the more will be accomplished."[33]

"We hear much of the higher education as the world regards the subject. But those who are ignorant of the higher education as it is taught and exemplified in the life of Christ, are ignorant of what constitutes the higher education. Higher education means conformity to the terms of salvation. It embraces the experience of daily looking to Jesus, and of working together with Christ for the saving of the perishing... Christ imparted instruction of the highest order... By pen and by voice labor to sweep back the false ideas that have taken possession of men's minds regarding the higher education. To every worker Christ gives the command, Go work today in my vineyard for the glory of my name. Represent before the world laden with corruption the blessedness of true higher education. Light is to shine forth from every believer. The weary, the heavy-laden, the broken-hearted and the perplexed, are all to be pointed to Christ, the source of all spiritual life and strength."[34]

"Our schools should have little to say now of degrees and long courses of study. The work of preparation for the service of God is to be done speedily. Let the work be carried forward in strictly Bible lines. Let every soul remember that the judgments of God are in the land. Let degrees be little spoken of."[35] "Workers–gospel medical missionaries, are needed now. You cannot afford to spend years in preparation. Soon the doors now open to the truth will be forever closed. Carry the message now. Do not wait, allowing the enemy to take possession of the fields now open to you. Let little companies go forth to do the work which Christ appointed His disciples. Let them labor as evangelists, scattering publications, and talking of the truth to those they meet. Let them pray for the sick, ministering to their necessities, not with drugs, but with nature's remedies, and teaching them how to regain health and avoid disease."[36]

---

[32] Ellen G. White, *Medical Ministry*, pp. 61, 62.
[33] Ellen G. White, *Series B*, no. 7, p. 63; 1905.
[34] Ellen G. White, *Spalding and Megan Collection*, p. 448.
[35] Ellen G. White, *Letter 38*, par. 11; December 23, 1908.
[36] Ellen G. White, *Counsels on Health*, p. 397.

"In this closing work of the gospel there is a vast field to be occupied; and, more than ever before, the work is to enlist the helpers from the common people. Both the youth and those older in years will be called from the field, from the vineyard, and from the workshop, and sent forth by the Master to give His message. Many of these may have little opportunity for education, but Christ sees in them qualifications that will enable them to fulfill His purpose. If they put their hearts into the work, and continue to be learners, He will fit them to labor for Him."[37]

"Following [Christ's] example in our medical missionary work, we shall reveal to the world that our credentials are from above... United with Christ in God, we shall reveal to the world that as God chose His Son to be His representative on the earth, even so has Christ chosen us to represent His character."[38]

The Educational Element comprises Four Requirements—

Individual enrollment in the school of Christ, with a strong personal commitment to following His plan precisely, realizing this will require living a life distinct from the world.

City-Mission focus: This is one of the *primary directives*. We will study it in chapter 12.

Simple and short courses of study to fit students of all ages to enter the work quickly.

Two-by-two field training model show-as-you-go mentoring program.

The Galilee Protocol Core Curriculum—

Christ's Method Alone! This course studies the *Galilee Protocol* concept, rationale, and method. It emphasizes strict conformity to Christ's own method of work, especially as it applies to the blueprint that He has given to the *Seventh-day Adventist Church*.

The Bible Witness: This is a basic study of the plan of salvation and prophecy's role in it. It is Christ centered and incorporates a strong focus on personal salvation and mission in a last-days context.

The History of Our Message: This is an exciting course that provides a very necessary grounding in the *Seventh-day Adventist* context.

God's Eight Doctors: These lessons present the eight natural remedies: trust in God, water, fresh air, sunshine, nutrition, exercise, temperance and rest as the model for life and health.

---

[37] Ellen G. White, *Welfare Ministry*, pp. 108-109.

[38] Ellen G. White, *Medical Ministry*, p. 23.

Anatomy, Physiology and Hygiene: This course provides a basic understanding of the major body systems and organs, and how to keep them healthy.

Hygienic Healthcare: This study looks at divine healing, nature's remedies, caring for the sick, temperance matters, specific diseases, and the conservation of health.

Hydrotherapy: Here we study hydrotherapy theory and technique.

Healthful Cookery: Cooking healthfully is more involved than most of today's convenience methods. This practical course will provide a simple, enjoyable eating plan built around good health.

Home Gardening: Gardening is not only a wonderful source for wholesome food, it is also an activity divinely engineered to promote many health benefits. This is an important study on the how, whys, wherefores, and prophetic significance for home gardening.

> **"Christ's workers should be well qualified, well trained men and women, enjoying the vigorous use of all their powers. They should be men and women who have denied self, who in a crisis will know, as did Daniel, what course to pursue in order to honor and glorify God."**
>
> **—Signs of the Times, October 24, 1900.**

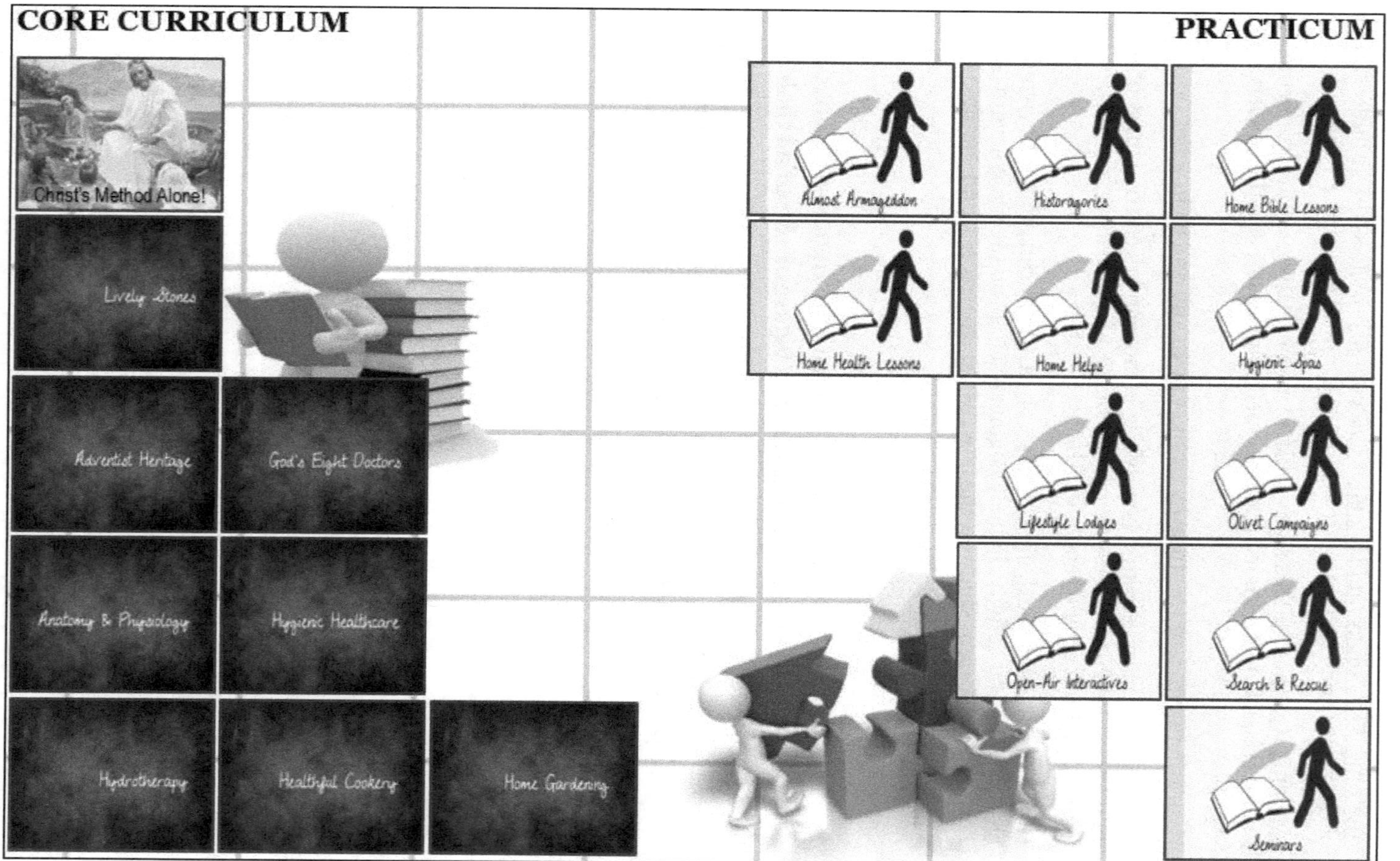
CORE CURRICULUM
Christ's Method Alone!
Lively Stones
Adventist Heritage
God's Eight Doctors
Anatomy & Physiology
Hygienic Healthcare
Hydrotherapy
Healthful Cookery
Home Gardening
PRACTICUM
Almost Armageddon
Historagories
Home Bible Lessons
Home Health Lessons
Home Helps
Hygienic Spas
Lifestyle Lodges
Olivet Campaigns
Open-Air Interactives
Search & Rescue
Seminars

CHAPTER TEN

Second Protocol—Ministerial

Jesus asked, "What went ye out into the wilderness to see? A reed shaken with the wind?... a man clothed in soft raiment?... But what went ye out into the wilderness to see? A prophet? Yea, I say unto you, and more than a prophet. For this is he, whom it is written, Behold, I send My messenger before Thy face, which shall prepare Thy way before Thee."[1]

Great numbers of people from Jerusalem, Judea, and from all around the Jordan river had earlier gone into the wilderness where John was preaching—to hear him and to be baptized.[2] What led such a multitude there? What did they expect to see?

There around the Jordan were reeds—tall reeds—swaying and bending at every breeze.[3] While such might be a fitting illustration of the rabbis of the day, swaying reeds did not represent *John the Baptist!* He wore no fancy, soft clothes. He did not bend to the winds of popular opinion. God called him to reprove sin and excess. His clothing was plain. His life was self-denying. He rightly portrayed the character of his mission.

---

[1] Matthew 11:7-10.

[2] Matthews 3:5.

[3] Ellen G. White, *The Desire of Ages*, p. 218.

> "The multitude who were gathered about Christ had been witnesses to the work of John. They had heard his fearless rebuke of sin. To the self-righteous Pharisees, the priestly Sadducees, King Herod and his court, princes and soldiers, publicans and peasants, John had spoken with equal plainness. He was no trembling weed, swayed by the winds of human praise or prejudice."[4]

Mark connects John with Isaiah's prophecy: "Behold, I send My messenger before Thy face, which shall prepare Thy way before Thee. The voice of one crying in the wilderness, Prepare ye the way of the Lord, make His paths straight."[5] Jesus calls John the greatest of prophets;[6] and quotes Malachi, saying, "Behold, I will send My messenger, and he shall prepare the way before Me."[7]

—The Elijah Connection.

Sometimes Jesus said things that needed careful unpacking. So He'd say, "He that hath ears to hear, let him hear."[8] This meant that not everyone will get this, only those who are paying attention. This was the case when He said, "If ye will receive it, this is Elijah, who was to come."[9] He referred here to another prophecy in Malachi:

> "Behold, I will send you Elijah the prophet before the coming of the great and dreadful day of the Lord: And he shall turn the hearts of the fathers to the children, and the hearts of the children to their fathers, lest I come and smite the earth with a curse."[10]

For those who *are* paying attention, this prophecy applies to those living at the end of time—just before the second coming. Its application to John marks a parallel between the work that needed doing when Christ came, and the work that needs doing before He comes again.

> "John the Baptist went forth in the spirit and power of Elijah to prepare the way of the Lord and to turn the people to the wisdom of the just. He was a representative of those living in these last days to whom God has entrusted sacred truths to present before the people to prepare the way for the second appearing of Christ... Those who are to prepare the way for the second coming of Christ are represented by faithful Elijah, as John came in the spirit of Elijah to prepare the way for Christ's first advent.[11]

---

[4] Ibid.

[5] Mark 1:2-3.

[6] Matthew 11:9-11.

[7] Malachi 3:1.

[8] Matthew 11:15. See Matthew 13:9, 43; Mark 4:9, 23; 7:16; Luke 8:8, 14:35, Revelation 2:7; 2:11; 2:17; 2:29; 3:6; 3:22; 3:29.

[9] Matthew 11:14. King James 2000 Bible.

[10] Malachi 4:5-6.

[11] Ellen G. White, *Testimonies for the Church*, vol. 3, pp. 61, 62.

Elijah saw that Israel had plunged into fearful apostacy. When God sent him to give a message to the people, they didn't listen to his warning. They thought he was "unnecessarily severe. He must, they thought, have lost his senses—that he would denounce them, the favored people of God, as sinners, and their crimes, so aggravating, that the judgments of God would awaken against them."[12]

Even though the ten tribes incorporated Baal into their worship, they still considered themselves God's chosen people. They were synchronistic—their worship mixed the religion of God with the religion of Baal. So on Mount Carmel, Elijah boldly declared, "How long halt ye between two opinions? If the Lord be God, follow Him: but if Baal, then follow him."[13]

Going before king Ahab, Elijah warned that the judgments of God *would awaken against them*. He saw the problem and determined to do all he could about it.

> "Elijah's faithful soul was grieved. His indignation was aroused, and he was jealous for the glory of God... He went before God, and with his soul wrung with anguish, plead for him to save his people *if it must be by judgment*. He pled with God to withhold from his ungrateful people dew and rain... that apostate Israel might look in vain to their idols of gold, wood, and stone, the sun, moon, and stars, their gods, to water the earth and enrich it... God told Elijah he had heard His prayer.[14]

—Where is the God of Judgment?

Notice the role of judgment here. Elijah figured out that Israel's course would not self-correct. Gentle nudging and encouragement alone would not prompt them to singular fidelity to God. When knocking fails, the only way to reach Laodicea is through judgment.[15]

Malachi declares: "Ye have wearied the Lord with your words. Yet, ye say... Everyone that doeth evil is good in the sight of the Lord, and he delighteth in them; or, Where is the God of judgment?"[16] This was the tenor of things in Malachi's time. This was the tenor of things when Christ came onto the scene. It is the tenor of things today.

> "The Jews tried to stop the proclamation of the message that has been predicted in the Word of God; but prophecy must be fulfilled. The Lord says, 'Behold, I will send you Elijah the prophet before the coming of the

---

[12] Ellen G. White, *The Laodicean Church*, Review and Herald, September 16, 1873.

[13] 1 Kings 18:21.

[14] Ellen G. White, *The Laodicean Church*, Review and Herald, September 16, 1873. Emphasis added.

[15] The previous reference was from an article Sister White wrote in the Review. Most of the article recounted the story of Elijah, though the title of the piece (that ran through several editions) was "*The Laodicean Church*."

[16] Malachi 2:17.

great and dreadful day of the Lord.' (Mal. 4:5). Somebody is to come in the spirit and power of Elijah, and when he appears, men may say, 'You are too earnest, you do not interpret the Scriptures in the proper way. Let me tell you how to teach your message.'"[17]

This tenor of things formed the context of Malachi's proclamation some verses later—that a messenger was coming to prepare the way for the Lord, saying that He shall suddenly come to His temple:

"But who may abide the day of His coming? and who shall stand when He appeareth? for He *is* like a refiner's fire, and like fullers' soap: And He shall sit *as* a refiner and purifier of silver: and He shall purify the sons of Levi, and purge them as gold and silver, that they may offer unto the LORD an offering in righteousness... And I will come near to you to judgment..."[18]

So also, this tenor of things influenced the preaching of *John the Baptist*, saying, "Repent ye: for the kingdom of heaven is at hand."

"I indeed baptize you with water unto repentance: but He that cometh after me is mightier than I, whose shoes I am not worthy to bear: He shall baptize you with the Holy Ghost, and with fire: Whose fan is in His hand, and He will thoroughly purge His floor, and gather His wheat into the garner; but He will burn up the chaff with unquenchable fire."[19]

—Before the Great and Dreadful Day of the Lord

And such are the tenor of things in Laodicea. Our message differs radically from the normal Christian fare of today—for we have received a clear understanding of the condition of things as they are now just ahead of the *second* coming of the Lord. With this understanding comes the same solemn responsibility that rested on Elijah and John.

"The word of the Lord came to Elijah; he did not seek to be the Lord's messenger, but the word came to him. God always has men to whom He entrusts His message. His Spirit moves upon their hearts, and constrains them to speak. Stimulated by holy zeal, and with the divine impulse strong upon them, they enter upon the performance of their duty without coldly calculating the consequences of speaking to the people the word which the Lord has given them. But the servant of God is soon made aware that he has risked something. He finds himself and his message made the subject of criticism. His manners, his life, his property are all inspected and commented upon. His message is picked to pieces and rejected in the most illiberal and unsanctified spirit, as men in their finite judgment see fit. Has that message done the work God designed it

---

[17] Ellen G. White, *Selected Messages*, book 1, p. 412,

[18] Malachi 3:2-5.

[19] Matthew 3:1, 11-12.

should accomplish? No; it has signally failed, because the hearts of the hearers were unsanctified.

"If the minister's face is not flint, if he has not indomitable faith and courage, if his heart is not made strong by constant communion with God, he will begin to shape his testimony to please the unsanctified ears and hearts of those whom he is addressing. In endeavoring to avoid the criticism to which he is exposed, he separates from God, and loses the sense of the divine favor, and his testimony becomes tame and lifeless. He finds that his courage and faith are gone, and his labors are powerless. The world is full of flatterers and dissemblers who have yielded to the desire to please; but the faithful men, who do not study self-interest, but love their brethren too well to suffer sin upon them, are few indeed.[20]

"Elijah prays, "Be it known this day that Thou art the God of Israel." The honor of God is to be exalted as supreme, but the prophet asks further *that his mission also may be confirmed.* "Let it be known that Thou art God in Israel," he prays," and that I am Thy servant, and have done all things at Thy word." "Hear me, O Lord," he pleads, "Hear me." Elijah is intense. As he prayed the silence of death seemed to be about him. As the Amen was spoken, lo, the fire of heaven descended on the sacrifices in sight of the multitude."[21]

"Those who will study the manner of Christ's teaching, and educate themselves to follow His way, will attract and hold large numbers now, as Christ held the people in His day.... When the truth in its practical character is urged upon the people because you love them, souls will be convicted, because the Holy Spirit of God will impress their hearts."

—Evangelism p. 124.

—Ministerial

The Bible says, "Jesus came into Galilee, preaching the gospel of the kingdom of God, and saying, The time is fulfilled, and the kingdom of God is at hand: repent ye, and believe the gospel."[22] This was good news because Jesus had come to "preach the gospel to the poor... to heal the brokenhearted, to preach deliverance to the captives, and recovering of

[20] Ellen G. White, *Review and Herold*, April 7, 1885.
[21] Ellen G. White, *Loma Linda Messages*, p. 572.
[22] Mark 1:14-15.

sight to the blind, to set at liberty them that are bruised, to preach the acceptable year of the Lord."[23]

His great offer of restoration was especially important because of the urgency of the time. In just a few short years, the Roman general, Titus, would destroy Jerusalem and the temple; and the Jewish people would be broken up and scattered. Their opportunity was almost past. Israel's clock was winding down—and she was failing her divine commission. In this last moment, Christ came to intervene. "He knew that unless there was a decided change in the principles and purposes of the human race, all would be lost."[24] It was judgment-hour for the Jews.

When Jesus preached the time was fulfilled, He was announcing the close of Daniel's seventy-week probation for that chosen people. When Jesus preached, "Repent for the kingdom of heaven is at hand,"[25] He was echoing the startling cry of *John the Baptist*:

> "O generation of vipers, who hath warned you to flee from the wrath to come? Bring forth therefore fruits meet for repentance: And think not to say within yourselves, We have Abraham to our father: for I say unto you, that God is able of these stones to raise up children unto Abraham. Now also the axe is laid unto the root of the trees: therefore every tree which bringeth not forth good fruit is hewn down, and cast into the fire..."

While riding triumphantly into Jerusalem that last week of His life, Christ clarified that He was fulfilling these very words. Judgment *had* come to the Jews. Their probation was at an end. Those who were spreading their coats and palm branches before Him were the stones He was raising up to be children unto Abraham.[26] By cursing the fruitless fig tree, He showed He was laying the ax to the root of the tree.[27]

The protocol's *Ministerial Element* reaches out to the public with the gospel message. It requires that the message "sound forth in earnest words of warning... We must persuade men everywhere to repent and flee from the wrath to come."[28] "Let those who present the truth enter into no controversy. They are to preach the gospel with such faith and earnestness that an interest will be awakened. By the words they speak, the prayers they offer, the influence they exert, they are to sow seeds that will bear fruit to the glory of God. There is to be no wavering. The

---

[23] Luke 4:18-19.
[24] Ellen G. White, *The Desire of Ages*, p. 92.
[25] Matthew 4:17.
[26] See Luke 19-28-44.
[27] See Mark 11:12-14; 20-26.
[28] Ellen G. White, *Evangelism*, p. 217.

trumpet is to give a certain sound. The attention of the people is to be called to the third angel's message. Let not God's servants act like men walking in their sleep, but men preparing for the coming of Christ."[29]

> "Most startling messages will be borne by men of God's appointment, messages of a character to warn the people, to arouse them. And while some will be provoked by the warning, and led to resist the light and evidence, we are to see from this that we are giving the testing message for this time... We must also have, in our cities, consecrated evangelists through whom a message is to be borne so decidedly as to startle the hearers."[30]

The *Ministerial Element* approaches the work of evangelism frugally, focused on two essentials: Christ and His Revelation.

> "There must be no time uselessly employed in the work. We must not miss the mark. Time is too short for us to undertake to reveal all that might be opened up to view. Eternity will be required that we may know all the length and breadth, the height and depth, of the Scriptures... To the apostle John, on the Isle of Patmos, were revealed the things that God desired him to give to the people. Study these revelations. Here are themes worthy of our contemplation, large and comprehensive lessons, which all the angelic hosts are now seeking to communicate. Behold the life and character of Christ, and study His mediatorial work. Here are infinite wisdom, infinite love, infinite justice, infinite mercy. Here are the depths and heights, lengths and breadths, for our consideration. Numberless pens have been employed in presenting to the world the life, the character, and the mediatorial work of Christ; yet every mind through whom the Holy Spirit has worked has presented these themes in a light that is fresh and new, according to the mind and spirit of the human agent."[31]

The Primary Thematic Patterns for Evangelism—

The Stories of Jesus: The stories of the Bible, especially those in the Gospels are told bringing out the fundamental principles of salvation and the special prophetic significance for our day.
The Olivet Pattern: In Matthew 24, Christ blends three prophecies in one, the destruction of Jerusalem, the whole history of the Christian church, and earth's final conflict in the last generation. We use this same pattern: the first two prophecies illustrating the third.

---

[29] Ibid p. 119.
[30] Ibid p. 168.
[31] Ellen G. White, *Evangelism*, p. 120.

The Book of Revelation: The prophecies of Revelation follow the Olivet pattern. We present Revelation, using history to bring out its special importance for the last days.
Great Controversy: Ellen White's inspired evangelistic masterpiece also follows the Olivet pattern. We also use this as a model for evangelism.

"Our Lord is cognizant of the conflict of His people in these last days with the satanic agencies combined with evil men who neglect and refuse this great salvation. With the greatest simplicity and candor, our Savior, the mighty General of the armies of heaven, does not conceal the stern conflict which they will experience. He points out the dangers, He shows us the plan of the battle, and the hard and hazardous work to be done, and then lifts His voice before entering the conflict to count the cost while at the same time encouraging all to take up the weapons of their warfare and expect the heavenly host to compose the armies of war in defense of truth and righteousness... While the vast confederacy of evil is arrayed against them He bids them to be brave and strong and fight valiantly for they have a heaven to win, and they have more than an angel in their ranks, the mighty General of armies leads on the armies of heaven."

—Bible Commentary, Vol. 2, pp. 995, 996.

CHAPTER ELEVEN

Third Protocol—Medical

As already noted,[1] Christ referred to the healing of *Naaman the Syrian*[2] and to the *Widow of Zarephath*[3] during His presentation to the synagogue in Nazareth.[4] He did this after saying, “Ye will surely say unto me this proverb, Physician, heal thyself.”[5]

Evidently Jesus touched a sensitive nerve, because “they in the synagogue, when they had heard these things, where filled with wrath, and rose up, and thrust Him out of the city, and led Him unto the brow of the hill whereon their city was built, that they might cast Him down headlong.”[6]

This was a sudden change of attitude. Moments before “all bare witness, and wondered at the gracious words which proceeded out of His mouth.”[7]

Jesus’ point is clear enough—God is in the healing business; and the only reason His people have to take their business elsewhere is because

---

[1] See chapter 3, *Sabbath—A Protocol for Service.*

[2] 2 Kings 5:1-14.

[3] 1 Kings 17:9.

[4] Luke 4:14-30.

[5] Luke 4:23.

[6] Luke 4:28-30.

[7] Luke 4:22.

"no prophet is accepted in his own country."[8] In this case, the "prophet" is Christ Himself. God's own people lacked faith in Him—the *Greatest Physician.*

Through Elijah, Christ brought the widow's son[9] back to life. Through Elisha, Christ healed Naaman's leprosy, and also cured the Shunamite woman's barrenness[10]—and later raised her son from the dead.[11] Christ healed Miriam from her leprosy.[12] Through an unnamed prophet, Christ healed the shriveled hand of King Jeroboam.[13] Christ even used the dead bones of Elisha to bring someone back to life.[14]

When king Hezekiah prayed to God for healing, Isaiah received word from God that he would live another fifteen years. This time Christ worked through a poultice of figs.[15] Christ healed Job.[16] Christ healed Nebuchadnezzar from his insanity.[17] Many barren women where healed by Christ: Hannah—the mother of Samuel,[18] Sarah,[19] Manoah's wife,[20] Rebekah,[21] Rachel,[22] "every womb in Abimelech's household,"[23] and in the New Testament—Elizabeth.[24]

To the Psalmist, God is the healer. "Bless the LORD, O my soul: and all that is within me, bless His holy name. Bless the LORD, O my soul, and forget not all His benefits: who forgiveth all thine iniquities; who healeth all thy diseases."[25] "He healeth the broken in heart, and bindeth up their wounds."[26] "Then they cry into the LORD in their trouble, and He saveth them out of their distresses. He set His word, and healed them, and delivered them from their destructions."[27]

---

[8] Luke 4:24.
[9] 1 Kings 17:17-24.
[10] 2 Kings 4:8-17.
[11] 2 Kings 4:18-37.
[12] Numbers 12:1-15.
[13] 1 Kings 13:4-6.
[14] 2 Kings 13:21.
[15] 2 Kings 20:1-7, 2 Chronicles 32:24-26, Isaiah 38:1-8.
[16] Job 42:10-17.
[17] Daniel 4:24, 36.
[18] 1 Samuel 1:9-20.
[19] Genesis 18:10,14, 21:1-3.
[20] Judges 13:5-25.
[21] Genesis 25:21.
[22] Genesis 30:1, 22.
[23] Genesis 20:1-18.
[24] Luke 1:7.
[25] Psalms 103:1-3.
[26] Psalms 147:3. See also Psalms 41; 116.
[27] Psalms 107:19-20.

The story of Israel in the wilderness exemplifies God's healing on a grand scale. "If thou wilt diligently harken to the voice of the LORD thy God, and wilt do that which is right in His sight, and wilt give ear to His commandments, and keep all His statutes, I will put none of these diseases upon thee, which I have brought upon the Egyptians: for I am the LORD that health thee."[28] God proved faithful. During their entire forty-year sojourn, even their shoe-leather stayed young and healthy![29]

In the New Testament, James admonishes us to have the elders pray for the sick and to anoint them "with oil in the name of the Lord. And the prayer of faith shall save the sick, and the Lord shall raise him up; and if he have committed sins, they shall be forgiven him."[30]

Unfortunately, God's people do not always turn to Him for their healthcare needs. King Asa—though generally a good, God-fearing king—when his feet became diseased in the thirty-ninth year of his reign, (even though the disease became great) "yet in his disease he sought not the LORD, but to the physicians."[31] He died in the forty-first year.

King Ahaziah fell through a lattice in his upper chamber and was sick. He sent his messenger to Baalzebub, the god of Ekron to find out whether he would recover from his disease. The angel of the Lord sent Elijah to intercept the king's messenger, and say to him: "Is it not because there is not a God in Israel, that ye go to inquire of Baalzebub the god of Ekron?" The king was informed that he would indeed die.[32]

"Is there no balm in Gilead; is there no physician there? why then is not the health of the daughter of my people recovered?"[33] While the context of this verse suggests it is a parable regarding the *spiritual wounds* of Israel, it does tend to reinforce the apocryphal proverb "He that sinneth before his Maker, let him fall into the hand of the physician."[34]

> "Christ is the same compassionate physician now that He was during His earthly ministry. In Him there is healing balm for every disease, restoring power for every infirmity."[35]
>
> "There is something better for us to engage in than the control of humanity by humanity. The physician should educate the people to look from the human to the divine. Instead of teaching the sick to depend

---

[28] Exodus 15:26. See Deuteronomy 7:15.
[29] Deuteronomy 29:5.
[30] James 5.
[31] 2 Chronicles 16:12.
[32] 2 Kings 1:1-4.
[33] Jeremiah 8:22.
[34] Ecclesiasticus 38:15.
[35] Ellen G. White, *The Ministry of Healing*, p. 226.

upon human beings for the cure of soul and body, he should direct them to the One who can save to the uttermost all who come unto Him. He who made man's mind knows what the mind needs. *God alone is the one who can heal.* Those whose minds and bodies are diseased are to behold in Christ the restorer."[36]

—Medical

The protocol's *Medical Element* involves the right arm of the gospel work. Not only did Jesus go "about all Galilee, teaching in the synagogues, and preaching the gospel of the kingdom," He also went "healing all manner of disease among the people."[37] It is absolutely necessary that we understand the rigid distinction between this *Galilee Protocol* element and modern *allopathic*[38] *medicine.* It has to be clear and obvious that this is the work of the God of heaven, and not the god of Ekron.

Ellen White once said,

> "I tried to make it plain that sanitarium physicians and helpers were to cooperate with God in combating disease not only through the use of natural remedial agencies He has placed within our reach, but also by encouraging their patients to lay hold of divine strength through obedience to the commandments of God."[39]

"Use nature's remedies,—water, sunshine, and fresh air. Do not use drugs. Drugs never heal; they only change the features of the disease."

—Paulson Collection, p. 17

Referring to Loma Linda, she writes,

> "It is in the order of God that this property has been secured, and He has given instruction that a school should be connected with the sanitarium. A special work is to be done there in qualifying young men and young women to be efficient medical missionary workers. They are to be taught how to treat the sick without the use of drugs."[40]

"Let *Seventh-day Adventist* medical workers remember that the Lord God omnipotent reigneth. Christ is the greatest Physician that ever trod

---

[36] Ellen G. White, *Counsels on Health*, p. 346. Emphasis added.

[37] Matthew 4:23.

[38] "*Allopathy*" is a term that refers to the mainstream medical system using pharmacology, radiation, and surgery to treat disease.

[39] Ellen G. White, *The Review and Herald*, June 21, 1906.

[40] Ellen G. White, *Letter 274*, 1906.

the sin-cursed earth. The Lord would have His people come to Him for their power of healing. He will baptize them with His Holy Spirit and fit them for a service that will make them a blessing in restoring the spiritual and physical health of those who need healing."[41]

"O how great are the possibilities that He has placed within our reach! He says, 'Whatsoever ye shall ask the Father in My name, He will give it to you.' He promises to come to us as a Comforter, to bless us. Why do we not believe these promises? That which we lack in faith we make up by the use of drugs. Let us give up the drugs, believing that Jesus does not desire us to be sick, and that if we live in accordance to the principles of health reform, He will keep us well."[42]

"The same power that upholds nature is working also in man. The same great laws that guide alike the star and the atom control human life. The laws that govern the heart's action, regulating the flow of the current of life to the body, are the laws of the mighty Intelligence that has the jurisdiction of the soul. From Him all life proceeds. Only in harmony with Him can be found its true sphere of action. For all the objects of His creation the condition is the same,—a life sustained by receiving the life of God, a life exercised in harmony with the Creator's will. To transgress His law, physical, mental, or moral, is to place one's life out of harmony with the universe, to introduce discord, anarchy and ruin."[43]

"There are many ways of practicing the healing art, but there is only one that Heaven approves. God's remedies are the simple agencies of nature, that will not tax or debilitate the system with their powerful properties."

—Counsels on Health, p. 323.

"We must have medical instructors who will teach the science of healing without the use of drugs... We are to prepare a company of workers who will follow Christ's methods."[44]

"God's people are to be genuine medical missionaries. They are to learn to minister to the needs of soul and body. They should know how to give the simple treatments that do so much to relieve pain and remove disease. They should be familiar with the principles of health reform, that they may show others how, by right habits of eating, drinking, and dressing, disease may be prevented, and health regained.

---

[41] Ellen G. White, *The Medical Evangelist*, Vol. 2, No. 1, 1910.

[42] Ellen G. White, *Manuscript 169*, July 12, 1902.

[43] Ellen G. White, *Medical Ministry*, p. 10.

[44] Ibid, p. 75.

> Demonstration of the value of the principles of health reform will do much toward removing prejudice against our evangelistic work. The Great Physician, the originator of medical missionary work, will bless everyone who will go forward humbly and trustfully, seeking to impart the truth for our time."[45]

"We cannot heal. We cannot change the diseased conditions of the body. But it is our part, as medical missionaries, as workers together with God, to use the means He has provided. Then we should pray that He will bless these agencies. We do believe in God; we believe in a God who hears and answers prayer."[46] Ellen White wrote:

> "The treatment we gave when the sanitarium was first established required earnest labor to combat disease. We did not use drug concoctions; we followed hygienic methods. The work was blessed by God. It was a work in which the human instrumentality could cooperate with God in saving life. There should be nothing put into the human system that would leave its baleful influence behind. And to carry out the light on this subject, to practice hygienic treatment, and to educate on altogether different lines of treating the sick, was the reason given me why we should have sanitariums established in various localities."[47]

"Drug medications have their origin in perverted knowledge—knowledge supposed by man to be wonderful, but that God did not mean that they should have."

—Letter to S. N. Haskell, 1898.

Basic Requirements of the Medical Element—

- The principles of health and healing we use must be wholly consistent with obedience to God's laws. "Health is a result of the obedience to law."[48] "The Lord has made it part of His plan that man's reaping shall be according to his sowing."[49]
- Medical missionary work must show Christ's loving character. "Christ is the same compassionate physician now that He was during His earthly ministry."[50] We're His hands and feet–His

[45] Ellen G. White, *Welfare Ministry*, p. 127.
[46] Ellen G. White, *Medical Ministry*, p. 13.
[47] Ellen G. White, *Manuscript Releases*, Vol. 21, p. 289.
[48] Ellen G. White, *The Ministry of Healing*, p. 128.
[49] Ellen G. White, *Healthy Living*, p. 25.
[50] Ellen G. White, *The Ministry of Healing*, p. 223.

ambassadors. We do not heal. God does. We constantly point to Christ, to His love, and to His healing power.

- Medical missionaries do not *practice allopathic medicine.* They follow, promote, and demonstrate basic hygienic health principles. They educate about basic hygienic health techniques. They assist people with basic hygienic health practices.
- Participating licensed medical professionals must fully support the *Galilee Protocol.* Their training and license privileges affords them a good opportunity to help in the training of medical missionaries; provide diagnostic expertise; work with difficult cases; and safely transition patients away from drug medications. We value our professional friends.

"God does not at one time send a message of warning, and later another message encouraging a movement against which He had previously given warning. His messages do not contradict one another. Cautions have been given that should cause our brethren to stop and consider their course."

—Series B, No. 5, P. 45, 1905

CHAPTER TWELVE

Directive One—City-Centric

The day was sunny and hot. Abraham was sitting outside by the door of his tent. Far in the distance he saw them—three messengers on their way to the cities of the plain. He didn't know it then, but they were the three angels.

While visiting Abraham, these messengers shared the nature of their divine mission. God said, "The cry of Sodom and Gomorrah is great, and because their sin is very grievous, I will go down now, and see whether they have done altogether according to the cry of it."[1]

The city-dwellers of Sodom and Gomorrah were not wholly ignorant of God's laws, or His past dealings with wonton wickedness. They knew about the wicked generation destroyed by the flood. They knew God manifested His wrath in that storm of judgment. Yet they followed the same wicked path of the antediluvian world.[2]

They also knew Abraham—how he, despite impossible odds, rescued Lot and the rest of the captives from the Elamites. They knew full-well that Abraham's victory was a blessing from God because of his

---

[1] Genesis 18:20-21.

[2] Ellen G. White, *Patriarchs and Prophets*, p. 157.

faithfulness. His noble and unselfish spirit (so foreign to the self-seeking inhabitants of Sodom) gave evidence to the superiority of his religion.[3]

Still, they openly defied God and His law. They delighted in violence. Sodom's mirth and revelry, feasting and drunkenness, and vile passions were unrestrained.

— Extravagant Patience and Mercy

God already knew the measure of Sodom and Gomorrah's guilt. His trip to the cities was not for the sake of His own enlightenment. He already knew the condition of each heart. He knew the terrible necessity for divine judgments to check sin. But before bringing judgment upon the transgressors "He [would express] Himself after the manner of men, that the justice of His dealings might be understood."[4]

Not only would God go there Himself to examine their case, He would show that "though God is strict to mark iniquity and to punish transgression, He takes no delight in vengeance. The work of destruction in a 'strange work' to Him who is infinite in love."[5]

The *give and take* exchange between the Lord and Abraham about the number of faithful souls needed to spare Sodom, showed God's extravagant patience and mercy. His following through with the destruction of those wicked cities showed that:

> "The non-execution of the penalty of sin would be a crime in the divine administration. God is a judge, the Avenger of justice... He cannot dispense with His law, He cannot do away with its smallest item in order to meet and pardon sin. The rectitude, justice, and moral excellence of the law must be maintained and vindicated before the heavenly universe and the unfallen worlds."[6]

We need to understand this context if we are to do the work God has assigned to our church. Those *three angel messengers* are again mighty heralds of divine judgment—sent to the world today. Like the cities of the plain, our great cities have passed the limits of divine forbearance. God is again ready to kindle the fires of vengeance like on the vale of Siddim.

---

[3] Ibid.

[4] Ibid., pp. 139, 160.

[5] Ibid., p. 139.

[6] Ellen G. White, *Manuscript 145*, December 30, 1897.

— Bringing it Home to Israel

The history of Sodom and Gomorrah proved a fitting allegory in the days of Christ's mission to the nation of Israel. As He sent the twelve to the lost sheep of the house of Israel, He spoke of any city that might not receive them. He said, "Verily I say unto you, it shall be more tolerable for the land of Sodom and Gomorrah in the day of judgment, then for that city."[7]

As we previously noted in chapter one,[8] Tyre and Sidon were renown cities—also targets for divine wrath. Jesus spoke of certain cities of Israel in terms of Tyre, Sidon, and Sodom.

> "Then began He to upbraid the cities wherein most of His mighty works were done, because they repented not: Woe unto thee, Chorazin! woe unto thee, Bethsaida! for if the mighty works, which were done in you, had been done in Tyre and Sidon, they would have repented long ago in sackcloth and ashes. But I say unto you, It shall be more tolerable for Tyre and Sidon at the day of judgment, than for you. And thou, Capernaum, which art exalted unto heaven, shalt be brought down to hell: for if the mighty works, which have been done in thee, had been done in Sodom, it would have remained until this day. But I say unto you, that it shall be more tolerable for the land of Sodom in the day of judgment, than for thee."[9]

Like in the days of old, it is not enough for God to show His commitment to righteousness and justice. He also has to show extravagant patience and mercy. He will first send warnings mixed with clear demonstrations of His extravagant love. We are His ambassadors in this work. This time, the three angels bring their messages though human instruments. God has given us clear and specific instruction and examples on how we are to do this. It is the *Galilee Protocol.*

Observe that Christ did not direct these warnings to the heathen or the pagan. They were to the cities of Galilee—the "Christian nation" of His day. Israel's probation[10] was fast closing. Rome's armies would soon plant their banner in the Holy Ground just outside Jerusalem's city wall. That was the context of this warning:

> "As it was in the days of Lot; they did eat, they drank, they bought, they sold, they planted, they builded; But the same day that Lot went out of Sodom it rained fire and brimstone from heaven, and destroyed *them* all. Even thus shall it be in the day when the Son of man is

---

[7] Matthews 10:15.

[8] Chapter One, *A Tale of Three Mountains.*

[9] Matthew 11:20-24.

[10] See the seventy-week prophecy in Daniel 9:24-27.

> revealed. In that day, he which shall be upon the housetop, and his stuff in the house, let him not come down to take it away: and he that is in the field, let him likewise not return back. Remember Lot's wife."[11]

— Bringing It Home to Us

So here, Jesus brings it to our house. The *abomination of desolation* spoken of by Daniel[12] was soon to be placed in connection with the destruction of Jerusalem and the temple—but not that only. He links it to an end-time placing of the *abomination of desolation*—one to take *place in the day when the Son of man is revealed.* It is in this connection that we read:

> "The time is not far distant, when, like the early disciples, we shall be forced to seek a refuge in desolate and solitary places. As the siege of Jerusalem by the Roman armies was the signal for flight to the Judean Christians, so the assumption of power on the part of our nation [the United States] in the decree enforcing the papal sabbath will be a warning to us. It will then be time to leave the large cities, *preparatory to leaving the smaller ones* for retired homes in secluded places among the mountains."[13]

The parallels are fascinating. Three angels come to Abraham with three messages. The *first* one (given by Christ Himself) was concerning the everlasting gospel—"Sarah thy wife, shall bear thee a son indeed; and thou shalt call his name Isaac: and I will establish my covenant with him for an everlasting covenant, and with his seed after him."[14] This is what the *Angel* told Abraham—and without question: Isaac typified Christ.

The other two angels carried the second and third messages to the faithful *still in Sodom*. They warned that because of the wickedness of the city, God would destroy it with fire and brimstone; and basically[15] said (to those who would): "Come out of her my people, that ye be not partakers of her sins, and that ye receive not of her plagues."[16]

Lot and his family were accustomed to city life. Apprehensive about the angel's instruction to "flee to the mountains,"[17] he asked if they might go instead to one of the smaller cities.[18] This the angel allowed, but the

---

[11] Luke 17:28-32.

[12] Daniel 9:27.

[13] Ellen G. White, *Maranatha*, p. 180. Emphasis added.

[14] Genesis 17:19.

[15] Compare Genesis 19:24-25 to Revelation 14:9-11.

[16] Compare Genesis 19:12-15 to Revelation 14 and 18.

[17] Genesis 19:17.

[18] Genesis 19:20.

arrangement proved only a temporary one. Before long, Lot left Zoar too, dwelling in the cave of a mountain.

It was just as Christ told the disciples concerning the destruction of Jerusalem. Lot and his family were to hasten—to leave quickly—not look back. Because they were leaving too slowly, the angels grabbed them by the hand and set them outside the city.[19] Lot's wife did look back; and instantly she became a pillar of salt.[20] Christ warns the final generation to *remember what happened to Lot's wife.* [21]

> **"In the darkness of misapprehension of God that is enshrouding the world. Men are losing their knowledge of His character. It has been misunderstood and misinterpreted. At this time a message from God is to be proclaimed, a message illuminating in its influence and saving in its power. His character is to be made known. Into the darkness of this world is to be shed the light of His glory, the light of His goodness, mercy, and truth."**
>
> **—Christ Object Lessons, p. 415.**

— City-Centric

The first directive is that the *Galilee Protocol* must be *City-Centric.* "Jesus went about all Galilee, teaching in the synagogues, and preaching the gospel of the kingdom, and healing all manner of disease among the people."[22] Jesus said specifically, "I must preach the kingdom of God to [the cities], for therefore am I sent."[23] Luke says that Jesus "went throughout every city and village, preaching and shewing the glad tidings of the kingdom of God."[24]

> "The work in the cities is the essential work for this time. When the cities are worked as God would have them, the result will set into operation a mighty movement such as we have not yet witnessed. God calls for self-sacrificing men converted to the truth to let their light shine forth in

[19] Genesis 19:14-16.
[20] Genesis 19:26.
[21] Luke 17:32.
[22] Matthew 4:23.
[23] Luke 4:43.
[24] Luke 8:1.

clear, distinct rays."[25]

"As a people we need to hasten the work in the cities, which has been hindered for a lack of workers and means and a spirit of consecration. At this time, the people of God need to turn their hearts fully to Him; for the end of all things is at hand. They need to humble their minds, and be attentive to the will of the Lord, working with earnest desire to do that which God has shown must be done to warn the cities of their impending doom."[26]

"O that God's people had a sense of the impending destruction of thousands of cities, now almost given to idolatry."[27] "When God shall bid His angels loose the winds, there will be such a scene of strife as no pen can picture... A moment of respite has been graciously given us of God. Every power lent us of heaven is to be used in doing the work assigned us by the Lord for those who are perishing in ignorance... God's people should make a mighty intercession to Him for help now. And they must put their whole energies into the effort to proclaim the truth during the respite that has been granted."[28] "In this work all the angels of heaven are ready to cooperate. All the resources of heaven are at the command of those who are seeking to save the lost."[29] "Angels have long been waiting for human agents... to cooperate with them in the great work to be done."[30]

"I was shown God's people waiting for some change to take place,—a compelling power to take hold of them. But they will be disappointed, for they are wrong. They must act; they must take hold of the work themselves. The scenes which are passing before us are of sufficient magnitude to cause us to arouse, and urge the truth home to the hearts of all who will listen. The harvest of the earth is nearly ripe."

—Testimonies, vol. 1, p. 261.

---

25 Ellen G. White, *Medical Ministry*, p. 304.
26 Ellen G. White, *Evangelism*, p. 30.
27 Ibid., p. 29.
28 Ellen G. White, *The Review and Herald*, November 23, 1905.
29 Ellen G. White, *Christ's Object Lessons*, p. 197.
30 Ellen G. White, *The Acts of the Apostles*, p. 154.

Five Components of the City-Centric Directive—

Starts at the Church: When Jesus would enter a city, He would go to the synagogue. This was an early priority. The record says, "He came to Nazareth... and as His custom was, He went to the synagogue on the Sabbath day, and stood up to read."[31]

Later, they came to Capernaum; and straightway on the Sabbath day He entered into the synagogue and taught.[32] Luke says that "Jesus returned of the Spirit to Galilee... and He taught in their synagogues, being glorified of all."[33]

When entering the city-field, workers should go to the local *Seventh-day Adventist* churches to recruit workers there. The church should become a training school,[34] and medical missionary work should be part of every church.[35] In the church there should be well-organized companies of workers to labor in the vicinity.[36]

Health Reform: "The principles of health reform are to be promulgated as a part of the work in the cities."[37] "Gospel workers should be able to give instruction in the principles of healthful living... Thousands are in need and would gladly receive instruction concerning simple methods of treating the sick—methods that are taking the place of the use of poisonous drugs."[38]

Door-to-door: "The purest unselfishness is to be shown by our workers as, with knowledge and experience gained by practical work, they go out to give treatments to the sick. As they go from house to house, they will find access to many hearts. Many will be reached who otherwise never would have heard the gospel message."[39]

"As the canvasser goes from place to place, he will find many who are sick. He should have a practical knowledge of the causes of disease and should understand how to give simple treatment, that he may relieve the suffering ones. More than this, he should pray in faith and simplicity for the sick, pointing them to the Great Physician."[40]

---

[31] Luke 4:16.
[32] Mark 1:21.
[33] Luke 4:14-15.
[34] Ellen G. White, *The Ministry of Healing*, p. 149.
[35] Ellen G. White, *Counsels on Health*, p. 514.
[36] Ellen G. White, *Welfare Ministry*, p. 107.
[37] Ellen G. White, *Evangelism*, p. 533.
[38] Ellen G. White, *The Ministry of Healing*, p. 146.
[39] Ellen G. White, *Welfare Ministry*, p. 125.
[40] Ellen G. White, *Counsels on Health*, pp. 463-464.

City-Centers: "In every city where we have a church, there needs to be a place where treatment can be given."[41] These city centers are to be useful for cooking schools[42] and reading libraries.[43] They should be a place to prepare simple, healthful, and inexpensive foods.[44] They should be small[45] and scattered throughout the larger cities.[46]

"Not only on health and temperance topics [should the people be taught] but also on other appropriate Bible subjects. As the people are taught to preserve health, many opportunities will be found to sow seeds of the gospel of the kingdom."[47] "True religion and the laws of health go hand in hand."[48]

> **"I was plainly instructed that there should be a decided change from past methods of working... I urge that companies be organized and diligently trained to labor in our important cities. These workers should go two by two, and then from time to time all should meet together to relate their experiences, to pray, and to plan how to reach the people quickly, and thus if possible redeem time... From city to city the work is to be carried quickly. Let companies be quickly organized to go out two by two, and labor in the spirit of Christ, following His plan."**
>
> **—Paulson Collection, p. 69.**

Country Outposts: The small city centers "will serve as feeders"[49] to outposts in the country. "We are not to erect large buildings in which to care for the sick, because God has plainly indicated that the sick can be better cared for outside the cities."[50] These must be outside the cities,[51] should

[41] Ibid., p. 468.
[42] Ibid., p. 443.
[43] Ibid., p. 482.
[44] Ibid., p. 493.
[45] Ellen G. White, *Testimonies for the Church*, vol. 7, p. 60.
[46] Ellen G. White, *Counsels on Health*, p. 485.
[47] Ibid., p. 481.
[48] Ellen G. White, *Testimonies for the Church*, vol. 7, p. 137.
[49] Ellen G. White, *Counsels on Health*, p. 488.
[50] Ibid.
[51] Ellen G. White, *Medical Ministry*, p. 159.

be associated with agriculture,[52] and have teaching facilities.[53] They should be small[54] homelike[55] facilities in pleasant places.

Christ would lead people out of the cities. Coming out of Nazareth, Jesus went "into a desert place apart: and when the people heard thereof, they followed Him on foot, *out of the cities*."[56] He ministered to them in mountain places,[57] sea-sides retreats,[58] and desert places.[59] In these places He would teach, and preach, and heal.

> **"The end is near, stealing upon us stealthfully, imperceptibly, like the noiseless approach of a thief in the night. May the Lord grant that we no longer sleep as do others, but that we will watch and be sober. The truth is soon to triumph gloriously, and all who now choose to be laborers together with God, will triumph with it. The time is short; the night soon cometh when no man can work."**
>
> **— Evangelism, p. 692.**

[52] Ellen G. White, *Counsels on Health*, p. 223.
[53] Ibid., pp. 242-243.
[54] Ibid., p. 255.
[55] Ibid., p. 211.
[56] Matthew 14:13-14. Emphasis added.
[57] Matthew 5:1-3.
[58] Luke 5:1-3.
[59] Luke 4:42.

CHAPTER THIRTEEN

Directive Two—Missionarial

Jesus said, "Go." It's an acton verb. It's not rhetorical. It's not proverbial. It's not even a semi-action verb. Jesus used it as a hyper-action verb. It's extreme. We know this because of the effect it had on His disciples. That word transformed them from disciples to missionarial apostles.

According to early historians,[1] Andrew was a missionary to modern-day Georgia and Bulgaria near Turkey. Bartholomew (Nathanael) was a missionary to India. James (son of Alphaeus) was a local missionary to Jerusalem; and James (son of Zebedee) was also a local missionary—to Judea.

John (son of Zebedee) was missionarial to Asia; Levi Matthew to areas in what is now Iran. Simon Peter was a missionary to Pontus, Galatia, Cappadocia, Betania, Italy, and Asia. Philip (from Bethsaida) was a missionary to areas now in Turkey; and Simon (the Zealot) to Jerusalem.

Thaddaeus (Judas, son of James) went to the surrounding Mesopotamian region—Iraq, Syria, Turkey, Iran. Thomas worked areas now part of Iran, Afghanistan and India. Matthias was also a local missionary in Jerusalem; and finally Paul—he was missionarial to Croatia, Italy, and

[1] Hippolytus of Rome, Eusebius of Caesarea, and Josephus of Jerusalem. See footnote #2 for source of this summery.

Spain. Paul preached the gospel for thirty-five years before being beheaded in Rome.

The apostles went where they were needed. It wasn't just about reaching out to neighbors and holding occasional evangelistic efforts at the local church. These are good things to do; but they are only semi-action behaviors. Christ's disciples today desperately need to become hyper-action *missionaries*. It was important back in the days of the thirteen apostles too—so important they risked everything. While many of them were martyred: *all* of them were missionaries. This was what being a disciple of Jesus required! They risked their lives. They forsook the norms of society. They traveled to the cities that needed them.[2]

The point is this: following Jesus is not a spectator sport. It's a point we all know; but our knowing is mostly theoretical—but not so with Peter, or John, or Paul. It was not so with countless millions through the centuries—the Waldensians, the Reformers, the Millerites. And it was not so with Enoch.

—Missionaries from the Mountains

The Waldenses were persecuted because they refused to contaminate their faith with the teachings of men.

> "Hundreds of years before the Reformation, they possessed the entire Bible in manuscript in their native tongue. They had the truth unadulterated, and this rendered them the special objects of hatred and persecution. They declared the Church of Rome to be the apostate Babylon of the Apocalypse, and at the peril of their lives they stood up to resist her corruptions... Through the ages of darkness and apostacy, there were Waldenses who denied the supremacy of Rome, who rejected image worship as idolatry, and who kept the true Sabbath."[3]

First, they had to flee from the cities to dwell in the plains. Later, they had to go to the safety of the mountains and caves. Doesn't this sound familiar?

It would have been easy for them to justify secluded lives. But Christ had said "Go." This they could not neglect!

---

[2] Tony Mariot, Researcher Biblical Antiquities as University of Oxford. Updated December 25, 2018. Accessed 2-7-19 at www.quora.com. (https://www.quora.com/Where-did-each-of-the-apostles-travel-after-Christs-ascension).

[3] Ellen G. White, *The Spirit of Prophecy*, vol. 1, p. 70. A primary source of evidence of Waldensian Sabbathkeeping during the first half of the thirteenth century comes from a collection of five books written against the Cathars and Waldensians about 1241-1244 by Dominican inquisitor Father Moneta of Cremona in northern Italy. See Moneta and Tommaso Agostino Ricchini, Venerabilis Patris Monetæ Cremonensis ordinis prædicatorum S. P. Dominico Æqualis adversus Catharos et Valdenses libri quinque: Quos ex manuscriptis codd. Vaticano, Bononiensi, ac Neapolitano (Rome: 1743; reprinted, Ridgewood, N.J.: 1964), pp. 475-477. See a summery by P. Gerard Damsteegt, Were Waldensians Sabbath-keepers? Adventist World, (https://www.adventistworld.org/were-waldensians-sabbath-keepers/). Accessed 2-8-2019.

> "The Waldenses felt that God required more of them than merely to maintain the truth in their own mountains; that a solemn responsibility rested upon them to let their light shine forth to those who were in darkness; that by the mighty power of God's word, they were to break the bondage which Rome had imposed... The missionaries began their labors in the plains and valleys at the foot of their own mountains, going forth two and two, as Jesus sent out his disciples. These co-laborers were not always together, but often met for prayer and counsel, thus strengthening each other in the faith... With naked feet and in coarse garments, these missionaries passed through great cities, and traversed provinces far removed from their native valleys. Everywhere they scattered the precious seed. Churches sprang up in their path, and the blood of martyrs witnessed for the truth."[4]

The Waldensians loved the Lord; and the truths of Scripture meant everything to them. "They believed it unfolded the perils and glories of the future... As the light illuminated their understanding and made glad their hearts, they longed to shed its beams upon those who were in the darkness of papal error."[5]

—A Missionary that Walked with God

The Bible tells of Enoch who was translated because he pleased God.[6] He walked with God.[7] During his activities, Enoch steadfastly maintained his communion with God.[8]

He had no written Scripture to use;[9] but by his constant communion with God, and his "hungering and thirsting for that divine knowledge which God alone can impart," God opened the future to him.[10] He was the first prophet—and he became a preacher of righteousness.[11] "In the land where Cain had sought to flee from the divine presence, the prophet of God made known the wonderful scenes that had passed before his vision."[12]

Jude gives the brunt of Enoch's message: "The Lord comes with ten thousand of His saints to execute judgment upon all."[13] This sounds familiar too.

---

[4] Ellen G. White. *The Spirit of Prophecy*, vol. 1, p. 76.

[5] Ibid., p. 77.

[6] Hebrews 11:5.

[7] Genesis 5:24

[8] Ellen G. White, *Gospel Workers*, p. 52.

[9] Ellen G. White, *Seventh-day Adventist Bible Commentary*, vol. 1, p. 1087.

[10] Ellen G. White, *Gospel Workers*, p. 52.

[11] Ellen G. White, *Patriarchs and Prophets*, p. 86.

[12] Ellen G. White. *Gospel Workers*, p. 52.

[13] Jude 1:14-15. Paraphrased by author.

"He was a fearless reprover of sin. While he preached the love of God in Christ to the people of his time, and pleaded with them to forsake their evil ways, he rebuked the prevailing iniquity and warned the men of his generation that judgment would surely be visited upon the transgressor. It was the Spirit of Christ that spoke through Enoch; that Spirit is manifested, not alone in utterances of love, compassion, and entreaty; it is not smooth things only that are spoken by holy men. God puts into the heart and lips of His messengers truths to utter that are keen and cutting as a two-edged sword.

"The power of God that wrought with His servant was felt by those who heard. Some gave heed to the warning, and renounced their sins; but the multitudes mocked at the solemn message, and went on more boldly in their evil ways. The servants of God are to bear a similar message to the world in the last days, and it will also be received with unbelief and mockery. The antediluvian world rejected the warning words of him who walked with God. So will the last generation make light of the warnings of the Lord's messengers."[14]

Enoch would be surrounded by people—working to help them by instruction and example; and then he would withdraw to a place of quiet communion with God. Sometimes he would exclude himself from all society.[15] The busier Enoch was, the stronger were his prayers.

"[Enoch] did not make his abode with the wicked. He did not locate in Sodom, thinking to save Sodom. He placed himself and his family where the atmosphere would be as pure as possible. Then at times he went forth to the inhabitants of the world with his God-given message. Every visit he made to the world was painful to him. He saw and understood something of the leprosy of sin. After proclaiming his message, he always took back with him to his place of retirement some who had received the warning. Some of these became overcomers, and died before the flood came. But some had lived so long in sin that they could not endure righteousness."[16]

"As God's commandment-keeping people we must leave the cities. As did Enoch, we must work in the cities but not dwell in them."[17] The cities are to be worked from outposts. Said the messenger of God, "Shall not the cities be warned? Yes, not by God's people living in them but by their visiting them, to warn them of what is coming upon the earth."[18]

"The question is asked, How shall we reach the people? As Enoch reached them. He did not live with them in close companionship lest he should become like them by hearing their godless words and their

[14] Ellen G. White, *Patriarchs and Prophets*, p. 86.
[15] Ellen G. White. *Gospel Workers*, p. 52.
[16] Ellen G. White, *Seventh-day Adventist Bible Commentary*, vol. 1, pp. 1087-1088.
[17] Ellen G. White, *Evangelism*, pp. 77-78.
[18] Ellen G. White, *Selected Messages*, book 2, p. 358.

ambitions projects. He had his retired place to commune with God, to walk with God. And when he came to the cities, he had a message to bear... From his retired place, Enoch came to cities, bore his testimony of warning and reproof, and [then] separated from the wicked to preserve his soul in righteousness, for he had warnings to give of reproof and messages of warning."[19]

—Impediments to Service

A popular hymn goes like this: "*This world is not my home, I'm just passing through. My treasures are laid up, somewhere beyond the blue.*"[20] This idea captures the Bible essence of discipleship, but for most of us it's a platitude. Mostly we are comfortable and content here. As a church we function amazingly well in this modern setting. We are up to date. We're relevant. The Lord's hand has been with us, and it shows. We're decent folks: responsible, busy, we take good care of our family; we're active at church. In this modern age—we're able to juggle both the things of God and the things of the world; or so we seem to think.

The real truth is that living with and near societal norms imposes serious impediments to Christian service; so most of us fall short of our spiritual responsibilities. It's tough to talk about—but Laodicea[21] is real. But the culture of Laodicea does not have to continue forever. Why hasn't the "message of the True Witness accomplished God's design?

> "[It] is because [the people of God] will not receive correction." "Very many feel impatient and jealous because they are frequently disturbed with warnings and reproofs which keep their sins before them." "This message must arouse the people of God from their security and dangerous deception in regard to their real standing before God. This testimony, if received, will arouse to action, and lead to self-abasement, and confession of sins." This alone will answer to the message to the Laodiceans. Wrongs must be reproved, sins must be called sins, and iniquity must be met promptly and decidedly, and put away from among us."[22]

We cannot hope to keep blending our religion with the societal norms in housing, eating, healing, dressing, playing, teaching, working, entertaining, and worshiping. Those who must offer the things of the world to their families are better off not pretending to be Christians.

---

[19] Ellen G. White, *Manuscript 233*, 1902.

[20] The text and tune (I'm Just a Passing Through) are both of unknown origin. Sometimes they are attributed to Albert Edward Brumley (1905-1977), though the first appearance of the song seems to have been in the 1919 *Joyful Meeting in Glory No. 1*, edited by Bertha Davis and published by C. Miller of Mount Sterling, Kentucky.

[21] See Revelation 3:14-22.

[22] Ellen G. White, The *Review and Harold*, September 16, 1873.

> "Can two walk together lest they be agreed?"[23]
> "No man can serve to masters... Ye cannot serve God and mammon."[24]
> "[A] house divided against itself cannot stand."[25]
> "What communion hath light with darkness? And what concord hath Christ with Belial? Or what part hath he that believes with an infidel? And what agreement hath the temple of God with idols? For ye are the temple of the living God... Wherefore come out from among them, and be ye separate, saith the Lord, and touch not the unclean thing, and I will receive you, and I will be a Father to you, and ye shall be my sons and daughters, saith the Lord Almighty."[26]

Jesus tells Laodicea that He would rather for them to be cold than lukewarm.[27] This is the issue with Laodicea. This is the issue with us—and it goes all the way back to the earliest years on our timeline. The world's glitter blinds us; and it deters us from our mission. It causes us to exclude Christ from His own church—and prevents us from even recognizing His absence:

> "The church is in the Laodicean state. The presence of God is not in her midst... Abridge the work, limit your labors, and you remove your Helper. The sickly, unhealthy state of the church reveals a church afraid to work, fearing that self-denial will be required. The presence of the Lord is ever seen where every energy of the church is aroused to meet the spiritual responsibilities. But many of the churches who have had the light of present truth are dwarfed and crippled by the evils existing in their midst, by the selfishness cherished, by spending on self that which should be given to the Lord... Angels of God are sent to measure the temple and the worshipers therein. The Lord looks with sadness upon those who are serving their idols, with no care for the souls perishing in darkness and error. He cannot bless a church who feels it no part of their duty to be laborers together with God. What a terrible thing it is to exclude Christ from His own temple. What a loss to the church![28]

—Missionarial

The second directive of the *Galilee Protocol is that it* must be *missionarial.* This is a staffing plan that is deliberately noncommercial and specifically patterned after the instructions Christ gave when He sent out the *twelve* and *seventy*.

---

[23] Amos 3:3.
[24] Matthew 6:24.
[25] Matthew 12:25.
[26] 2 Corinthians 6:14-18.
[27] Revelation 3:15.
[28] Ellen G. White, *Manuscript 156*, 1898.

Christ left His comfortable home and position in Heaven "to seek and save that which was lost."[29] And while on earth, "the Savior, though possessing 'all power.' never used this power for self-aggrandizement. No dream of earthly conquest, of worldly greatness, marred the perfection of His service for mankind. 'Foxes have holes, and the birds of the air have nests,' He said, 'but the Son of man hath not where to lay His head.' Those who, in response to the call of the hour, have entered the service of the Master Worker, may well study His methods."[30]

"We are nearing the end of this earth's history, and the different lines of God's work are to be carried forward with much more self-sacrifice than is at present manifest. The work for these last days is in a special sense a missionary work. The presentation of present truth, from the first letter of its alphabet to the last, means missionary effort. The work to be done calls for sacrifice at every advance step. From this unselfish service the workers will come forth purified and refined as gold tried in the fire."[31]

> **"If every watchman on the walls of Zion had given the trumpet a certain sound, the world might ere this have heard the warning message. But the work is years behind. While men have slept, Satan has stolen a march upon us."**
>
> **— Evangelism, p. 692.**

"The forces of the enemy of all righteousness are strongly entrenched; only by the power of God can the victory be gained. The conflict before us calls for the exercise of a spirit of self-denial, for distrust of self and for dependence on God alone, for the wise use of every opportunity for the saving of souls. The Lord's blessing will attend His church as they advance unitedly, revealing to a world lying in the darkness of error the beauty of holiness as manifested in a Christlike spirit of self-sacrifice, in an exaltation of the divine rather than the human, and in loving and untiring service for those so much in need of the blessings of the gospel."[32]

"When the Lord sees His people restricting their imaginary wants and practicing self-denial, not in a mournful, regretful spirit, as Lot's wife left Sodom, but joyfully, for Christ's sake, and because it is the right

---

29 Luke 19:10.

30 Ellen G. White, *Prophets and Kings*, pp. 71-72. Quoting Matthew 8:20.

31 Ellen G. White, *Counsels on Health*, p. 216.

32 Ellen G. White, *Prophets and Kings*, p. 74.

thing to do, the work will go forward with power."[33] "Let every church member practice self-denial... The presence of the Lord is ever seen where every energy of the church is aroused to meet the spiritual responsibilities."[34]

> "The purest unselfishness is to be shown by our workers as, with knowledge and experience gained by practical work, they go out to give treatments to the sick. As they go from house to house, they will find access to many hearts. Many will be reached who otherwise would never have heard the gospel message."[35]
>
> "Many have lost the sense of eternal realities, lost the similitude of God, and they hardly know whether they have souls to be saved or not. They have neither faith in God nor confidence in man. As they see one with no inducement of earthly praise or compensation come into their wretched homes, ministering to the sick, feeding the hungry, clothing the naked, and tenderly pointing all to Him whose love and pity the human worker is but the messenger—as they see this, their hearts are touched. Gratitude springs up. Faith is kindled. They see that God cares for them, and they are prepared to listen as His Word is opened."[36]

"There are those, even among Seventh-day Adventists, who are under the reproof of the word of God, because of the way they acquired their property and use it, acting as if they own it, and created it, without an eye to the glory of God, and without earnest prayer to direct them in acquiring or using it. They are grasping at a serpent, which will sting them as an adder."

— Counsels on Stewardship, p. 141.

The Missionarial Directive Has Three Components—

Purseless: A funding arrangement for *missionarial* participants that relies upon field-local hospitality for personal food and supplies. To the twelve Jesus said, "Provide neither gold, nor silver, nor brass in your purses, Nor script for your journey, neither two coats, neither shoes, nor yet staves: for the workman is worthy of his meat."[37] And to the seventy

---

[33] Ellen G. White, *Testimonies for the Church*, vol. 8, p. 53.
[34] Ellen G. White, *Notebook Leaflets*, vol. 1, p. 99.
[35] Ellen G. White, *Welfare Ministry*, p. 125.
[36] Ellen G. White, *Evangelism*, p. 517.
[37] Matthew 10:9-10.

He likewise said, "Carry neither purse, nor script, nor shoes: and salute no man by the way."[38]

Nestless: A housing arrangement for *missionarial* participants that relies upon field-local hospitality. To the twelve Jesus said, "Into whatsoever city or town ye shall enter, inquire who in it is worthy; and there abide till ye go thence."[39] And to the seventy He likewise said, "into whatsoever house ye enter, first say, Peace be to this house... and in the same house remain, eating and drinking such things as they give: for the laborer is worthy of his hire. Go not from house to house."[40]

Disinterest: There is to be no intent for personal gain. Selflessness; involvement not motivated by personal pecuniary interest—this has to be what distinguishes us. The *Galilee Protocol* is not a business or commercial enterprise. It is to be guarded diligently against all forms of commercialization. *Missionarial* participants are not employees. "All heaven is looking on with intense interest to see what character medical missionary work will assume under the supervision of human beings. Will men make merchandise of God's ordained plan for reaching the dark parts of the earth with a manifestation of His benevolence? Will they cover mercy with selfishness and call it medical missionary work?"[41]

> **"In no way would the Lord be better glorified and the truth more highly honored than for unbelievers to see that the truth has wrought a great and good work upon the lives of naturally covetous and penurious men. If it could be seen that the faith of such had an influence to mold the characters, to change them from close, selfish, overreaching, money-loving men to men who love to do good, who seek opportunity to use their means to bless those who need to be blessed, who visit the widow and fatherless in their affliction, and who keep themselves unspotted from the world, it would be evidence that their religion was genuine."**
>
> **—Testimonies, vol. 2, p. 239.**

---

[38] Luke 10:4.
[39] Luke 10:5.
[40] Matthew 10:11.
[41] Ellen G. White, *Series B*, No. 1, p. 19.

"Satan and his angels will come down with power and signs and lying wonders to deceive those who dwell on the earth, and if possible the very elect. The crisis is right upon us. Is it to paralyze the energies of those who have a knowledge of the truth? Is the influence of the powers of deception so far reaching that the influence of truth will be overpowered?"

— Evangelism, p. 692.

CHAPTER FOURTEEN

Directive Three—Provocative

The earth was young. "The hills were crowned with majestic trees supporting the fruit-laden branches of the vine. The vast, gardenlike plains were clothed with verdure, and sweet with the fragrance of a thousand flowers... Gold, silver, and precious stones existed in abundance."[1]

Humanity was in its infancy. The race "yet retained much of its early vigor. But a few generations had passed since Adam had access to the tree which was to prolong life; and man's existence was still measured by centuries."[2] It was the prime of life. Physically, men were of great stature and strength. Intellectually, they were renown for wisdom; and skilled in the most cunning and wonderful works. But their wickedness grew exceedingly great.

Cain was first a tiller of soil. After he murdered his brother, God cursed him; and the ground no longer yielded its fruit to him.[3] So Cain left his father's house and founded a city. He left the Lord and abandoned the promise of Eden restored. He decided to make the best of his possessions and enjoyment in the earth cursed by sin. He became the father of all who worship the god of this world; and his descendants became

---

[1] Ellen G. White, *Patriarchs and Prophets*, p. 90.

[2] Ibid.

[3] Genesis 4:11, 12.

distinguished in the things that pertain merely to earthly and material progress. They were regardless of God and opposed His purposes for man.[4]

—Sin Without Restraint

In those days, because men lived to nearly a thousand years old, it was easy for sin and rebellion to grow without restraint. Men sought only to gratify the desires of their own proud hearts, and reveled in scenes of pleasure and wickedness. Desiring not to keep God in their knowledge, they soon denied His existence. They adored nature instead of the God of nature. They glorified human genius, worshiped the works of their hands, and taught their children to bow down to carved stone images.[5]

As men put God from their minds, they worship the creatures of their imagination; and so they become more and more debased. They clothed their deities with human attributes and passions—degraded to the forms of sinful humanity.

Amid the prevailing corruption, Enoch, Methuselah, Noah, and many others labored to keep alive the knowledge of the true God and to stay the tide of moral evil.[6] But the Bible says:

> "It came to pass, when men began to multiply on the face of the earth, and daughters were born to them, that the sons of God saw the daughters of the sons of men that they were fair; and they took them wives of all whom they chose... And God saw that the wickedness of man was great in the earth, and that every imagination of the thoughts of his heart was only evil continually... And He said, I will destroy man whom I have created from the face of the earth."[7]

—Preaching Righteousness

The Lord called Noah to be a preacher of righteousness to that wicked generation—to warn them of coming judgment, and that God would destroy the world. His alarmist message was provocative. He faithfully preached this final warning message to those upon whom probation[8] was closing. "God spared not... the old world, but saved Noah [one of eight people], a preacher of righteousness, bringing in the flood upon the world of the ungodly."[9]

---

[4] Ellen G. White, *Patriarch and Prophets*, p. 81.
[5] Ellen G. White, *Patriarch and Prophets*, p. 90.
[6] Ibid., p. 92.
[7] Genesis 6:1-7.
[8] Ellen G. White, *The Great Controversy*, p. 491.
[9] 2 Peter 2:4-5

"Satan, when tempting Eve to disobey God, said to her, 'Ye shall not surely die.'[10] Great men, worldly, honored, and wise men, repeated the same. 'The threatenings of God,' they said, 'are for the purpose of intimidating, and will never be verified. You need not be alarmed. Such an event as the destruction of the world by the God who made it, and the punishment of the beings He has created, will never take place. Be at peace; fear not. Noah is a wild fanatic.' The world made merry at the folly of the deluded old man...

"But Noah stood like a rock amid the tempest. Surrounded by popular contempt and ridicule, he distinguished himself by his holy integrity and unwavering faithfulness. A power attended his words, for it was the voice of God to man through His servant. Connection with God made him strong in the strength of infinite power, while for one hundred and twenty years his solemn voice fell upon the ears of that generation in regard to events, which, so far as human wisdom could judge, were impossible."[11]

—Provocative

The third and fourth directives speak to the distinctive nature of the *Galilee Protocol's* missionary work to the cities. The power of the gospel message is its ability to show God's character to fallen humanity to draw them from sin and into a redeeming relationship with God. The difficulty lies in the sinner's tendency to fragment the divine attributes into two apparently incompatible parts—justice and mercy. Either the sinner sees God as an exacting judge or as an indulging enabler. Both views short circuit the gospel.

Christ came to remedy this very thing. He came to repair the sinner's misconception of God. He came to show us the Father.[12] He came to bear witness to the truth.[13] Of Christ the psalmist declares, "Mercy and truth are met together; righteousness and peace have kissed each other."[14] The apostle John confirms this, "And the Word was made flesh, and dwelt among us, (and we beheld His glory, the glory as of the Only Begotten of the Father,) full of grace and truth."[15]

In Scripture, truth, righteousness and justice are synonymous terms.[16] Says the psalmist about God: "Righteousness and justice are the foundation of Your throne."[17] According to the KJV dictionary, that is what

---

[10] Genesis 3:4.

[11] Ellen G. White, *Patriarch and Prophets*, p. 96.

[12] John 14:9.

[13] John 18:37.

[14] Psalms 85:1.

[15] John 1:14.

[16] Isaiah 59:14.

[17] Psalms 89:14.

righteousness means: "just, accordant to the divine law."[18] Truth means exactness; conformity to rule; real fact of just principle.[19] So we see that Christ came to present the glory of the Father—His character—as the perfect blending of justice and mercy.

The third directive brings out the justice side of God's character. The three angels' messages are earth's final warnings and they boldly assert this side of God. It is the hour of His judgment[20]—and the warning is *provocative*. The third angel sternly warns those who do not comprehend His uncompromising commitment to law and justice: that they "shall drink of the wine of the wrath of God... poured out without mixture into the cup of His indignation; and shall be tormented with fire and brimstone in the presence of the holy angels, and in the presence of the Lamb."[21] But God will reward those who "keep the commandments of God, and the faith of Jesus"[22] with glorious life eternal.

The three angels' messages are provocative. God would have worded them differently if His intent was otherwise. While we usually consider *provocative* to be negative, the KJV dictionary gives more constructive connotations: to call into action; to arouse; to excite; to challenge; to move; to stir up; to induce by motives; to appeal.[23] Given the urgency of the hour, and the high stakes involved—especially as Christ's Spirit is being withdrawn from the world—mercy's tenderest appeal comes in the form of a provocative alarm to wake up those who are running headlong toward eternal annihilation. It is our work to draw the world's attention to this urgent alarm.

> "In a special sense Seventh-day Adventists have been set in the world as watchmen and light-bearers. To them has been entrusted the last warning for a perishing world. On them is shining wonderful light from the Word of God. They have been given a work of the most solemn import,—the proclamation of the first, second, and third angels' messages. There is no other work of so great importance. They are to allow nothing else to absorb their attention.
>
> "The most solemn truths ever entrusted to mortals have been given us to proclaim to the world. The proclamation of these truths is to be our work. The world is to be warned, and God's people are to be true to the trust committed to them...

---

[18] (http://av1611.com/kjbp/kjv-dictionary/righteous.html).
[19] (http://av1611.com/kjbp/kjv-dictionary/truth.html).
[20] Revelation 14:7.
[21] Revelation 14:10.
[22] Revelation 14:12.
[23] (http://av1611.com/kjbp/kjv-dictionary/provoke.html).

"Shall we wait until God's judgments fall upon the transgressor before we tell him how to avoid them? Where is our faith in the Word of God? Must we see things foretold come to pass before we will believe what He has said? In clear, distinct rays light has come to us, showing us that the great day of the Lord is near at hand, 'even at the door.'"[24]

"We are living in the close of this earth's history... Prophecy is fulfilling. Soon Christ will come with power and great glory. We have no time to lose. Let the message sound forth in earnest words of warning... We must persuade men everywhere to repent and flee from the wrath to come. They have souls to save or to lose. Let there be no indifference in this matter. The Lord calls for workers who are filled with an earnest, decided purpose."[25]

"Most startling messages will be borne by men of God's appointment, messages of a character to warn the people, to arouse them. And while some will be provoked by the warning, and led to resist the light and evidence, we are to see from this that we are giving the testing message for this time... We must also have, in our cities, consecrated evangelists through whom a message is to be borne so decidedly as to startle the hearers."[26]

"Agitate, agitate, agitate the public mind. There must be no spiritual stupor now. Bring out important points of truth bearing directly upon genuine conversion."[27]

"Let those who present the truth enter into no controversy. They are to preach the gospel with such faith and earnestness that an interest will be awakened. By the words they speak, the prayers they offer, the influence they exert, they are to sow seeds that will bear fruit to the glory of God. There is to be no wavering. The trumpet is to give a certain sound. The attention of the people is to be called to the third angel's message. Let not God's servants act like men walking in their sleep, but like men preparing for the coming of Christ."[28]

"We are under obligation to declare faithfully the whole counsel of God. We are not to make less prominent the special truths that have separated us from the world, and made us what we are; for they are fraught with eternal interests. God has given us light in regard to the things that are now taking place in the last remnant of time, and with pen and voice we are to proclaim the truth to the world, not in a tame, spiritless way, but in demonstration of the Spirit and power of God."[29]

In the year 1900, Sister White called for a more direct approach to presenting the final message. She said,

---

[24] Ellen G. White, *Evangelism*, pp. 119, 120.
[25] Ibid., p. 217.
[26] Ibid., p. 168.
[27] Ellen G. White, *Letter 34*, October 12, 1875.
[28] Ellen G. White, *Evangelism*, p. 119.
[29] Ibid., p. 121.

> "I am more and more decided we must make one more final effort to get the truth in clearness before the people. They must have another opportunity to hear the reasons of our faith, straight and clear from the living oracles. But I know we have made a mistake in not presenting the strongest points of our faith—the Sabbath question as the first subject and then bring in the subjects that are not a life and death question.[30]

"The power which stirred the people so mightily in the 1844 movement will again be revealed. The third angel's message will go forth, not in whispered tones, but with a loud voice."[31]

"Let the gospel message ring through our churches, summoning them to universal action. Let the members of the churches have increased faith, gaining zeal from their unseen, heavenly allies, from a knowledge of their exhaustless resources, from the greatness of the enterprise in which they are engaged, and from the power of their Leader. Those who place themselves under God's control, to be led and guided by Him, will catch the steady trend of the events ordained by Him to take place. Inspired with the Spirit of Him who gave His life for the life of the world, they will no longer stand still in impotency, pointing to what they cannot do. Putting on the armor of heaven, they will go forth into the warfare, willing to do and dare for God, knowing that His omnipotence will supply their need."

—Review and Herald, August 5, 1902.

---

[30] Ellen G. White, *Letter 179*, 1900.
[31] Ellen G. White, *Evangelism*, p. 693.

CHAPTER FIFTEEN

Directive Four—Advocative

Moses "discerned ground for hope where there appeared only discouragement and wrath."[1] Only weeks after God proclaimed His holy law from Sinai, and His chosen people covenanted with Him, they already broke the vital agreement. Grievous sins now separated them from God.

God said to Moses, "Let Me alone, that my wrath may wax hot against them, and that I may consume them: and I will make of thee a great nation."[2] "The words of God, 'Let Me alone,' he understood not to forbid but to encourage intercession, implying that nothing but the prayers of Moses could save Israel, but that if thus entreated, God would spare His people."[3]

The Bible testifies: "Moses besought the Lord His God and said... Turn from Thy fierce wrath, and repent of this evil against Thy people."[4] As God's faithful servant, Moses shows God's attitude as *advocate* when only His attitude as *judge* is apparent.

---

[1] Ellen G. White, *Patriarchs and Prophets*, p. 318.

[2] Exodus 32:10.

[3] Ellen G. White, *Patriarchs and Prophets*, p. 318.

[4] Exodus 32:11.

> "As Moses interceded for Israel, his timidity was lost in his deep interest and love for those for whom he had, in the hands of God, been the means of doing so much. The Lord listened to his pleadings, and granted his unselfish prayer. God had proved His servant; He had tested his faithfulness and his love for that erring, ungrateful people, and nobly had Moses endured the trial. His interest in Israel sprang from no selfish motive. The prosperity of God's chosen people was dearer to him than personal honor, dearer than the privilege of becoming the father of a mighty nation. God was pleased with his faithfulness, his simplicity of heart, and his integrity, and He committed to him, as a faithful shepherd, the great charge of leading Israel to the Promised Land."[5]

Moses' intercession did not entirely release Israel from the consequences of their situation. God told Moses to grind the golden calf into powder and mix it with water and make them drink it. He was then to separate to himself those who were on the Lord's side. The Levites joined him. With their swords they went through the camp. Three thousand men died that day... and then the plague began!

Again Moses went to the Lord and asked that He forgive Israel, saying, and if not, "blot me, I pray Thee, out of Thy book which Thou hast written."[6] Moses could not endure to see Israel rejected by the Lord or for the judgments of God to fall upon them. God told him to return to the people and lead them as He directed, but that an angel (not the Lord Himself) would go before them.

> "In deep sorrow the people buried their dead," and learned that "the divine Presence would no longer accompany them in their journeyings."
>
> "By divine direction, the tent that had served as a temporary place of worship was removed 'afar off from the camp.' This was still further evidence that God had withdrawn His presence from them."[7]

Moses continued to plead with God, and eventually God restored the tokens of His presence.

"'Let Me alone, ... that I may consume them,' were the words of God. If God had purposed to destroy Israel, who could plead for them? How few but would have left the sinners to their fate! How few but would have gladly exchanged a lot of toil and burden and sacrifice, repaid with ingratitude and murmuring, for a position of ease and honor, when it was God Himself that offered the release."[8]

---

[5] Ellen G. White, *Patriarchs and Prophets*, p. 319.

[6] Exodus 32:32.

[7] Ellen G. White, *Patriarchs and Prophets*, p. 327.

[8] Ibid.

Justice does not allow mercy to obscure the consequences of sin. In this age, as probation's close looms ever so near, and God's wrath is soon to visit the wicked cities of our nation: God needs faithful people to show His attitude as *advocate* when only His attitude as *judge* is apparent. The *Galilee Protocol* must be advocative.

—Advocative

Most of the parables of Jesus have a judgment theme. He often said, "And there will be wailing and gnashing of teeth."[9] Given the urgency and the situation, such startling warnings were necessary. They also brought credibility to His work. Consequences are integral to the natural world. Though people try to deceive themselves, they instinctively sense that there will be a day of reckoning. Our guilty natures only add to our sense of foreboding.

Our message to the world is also a startling warning. The *three angels' messages* contain "the most fearful threatening ever addressed to mortals."[10] But like Christ's, our message must be that of an *advocate*. He came to show the world how much He loves us. Our fallen human natures do not easily sense this part of the God equation. Our guilt fills us with fear and condemnation.

While we have to do it in the context of justice and even judgment, our real challenge is to present the love of Christ in an authentic, convincing manner.

> "It is the darkness of misapprehension of God that is enshrouding the world. Men are losing their knowledge of His character. It has been misunderstood and misinterpreted. At this time the message from God is to be proclaimed, a message illuminating in its influence and saving in its power. His character is to be made known. Into the darkness of the world is to be shed the light of His glory, the light of His goodness, mercy and truth."[11]

Jesus was superb at this. "Christ's method alone will give true success in reaching the people. The Savior mingled with men as one who desired their good. He showed His sympathy for them, ministered to their needs, and won their confidence. Then He bade them, 'Follow Me.'"[12] Around Him there "were whole villages where there was not a moan of

---

[9] Matthew 8:12, 13:42, 22:13, 24:51, 25:30, Luke 13:28.

[10] Ellen G. White, *The Great Controversy*, p. 449.

[11] Ellen G. White, *Christ's Object Lessons*, p. 415.

[12] Ellen G. White, *The Ministry of Healing*, p. 143.

sickness in any house; for He had passed through them, and healed all their sick."[13]

It is important to present an accurate picture of the relationship between justice and mercy as it pertains to the character of God and the process of atonement. To illustrate this, consider the vital distinction between Lucifer and Adam.

> "Lucifer in heaven had sinned in the light of God's glory. To him as to no other created being was given a revelation of God's love. Understanding the character of God, knowing His goodness, Satan chose to follow his own selfish will. This choice was final. There was nothing else that God could do to save him. But man was deceived; his mind was darkened by Satan's sophistry. The height and depth of the love of God he did not know. For him there was hope in a knowledge of God's love. By beholding His character he might be drawn back to God."[14]

While justice allows forgiveness in cases of deception, it does not for fully informed, willful and persistent rebellion. "The wrath of God is not declared against unrepentant sinners merely because of the sins they have committed, but because, when called to repent, they choose to continue in resistance, repeating the sins of the past in defiance of the light given them."[15]

> "Through Jesus, God's mercy was manifested to men; but mercy does not set aside justice. The law reveals the attributes of God's character, and not one jot or tittle of it could be changed to meet man in his fallen condition."[16]

—A Second Probation

But justice allows for a limited period of safety from the law's retributive judgment—a sanctuary—in which God gives the guilty the time and means to reconnect with Him. "Infinite wisdom devised a plan of redemption, which places the race on a second probation by giving them another trial."[17] It is this period of safety that poses one of the greatest difficulties in the plan of salvation. It appears to set aside the strict demands of the law—potentially weakening its authority. This is why even the altars and the sanctuary itself needs cleansing on the day of atonement. The whole system tends to accommodate continuing sinfulness. After Calvary, "Satan declared that mercy destroyed justice, that the

---

[13] Ellen G. White, *The Desire of Ages*, p. 241.
[14] Ibid., pp. 761-762.
[15] Ellen G. White, *The Acts of the Apostles*, p. 62.
[16] Ellen G. White, *The Desire of Ages*, p. 762.
[17] Ellen G. White, *Testimonies for the Church*, vol. 3, p. 484.

death of Christ abrogated the Father's law."[18] So provision had to be built into the atonement process to preserve the law's integrity.

> "The transgression of God's law in a single instance, in the smallest particular, is sin. And the non-execution of the penalty of that sin would be a crime in the divine administration. God is a judge, the Avenger of justice... He cannot dispense with His law; He cannot do away with its smallest item in order to meet and pardon sin. The rectitude, justice, and moral excellence of the law must be maintained before the heavenly universe and the worlds unfallen."[19]

Christ's atoning life and death contained all the provisions to preserve the law while also offering a second chance to sinners. Since "the law of God [is] the transcript of the divine character,"[20] and since "the life of Christ on earth was a perfect expression of God's law,"[21] Christ and the law are equal. So, "Christ alone could... make an offering equal to the demand of the law."[22] "Christ has made a sacrifice to satisfy the demands of justice... [the] holy law could not be maintained by any smaller price... [Instead] of the law being abolished to meet sinful man in his fallen condition, it has been maintained in all its sacred dignity."[23] But an inaccurate understanding of atonement theology allows for its substitutionary elements to do damage to the perceived sanctity of the law.

> "Man's substitute and surety must have man's nature, a connection with the human family whom He was to represent, and, as God's ambassador, He must partake of the divine nature, have a connection with the Infinite, in order to manifest God to the world, and be a mediator between God and man. These qualifications were found alone in Christ. Clothing His divinity with humanity, He came to earth to be called the Son of man and the Son of God. He was the surety for man, the ambassador for God—the surety for man to satisfy by His righteousness in man's behalf the demands of the law, and the representative of God to make manifest His character to a fallen race."[24]

Because of Christ's sacrifice, "the church is justified through Him, its representative and head... [The] Father ratifies the contract with His Son, that He will be reconciled to repentant and obedient men, and take them into divine favor through the merits of Christ. Christ guarantees that He will make man 'more precious than fine gold, even a man, than

[18] Ellen G. White, *The Desire of Ages*, p. 762.

[19] Ellen G. White, *Manuscript 145*, December 30, 1897, note of work.

[20] Ellen G. White, *Ministry to the Cities*, p. 30.

[21] Ellen G. White, *Christ's Object Lessons*, p. 315.

[22] Ellen G. White, *Spirit of Prophecy*, vol. 2, pp. 11-12.

[23] Ellen G. White, *Manuscript Releases*, vol. 21, p. 194.

[24] Ellen G. White, *Selected Messages*, vol. 1, p. 257.

the golden wedge of Ophir.'"[25] Mercy is justified by the finished work Christ promises in those who reconnect with Him. He will bring them back into harmony with the law—written in their hearts and minds.

> "The trials and sufferings of Christ were to impress man with a sense of his great sin in breaking the law of God, and to bring him *to* repentance and obedience to that law, and through obedience to acceptance with God. He would impute His righteousness to man and so raise him in moral value with God that his efforts to keep the divine law would be acceptable. Christ's work was to reconcile man to God through His human nature, and God to man through His divine nature."[26]

Christ is the mediator between God and man. The apostle John calls Him our "advocate with the Father."[27] In the blending of His human and divine natures, He presents the divine character in ways to draw humanity back. As disciples, we are His ambassadors. "The world has keenness of perception, and will take knowledge to some purpose of those who sit together in heavenly places in Christ Jesus. The character of God's human agencies must be a transcript of the character of their Savior."[28]

Judgment is a looming reality and should strengthen our passion to advocate for those who know not the truth. This *Galilee Protocol* directive is vitally important to the cause. We must be *advocative*.

> "There is need of coming close to the people by personal effort. If less time were given to sermonizing, and more time were spent in personal ministry, greater results would be seen. The poor are to be relieved, the sick cared for, the sorrowing and the bereaved comforted, the ignorant instructed, the inexperienced counseled. We are to weep with those that weep, and rejoice with those that rejoice. Accompanied by the power of persuasion, the power of prayer, the power of the love of God, this work will not, cannot, be without fruit."[29]
>
> "The love of a holy God is an amazing principle... But after the season of our probation, if we are found transgressors of God's law, the God of love will be found a minister of vengeance. God makes no compromise with sin. The disobedient will be punished. The wrath of God fell upon His beloved Son as Christ hung upon the cross of Calvary in the transgressors place. The love of God now reaches out to embrace the lowest, vilest sinner that will come to Christ with contrition. It reaches out to transform the sinner into an obedient, faithful child of God; but not a soul can be saved if he continues in sin."[30]

---

[25] Ellen G. White, *Spirit of Prophecy*, vol. 3, p. 203.
[26] Ellen G. White, *Selected Messages*, book 1, p. 272.
[27] 1 John 2:1.
[28] Ellen G. White, *Medical Ministry*, p. 46.
[29] Ellen G. White, *The Ministry of Healing*, p. 143.
[30] Ellen G. White, *Selected Messages*, book 1, p. 313.

CHAPTER SIXTEEN

Directive Five—Representative

A vital part of correcting the sin problem lies in correcting a sinner's misconception about the character of God.

Many echo Satan's original claim. He said that "God was not just in imposing laws... that in requiring submission and obedience from His creatures, He was seeking merely the exhalation of Himself."[1] Furthermore they claim that "God's law could not be obeyed, that justice was inconsistent with mercy, and that, should the law be broken, it would be impossible for the sinner to be pardoned."[2]

"By His life and His death, Christ proved that God's justice did not destroy His mercy, but that sin could be forgiven, and that the law is righteous, and can be perfectly obeyed. Satan's charges were refuted. God had given man unmistakable evidence of His love."[3]

Others echo the new claim Satan made *after* Calvary: "that mercy destroyed justice, that the death of Christ abrogated[4] the Father's law."[5] In this view, God is seen as now being soft on the sin problem—a

[1] Ellen White, *Patriarchs and Prophets*, p. 42.
[2] Ellen G. White, *The Desire of Ages*, p. 761.
[3] Ibid., p. 762.
[4] or a*bolished.*
[5] Ibid.

permissive parent who prefers that His children do good, but forever forgiving them regardless of what they do.

We have already seen God's true character (His glory) is the perfect balance of both justice and mercy. This He proclaimed when His glory passed before Moses.[6] Calvary showed both attributes of God.[7] In giving His Son as a ransom for sin, God showed His great mercy. But if the law could have been abolished, He would not have had to die in the first place. In requiring the life of His Son, He showed that He could not lay aside the demands of the law even in the case of overwhelming affection.

—Preaching and Showing

Christ's death is not the only way He showed God's balanced character. His ministry showed both attributes. He *preached* judgment while *showing* mercy to the poor, the lame, and those possessed by devils. Consider the parables of Christ—how so many of them dealt with themes of judgment; but consider them as told by a *Savior*—the sinner's best friend and only hope! Presenting this blended picture of God's character is what the *Galilee Protocol* is all about.

The fifth directive emphasizes our responsibility to portray Christ accurately. This we must do "according as His divine power hath given unto us all things that pertain to life and godliness, through the knowledge of Him who hath called us to glory and virtue: Whereby are given unto us exceeding great and precious promises: that by these ye might be partakers of the divine nature, having escaped the corruption that is in the world through lust."[8]

Peter continues this greeting to the saints by promising not to be negligent as long as he is "in this tabernacle" (alive in his body of flesh), but rather to stir them up and establish them in the present truth. How does he do this? By challenging them to add to their "faith virtue; and to virtue knowledge; and to knowledge temperance; and to temperance patience; and to patience godliness; and to godliness brotherly kindness; and to brotherly kindness charity."[9]

---

[6] Exodus 34:5-7.

[7] See Ellen G. White, *The Desire of Ages*, chapters 78 and 7.

[8] 2 Peter 1:3-4.

[9] 2 Peter 1:12-13, 5-7.

—Godhead-Power for Living

In this context, consider this statement: "The Father is all the fullness of the Godhead bodily, and is invisible to mortal sight. The Son is all the fullness of the Godhead manifested. The Word of God declares Him to be 'the express image of His person'... The Comforter that Christ promised to send after He ascended to heaven, is the Spirit in all the fullness of the Godhead, making manifest the power of divine grace to all who receive and believe in Christ as a personal Savior. There are three living persons of the heavenly trio; in the name of the Father, the Son, and the Holy Spirit—those who receive Christ by living faith are baptized, *and these powers will cooperate with the obedient subjects of heaven in their efforts to live the new life in Christ.*"[10]

So we see that we are living temples—or *lively stones* built up into a spiritual house, a holy nation, a peculiar people, shewing forth the praises of Him who hath called us out of darkness and into His marvelous light.[11] This we do by becoming partakers of the divine nature even as the three great Powers of heaven cooperate with our efforts to live as Christ lived.

The Father presents the unveiled standard of righteousness. We cannot directly behold Him because our God is a consuming fire.[12] But in mercy, God veiled divinity in the garb of humanity.[13] Christ presents divine righteousness to man.

The Son both showed the Father's glory[14] and showed the path[15] we follow to have the image of God restored in us. Jesus "brought into His human nature all the life-giving energies that human beings will need and must receive."[16]

> "All who receive Him would partake of His nature, and be conformed to His character. This involved the relinquishment of their cherished ambitions. It required the complete surrender of themselves to Jesus. They were called to become self-sacrificing, meek and lowly in heart. They must walk in the narrow path traveled by the Man of Calvary, if they would share the gift of heaven."[17]

---

[10] Ellen G. White, *Evangelism*, p. 614-615, (from *Manuscript 21*, November 1905). Emphasis added.

[11] 1 Peter 2:5, 9.

[12] Hebrews 12:29; Deuteronomy 2:24.

[13] Ellen G. White, *The Review and Herald*, June 15, 1905.

[14] John 8:28, 50; 6:57; 7:18.

[15] Hebrews 5:8-9.

[16] Ellen G. White, *The Review and Herald*, June 15, 1905.

[17] Ellen G. White, *The Desire of Ages*, p. 391.

The Holy Spirit comes personally to each believer bringing the divine power we need in order to live the character of Christ. This gift "would come with no modified energy, but in the fullness of divine power...Through the Spirit, the believer becomes a partaker of the divine nature."[18]

> "The love of pleasure is infectious. Given up to this, the mind hurries from one point to another, ever seeking some amusement. Obedience to the law of God counteracts this inclination and builds barriers against ungodliness. Each person, as a rational human being, is under the most sacred obligation to obey the law. The Spirit has been provided to enable all to do this. Christ is our personal Savior, and if we are His disciples, our wrongdoing will cease, unrighteousness will come to an end. The strife to be first will no longer exist; for Christ will be formed within, the hope of glory. Pure and undefiled religion will be seen in our lives."[19]

—The Pattern-Man

This is vital to the work of the *Galilee Protocol*. We must be living representatives of Christ—we must be like Him. "All the strength of passion of humanity clamored for expression," in Jesus, just like it does in us. And like Him, we should purpose to—"never yield to temptation to do one single act that [is] not pure and elevating and ennobling.[20]

> "Our loyalty or disloyalty will decide our destiny. Since the fall of Adam, men in every age have excused themselves for sinning, charging God with their sin, saying they could not keep His commandments. This is the insinuation Satan cast at God in heaven. But the plea, 'I cannot keep the commandments,' need never be presented to God; for before Him stands the Savior, the marks of the Crucifixion upon His body, a living witness that the law can be kept. It is not that men cannot keep the law, but that they will not."[21]
>
> "In His human nature Christ rendered perfect obedience to the law of God, thus proving to all that this law can be kept. He endured the death penalty Himself, not to abrogate the law, not to immortalize sin, but to take away sin. It is because He has borne the punishment that man can have a second probation. He may, if he will, return to his loyalty. But if he refuses to obey the commands of God, if he rejects the warnings and messages God sends, choosing rather to echo the word of the deceiver, he is willingly ignorant, and the condemnation of God is upon him. He chooses disobedience because obedience means lifting the cross, practicing self-denial."[22]

---

[18] Ibid, p. 671.

[19] Ellen G. White, *The Youth Instructor*, December 8, 1898.

[20] Ellen G. White, *In Heavenly Places*, p. 155.

[21] Ellen G. White, *The Review and Herald*, May 28, 1901

[22] Ibid.

> **"Consecrate yourself to God in the morning; make this your very first work. Let your prayer be, "Take me, O Lord, as wholly Thine. I lay all my plans at Thy feet. Use me today in Thy service. Abide with me, and let all my work be wrought in Thee." This is a daily matter. Each morning consecrate yourself to God for that day. Surrender all your plans to Him, to be carried out or given up as His providence shall indicate. Thus day by day you may be giving your life into the hands of God, and thus your life will be molded more and more after the life of Christ."**
>
> **—Steps to Christ, p. 70.**

The plan of salvation is the work of restoring in man the image of God. This happens when we become partakers of the divine nature. Four things are necessary for this to happen; and the sanctuary model illustrates them.

—Steps to Restoration

Step one takes place in the courtyard where we confess our sins and offer ourselves in simple obedience to God's commands. Obedience is important. Remember? *Obedience to the law of God counteracts the inclination for sinful pleasure and amusement and builds barriers against ungodliness.* The Old-Testament emphasizes this basic commitment to *courtyard obedience.*

The second step happens in the first apartment. In it we find the instruments of truth and light for gaining and imparting a knowledge of the things of God. "All truth is to be received as the life of Jesus. Truth cleanses us from impurity, and prepares the soul for Christ's presence. Christ is formed within, the hope of glory."[23]

> "The whole Bible is a manifestation of Christ, and the Savior desired to fix the faith of His followers on the word. When His visible presence should be withdrawn, the word must be their source of power... As they feed upon His word, they find that it is spirit and life. The word destroys the natural, earthly nature, and imparts a new life in Christ Jesus. The Holy Spirit comes to the soul as a Comforter. By the transforming agency of His grace, the image of God is reproduced in the disciple; he becomes

[23] Ellen G. White, *Manuscript 103*, 1902.

> a new creature. Love takes the place of hatred, and the heart receives the divine similitude."[24]

We receive the word at the table of shewbread. At the altar of incense we pray. As with the candlestick, the oil of the Holy Spirit flows into us as we shine with the light of God.

> "Prayer is the breath of the soul. It is the secret of spiritual power. No other means of grace can be substituted, and the health of the soul preserved. Prayer brings the heart into immediate contact with the Well-spring of life, and strengthens the sinew and muscle of the religious experience. Neglect the exercise of prayer, or engage in prayer spasmodically, now and then, as seems convenient, and you lose your hold on God."[25]

The first apartment brings the seeker before the veil. Here Paul admonishes us to "draw near with a true heart in full assurance of faith, having our hearts sprinkled from an evil conscience" [first apartment], "and our bodies washed with pure water" [courtyard], "having therefore, brethren, boldness to enter into the holiest [second apartment] by the blood of Jesus, by a new and living way, which He hath consecrated for us, through the veil, that is to say, His flesh; and having an high priest over the house of God."[26]

This is day-of-atonement stuff. This is blotting-out-of-sins stuff. Here we actively engage in a bold move through the veil into the fullness of the divine Presence. In this context we look for the full indwelling of the Spirit of God in the lives of His church—we're looking for the latter-rain power as the Spirit works through us in a capacity that exceeds all historical precedence.

—The Hope of Glory

When promising to send the Holy Spirit, Christ said, "But ye know Him; for He dwelleth *with* you, and shall be *in* you."[27] The early rain poured out at Pentecost is symbolic of the latter rain at the end of time. Here Christ makes a distinction of degree: prior to this outpouring, the Spirit is said be *with* us; but after—He is *in* us. Christ prayed for the Father to send this greater measure of the Holy Spirit to His disciples.[28] We should pray for this too.

---

[24] Ellen G. White, *The Desire of Ages*, p. 391.

[25] Ellen G. White, *Gospel Workers*, p. 254.

[26] Hebrews 10:22, 19-21.

[27] John 14:16-18. Emphasis added.

[28] Ibid.

His image is restored in us when we become partakers of the divine nature through obedience, Bible study, and prayer for the indwelling Holy Spirit; and when we let our light shine in active witness to others.

These four things are essential daily behaviors to bring changes manifest in our lives as the fruit of the Spirit. Christ said "make the tree good and its fruit good, or make the tree bad and its fruit bad. For the tree is known by the fruit.[29] The Christian must show visible evidence of His connection to God.

> "For though we walk in the flesh, we do not war after the flesh: (for the weapons of our warfare are not carnal, but mighty through God to the pulling down of strongholds;) casting down imaginations, and every high thing that exalteth itself against the knowledge of God, and bringing into captivity every thought to the obedience of Christ."[30]

These are the fruit of the Spirit:[31]

Love	Joy,	Peace,
Longsuffering,	Gentleness,	Goodness,
Faith,	Meekness,	Temperance.

Also notice what Paul expected of the Colossian Christians:[32]

Mercy,	Kindness,	Meekness,
Longsuffering,	Forbearance	Forgiveness,
Charity,	Peace,	Thanksgiving,
Teaching,	Admonition,	Sing unto the Lord,
Prayer,	Wisdom,	Graceful speech,

Wives submit to husbands,	Husbands love wives,
Children obey parents,	Fathers don't provoke children,
Servants obey masters,	Masters treat servants fairly.

> **"Daily [Christ] received a fresh baptism of the Holy Spirit. In the early hours of the new day the Lord awakened Him from His slumbers, and His soul and His lips were anointed with grace, that He might impart to others. His words were given Him fresh from the heavenly courts, words that He might speak in due season to the weary and oppressed."**
>
> **— Christ Object Lessons, p. 139.**

29 Matthew 12:33.

30 2 Corinthians 10:3-5.

31 Galatians 5:22-23.

32 Colossians 3:12-4:6

Dress and adornment are also important considerations.[33]
Christians show modesty and discretion in their clothing and hairstyles. They do not adorn themselves with gold or pearls or costly clothing—but rather with good works. They do not wear tattoos.[34]

Christians recognize that they are not their own.[35]
They have been bought with a price; and their bodies are the temples of God. They care for their bodies and avoid those things harmful to their health.

Paul also lists the fruit of the flesh that war against the Spirit:[36]

Adultery,	Fornication,	Uncleanness,
Lasciviousness,	Idolatry,	Witchcraft,
Hatred,	Variance,	Emulations,
Wrath,	Strife,	Seditions,
Heresies,	Envyings,	Murders,
Drunkenness,	Revelings,	Homosexuality,
Robbery,	Extortion,	Lying,
Blasphemy,	Malice,	Filthy Communication.

The Bible is clear that God is ever ready to redeem a sinner; but it is a mistake to think God is tolerant of sin.

> "The history of Achan teaches the solemn lesson, that for one man's sin, the displeasure of God will rest upon a people or a nation till the transgression is searched out and punished. Sin is corrupting in its nature. One man infected with its deadly leprosy may communicate the taint to thousands. Those who occupy responsible positions as guardians of the people are false to their trust, if they do not faithfully search out and reprove sin. Many dare not condemn iniquity, lest they shall thereby sacrifice position or popularity. And by some it is considered uncharitable to rebuke sin. The servant of God should never allow his own spirit to be mingled with the reproof which he is required to give; but he is under the most solemn obligation to present the word of God, without fear or favor. He must call sin by its right name. Those who by their carelessness or indifference permit God's name to be dishonored by his professed people, are numbered with the transgressor,—registered in the record of Heaven as partakers in their evil deeds."[37]

---

33 1 Timothy 2:9; 1 Peter 3:3.

34 Leviticus 19:28.

35 1 Corinthians 3:16-17; 1 Corinthians 6:19-20.

36 Galatians 5:19; 1 Corinthians 6:9-11; Colossians 3:8-9.

37 Ellen G. White, *The Signs of the Times*, April 21, 1881.

CHAPTER SEVENTEEN

Directive Six—Organized

After everyone who sided with the ten faithless spies died in the wilderness, a new generation of Hebrews resumed the march toward Canaan. God told them to turn toward Edom and pass through that land. Edom was a well-watered and fertile country. So when the miraculous flow of water from the smitten rock ceased, they should have known it was a token their wilderness wandering had ended. "The water ceased before they had reached Edom. Here was an opportunity for them, for a little time, to walk in faith instead of sight."[1]

But the new generation also failed the test. "Had the people, when brought into trial, trusted in God, the Captain of the Lord's host would have led them through Edom, and the fear of them would have been upon the inhabitants of the land, so that, instead of manifesting hostility, they would have shown them favor."[2] Now the king of Edom refused them passage. They had to go around through desert and sterile wastes.[3]

On the way, they suffered defeat in an engagement with Arad—one of the Canaanite kings. They sought the Lord earnestly, and He heard them and routed their enemies. But this didn't cause them to feel gratitude.

---

[1] Ellen G. White, *Patriarchs and Prophets*, p. 414.
[2] Ibid., p. 422-223.
[3] Ibid., p. 423-424.

Instead of acknowledging their dependence upon God, this victory made them boastful and self-confident. They began to murmur about their long wilderness sojourn. "They flattered themselves that if God and Moses had not interfered [forty years before], they might now have been in possession of the Promised Land."[4]

—Protection Withdrawn

God shielded them for many years. They did not realize the countless dangers that surrounded them. The stings of the wilderness serpents were poison, and would cause inflammation and a speedy death. "As the protecting hand of God was removed from Israel, great numbers of the people were attacked by these venomous creatures."[5]

The people humbled themselves before God; and He told Moses to fashion a brazen serpent and put it upon a pole—even as the Son of man would be "lifted up: that whosoever believe on Him should not perish, but have eternal life."[6] There was no power in the serpent of brass—and the people knew this. *Healing virtue is from God alone.*

The Israelites learned the lesson of faith; and they moved forward as the Captain of the Lord's host vanquished the enemies of His people. They were victorious over the nations on the borders of Canaan—the Amorites at Heshbon, and the giants at Bashan and Edrei. The people then returned to the Jordan to prepare for the immediate invasion of Canaan. Their camp was beside the river—just opposite of Jericho—and on the borders of Moab. The Moabites were terrified.[7]

Balak, king of Moab, hired Balaam to curse Israel. Perched in the "high places of Baal," Balaam could survey the entire camp of the Hebrew host.

> "He beheld with astonishment the evidence of their prosperity. They had been represented to him as a rude, disorganized multitude, infesting the country in roving bands that were a pest and terror to the surrounding nations; but their appearance was the reverse of this. He saw the vast extent and perfect arrangement of their camp, everything bearing the marks of thorough discipline and order. He was shown the favor with which God regarded Israel, and their distinctive character as His chosen people. They were not to stand upon a level with the other nations, but to be exalted above them all. 'The people shall dwell alone, and shall not be reckoned among the nations.'"[8]

---

[4] Ibid., p. 428.
[5] Ibid., p. 429.
[6] John 3:15.
[7] Ellen G. White, *Patriarchs and Prophets*, p. 438.
[8] Ibid., p. 447.

—God of Order

This is the sixth and final directive: The *Galilee Protocol* must be well organized. "God is a God of order. Everything connected with heaven is in perfect order; subjection and thorough discipline mark the movement of the angelic host. Success can only attend order and harmonious action. God requires order and system in His work now no less than in the days of Israel. All who are working for Him are to labor intelligently, not in a careless, haphazard manner. He would have His work done in faith and exactness, that He may place the seal of His approval upon it."[9]

"As we near the final crisis, instead of feeling that there is less need of order and harmony of action, we should be more systematic than heretofore."[10] "Diligent work is now called for. In this crisis, no halfhearted efforts will prove successful. In all our city work, we are to hunt for souls. Wise plans are to be laid, in order that such a work may be done to the best possible advantage."[11]

> "In every large city there should be corps of organized, well-disciplined workers; not merely one or two, but scores should be set to work... Each company of workers should be under the direction of a competent leader, and it should ever be kept before them that they are to be missionaries in the highest sense of the term. Such systematic labor, wisely conducted, would produce blessed results."[12]
>
> "It is essential to labor with order, following well organized plans and a definite object. No one can properly instruct another unless he sees to it that the work to be done shall be taken hold of systematically and in order... Well-defined plans should be freely presented to all whom they may concern, and it should be ascertained that they are understood. Then require of all those who are at the head of the various departments to operate in the execution of these plans. If this sure and radical method is properly adopted and followed up with interest and good will, it will avoid much work being done without any definite object, much useless friction."[13]

---

[9] Ibid., p. 376.

[10] Ellen G. White, *Selected Messages*, vol. 3, p. 26.

[11] Ellen G. White, *Evangelism*, p. 59.

[12] Ellen G. White, *Medical Ministry*, p. 300-301.

[13] Ellen G. White, *Evangelism*, p. 94.

The Organized Directive Has Five Components—

Planning: a board of trustees provides general oversight for the entire program. They work diligently to maintain that the principles of the work conform to the divine council; and seek to direct all activity according to God's leadership and will.

Training: Those who wish to be involved take part in the core training. There are two designations for those who are trained: *Certified Medical Missionaries* have successfully completed the theory (or bookwork) portion of the core training. This is accomplished through self-study, small groups, or seminar; *Registered Medical Missionaries* have also successfully completed the required fieldwork (lab or practicum) under the direction of a qualified coach.

Evaluating: Both Certified and Registered Medical Missionaries have to show their ability with the core competencies in order to receive and maintain their designation.

Leadership: The trustees appoint the leaders. District managers oversee various geographical regions. Program managers oversee training, recruiting, logistics and various other programs. Event managers oversee each major mission-event.

Accountability: The *Galilee Protocol* officially operates as a non-profit unincorporated association: *Galilee Protocol Medical Missionary Association*. In order to protect its name, its mission, and all those it seeks to minister to, it is necessary that all those who operate as part of its scope of influence be credentialed as official association members in good and regular standing.

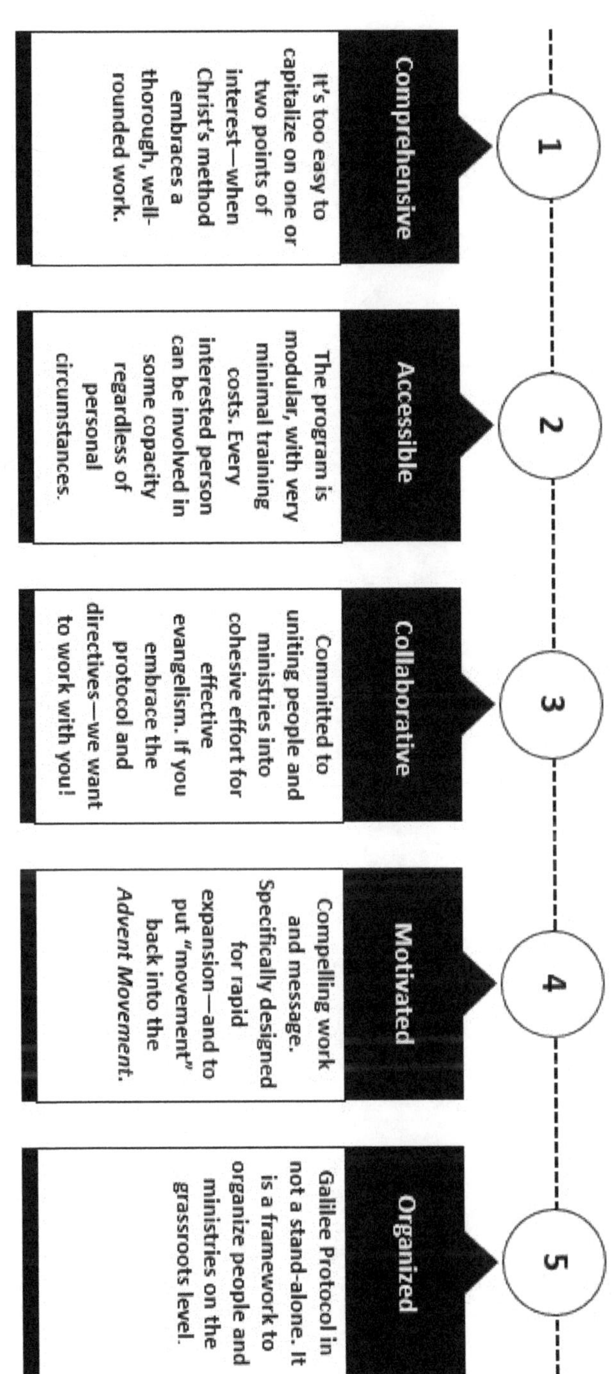
1
Comprehensive
It's too easy to capitalize on one or two points of interest—when Christ's method embraces a thorough, well-rounded work.
2
Accessible
The program is modular, with very minimal training costs. Every interested person can be involved in some capacity regardless of personal circumstances.
3
Collaborative
Committed to uniting people and ministries into cohesive effort for effective evangelism. If you embrace the protocol and directives—we want to work with you!
4
Motivated
Compelling work and message. Specifically designed for rapid expansion—and to put "movement" back into the *Advent Movement*.
5
Organized
Galilee Protocol in not a stand-alone. It is a framework to organize people and ministries on the grassroots level.

CHAPTER EIGHTEEN

The Storm

People cannot manage the luxury of being on the fence during a full-fledged, fully-developed crisis. Consider the war in heaven: Satan's "underworking was so subtle that it could not be made to appear before the heavenly host as the thing it really was."[1] "The evil continued to work until the spirit of disaffection ripened into active revolt."[2] "It was necessary for his plans to be fully developed, that their true nature and tendency might be seen by all."[3] "Then it was that there were two parties. One was warring on the one hand, and God and His angels on the other hand."[4] "There was war in heaven. Angels were engaged in battle."[5]

There were only two sides when the flood came in the days of Noah; and there will only be two sides at the very end of time. Indeed, there is always only two sides—but like it was in Heaven, it is often difficult to differentiate between the rebellious and the loyal. Unfortunately, we often do not even know our own condition. "There are only two parties in our world, those who are loyal to God, and those who stand under the banner of the prince of darkness. Satan and his angels will come down

---

[1] Ellen G. White, *The Faith I live By*, p. 69.
[2] Ellen G. White, The Seventh-day Adventist Bible Commentary, vol. 7, p. 973.
[3] Ellen G. White, *Patriarchs and Prophets*, p. 41.
[4] Ellen G. White, *Manuscript 142*, 1906.
[5] Ellen G. White, *Early Writings*, p. 145.

with power and signs and lying wonders to deceive those who dwell on the earth, *and if possible the very elect*. The crisis is right upon us. Is it to paralyze the energies of those who have a knowledge of the truth? Is the influence of the powers of deception so far reaching that the influence of the truth will be overpowered?"[6]

> "All the world will be on one side or the other of the question. The battle of Armageddon will be fought, and that day must find none of us sleeping. Wide awake we must be... The power of the Holy Ghost must be upon us, and the Captain of the Lord's host will stand at the head of the angels of heaven to direct the battle. Solemn events before us are yet to transpire. Trumpet after trumpet is to be sounded, vial after vial poured out one after another upon the inhabitants of the earth. Scenes of stupendous interests are right upon us."[7]
>
> "The present is a solemn, fearful time for the church. The angels are already girded, awaiting the mandate of God to pour their vials of wrath upon the world. Destroying angels are taking up the work of vengeance; for the Spirit of God is gradually withdrawing from the world. Satan is also mustering his forces of evil, going forth 'unto the kings of the earth and of the whole world,' to gather them under his banner, to be trained for 'the battle of the great day of God Almighty.' Satan is to make a most powerful effort for the mastery in the last great conflict. Fundamental principles will be brought out, and decisions made in regard to them. Skepticism is prevailing everywhere. Ungodliness abounds. The faith of the individual members of the church will be tested as though there were not another person in the world."[8]

Deciding who is on which side is not arbitrary. All choose based on their relationship to the evidence. Like the days of Noah—the last generation will not have a lifetime to manifest their choice. They will simultaneously be brought to a point of final decision. The principles will be fully developed—and fully demonstrated by the two groups. The *mystery of God* and the *mystery of iniquity* will be on full display.

Getting there from here requires a massive movement progressively developing through three stages. The crises in each stage will concern the *fundamental principles*—the heaven-fought issues of whether *physical, mental,* and *spiritual* glory come from God alone, or whether Satan's merchandise is a suitable alternative.

In His day, Christ caused an educational crisis, a ministerial crisis, and a medical crisis—in the church, the nation, and the world. God's last-day people—properly using the *Galilee Protocol*—will to do the same in our

---

[6] Ellen G. White, *Manuscript* 178, 1899. Emphasis added.

[7] Ellen G. White, *Letter 112*, 1890.

[8] Ellen G. White, *Manuscript* 1a, 1890.

church, our nations, and then the whole world. This movement will crescendo into the final test.

Concerning the church phase of the crisis, the biblical types tend to favor the imagery of *a storm* over images of war. Storms emphasize divine judgment as an essential element. The stormy crisis that turned Jonah back to his mission clearly displays the divine fingerprint. This is not only true of the church crisis. Storms also happen to cities. "Abraham sought to save" the dwellers in Sodom "from the storm of divine judgment."[9] And there will be a global storm at the very end of time. Revelation 7:1-3 tells of four angels "restraining the winds of strife, until the world shall be warned of its coming doom; but a storm is gathering, ready to burst upon the earth."[10]

—The Storm of Jonah

Jonah would probably have made a good Seventh-day Adventist. There are some striking similarities between his story and ours. His people were the keepers of God's precious oracles, the sanctuary truth, the Sabbath; and they looked for the soon coming Messiah. They also had the Spirit of Prophecy. Jonah was God's chosen instrument to take a warning message to city-dwellers. He lived when God's destructive judgments were about to fall on the city of Nineveh; and Jonah preferred the ease and wealth of Tarshish, resisting the work God called him to do.

We all know the story of Jonah: how God sent a storm to intercept his flight-by-sea to Tarshish;[11] how sailors threw him from the ship into the sea;[12] how he was swallowed by a large fish; and how he stayed (and prayed) in the fish's belly for three days and three nights[13] before being coughed up on land.[14]

Nineveh worshiped a god they called Dagon. He was half man and half fish. When the news of this seaweed incrusted, fish-spat evangelist hit the front pages at Nineveh, they were all ears.

Jonah, hopelessly unwilling to do city-evangelism, became willing.[15] Nineveh, presumably disinterested in Jonah's warning, became very attentive to this fish-prophet. This is the point of the story. God sent *a*

---

[9] Ellen G. White, *From Eternity Past*, p. 84.
[10] Ellen G. White, *Maranatha*, p. 259.
[11] Jonah 1:3.
[12] Jonah 1:15.
[13] Jonah 1:17; 2:2.
[14] Jonah 2:10.
[15] Jonah 3:3.

storm to convince His unfaithful servant to do city missionary work—and in so doing also set up things for some very effective evangelism![16]

—The Sign of Jonah

When Christ spoke of the *sign of Jonah*, He tied the traumatic three-day, three-night experience of Jonah to the eminent three-day, three-night trauma coming to His followers. When Christ hung upon Calvary's cross, there was a terrible storm that day too. "Inanimate nature expressed sympathy with its insulted and dying author. The sun refused to look upon the awful scene... Complete darkness, like a funeral pall, enveloped the cross." "A nameless terror held the throng that was gathered about the cross... Vivid lightnings occasionally flashed forth from the cloud... Priests, rulers, scribes, executioners, and the mob, all thought that their time of retribution had come."[17]

> "No eye could pierce the gloom that surrounded the cross, and none could penetrate the deeper gloom that enshrouded the suffering soul of Christ. The angry lightnings seemed to be hurled at Him as He hung upon the cross. Then 'Jesus cried with a loud voice, saying, Eloi, Eloi, lama sabachthani?' 'My God, My God, why hast Thou forsaken Me?'"[18]

After a time, "suddenly the gloom lifted from the cross, and in clear, trumpetlike tones, that seemed to resound throughout creation, Jesus cried, 'It is finished.' 'Father, into Thy hands I commend My spirit.'"[19]

> "Never before had the earth witnessed such a scene. The multitude stood paralyzed, and with bated breath gazed upon the Savior. Again the darkness settled upon the earth, and a hoarse rumbling, like heavy thunder, was heard. There was a violent earthquake. The people were shaken together in heaps. The wildest confusion and consternation ensued. In the surrounding mountains, rocks were rent asunder, and went crashing down into the plains. Sepulchers were broken open, and the dead were cast out of their tombs. Creation seemed to be shivering to atoms. Priests, rulers, soldiers, executioners, and people, mute with terror, lay prostrate upon the ground."[20]

On the morning of His arrest, Jesus said, "All ye shall be offended because of me this night: for it is written, I will strike the shepherd and the

[16] Jonah 3:10.
[17] Ellen G. White, *The Desire of Ages*, p. 754.
[18] Ibid.
[19] Ellen G. White, *The Desire of Ages*, p. 756.
[20] Ibid.

sheep of the flock will be scattered." He then added, "But after I am risen again, I will go before you into Galilee."[21]

While in the whale's belly Jonah had to come to grips with his faulty ideas and with his responsibility. Likewise, while Christ was in the earth's belly, His disciples had to confront their misguided assumptions about their role and the kingdom of God. Before Calvary, the things of this world preoccupied even Christ's followers—wealth, power, and position. They were prideful of their religion and their nation; and they hoped for temporal superiority among the nations. They wanted a Messiah who would bring victory over Roman aggression. They were not interested in ideas of national judgment, nor eager to warn cities of soon coming destruction. They had trouble embracing, and evangelizing for, a kingdom not of this world.

National judgment was an unpopular message that even the disciples had trouble embracing. Notwithstanding the whole people—the disciples included—were stubbornly persisting in rebellion and insubordination, *a storm* was coming that would aggressively boot them (as many as would) into a position of active missionary labor. After the storm, the early Christians closely followed the prototype established by Jesus. Using the *Galilee Protocol* they reached the entire world in one generation.

—The Last-day Storm

The *Great Controversy* describes a storm that will take place even as the forth angel is about to sound—"the angel... that unites in the proclamation of the third message is to lighten the whole earth with His glory."[22] It helps us know what will precipitate the *storm:*

> "As the time comes for the loud cry to be given, the Lord will work through humble instruments, leading the minds of those who consecrate themselves to His service. The laborers will be qualified rather by the unction of His Spirit than by the training of literary institutions. Men of faith and prayer will be constrained to go forth with holy zeal, declaring the words which God gives them. The sins of Babylon will be laid open."[23]

As these humble instruments mobilize with holy zeal, events will follow the pattern of things seen in Christ's three-and-a-half-year ministry; and a similar opposition will build into *a storm* like that of A.D. 31.

---

[21] Matthew 26:31.

[22] Ellen White, *The Great Controversy*, pp. 378-379. 1884 edition.

[23] Ibid., p. 606.

"Thousands upon thousands have never listened to words like these... The people go to their former teachers with the eager inquiry, Are these things so? The ministers present fables, prophesy smooth things, to soothe their fears, and quiet the awakened conscience. But many refuse to be satisfied with the mere authority of men, and demand a plain 'thus saith the Lord.' The popular ministry, like the Pharisees of old, are filled with anger as their authority is questioned."[24]

"The clergy put forth almost superhuman effort to shut away the light, lest it should shine upon their flocks. By every means at their command they endeavor to suppress the discussion of these vital questions. The church appeals to the strong arm of civil power, and in this work, papists are solicited to come to the help of Protestants... [Commandment-keepers] are threatened with fines and imprisonment, and some are offered positions of influence, and other rewards and advantages, and inducements to renounce their faith."[25]

"As the defenders of truth refuse to honor the Sunday-Sabbath, some of them will be thrust into prison, some will be exiled, some will be treated as slaves. To human wisdom, all this now seems impossible; but as the restraining spirit of God shall be withdrawn from men, and they shall be under the control of Satan, who hates the divine precepts, there will be strange developments. The heart can be very cruel when God's fear and love are removed."[26]

"As the *storm* approaches, a large class who have professed faith in the third angel's message, but have not been sanctified through it, abandon their former position, and take refuge under the banner of the powers of darkness. By uniting with the world and partaking of its spirit, they come to view matters in the same light; and when the test is brought, they choose the easy, popular side."[27]

"The Lord's servants have faithfully given the warning, looking to God and to His word alone. They have not coolly calculated the consequences to themselves. They have not consulted their temporal interests, or sought to preserve their reputations or their lives. Yet when the *storm* of opposition and reproach bursts upon them, they are overwhelmed with consternation... They are hedged in with difficulties. Satan assails them with fierce temptations. The work which they have undertaken seems far beyond their ability to accomplish. They are threatened with destruction. The enthusiasm which animated them is gone; yet they cannot turn back. Then feeling their helplessness, they flee to the Mighty One for strength."[28]

"As the opposition rises to a fiercer height, the servants of God are again perplexed; for it seems to them that they have brought the crisis. But conscience and the word of God assures them that their course is right; and although the trials continue, they are strengthened to bear

[24] Ellen White, *The Great Controversy*, p. 379. 1884 edition.

[25] Ibid.

[26] Ibid., p. 380.

[27] Ibid., Emphasis Added.

[28] Ibid., pp. 380-381. Emphasis added.

them. The contest grows closer and sharper, but their faith and courage rise with the emergency."[29]

"As long as Jesus remains man's intercessor in the sanctuary above, the restraining influence of the Holy Spirit is felt by the rulers and people. It still controls, to some extent, the laws of the land... The enemy moves upon his servants to propose measures that would greatly impede the work of God; but statesmen who fear the Lord are influenced by holy angels to oppose such propositions with unanswerable arguments. Thus a few men will hold in check a powerful current of evil. The opposition of the enemies of truth will be restrained that the third message may do its work. When the loud cry shall be given, it will arrest the attention of these leading men through whom the Lord is now working, and some will accept it, and stand with the people of God through the time of trouble."

"The angel who unites with the third message is to lighten the whole earth with His glory. A work of world-wide extent and unwonted power is here brought to view. The Advent movement of 1840-44 was a glorious manifestation of the power of God; the first message was carried to every mission station in the world, and in this country there was the greatest religious interest which has been witnessed in any land since the Reformation of the sixteenth century; but these are to be far exceeded by the mighty power under the loud cry of the third message. The work will be similar to that of the day of Pentecost. Servants of God, with their faces lighted up and shining with holy consecration, hasten from place to place to proclaim the warning from Heaven. By thousands of voices, all over the earth, the message will be given. Miracles are wrought, the sick are healed, and signs and wonders follow the believers. Satan also works with lying wonders, even bringing down fire from heaven in the sight of men. Thus the inhabitants of the earth are brought to take their stand."[30]

—Before the Storm

The term *Galilee Protocol* not only describes Christ's method of teaching, preaching, and healing: it also describes the tactically necessary storm. *This* storm is not primarily aimed at the cities or the world. This one is aimed at unfaithful "Jonah"; and is necessary to reform "Jonah"—even though it will also effectively set up things to reach "Nineveh."

We ask you to adopt the *Galilee Protocol* today—aiming it at the largest and most sinful cities of America—not because we expect to see it result in the immediate outpouring of the latter rain, but because it is a necessary work that we must do before the storm. Prior to Calvary, Christ worked for three and a half years to lay the groundwork for Pentecost and beyond. His preparatory work (the *Galilee Protocol*)

[29] Ibid., pp. 381-382.
[30] Ibid., pp. 382-383.

established the required context so the Calvary-storm would be effective and to provide the pattern of work for His people to follow during the early rain.

—Shaking

We've known there is going to be a shaking in the church, but to compare our condition with that of the Jews in Christ's day—that is going too far isn't it? Maybe not.

> "Very few of those who have received the light are doing the work entrusted to their hands. There are few men of unswerving fidelity... But the sins that control the world have come into the churches, and into the hearts of those who claim to be God's peculiar people. Many who have received the light exert an influence to quiet the fears of worldlings and formal professors. There are lovers of the world even among those who profess to be waiting for the Lord. There is ambition for riches and honor... This world is their home. They make it theirs to secure earthly treasures. They erect costly dwellings and furnish them with every good thing; they find pleasure in dress and the indulgences of appetite. The things of this world are their idols. These interpose between the soul and Christ, and the solemn and awful realities that are crowding upon us are but dimly seen and faintly realized. *The same disobedience and failure which were seen in the Jewish church have characterized in a greater degree the people who have had this great light from heaven in the last messages of warning.* Shall we, like them, squander our opportunities and privileges until God shall permit oppression and persecution to come upon us? Will the work which might be performed in peace and comparative prosperity be left undone until it must be performed in days of darkness, under the pressure of trial and persecution?"[31]

When all else fails, God sends a storm. As we move into line with the *Galilee Protocol*, we should be clear in our understanding and expectation. Before we will see the full power and glory of the latter rain, we must endure the storm.

The *Galilee Protocol* will bring a great crisis on three fronts and in three theaters: it will cause an educational crisis, a ministerial crisis, and a medical crisis—in the church, in the nation, and in the world. This crisis will swell into a full-fledged storm.

"The storm is coming, the storm that will try every man's faith of what sort it is. Believers must now be firmly rooted in Christ or else they will be rooted in some phase of error."[32]

---

[31] Ellen G. White, *Testimonies for the Church*, vol. 5, p. 456. Emphasis added.
[32] Ellen G. White, *Evangelism*, pp. 361-362.

CHAPTER NINETEEN

Deliverables

Deliverables are specific, tangible actions and activities that engage the target(s) with real missionary value. They are divided into two general categories.

Category one is *On-Boarding.* This category targets people within the Seventh-day Adventist community. They may be individuals, small groups, congregations, multi-congregational groups or school groups. Here the *Deliverables* are activities to recruit and train Adventists for involvement in domestic medical missionary work.

Category two is *Protocol Evangelism.* Here the targets are people outside the Seventh-day Adventist community. They may be individuals, families, small community groups, or even whole cities. Here the *Deliverables* are missionary activities for reaching people with Christ's final warning message.

These Deliverables are fluid action-ideas for well-rounded ministry, attempting to bring together all the necessary elements according to God's revealed plan. It would be a mistake to treat them as static, unbending programs since they are (in most cases) uninspired applications for inspired principles. While it is vital to apply the principles faithfully, creativity in programming is a good thing.

—On-boarding

What Doest Thou Here, Elijah? This is a propagational event for church congregations and church groups. It is an entry level interest building seminar based on the first and third sections of this book.

Almost Armageddon: This is an event for schools or groups of school-aged young people. It is an entry level multimedia presentation exposing Hollywood's preoccupation with Armageddon and the physical, mental, and spiritual repercussions. This series presents the *Great Controversy* in a way that will engage and motivate young *Adventists* for revival, reformation and missionary ministry.

Christ's Method Alone! This is an orientation seminar intended for church congregations, church groups, and school groups. It presents the *Galilee Protocol Orientation Study Guides* culminating in an exam and the opportunity to join the *Galilee Protocol Medical Missionary Association* as an *Enrolled Medical Missionary*. These study guides are based on the second section of this book.

Galilee Protocol Core Curriculum: This is the fairly intensive training program for *Enrolled Medical Missionaries (EMM)*. After successful completion of the theory portion of the *Core Curriculum* they will be given the opportunity for an upgraded membership as a *Certified Medical Missionary (CMM)*. Here are some of the important topics in this curriculum:

1. The Bible Witness
2. *The History of Our Message*
3. *God's Eight Doctors*
4. *Anatomy, Physiology and Hygiene*
5. *Hygienic Healthcare*
6. *Hydrotherapy*
7. *Healthful Cookery*
8. *Home Gardening*

Galilee Protocol Practicum: This is a hands-on, mentoring style, field training to prepare medical missionaries for specific *protocol evangelism* activities. It uses the *Galilee Protocol Field Manual* as a training text. After successful completion of the practicum portion of the Core Curriculum, CMM's will be given the opportunity for an upgraded membership as a *Registered Medical Missionary* (RMM). The areas of training for *protocol evangelism* are described in the following section.

—Protocol Evangelism

Home Health Lessons: These are basic health studies to be taught in a home-like setting. It is ideal to conduct them in an interest's home encouraging them to invite friends or family. They cover *God's Eight*

Doctors, introducing several practical techniques for each one. These should be followed up with seminars and campaigns.

Home Bible Lessons: These are basic Bible studies to be taught in a home-like setting. It is ideal to conduct them in an interest's home encouraging them to invite friends or family. They use the *sanctuary* as a model to teach important Bible topics relevant to salvation and worship. These should be followed up with seminars and campaigns.

Home Helps: *Home Helps* emphasize doing. It could be help with cleaning or cooking, tending someone who is sick, yard work or home repairs. Maybe it is help getting food or clothes for someone in need or visiting someone in jail. Whatever the case, these helps need to stay focused on *Galilee Protocol* evangelism goals.

Historagories: Think *history stories of an allegorical nature*. These are special because everybody loves a story. This is a focused use of stories from the Bible or history to pull out important apocalyptic points relevant for today. It is amazing how many Bible stories have built-in end-time symbolism.

Search & Rescue: Door-to-door work is vital to seeking and saving the lost. Yes, sometimes intimidating, but it can also be fun and rewarding. The emphasis is on ways to engage people who are open to what we have to share concerning health and the gospel.

Open-Air Interactives: Ever consider street evangelism? Here we capitalize on very brief encounters with people just to spark their interest in following up with us at a seminar or study event. In this area we can get creative—especially with the help of schools and youth groups.

Bible Answers Seminars: This is not a venue for whole-message evangelism. Rather, they are short, focused seminars on various relevant Bible topics. With these we work with the more difficult studies like the state of the dead, the Sabbath, hell fire, spiritualism, and so on.

Ten Times Better Health Seminar: These are short focused seminars on various health topics that work well in more formal settings. They cover things like hydrotherapy techniques, cooking classes, healing herbs, and so forth.

Almost Armageddon: Similar idea to the *On-Boarding* seminar for *Adventist* youth except this one targets young people from the public. Several multimedia presentations can be made into a series; but these can also stand on their own. These point out Hollywood's preoccupation with Armageddon—and Satan's diabolical agenda for the end of the world.

Olivet Prophecy Campaigns: This is a new twist on an evangelistic campaign. Well, new but not new. It approaches evangelism more like the book, *Great Controversy*. These are powerful presentation of the most vital issues for our time. This series is shorter than the traditional campaign and is to be presented tent-meeting style away from the bustle of city life. These are not full-message campaigns so baptismal interests will need to cover some of our beliefs in another way.
Ten Times Better Hygienic Spas: These are city centers. Usually simple rented properties where there is room enough to hold seminars and equipped to do cooking and hydrotherapy demonstrations. They have rooms where simple treatments can be done; and they serve as resource centers for both medical missionaries and those for whom they are laboring.
Siloam Therapeutics Lifestyle Lodges: These are country outposts. Repurposed farms or some land suitable for a rapid-deployment base camp: these are for training and treatment facilities. They are equipped much like the city centers but designed to accommodate people who need to stay for a while. They incorporate gardening programs, are able to accommodate training, tent-meetings and camping.
Field Expeditions: A *field expedition* is a missionary campaign that is conducted at some target ministry location, usually quite some distance from home. Since the *Galilee Protocol* primarily targets the large cities, *Field Expeditions* are generally short-term (6-month) city campaigns. These are the main events where all the *deliverables* converge to blitz a target area with intensive, focused, and organized missionary activity.

—Modularity and Affordability

Every attempt is to be made to keep the *Galilee Protocol* programs as modular as possible and training cost to an absolute minimum. This is so that it can grow quickly and so that every interested person can be involved in some capacity regardless of their personal circumstances. When a *field expedition* occurs, we simply assemble the various modules (with those who are available to work them) into a well-organized missionary event.

Home Health Lessons

Basic health studies oriented around the eight laws of health.

Home Bible Lessons

Basic Bible studies teaching important topics relevant to salvation and worship.

Home Helps

Cooking, cleaning, repairs, tending the sick. Helping that stays focused on evangelism goals.

Historagories

"History stories of an allegorical nature." Parables told with important apocalyptic points.

Search & Rescue

Door-to-door effort to find people who are open to our health and gospel offerings .

Open-Air Interactives

Street evangelism for brief encounters with people to spark interest in our events.

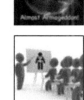

Almost Armageddon Multimedia Events

Stand alone, attention-getting presentations to point out society's rapid race to Armageddon.

Ten Times Better Health Seminars

Short, focused seminars on various *more difficult* health topics.

Bible Answers Seminars

Short, focused seminars on various *more difficult* Bible topics.

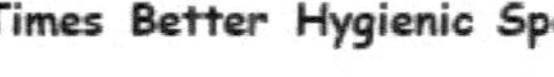

Ten Times Better Hygienic Spa

City centers that serve as venues for medical missionary activity.

Siloam Therapeutics Lifestyle Lodge

Country outpost centers that serve as venues for medical missionary activity.

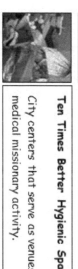

Olivet Prophecy Campaigns

Short prophecy campaigns presented tent-meeting style, *Great Controversy* type topics.

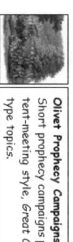

"The plan of holding Bible readings was a heaven-born idea. There are many, both men and women, who can engage in this branch of missionary labor... Men are entreated to read, examine, and judge for themselves, and they must abide the responsibility of receiving or rejecting the divine enlightenment... God will not permit this precious work to go unrewarded."

—Christian Service, p. 141.

PART THREE

APPLICATION

CHAPTER TWENTY

When Nets Break

Some people have unusual warmth and presence. They draw others to them like a magnet. People like to be around them. Jesus was like that. When He was on earth, people loved being with Him. Jesus was *vivacious!*

Vivacious comes from the French verb, *vivre*. It means "to live." It's a good word for Jesus. Not only is He full of life—He is life! He said: "I am the way and the truth and the life. No one comes to the Father except by Me."[1]

Jesus said, "I am the resurrection and the life, he that believes in me, though he were dead, yet shall he live."[2] This vivacious Jesus also said, "I have come that they [the people] might have life, and that they might have it more abundantly."[3]

Vivacious Jesus mingled daily with people—lots of people—sharing warmth and understanding; a healing touch; a compassionate look. He was a likeable guy; and He liked others too. Jesus loved people. Jesus helped people. Jesus gave them life!—abundant life, full and free!

---

[1] John 14:6.

[2] John 11:25.

[3] John 10:10.

This is the Jesus that stood beside the lake that day—a warm, compassionate, *vivacious* Jesus. The crowd just had to be near Him as they pressed Him against the water's edge.

With a healing touch, He brought life to their withered and broken bodies (physical). His healing words brought light, and life, and order into their twisted and confused understanding (mental). And that look—that healing look, thrilled their desperate hearts so recently weighed down with guilt and shame and loneliness (spiritual).

—In Peter's Boat

They were on the shore of lake Gennesaret. We usually call it the Sea of Galilee. Jesus was there to meet Peter, Andrew, James, and John who had been working all night plying their trade as fishermen. Morning now, Jesus is walking by the shore. He finds these disciples out of their boats, washing and mending their nets.

Not far behind Him is a throng of excited people. Before you know it, there is barely room enough to stand. So Jesus climbs into Peter's fishing boat and moves back a bit from the land.

Try to imagine Peter telling the story himself. It might have gone something like this:

Me and Andrew, we'd been fishin',
the best part of last night.
We'd caught nothin' for all our tryin',
come the morning, and the light—
Then I saw Him, and He asked me,
to take Him out a little way from the land.
He was teachin' all the People.
They listened there in silence on the sand.

"Come and follow, come and follow,
come and follow, come and follow Me.
Come and follow, come and follow,
come and follow, come and follow Me!"

When He'd ended all His teachin',
He turned around and spoke again to me.
He said, "Simon, row out farther—
drop your nets once again into the sea!"
I said, "Master, we've been workin'

since the sundown yesterday!
But one more time, I'll throw them over,
just because, it's You, who says:

Come and follow, come and follow,
come and follow, come and follow Me.
Come and follow, come and follow,
come and follow, come and follow Me!"

James and John, they're both my witnesses,
to the truth in what I've told—
how our nets were filled to bursting
more than both our boats could ever hold!
And I fell down, there before Him,
crying, "Leave me, Lord— I'm full of sin!"
He said, "Simon, don't be frightened,
follow Me and you will learn to fish for men."

"Come and follow, come and follow,
come and follow, come and follow Me.
Come and follow, come and follow,
come and follow, come and follow Me!"[4]

All this happened at the start of Jesus' public ministry to Galilee. He had already been working for about a year in Judea. Andrew and Peter, anyway, had been among Christ's earliest disciples—going all the way back to when John the Baptist said, "Behold, the Lamb of God, who taketh away the sins of the world."[5]

They were His earliest disciples—but they were part-time, pass-time disciples. They had jobs. They were still professional fishermen. And at night they fished. And last night... they caught nothing! So Jesus sends them back out, and Jesus tells them *how* to fish!

—Teaching Fishers to Fish

Today we still have professional fishermen. And if there is one thing professional fishermen know, it's this business of how to fish! And today we have spiritual fishermen—who are also professionals at what they do. *Spiritual fishermen know how to catch spiritual fish!*

---

[4] Don Francisco, *Come and Follow,* from his album: *He's Alive: Don Francisco Collection*, vol. 1. 1998.

[5] John 1:29, 36.

So here are Peter, Andrew, James and John, just finishing a difficult fishing campaign. Jesus finds them tired and discouraged. They are cleaning and mending their empty nets. Not catching fish is not their only problem.

Peter and Andrew were disciples of John the Baptist *before* they were disciples of Jesus. And during that long night, Peter was thinking about John[6]—who was languishing alone in a dungeon cell. He was thinking also of Judea, of the ill-success of the mission there—and of the malice of the priests and rabbis. Now even his own occupation was failing him. The future seemed dark with discouragement.

Maybe there are some parallels to today? Times for us aren't what they used to be! In our own Christian nation, the *Christian mission* isn't going so well. Even in America, Christ's followers are mocked and derided and locked up in proverbial prisons of *political correctitude*.

And let's be honest—the *Seventh-day Adventist mission* isn't really going so well here either! We're not making an impact that lives up to our prophetic expectations. And about our evangelism—it's clear that the old nets just don't bring in the fish like they used to.

—Sneaking Up on the Fish

Peter and his associates fished at night. No, they weren't insomniacs—it's just because that was how professional fishermen caught fish! The waters of Gennesaret were crystal clear. Fishermen couldn't use nets during the day because the fish could see them. So they had to work in the dark.

Do you ever tire of having to sneak up on the fish? Do you ever wish you could let daylight shine on the clear bold truth so needed in our time? And the catch, wouldn't you like to see us bring in a great catch of fish—big enough to overfill the boat?

Well, Jesus didn't sneak up on fish. During His trial before the high priest He said, "I spake openly to the world... and in secret have I said nothing."[7]

Man's wisdom tells us to soften and subdue the message—so it is easy to accept. But inspiration says:

---

[6] Ellen G. White, *The Desire of Ages*, p. 249.

[7] John 18:20.

> "Most startling messages will be borne by men of God's appointment, messages of a character to warn the people, to arouse them. And while some will be provoked by the warning, and led to resist the light and evidence, we are to see from this that we are giving the testing message for this time... [and that we must] have, in our cities, consecrated evangelists through whom a message is to be borne so decidedly as to startle the hearers." [8]

"Agitate, agitate, agitate the public mind," we are told, "there must be no spiritual stupor now."[9]

Wherever Jesus went, He upset the status quo, and He challenged the conventions of the experts and the worldly wise. And great multitudes flocked to hear Him—for He taught having authority, not as the scribes did.[10]

> "Those who will study the manner of Christ's teaching, and educate themselves to follow His way, will attract and hold large numbers now, as Christ held people in His day."[11]

Now that's what I am talking about!

Please don't misunderstand. The intent is not to be critical. But the truth of the matter is that we just do not catch all that many fish anymore. And that's a problem!

It's a problem because we accept less than what's promised—Christ promises that *if we educate ourselves about His method, and obey His instructions on how to fish, we will attract and hold large numbers now, as He did in His day.*

—In the Full Light of Day

So back on that lake, Jesus, sends those professional fishermen out there—*this time in the full light of day!*

> "The trumpet is to give a certain sound. The attention of the people is to be called to the third angel's message. Let not God's servants act like men walking in their sleep, but men preparing for the coming of Christ."[12]

Well, tired Peter—he's discouraged, irritated, argumentative. Peter is certain he knows way more about fishing than Jesus does. All the

---

[8] Ellen G. White, *Evangelism*, p. 217.

[9] Ibid., p. 168.

[10] Matthew 7:29, Mark 1:22, Luke 4:32.

[11] Ellen G. White, *Evangelism*, p. 124.

[12] Ibid., p. 119.

disciples know they have about a zero percent chance of catching fish in broad daylight. But they love their Master. His instructions are clear. So they obey.

What a lesson for us. Do we love the Master? Has He given us clear instructions?

—Tactically Crazy and Dangerous

This was not the first time Jesus ever gave people baffling instructions. He did it in the Old Testament too.

When God sent Gideon out against the host of Midian, His tactics were crazy and even dangerous. Gideon's forces were pitiful against such a vast enemy. The Bible says:

> "The Midianites and the Amalekites and all the children of the east lay along in the valley like grasshoppers for multitude; and their camels were without number, as the sands by the sea for multitude."[13]

Gideon sent word to the tribes; and they could only raise an army of a mere 32,000 men. It is easy to see that they will be no match for a grasshopper-multitude of Midianites. So, Gideon could hardly believe his ears when the Lord told him he had *too many.*

The problem was that those unwilling to face danger and hardships, or whose worldly interests drew their hearts from their God-ordained mission—wouldn't add strength to the armies of the Lord. They would only be a cause of weakness. Hear this point—it's important: distraction, selfishness, and disinterest weaken us collectively and limits God's ability to work through us.

So God helped Gideon remove the weeds. Gideon invited those who were afraid or who felt that they had more pressing business to go home; and two-thirds of his already-pitiful army left. Now with only ten thousand men, Gideon learns that God thinks he still has too many. The men expect to make an immediate advance. While on the way, they come to the side of a brook. Only three hundred out of ten thousand scoop up water in their hand—drinking quickly so they can eagerly do the Lord's work. The others leisurely lay on their faces lapping water from the stream.

---

[13] Judges 7:12.

Only the *serious* need to apply, for only the *eager* are retained. Gideon now has but a small troop of three hundred men. With just a trumpet in one hand, and a light hidden in a clay pitcher in the other, they divide into three groups: and they advance into the dark and lonely territory of the enemy.

—Old-Testament Breadcrumbs

In Bible imagery, vessels of clay often represent people—usually those who have been (or are being) worked and formed by the hands of the Master Potter. Light represents the power and illumination that come from the Word and the indwelling Holy Spirit. Trumpets pierce though the darkness with alarm—they blast the warning message.

The details of this fantastic Bible story are like breadcrumbs for the last generation—breadcrumbs helping us *to discover* the *nature of the final battle* of the great controversy.[14]

In the final battle, God's warriors will not fight with machine guns, or grenades, or tanks. *The sword of the Lord and of Gideon* is a trumpet-like warning message proclaimed by vessels of broken clay who are filled with the radiance of God's glory.

And *the sword of the Lord and of Gideon* cannot be wielded by those who are distracted by worldly interests or fearful of hardship and inconvenience. Self and selfish ambition must be put away. Only vessels of broken clay will shine with the light of heaven.

—Like a Rosetta Stone

Years before Gideon, Joshua led Israel against the fortified city of Jericho. That story is another example of *fishing in broad daylight*.

Again, the plan of attack makes no sense to military strategists. And again we find a story that is just riddled with breadcrumbs for us who face earth's final battle—a Rosetta Stone for the prophecies of the last days.

The procession that compassed the doomed city must have been as impressive as it was significant.

[14] 1 Corinthians 10:11, "Now all these things happened unto them for ensamples: and they are written for our admonition, upon whom the ends of the world are come".

> "First came the warriors, a body of chosen men, not now to conquer by their own skill and prowess, but by *obedience to the directions given from God*. Seven priests with trumpets followed. Then the ark of God, surrounded by a halo of divine glory, was born by priests clad in the dress denoting their sacred office. The army of Israel followed, each tribe under its standard."[15]

On the final day—just prior to the demise of the wall surrounding Jericho—the seven priests blast their seven trumpets. This was the signal for the army of Israel (stationed behind the halo-encircled ark) to give their loud cry.

There was no need to consult with the PhD's. It was pointless to confer with the leading scientists and experts.

> "How unscientific, how inconsistent, would they have thought the movements of Joshua and his armies at the taking of Jericho!... Where were the scientific methods of this warfare? The Lord works in His own way in order that man shall not lift themselves up in pride of intellect and take credit and the glory to themselves. The Lord would have every human being understand that his capabilities and endowments are from the Lord. God works by whom He will."[16]

Their strength rested in their simple obedience to the directions of God.[17] They were not to fight for themselves. They were to be instruments to execute the will of God—not to seek riches or self-exultation, but to bring glory to Jehovah their King.[18]

—Giving the Lie to the Christian Profession

Disregarding the Lord's instructions, one warrior took spoils—some gold, some silver, a goodly Babylonish garment. Here is commentary from the Spirit of Prophecy:

> "For a goodly Babylonish garment, multitudes sacrifice the approval of conscience and their hope of heaven. Multitudes barter their integrity, and their capabilities for usefulness, for a bag of silver shekels. The cries of the suffering poor are unheeded; the gospel light is hindered in its course; the scorn of worldlings is kindled by practices that give the lie to the Christian profession; and yet the covetous professor continues to heap up treasure...

---

[15] Ellen G. White, *Patriarchs and Prophets*, p. 488. Emphasis added.
[16] Ellen G. White, *Letter 54*, 1894.
[17] Ellen G. White, *Patriarchs and Prophets*, p. 488.
[18] Ibid., p. 491.

> "Achan's sin brought disaster upon the whole nation. For one man's sin the displeasure of God will rest upon His church till the transgression is searched out and put away. The influence most to be feared by the church is not that of open opposers, infidels, and blasphemers, but of inconsistent professors of Christ. These are the ones that keep back the blessing of the God of Israel and bring weakness upon His people.
>
> "When the church is in difficulty, when coldness and spiritual declension exist, giving occasion for the enemies of God to triumph, then, instead of folding their hands and lamenting their unhappy state, let its members inquire if there is not an Achan in the camp. With humiliation and searching of heart, let each seek to discover the hidden sins that shut out God's presence."[19]
>
> "The Captain of the Lord's host communicated only with Joshua; He did not reveal Himself to all of the congregation, and it rested with them to believe or doubt the words of Joshua, to obey the commands given by him in the name of the Lord or to deny his authority."[20]

God has given us ample evidence concerning the inspiration of the Bible and of the words of His prophets. He has given us detailed and explicit instruction about our work—and we need not expect that He will send an angel to us personally to tell us what we ought to know already.

—Recruiting Full-Time Fishers

The story of the early disciples' fishing campaign took place at the beginning of Christ's public ministry to Galilee. It was His purpose to call those who had been part-time, spare-time workers into full-time labor with Him. But before He would ask these simple fishermen to leave their livelihoods and to join an itinerant ministry—one not sanctioned by the religious authorities, one that had just suffered a miserable defeat in Judea—He would show them He really did know how to catch fish. He really was the Son of God, able even to command the forces of nature and effect the swimming patterns of the deep.

The fishermen dropped their nets again into the sea, just like Jesus asked. And so great was the catch that the nets broke; and both boats were filled to the point of nearly sinking. There were more fish than they could handle. Peter, overwhelmed with his own sinfulness, fell prostrate at the feet of Jesus.

---

[19] Ibid., p. 497.

[20] Ibid., p. 493.

—A Prophetic Roadmap

The Old Testament stories are not the only ones with breadcrumbs for the last generation. In fact, the footprints of Jesus put down a kind of prophetic roadmap, and the stories He told always contained last-days significance.

The Gospels record two grand fishing campaigns—separated by the storm of Calvary. One was *this* fishing expedition on Gennesaret in Galilee. The other was on the Sea of Tiberius just before Pentecost—before the *early rain* outpouring of the Holy Spirit.

We Seventh-day Adventist speak longingly of (and pray earnestly for) the latter rain—as if we wrap all our hope for successful evangelism into that great event. But while we wait for that "glory which is to fill the whole earth,"[21] we neglect fishing on Gennesaret. Oh yes, we fish, but we fail to catch; we fail because we don't fish the way Jesus fished. We don't follow the blueprints for the vital work that God has given us to do.

We consider ourselves expert fishermen. But what of the catch?

We consider ourselves expert healers—world class medical facilities and professionals. But what of the catch?

We consider ourselves expert educators—world class universities and professors. But what of the catch?

We consider ourselves expert evangelists—multimedia prophecy extravaganzas. But what of the catch?

—The Galilee Protocol

Gennesaret was the beginning of the work in Galilee. From there Jesus went "about all Galilee, *teaching* in the synagogues, and *preaching* the gospel of the kingdom, and *healing* all manner of disease among the people."[22] He did not use the systems or conventions of the world. He did not borrow techniques or procedures from the preachers, teachers, or physicians of His time. "By methods peculiarly His own, Christ helped all those who were in sorrow and affliction."[23]

---

[21] In Revelation 18:1, there is an angel with great power that fills the earth with his glory. This angel repeats the three angels' messages from chapter 14, but this time they go forth with the great power of the Holy Spirt during the latter rain. See also Ellen G. White, *1888 Materials*, p. 946; and *Letter 76*, 1898.

[22] Matthew 4:2.

[23] Ellen G. White, *The Ministry of Healing*, p. 23.

> "We are to work as Christ worked, in the same practical lines. Then we will be safe. The divine commission needs no reform. Christ's way of presenting the truth cannot be improved upon."[24] "Christ's method alone will give true success in reaching the people."[25]

We must reactivate this *Galilee Protocol!* Our work today is the same as Christ's work during His earthly ministry.

The *Galilee Protocol* vision is to use the cities of America as a stage upon which to unite a glorious display of Christ's righteousness so as to set the global context for the last conflict in the great controversy.

The *Galilee Protocol* is an urgent intervention plan. It sounds the alarm to the people of this world: that unless they turn to the Great Physician for physical healing; enroll in the School of Christ for restoration of their minds; and come to Christ (the only mediator between God and man) for spiritual regeneration: the judgments of God are soon to fall upon them.

The *Galilee Protocol* operates as these three primary elements: educational, ministerial, and medical. It uses specific activity to present Jesus as man's only hope for mental, spiritual, and physical restoration.

The *Galilee Protocol* has certain program absolutes—those clear *directives* that must be in place and cannot be compromised. These are found in the inspired blueprints.

The *Galilee Protocol* is city-centric. Christ said He was sent to the cities. He sends us there too.

The *Galilee Protocol* is missionarial. Christ was a missionary—sacrificing everything for the benefit of lost humanity. Our work is also missionarial.

The *Galilee Protocol* is provocative. Christ did not work quietly behind the scenes. His message and methods demanded attention. We must also catch the world's attention.

The *Galilee Protocol* is advocative. Though provocative, Christ made it clear that He was an advocate for man. We must present Christ as the sinner's best friend and only hope.

The *Galilee Protocol* is representative. Christ is waiting with a longing desire for the manifestation of Himself in His church. There must be a

---

[24] Ellen G. White, *Letter 123*, June 25, 1903.

[25] Ellen G. White, *The Ministry of Healing*, p. 143.

revival of primitive godliness in the lives of His messengers. In our lives we need to reverse the popular war against Christian standards.

The *Galilee Protocol* is organized. Inspiration tells us that "diligent work is now called for. In this crisis, no halfhearted effort will prove successful. In our cities we are to hunt for souls. Wise plans are to be laid, in order that such a work may be done to the best possible advantage."[26]

—Fishing After the Storm

It is a mistake for us to wait for the latter rain before we put everything into the work of evangelism. The gospel stories of the two great fishing campaigns help us understand this. When we compare the two stories—we see some significant contrasts.

Fast-forward roughly two years. Now we're at the Sea of Tiberius. Much has happened since that early call by Lake Gennesaret. Mighty has been Christ's teaching, and the preaching, and the healing. But not only Christ—His disciples too.

Everyone in the region knows of these itinerant *medical missionaries* and of their peculiar ministry. Scarce are those left untouched by these demonstrators of Christ's love and power through His *Galilee Protocol.*

Everybody also knows that things didn't end well. That last week, the people suddenly went from proclaiming Him King (coats and palm branches and all), to executing Him on the charges of sedition and treason. Jesus had challenged the authority of the teachers and preachers and physicians of His time. He got in the way of ambitious people. His way offered no opportunity for earthly greatness, no earthly wealth, no earthly kingdom—so they turned against Him. They murdered Him; and His disciples scattered.

But at the Sea of Tiberius—after things had settled—very early in the morning, Christ was again by the water's edge. Peter and company were coming in after another night of fishing. And again, there was no fish.

They didn't recognize Jesus standing on the shore. Calling out to them, He said, "Children, have ye any meat?"

"No," they answered.

"Cast your net on the right side of the ship and you will find!"

---

[26] Ellen G. White, *Evangelism*, p. 59.

Here, the right side was toward the shore. It would have made better sense to cast the nets toward the deep water. But Jesus was on the shore—so that was the side of faith.

We must not think of fishing success as science. We must think of it as faith. If we will but labor in connection with Christ—His divine power combining with our human effort—we cannot fail of success.[27]

—Comparing Fishing Trips

The *first* fishing campaign (Lake of Gennesaret) was during the three-and-a-half-year ministry of Christ. It was at the beginning of His work in Galilee. The *second* fishing campaign (Sea of Tiberias) was after the storm (Calvary), just before *Pentecost* and the *Early Rain.*

Lake Gennesaret and the Sea of Tiberius are both the same body of water—*Gennesaret* being a local, national name (Galilean), and *Tiberius* being the name given by the Global Roman Empire. The *first* campaign represented *fishing for men* in Galilee; the *second* campaign represented *fishing for men* throughout the "then known world."

During the *first* fishing campaign (Lake of Gennesaret), the nets broke, and the fish came into the boats nearly sinking them. During the *second* fishing campaign (Sea of Tiberias), the Bible specifically notes that the nets did *not* break; and that the fish did not come into the boat. Instead, they were dragged ashore, still in the nets.

In the *first* fishing campaign, each fish was part of a great, unnumbered multitude. In the *second* campaign, they were counted.[28] (153 fish).

Peter (in the *first* campaign), falls down before Jesus, saying "Depart from me, for I am a sinful man, O Lord." But in the *second* campaign, although he was naked in the boat, (and he again quickly swims to Jesus), this time, there is no mention of His sin or confession.

We need to dig deep here to understand the symbolism. The Roman Church teaches an erroneous doctrine that Peter was the head of the church. They claim the popes are his successors. In Acts, we can see that Peter did not hold this dominate authority. When the assembly met at Jerusalem to consider disputations about what the converting Gentiles would need to do, Peter was there to testify—as were also James,

[27] Ellen G. White, The *Desire of Ages*, p. 811.

[28] John 21:11.

Barnabas, and Paul. But on this occasion, it was James who was chosen to preside over the council and to announce its decision.[29]

Christ is Himself the real and only head of the church.[30] The Bible is clear about this. While not the head, Peter is sometimes used to symbolize the church. When he said to Jesus, "Thou art the Christ, the Son of the living God," he "expressed the truth which is the foundation of the church's faith."

> Then Jesus "honored him *as the representative of the whole body of believers*. He said, 'I will give unto thee the keys of the kingdom of heaven: whatsoever thou shalt bind on earth shall be bound in heaven: and whatsoever thou shalt loose on earth shall be loosed in heaven.'
>
> "'The keys of the kingdom of heaven' are the words of Christ. All the words of Holy Scripture are His, and are here included.... They declare the conditions upon which men are received or rejected. Thus the work of those who preach God's word is a savor of life unto life or of death unto death...
>
> "The Savior did not commit the work of the gospel to Peter individually. At a later time, repeating the words that were spoken to Peter, He applied them directly to the church."[31]

When considering the footsteps of Jesus as a prophetic roadmap, we can often see Peter symbolically representing the church—not as head, but as the body. In the stories of the fishing campaigns—Peter helps us see something of the *condition* of the church.

Since we've already gone deep, we should notice one other important point. We think of nakedness as having to do with shame. In Genesis, Adam and Eve sew together fig leaves to cover their nakedness—while hiding themselves from the Lord.[32] Isaiah and Revelation links shame with nakedness.[33] Ezekiel links nakedness with whoredoms and pollution.[34] This is because of guilt.

Conversely, there is a nakedness in scripture that denotes purity. Before the fall, "they were both naked, the man and his wife, and were *not* ashamed."[35] When Joseph fled from Potiphar's wife, he was naked—but

---

[29] Acts 15; Ellen G. White, *The Acts of the Apostles*, pp. 194, 195.

[30] Ephesians 1:22, 5:23, 1 Corinthians 11:3, Colossians 1:18, 2:10.

[31] Ellen G. White, The *Desire of Ages*, pp. 413-414, emphasis added; see also Matthew 16:19; John 20:23.

[32] Genesis 3:7-10.

[33] Isaiah 47:3; Revelation 3:18.

[34] Ezekiel 16:36; 22:10.

[35] Genesis 2:25.

pure in heart. The Son of God was naked[36] on Calvary's cross—shameless because of His spotless life; and ashamed because He bore our sins.

The *first* call (at Gennesaret) inaugurates a national campaign when the church (Peter) is sinful, but repenting and confessing at the feet of Jesus. In careful obedience to Christ's specific (although unorthodox) instructions, His disciples go fishing. That campaign catches many fish, but it also breaks the nets and nearly sinks the ship. They catch a great unnumbered multitude.

The *second* call (at Tiberius) inaugurates an international campaign when the church is pure having no spot or wrinkle or any such thing. It is no longer clothed with fig leaves or animal skins; it wears rather the *light of God's glory*—even as the power of the Holy Spirit fell on the church at Pentecost. This campaign also catches many fish, but this time the nets don't break, and the fish—though caught and brought ashore—are not brought into the boat. This catch is numbered. Though not elaborated here, all these symbols are worthy of attention and study.

—Let's Go Fishing

For us today it is still too early for Sea-of-Tiberius fishing. But God still asks us to fish. It's time. In fact, we're overdue for a Gennesaret fishing campaign. Yes, the church is weak, and we make mistakes, and we still haven't made our way past our Laodicea problem. And no, we cannot expect the *latter rain* to fall on an impure people. But at Gennesaret, Christ intervenes for His own name's sake. He intervenes in response to the disciple's simple act of obeying His call to go fishing—not their way, but according to His peculiar *protocol.*

It's time to reactivate the *Galilee Protocol.* Our old way of fishing is not working anymore. Under the *Galilee Protocol,* Christ wants His spare-time disciples to become full-time workers for Him. But first He bids us go fishing—not like the worldly-wise professional fishermen do, but following *Christ's method alone!* When we do, He will supply the fish in so marvelous a manner, that like Peter, we will surrender our all to the Master Fisherman.

---

[36] Most sources state that the common and expected form of crucifixion by the Romans involved total nakedness. There is some disagreement as to whether Jesus had on a loin cloth. It is also doubtful that Peter was totally naked on the boat—as working that way would be unlikely. The Bible account does say Peter was naked—as men were considered to be in those times if they only wore a loin cloth. This is likely true of Joseph as well. This still preserves the usefulness of the symbolism.

CHAPTER TWENTY-ONE

Magnum Opus

The year is 1901. The San Francisco earthquake is still five years away. Elder John Corliss addresses the delegates of the General Conference Session assembled at Battle Creek, Michigan. Our interest in John has to do with his connection to the mission in San Francisco. He plays a key role there; and he's here to speaks about it to the delegates. Our interest in the San Francisco mission is very much tied to the earthquake that will strike the *"City by the Bay"* in just a few years.

We are interested in that mission because it has been said to be, "perhaps the most fully developed program of Gospel-Medical Missionary Evangelism ever carried out in modern times."[1] We're interested in this earthquake because out of all the disasters to hit our world in modern times, it most clearly bears the signature of heaven.[2]

We have previously concluded that we must present the three angels' messages as the perfect blend of God's justice and mercy. We have noticed that Jesus combined a judgment-hour message with His own brand of medical missionary work; and we realize that, as His last-day people, God has commissioned us to do the same in the large cities of America. We have also observed that His *Galilee Protocol* is the only

---

[1] Dave Fiedler, *D'Sozo -Reversing the Worst Evil*, p. 161, (Remnant Publications, 2012).

[2] See chapter four, *Mistaken Identity*.

method that properly presents the cohesion that must exist between the law and the grace of God's righteous character.

The end-time rendition of the *Galilee Protocol* will be properly suited for the last generation; it will be the *Magnum Opus* of Seventh-day Adventism. The San Francisco mission was a precursor to our end-time work; and in this chapter we will use it to help describe the characteristics of the final product.

—John Corliss (Battle Creek, Michigan)

John Corliss is a key figure to our story. We first run into him in Battle Creek, Michigan—some thirty-six years before the 1901 General Conference Session. A new convert—and recently discharged from the army—he ends up living with James and Ellen White for about two years. James is in poor health (recovering from his first stroke), and the Whites are busy with much travel and a new project.

In 1863, Ellen received the famous health vision; and in December 1865, she was instructed that Adventists were to build a health institute to care for the sick and to educate people about health. So the Whites' new project was this *Western Health Reform Institute*—later to become known as the *Battle Creek Sanitarium.* For a sort time, John Corliss served as superintendent and chaplain there.[3]

—John Corliss (Australasia)

We run into John again in the 1890s. This time in the Australasian South Pacific—in New Zealand and Australia. He is here with Ellen White, Ellen's son Willie, and Elder A. G. Daniells. Also, with them are Arthur and Emma Semmens, nurses—recently trained by Dr. Kellogg at the *Battle Creek Sanitarium.* How they are in "Australia" is a complicated story; but while here, God intends for them to plot a new course, as it looks certain back home, that the *U.S.S. Galilee Protocol* will not sail any time soon.

In the United States there was some semblance of the three-components required for *Isaiah 58 style* medical missionary work; but each component was isolated and running pretty-well off-course. The health work in Battle Creek was a self-absorbed monster and deaf to the cries of the prophet. The benevolence work in Chicago was separated from

[3] Fiedler, p. 159.

the gospel—and gobbling up time and money while making little progress in saving souls. The ministerial department had a real need for "*Christ our Righteousness*"—something our ministerial leaders proved all too determined to resist at the then recent 1888 General Conference. They too turned a deaf ear—and sending Sister White to Australia seem like a good way to turn the 1888 volume down.

—A True Pattern

To be successful, the work must be symmetrical—that's the word Sister White used. She said,

> "It is [God's] purpose that there shall be a true pattern in Australia—a sample of how other fields shall be worked. The work should be symmetrical, and a living witness for the truth."[4]

It also must differ from what was happening in America:

> "The light that has been given to me regarding the work of the Avondale school is that we must not pattern it after the similitude of any school which has already been established."[5]

Arthur and Emma Semmons had received their nursing training at one of those *already established* schools. Working according to the new pattern proved to challenge them. They later wrote:

> "Our first work began in the Australian Bible School, located at St. Kilda, Victoria. Here we had many varied experiences... Later we labored in tent and Bible work in Sydney, under the direction of J. O. Corliss, doing much work among the sick. We did not understand why we could not enter upon strictly medical work; we know now. God was training us, that we should not be one-sided workers, but have an all-around experience."[6]

The Whites were there to make sure the work followed the blueprint. The Semmons supplied the medical background. John Corliss was there for his evangelistic expertise. And Australia provided the perfect environment to force them all to work together.

The Australian banking system had just crashed so the development of the humanitarian arm of the work was a simple necessity. Because Australia was broke (and the churches in America were holding on to their money), the Australian team had to work on a lean financial basis.

---

[4] Ellen G. White, *General Conference Bulletin*, March 2, 1899.

[5] Ellen G. White, *Manuscript Releases*, vol 8, p. 150.

[6] Arthur Semmons, *General Conference Bulletin*, June 2, 1909, p. 284.

This helped to further the cause for symmetry. Here is what Elder Daniells said about it:

> "Our medical work [in Australasia] stands in the same relation to the evangelical work and organizations that all the rest of the work does. We have no separate medical organization... When we first started out, the first man that came to us was Brother A. W. Semmens, a nurse who graduated from Battle Creek Sanitarium. When he came out there, I did not know what to do, to get him started in the medical work. Some of our brethren had a little more light, and they said, 'Let us make him a preacher and a medical worker combined. Let us have him work in the churches, and tell the brethren of the gospel of health, and let us help support him from the tithes of the Conference."[7]

—John Corliss (San Francisco)

When John Corliss returned to America in 1897, he brought the pattern with him. This is the J.O. Corliss that joined the work in San Francisco in 1899. And this is the J.O. Corliss that addressed the delegates at the 1901 General Conference Session. His experience in the work had taught him well. To the delegates, he said,

> "I have been struck with the thought that in every instance where the Savior has given the gospel commission, and sent out His workers, he told them to heal the sick... Thus the Savior gave his ministers just the same authority to heal the sick as to preach the gospel. He has united the two things in gospel work, so that it would seem almost impossible to separate them. There is no one thing which has all the elements in it for city work."[8]

John brought the pattern from the "*Land Down Under*" to America—specifically to San Francisco. After visiting the San Francisco mission in December 1900, Ellen White described it like this:

> "There are many lines of Christian effort being carried forward by our brethren and sisters in San Francisco. These include visiting the sick and destitute, finding homes for orphans, and work for the unemployed; nursing the sick, and teaching the love of Christ from house to house; the distribution of literature; and the conducting of classes for healthful living and the care of the sick. A school for the children is conducted in the basement of the meeting-house. In another part of the city a workingmen's home and medical mission is maintained. On Market Street, near City Hall, there is a bath establishment, operating as a branch of the St. Helena Sanitarium. In the same locality is a depot of the Health Food Company, where health foods are not only sold, but instruction is given as to reform and diet.

---

[7] A. G. Daniells, *General Conference Bulletin*, April 7, 1901, p. 91-92. See Ellen G. White, *Manuscript Releases*, vol 13, p. 281.
[8] John Corliss, *General Conference Bulletin*, April 21,1901, p. 370-372.

"Nearer the center of the city, our people conduct a vegetarian cafe, which is open six days in the week, and entirely closed on the Sabbath. Here about five hundred meals are served daily, and no flesh-meats are used.

"Dr. and Mrs. Dr. Lamb are doing much medical work for the poor in connection with their regular practice; and Dr. Buchannan is doing much free work at the workingmen's home. At the medical and dental schools in the city, there are about twenty of our young people in attendance.

"We earnestly hope that the steps taken in the future in the work in San Francisco will still be steps of progress. The work that has been done here is but a beginning. San Francisco is a world in itself, and the Lord's work there is to broaden and deepen."[9]

Writing of the same visit, she concludes,

"We have every reason to believe that the work carried on in San Francisco by Brother Corliss and his brethren is the work that needs to be done. San Francisco is a center, and must be thoroughly worked. A much more extensive work should be done in this great and wicked city."[10]

—Already Many Years Behind

Sometimes, timing is everything. There was a time when San-Francisco-style mission work was the best and most appropriate—but by the time we figured it out in San Francisco, we were already many years behind. As early as 1903 we learn that we had missed our window of opportunity:

"A great work is to be done. I am moved by the Spirit of God to say to those engaged in the Lord's work, that the favorable time for our message to be carried to the cities has passed by, and this work has not been done. I feel a heavy burden that we shall now redeem the time."[11]

The favorable time *passed*; but the importance of city work had not. It was still important on November 17, 1910, when an article by Sister White appeared in *The Review and Herald* declaring:

"The work in the cities is the essential work for this time. When the cities are worked as God would have them, the result will be the setting in operation of a mighty movement such as we have not yet witnessed."[12]

It was also important in 1910, when Ellen White awoke from another nighttime vision.

---

[9] Ellen G. White, *Australasian Union Conference Record*, March 1, 1901.

[10] Ellen G. White, *Manuscript Releases*, vol. 17, p. 41.

[11] Ellen G. White, *Manuscript 62*, 1903.

[12] Ellen G. White, *The Review and Herald*, November 17, 1910.

> "During the night of February 27, a representation was given me in which the unworked cities were represented before me as a living reality, and I was plainly instructed that there should be a decided change from past methods of working. For months the situation has been pressed upon my mind, and I urge that companies be organized and diligently trained to labor in our important cities. These workers should go two by two, and then from time to time all should meet together to relate their experiences, to pray, and to plan how to reach the people quickly, and thus if possible, redeem time.
>
> "There is no time to colonize. From city to city the work is to be carried quickly. Let companies be quickly organized to go out two by two, and labor in the spirit of Christ, following His plans."[13]

By 1910, God had also been letting a bit of His wrath show through. The Battle Creek Sanitarium already burned to the ground—as had the Review and Herald, and yes—even the Pacific Press. He called for a reorganization of the General Conference; and there was a stream of pointed rebukes and warnings from the pen of respiration. Dr. Kellogg and Battle Creek were abandoned; and the center for the medical work relocated to California. And let's not forget the San Francisco earthquake.

God's wrath was showing—but He had not given up. The new school in California was hopeful. As it turns out, "before a single MD ever graduated from the *College of Medical Evangelists*, the principles for which the school was founded had been turned loose on an unsuspecting world—to a small degree"[14] anyway. The San Francisco rendition of *city work* had come and gone; but the next rendition was about to emerge—updated for the times. It would incorporate the decided changes called for in the February 27th vision.

—Enter, John Tindall

The administrators of the *College of Medical Evangelists* needed a man to pioneer this new approach. One student stood out: John Tindall.

Though raised a Methodist, Tindall's religion began to fall apart when his little brother died. An old-fashioned hellfire and brimstone preacher fully cinched it for him. John had trouble relating to God and religion. He became an atheist. In his own words he later said, "I was honestly at war with what I believed to be the greatest fraud ever perpetrated on mankind."[15]

---

[13] Ellen G. White, *The Paulson Collection*, p. 69.

[14] Fiedler, p. 219.

[15] *Gospel-medical Evangelistic Campaign, conducted jointly by the Southeastern California Conference and the*

While traveling on a train one day, John was ranting to a car full of spectators with all his militant, evolutionist, existentialist, atheist rhetoric. A tall, stately gentleman—with a pleasing countenance—took a seat almost directly in front of him. In just three questions, the man completely upset John's arguments and left him speechless. A few minutes later, the gentleman got up and quietly left.

The more John thought about it the more humiliated he became. Anger and grim determination prompted him to find this man. He searched the entire train in vain. He later said, "The train was running at least forty-five or fifty miles an hour—the man did not get off: who he was, where he came from, what became of him, is a mystery, but I believe him to have been a messenger from God to me, and no ordinary being."[16] John became an agnostic: He could no longer say that "there is no God."

Sometime later, a prospecting trip took him to the mountains of San Diego. The group would stop at the "humble home of a very peculiar man—a man of about 64 years, who would not wish him to smoke in his house, who ate no meat, and who was very peculiar in his religion and in many other ways, but who would make [them] in every way comfortable and at home."[17]

John saw that the old man was bright and strong and set out to test his character—and his peculiar religion. Day after day he purposely tried to displease the old man—to try his temper. He made fun of his religion. But "Daddy Bell" was always of the same sweet temper.

Fate would have it that Tindall received a leg injury. It laid him up for some time out there in the mountains—and at the older gentleman's cabin. Tindell's host, Daddy Bell, turned out to be a good nurse. He was also a good evangelist—unafraid to tackle Tindall's objections and concerns. He eventually convinced him concerning the inspiration of the Bible—and as an added bonus: the *Spirit of Prophecy*.

> "The idea of a contemporary prophet had an obvious appeal. What an opportunity! A way to actually know what was what, from God's perspective. More than that, it was the *Desire of Ages* that reached his heart."[18]

College of Medical Evangelists, under the direction of Evangelist John Tindall, p. 161-162, (Redlands, California, 1922).

[16] Ibid.

[17] Ibid.

[18] Fiedler, p. 222.

—Company Evangelism

Tindall's appreciation for the *Spirit of Prophecy* never left him. Learning that there was an Adventist school in California training medical evangelists, John Tindall signed up. The timing was providential. He finished his course in the spring of 1910—when "four hundred twenty-five miles north-northwest of him, the woman whose writings had been instrumental in his conversion was having a restless night." Sister White was receiving special instructions regarding the need for that decided change in our methods of working the cities.

The administrators of the college asked John Tindall to pioneer this new work. After prayer and deliberation, he accepted the call. Unswerving in his confidence in the *Testimonies,* John determined to do it right. He united the recent call for new methods with the earlier instruction on reaching the cities—and thus was born a concept that eventually became known as "company evangelism."

—Providential Mothballs

Before the end-time time-line was fully reset (giving us the proverbial forty years of wilderness wandering); and before the denomination fully turned back toward Egypt (by formally making educational and medical alliances with the world); and before the living flame of inspiration quietly extinguished (at the passing of an old and tired Sister White); God left—for a later generation—the record of what a faithful few learned in those early days.

In the last generation, a fresh group of people will emerge to take up the work at a late moment in time. It will be when the final storm cloud is just about to burst—this time for real—and the world will see trouble such as it has never seen. This fresh group will not have the luxury of slowly assimilating the principles of work as they unfold over decades of patient revelation. But they will have the models—carefully preserved in providential mothballs. They'll discover the detailed battle plans.

The *company evangelism* that was the *Galilee Protocol* of Tindall's day, will be a great starting point for a *Galilee Protocol* for the last generation. Here are the details of that company-evangelism model.[19]

[19] Fiedler, see chapters 18-20.

—A Synopsis

Company evangelism comprised six-month campaigns. A team had two groups—a visiting group and a local group. In a small team, the visiting group would typically have an evangelist, a medical helper, and a Bible worker. Already trained, these would lead and teach the local group—usually volunteers.

Added to the visiting group would be this local group of volunteers—one business manager, one singer, six medical missionaries or nurses, and ten general purpose volunteers.

1. Preliminary work in the city would comprise contacting various clubs, schools, lodges and other organizations to arrange appointments for health lectures. Friends would be made through these lectures, and interests would be gathered. A medical missionary training program would be conducted for church members while the health lectures are given throughout the city.

They would stress the positive, practical side of health reform. Those from the visiting group would work with the church members visiting their friends and neighbors—especially those who have asked for physical help. Thus the church and the visiting group would fuse and unite their efforts for soul winning.

2. A public effort would be conducted. A broad, well-balanced program of health would be presented through this series—based on a knowledge of the human body. Physiology would be the basis for every lecture; and they would teach the audience the laws of the body are as divine as the precepts of the Decalogue. They would keep this thought before the people: The Creator has made us for health and happiness, not disease and misery. This would lay a strong foundation for an appreciation of the moral law.

As those attending the meeting would change their habits of life, their health would improve. Some would abandon liquor, tobacco, tea, coffee, and other poisons even before the subject of the Sabbath would be presented. In those cases, their minds would be in a much better condition to weigh and appreciate the special message for this time. Having experienced the beneficial results of obedience to natural laws—they would see the importance of obeying every command of the moral law.

3. Many would desire further instruction. This opens the way for a more personal work in their homes. Classes on cooking and other phases of health would be held—using *Ministry of Healing* and inexpensive

tracts. It is best to do these in their homes too. Close contact with people is important and gives precious opportunity to help them personally.

There is sickness in many homes. Acute and chronic illness furnish opportunities for simple treatments—given by nurses or other trained workers. One treatment in the home often does more to break down prejudice than many public lectures or sermons.

Meanwhile, there would be an ever-ongoing aspect to the work. Monday morning meetings would be held with all team members for instruction, coordination, and prayer. Also, classes would be offered on Bible topics, cooking, and home nursing—some for the public, and often separately for church members. Doctors and nurses would give free health consultation and treatments; in-home physician or nurse visitation would be offered for free; and in-home Bible reading, and Bible studies would be offered.

4. The Savior spent much of His time among the poor ministering to their physical and spiritual necessities. In large cities today many poor need health instructions and more. Food and clothing often need to be provided. This is an essential part of medical missionary work—and it is a phase every church member can share in. The great medical missionary chapter—Isaiah 58—is very practical in its instruction. "Deal thy bread to the hungry," clothe the naked, "bring the poor that are cast out into thy house."—these are the commands of our heavenly Father.

5. In every city there are those we cannot reach by meetings. Business and social life keep them occupied—we must reach these higher classes by special efforts. Health lectures given before their businesses or social groups are a means of contact with some. Most important for this class—is personal ministry in the home.

Efforts to help these neglected classes build goodwill even among those who do not accept the full message. It is important for us to become known as a medical missionary people by judges, legislatures, physicians, and ministers of other denominations.

6. Teams of varied talent and training are needed to carry on the medical-evangelistic program as outlined by the Spirit of Prophecy. The instruction on this matter is clear: "There should be companies organized and educated most thoroughly to work as nurses, as evangelists, as ministers, as canvassers, as gospel students, to perfect a character after the divine similitude."[20]

---

[20] Ellen G.White, *Counsels on Health*, p. 541.

It is essential that we do more than put together the minister and the physician, the nurse and the Bible worker, and call the group a medical missionary company. In the ideal program, every evangelistic worker is to be a health worker, and every health worker must be a soul winner.

—I Wonder

Tindall's model never really caught on. The new world—with its industrial and scientific revolution—infiltrated the church. The glitter and comforts of normal living attracted us; and the careers that would make it all possible enticed us. We lacked the faith to trust God's choices for our lives—and His ability and commitment to supply our need. We proved unwilling to depend fully on Him, or accept that He would make us successful even without entangling with the education and medicine of the world. We learned to despise the *Testimonies;* and we shunned the self-sacrificing life of the missionary.

When the time comes again for us to take up the work of the medical missionary company, maybe some things will have changed for the better. For starters, now our denomination has deep roots all over the globe. This opens up a vast field before us. Our experience with foreign missions has taught us techniques of labor that frugally use money and time. And in America, the Adventist living standard is already comfortable. Maybe for some, the new-worldly glitter has faded; and there are among us a growing group of earnest souls who grow tired of this world, and who *sigh and cry*[21] over the condition of the church.

Is there today, a ready group large enough to start the ball rolling with the *Galilee Protocol*? I wonder. In America we need to target our cities with a special *Galilee Protocol* geared to our time. Such a protocol must follow the pattern of Christ when He walked in Galilee. We see His principles at work in the Australian pattern—adapted for that time and place. We see His principles at work in the San Francisco pattern—adapted for another time and place. We see His principles at work in Tindall's pattern of company evangelism—adapted for the needs of his time. Today's *Galilee Protocol* must be true to the same principles used by these great models of yesteryear—while adapting to our world right now.

Such a protocol would be some kind of domestic synthesis of Christ's work, the mission of the twelve disciples, the seventy, and the early

---

[21] Ezekiel 9:4.

Christian church. It would share the principle characteristics of the Australian pattern, the San Francisco pattern, company evangelism, maybe even *Maranatha International*, and *Adventist Frontier Missions*. It would be a visionary missionary movement aimed squarely at America's largest and most sinful cities.

Such a protocol would make it possible for all to take part who catch the vision and desire to labor. Adventist young people from our schools, and members of all ages from our churches, would be trained to work variously sized blocks of time, plugged into well-organized, short-term city mission campaigns. Today's *Galilee Protocol* would follow Christ's financial model—relying upon the homes, and food, and hospitality of friendly partners wherever God calls His workers to labor for Him. Today's *Galilee Protocol* would have small training teams working with interested schools and churches to prepare students and church members to deploy for medical missionary work.

Near the close of every six-month city blitz, today's *Galilee Protocol* would conduct short campmeetings near—but outside the cities. In rural settings—by some lake, or in a mountain retreat, or even in a desert place—interested souls would come away from the hustle and bustle of city life to reinforce what they have learned. They'd come to hear a concluding series of presentations proclaiming the warning of the three-angels with much love, but "borne so decidedly as to startle the hearers."[22]

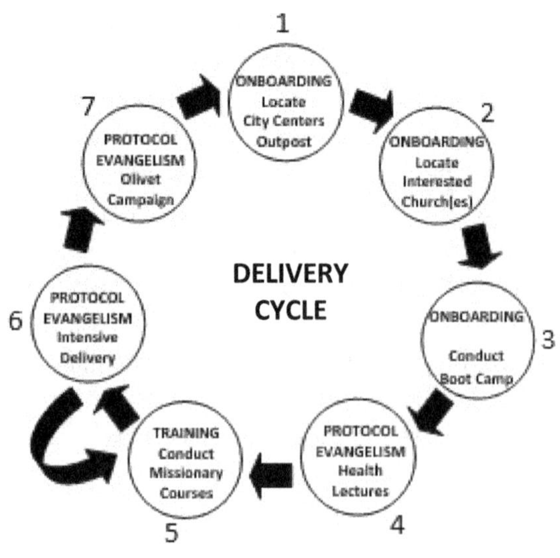

Everything would be calculated—in today's *Galilee Protocol*—to present clearly (by word and service) Christ, the selfless friend of sinners: mankind's redeeming friend; Christ: willing and able to save to the uttermost the body, mind, and soul; and Christ, the righteous judge: unwilling to compromise with

[22] Ellen G. White, *Evangelism*, p. 169.

wickedness. We must warn the world that God's judgments are about to full upon the guilty, and we must tell the cities that God's wrath will fall on them first. The cries of the three angels would sound boldly in today's *Galilee Protocol.* We must bring the world to test in the three areas of reform: body, mind and soul—in worship, education and health reform.

Today's Galilee Protocol would plan to make a substantial and notable impact—seen and heard across the country in just a few years' time. We should expect that by using Christ's special method for working the cities, medical missionaries will attract—by divine providence—national attention. They will "[set into] operation a mighty movement such as we have not yet witnessed." Today's *Galilee Protocol* would be a living, breathing movement—one led by Christ through the Holy Spirit. Such a movement would grow exponentially.

> "We [would] see the medical missionary work broadening and deepening at every point of its progress, because of the inflowing of hundreds and thousands of streams, until the whole earth is covered as the waters cover the sea."[23]

Today's Galilee Protocol could...

Today's Galilee Protocol should...

Today's Galilee Protocol would...

If... If only...

> **"I was shown God's people waiting for some change to take place,—a compelling power to take hold of them. But they will be disappointed, for they are wrong. They must act; they must take hold of the work themselves. The scenes which are passing before us are of sufficient magnitude to cause us to arouse, and urge the truth home to the hearts of all who will listen. The harvest of the earth is nearly ripe."**
>
> **—Testimonies for the Church, vol 1, p. 261.**

[23] Ibid, p. 317.

CHAPTER TWENTY-TWO

A City, A Tower, and A Name

One day a king was walking in his palace admiring the splendor of his kingdom. His palace was a fortress built into the northern wall of the capital city. Part of it was inside the city, part of it was outside. Archeologists call the outside part, the northern fortress. The inside part, they call the southern fortress. And the palace was a fortress to be sure—since that king was the most powerful man in the world.

His palace was a symbol of military might; and it was an icon of beauty and luxury. When his queen missed the mountains and greenery of her homeland, Nebuchadnezzar built her the legendary hanging gardens of Babylon—one of the seven wonders of the world.

This capital fortress embodied a sense of the *physical* strength, wealth, and comfort of that global superpower: Babylon the Great.

Perhaps, looking out a window toward the south (towards the city center), the king sees a mighty monument looming high above the the skyline. It's E-temen-an-ki, a 300-foot-tall ziggurat with seven steps or layers. Its name means "*house of the platform of heaven and earth.*"

E-temen-an-ki was old. It had been a crumbling artifact from antiquity until Nebuchadnezzar renovated it. The original builders never finished the structure; but Nebuchadnezzar did.

Archeologists have a clay tablet containing Nebuchadnezzar's own words telling about E-temen-an-ki. He said:

> "A former king built it, (they reckon 42 ages) but he did not complete its head. Since a remote time, the people had abandoned it, without order expressing their words. Since that time the earthquake and the thunder had dispersed the sun-dried clay. The bricks of the casing had been split, and the earth of the interior had been scraped in heaps. Merodach, the great god, excited my mind to repair the building.
>
> "I did not change the site, nor did I take away the foundation. In a fortunate month, in an auspicious day, I undertook to build porticoes around the crude brick masses, and the casing of burnt bricks. I adapted the circuits, I put an inscription of my name in the Kitir of the portico. I set my hand to finish it, and to exalt its head. As it had been done in ancient days, so I exalted its summit."[1]

Both the ancient city of Babylon—and before that, the tower of Babel—where in the plain of Shinar, and evidently built in the same place. Notice how Nebuchadnezzar said the former builder did not complete the head, and that the people had abandoned it "without order expressing their words." In other words, they stopped building because the Lord confounded their language. In Genesis 11:6-9, the Bible says:

> "The whole earth was of one language, and of one speech. And it came to pass, as they journeyed from the east, that they found a plain in the land of Shinar; and they dwelt there. And they said one to another, Go to, let us make brick, and burn them thoroughly. And they made brick for stone, and slime had they for mortar. And they said, Go to, let us build a city and a tower, whose top may reach unto the heaven; and let us make a name, lest we be scattered abroad upon the face of the whole earth.
>
> "And the Lord came down to see the city and the tower, which the children of men builded. And the Lord said, Behold, the people is one, and they have all one language; and this they begin to do: and now nothing will be restrained from them, which they have imagined to do. Go to, let us go down, and confound their language, that they may not understand one another's speech. So the Lord scattered them from thence upon the face of all the earth: and they left off to build the city. Therefore is the name of it called Babel; because the Lord did confound the language of all the earth: and from thence did the Lord scatter them abroad upon the face of all the earth."[2]

---

[1] John McClintock, James Strong, *McClintock and Strong Cyclopaedia*, pp. 465–*469.* (1894). Emphasis Added.

[2] Genesis 11:6-9.

—The Power of Language

The *Tower of Babel* was a monument to human wisdom and knowledge. The role that language played at Babel helps us understand this. Scientists like to ponder the intellectual differences between the various species of animals. Daniel Dennett, in a piece entitled *The Role of Language in Intelligence*, says human beings "are without any doubt at all the most intelligent. We are also the only species with language."

He suggests that rather than getting bogged down about the biological differences in the brains of various species, we should simply consider that it is language that takes "our species right off the scale of intelligence that ranks the pig above the lizard, and the ant above the oyster."

> "Comparing our brains with bird brains or dolphin brains is almost beside the point, because our brains are in effect joined... in a single cognitive system that dwarfs all others. They are joined by [an] innovation that [other animal brains do not have]: language... Each individual human brain, thanks to its communicative links, is the beneficiary of the cognitive labors of the others."[3]

With language we can pool our collective knowledge and teach each other from our experiences. God saw that humanity's singleness of language fostered an *intellectual* environment where nothing would "be restrained from them, which they [would] imagine to do." By confounding our language, God confused our collective enterprise.

In the book, Patriarch and Prophets, we read how after the flood,

> "God had directed men to disperse throughout the earth, to replenish it and subdue it; but these Babel builders determined to keep their community united in one body, and to found a monarchy that should eventually embrace the whole earth. Thus, their city would become the metropolis of a universal empire; its glory would command the admiration and homage of the world and render its founders illustrious. The magnificent tower, reaching to the heavens, was intended to stand as a monument of the power and *wisdom* of its builders, perpetuating their fame to the latest generations...
>
> "One object before them in the erection of the tower was to secure their own safety in case of another deluge... As they would be able to ascend to the region of the clouds, they hoped to *ascertain* the cause of the Flood."[4]

Where the Babel builder failed (because God intervened), Nebuchadnezzar succeeded. As the Fortress in the city of Babylon embodied a

---

[3] Daniel C. Dennett, *The Role of Language in Intelligence*, 1994. (https://ase.tufts.edu/cogstud/dennett/papers/rolelang.htm). Accessed 3/6/2019.

[4] Ellen G. White, *Patriarch and Prophets*, p. 119. Emphasis added.

sense of her *physical* strength, so E-teman-an-ki, embodied a sense of her *intellectual* strength—knowledge, wisdom and education.

—E-sag-il-a

Perhaps still lingering at the south window in the palace, the king is also thinking about the E-sag-il-a—even future south. It is on the other side of E-temen-an-ki. E-sag-il-a means "*the temple that raises its head.*" Nebuchadnezzar also completed its final version. It was sacred to Marduk—the sun god (father) and to his consort Sarpanit—the moon god (mother).

In France (at the Louvre), there is an artifact called the Esagila tablet. It's a Neo-Babylonia mathematical text describing both the temple of Marduk and the dimensions of E-temen-an-ki. The text illustrates the mathematical calculating methods used by the Babylonians; and the tablet reveals a more mysterious aspect of the art of the scribe. The dimensions were considered "sacred;" and on the back of the tablet, the recapitulation of the dimensions to be calculated are accompanied by the phrase, "let the *initiate* show the *initiate*, the *non-initiate* must not see this."

There existed a closed, learned system for the sole use of the "wise men,"—the guardians of tradition. Many cultures have similar secrets. These *mystery religions* date all the way back to the tower of Babel.

Ellen White tells us that the Egyptians also had these closed mystery religions. "The king of Egypt was also a member of the priesthood; and Moses, though refusing to participate in the heathen worship, was *initiated* into all the *mysteries* of the Egyptian religions."[5]

According to the *Louvre*, the guardians of the secrets of Babylon so safeguarded them they omitted to pass them on to their Greek colleagues. The entire Mesopotamian culture disappeared for nearly two thousand years.

The temple of Marduk—E-sag-il-a— was thought to be the cosmic center of the world.[6] They believed that E-sagil-a was on the very spot where Marduk created the world; and there alone, heaven and earth could interconnect.[7]

---

[5] Ellen G. White, *Education*, p. 62. Emphasis added.

[6] *Visit the Louvre with the Bible*, (https://english.louvrebible.org/index.php/louvrebible/default/visiteguidee?id_menu=VISGO2&&id_oeuvre=137&id_rubrique_menu=148). Accessed 3/6/2019.

[7] Mark Oliver, *Inside Etemenanki: The Real-Life Tower of Babel*, May 10, 2018. (https://www.ancient-origins.net/ancient-places-asia/inside-etemenanki-real-life-tower-babel-0010025). Accessed 3/6/2019.

As the Fortress in the city of Babylon embodied a sense of her *physical* strength, and as E-teman-an-ki, embodied a sense of her *intellectual* strength, so this E-sag-il-a embodied a sense of Babylon's *spiritual* strength—special mystery religions thought to connect them directly to heaven itself.

—Worthy Representatives

Babylon (the city), was a microcosm of the *physical*, *intellectual*, and *spiritual* power of Babylon. Daniel and his three friends understood this. Nebuchadnezzar brought these captives back from his exploits against Israel. He told the master of his eunuchs,

> "that he should bring certain of the children of Israel... [those] well favored, and skillful in wisdom, and cunning in knowledge, and understanding science, and such as had ability to stand in the king's palace, and whom they might teach the learning of the Chaldeans. The king appointed them daily provisions of the king's meat, and of the wine which he drank: so to nourish them three years, that at the end thereof they might stand before the king."[8]

Daniel and friends determined not to eat or drink what God said not to. This made the overseer afraid of what would happen if they didn't eat the king's diet. Liking the boys, he arranged for them to eat vegetables and drink water for ten days to see how they would compare. They turned out to be fairer and healthier than the others. By the end of their training period—the difference was obvious even to the king:

> "As for these four children, God gave them knowledge, and skill in all learning and wisdom: and Daniel had understanding in all visions and dreams. Now at the end of the days that the king had said he should bring them in... among them all was found none like Daniel, Hananiah, Mishael, and Azariah... And in all matters of wisdom and understanding, that the king enquired of them, he found them ten times better than all the magicians and astrologers that were in his realm."[9]

Later, "Nebuchadnezzar... made an image of gold... He set it up in the plain of Dura, in the providence of Babylon." He commanded all his officials to come to its dedication. When music played, everyone was to bow down and worship the golden image. The king would throw dissenters into a fiery furnace. Again, Hananiah, Mishael, and Azariah were unwilling to disobey God; so they did not bow. When taken to the king, they said:

---

[8] Daniel 1:3-5.
[9] Daniel 1:17-20.

> "Our God whom we serve is able to deliver us from the burning fiery furnace, and He will deliver us out of thine hand, O king. But if not, be it known to thee, O king, that we will not serve thy gods, nor worship the golden image which thou hast set up."[10]

The king had them thrown into the fire; and he saw "One like the Son of God" in the fire with them. This made an impression of the king. Their faithfulness was a monument to the *ministerial* element of the *Galilee Protocol*—just as their choice of food and drink was a monument to the *medical* element; and their being ten times wiser was a monument to the *educational* element.

These things made an important and necessary impression upon Nebuchadnezzar, but they did not have the full desired effect until there was a storm.

—Three-Protocol Connection

The *Galilee Protocol* gets its name from being patterned after Christ's method of work in Galilee. The Bible tells us "Jesus went about all Galilee *teaching* in the synagogues and *preaching* the gospel of the kingdom, and *healing* all manner of sickness and all manner of disease among the people."[11]

This verse reveals the three protocols. From teaching we get the first protocol: *educational*. From preaching we get the second protocol: *ministerial*. And from healing we get the third protocol: *medical*.

In the story of the *Worthies*, we see these same three protocols. They were ten times wiser—the first protocol—*educational*. They were faithful witnesses under fire—the second protocol—*ministerial*. And they were proper in diet—the third protocol—*medical*.

—Provocative & Advocative

Christ powerfully showed the *mercy* of God by His medical missionary approach to ministry; He also presented the *justice* of God through His judgment-hour preaching. During the sermon on the mount He boldly declared:

> "For I say unto you, that except your righteousness shall exceed the righteousness of the scribes and Pharisees, ye shall in no wise enter the kingdom of heaven. Ye have heard that it was said by them of old time, Thou shalt not kill; and whosoever shall kill shall be in danger of the judgment: But I say unto you, that whosoever is angry with his brother

---

[10] Daniel 3:17-18.

[11] Matthew 4:23. Emphasis added.

> without a cause shall be in danger of the judgment... and whosoever shall say, Thou fool, shall be in danger of hell fire."[12]

When healing the Centurion's servant, Jesus marveled at the faith of the non-Israelite soldier. He said,

> "Many shall come from the east and the west, and shall sit down with Abraham, and Isaac, and Jacob, in the kingdom of heaven. But the children of the kingdom shall be cast out into outer darkness: there will be weeping and gnashing of teeth."[13]

Explaining the parable of the tares, Jesus said,

> "The Son of man shall send forth His angels, and they shall gather out of his kingdom all things that offend, and them which do iniquity; and shall cast them into a furnace of fire: there shall be weeping and gnashing of teeth."[14]

Of the evil servant that says in his heart, "My Lord delays his coming," Jesus warned that the Lord of that servant would come in a day and hour not expected, and would "cut him asunder, and appoint him his portion with the hypocrites: there will be weeping and gnashing of teeth."[15]

In the parable of the ten virgins, the bridegroom told the five foolish virgins that He knew them not.[16]

In the parable of the talents, the unprofitable servant was cast into outer darkness, where there was weeping and gnashing of teeth.[17]

Matthew tells us that Jesus went through "*all* the cities"[18]... teaching in the synagogues, preaching the gospel of the kingdom, and healing every disease and every sickness. Luke says it too—but this way: "He went throughout *every* city... preaching and shewing the *glad tidings* of the kingdom of God."[19]

His words warned of judgment, while His deeds offered justification and restoration. This was *good news because although judgment was looming*, Christ was there—willing and able to make people judgment-proof.

---

12 Matthew 5:20-22.
13 Matthew 8:11-12.
14 Matthew 13:41-42.
15 Matthew 24:50-51.
16 Matthew 25:12.
17 Matthew 25:30.
18 Matthew 9:35. Emphasis added.
19 Luke 8:1. Emphasis added.

—Axe to the Tree

John the Baptist understood the nature of Christ's message. He warned the people, saying, "Repent ye: for the kingdom of heaven is at hand."[20] He said:

> "The axe is laid unto the root of the trees: therefore every tree which bringeth not forth good fruit is hewn down and cast into the fire. I indeed baptize you with water unto repentance: but He that cometh after me is mightier than I... He shall baptize you with the Holy Ghost and with fire: Whose fan is in His hand, and He will thoroughly purge the floor, and gather His wheat into His garner; but He will burn up the chaff with unquenchable fire."[21]

So back to Nebuchadnezzar walking in his palace. The Worthies had exposed him to the three-protocols: *educational*, *ministerial*, and *medical*. The stark contrast glared at him as he beheld the secure battlements of the *Fortress*, the intellectual wonders of *E-tamen-an-ki*, and the spiritual mysteries of *E-sag-il-a*. The magnificence of these Babylonian counterfeits impressed the king. The teachers, the preachers, and the doctors in his own glorious and prestigious city were the best the world offered. But judgment was fast approaching.

He should have known this. God had warned him in a dream. Daniel warned him—explaining the prophecies, and pleading with him to change his prideful and presumptuous ways. In his dream, Nebuchadnezzar was like a strong and great tree in the midst of the earth. His greatness grew until it reached unto heaven—and his dominion to the ends of the earth. A holy watcher from heaven cried, "Hew down that tree and cut off its branches."[22] The axe was indeed laid to the root.

—Sign of Jonah

Judgement-hour warnings are integral to the *Galilee Protocol*. They were at play in the plan to save Nebuchadnezzar.

An earlier chapter looked at the sign of Jonah—the tactically necessary storm sent to convince Jonah to do city missionary work. In that story we saw how the same storm also helped prepare Nineveh for successful evangelism.

Christ referred to the *sign of Jonah* in connection with the people of His day. Like Jonah, His people stubbornly refused their mission to

---

[20] Matthew 3:2-3.
[21] Matthew 1:10-12.
[22] Daniel 4:10-16.

evangelize the world. They rejected His *Galilee Protocol* and His efforts to bring them back into God's will. But after the Calvary storm, the disciples (like Jonah) were ready to work. They received the early rain and activated the *Galilee Protocol* on a grand scale. The same storm also set up the circumstances so that the disciples could reach the entire known world in a single generation.

Sometimes it takes a storm! Sometimes that's the only way to get people's attention. This was true of Nebuchadnezzar. Notwithstanding the Worthies—their faithful witness with the three-protocols; notwithstanding the judgment hour warnings—the dreams, the prophecies, Daniel's pleadings: still the storm happened. Walking around in his palace that day, king Nebuchadnezzar said to himself, "Is this not great Babylon, which I myself have built by the might of my own power, as a royal residence and for the *glory* of my majesty?"[23] Even while the words were still in his mouth—the storm hit. For seven years his reason left him (mental). He was—not as a man—but like a cow (spiritual); and the grass was his food (physical).

It was a tough road, but it led to where he needed to go. Storms can be like that. Ellen White tells us that "King Nebuchadnezzar... was finally thoroughly converted, and learned to extol and honor the King of heaven."[24]

—A City, A Tower and A Name

So far, we've looked at the *three-protocol connection* to the Worthies. We've looked at ancient Babylon's *three-protocol counterfeit* symbolically represented by the *Fortress, E-temen-an-ki,* and *E-sag-il-a.* We've looked at judgment relating to Nebuchadnezzar's three-protocol fall. And we've touched briefly on the *three-protocol counterfeit* at the Tower of Babel. At Babel, the children of men determined to build a city. Cities are man-made fortresses built for *physical* security, wealth, and comfort. At Babel, they determined to build a tower—towers are man-made monuments to *intellectual* accomplishment. And at Babel, they determined to make a name.

Names signify character, will, ownership, and authority. Christians take the name of Christ showing their spiritual connection to Him. They are baptized in the name of the Father, the Son, and the Holy Ghost—

---

23 Daniel 4:30. Berean Study Bible. Emphasis added.

24 Ellen G. White, *The Review and Herald*, January 11, 1906.

acknowledging God's ownership and His redeeming power. They pray and preach in Jesus' name. But the Babel-Builders wished to declare their spiritual independence from God. In making a name, they established their own *spiritual* authority.

All false religion has this in common—they are religions of human accomplishments, human authority. The final battle will pit human authority against God's authority. It's really that simple. Jesus challenged man's authority. With His unique protocols, He caused an *educational crisis*, a *ministerial crisis*, and a *medical crisis*—in the church, in the nation, and in the world. All three opposed Him, all three put Him on trial, and all three determined to kill Him.

—City-Centric

We've also touched on the *city-component*. Christ told Capernaum that He was sent to the cities; and He went throughout every city in Galilee. The Babel Builders said, "let us make us a city." They envisioned a city that would become the metropolis of a universal empire.

Ancient Babylon was a mighty global empire—and the city-Babylon was emblematic of all that the empire was. Really, this is the crux of the thing about cities—they are almost complete microcosms of global culture. They're big enough to import every flavor, but small enough to have a local taste.

Genesis tells us that Cain built the first city in the land of Nod, east of Eden.[25] He named it after his son, Enoch (not the Enoch who walked with God). Five generations after Cain's Enoch—Jabel, Jubal, and Tubalcain established counterfeit world-systems for the three-protocols.[26] This was all before the flood. Everyone still spoke

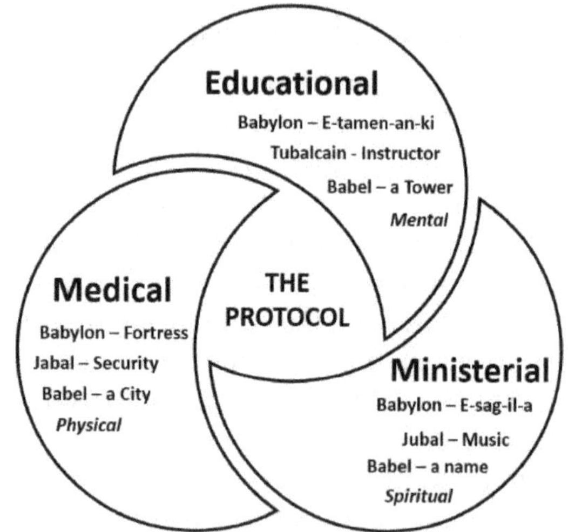

[25] Genesis 4:16-17.

[26] Genesis 4:20-22. Jabel's enterprise concerned physical security—food and shelter. Jubal's enterprise concerned spiritual things, the Bible links music with both true and false worship. Tubalcain was an educator—an *instructor* of every artificer of brass and iron.

the same language; and to make matters worse, people were generally living nine hundred or more years before they died. Before long "the wickedness of man was great in the earth, and... every imagination of the thoughts of his heart was only evil continually."[27]

—Quest of Solon

The Bible says little about the condition of things before the flood; and the deluge did a good job of erasing most of the would-be archeological puzzle pieces. But the stream of time has passed along some obscure bits and pieces of information. Symbols provide a universal language incorporated into the histories and traditions of the various people groups scattered when God confounded the language. In this way they have been in plain sight but hidden from the uninitiated.

> "Twenty-five hundred years ago, the Greek philosopher named Plato set down a dialog called the *Critias*. He recounted the story of an ancient poet and statesman named Solon. Solon had journeyed to Egypt in search of wisdom, to help the government of his beloved Greece. The Greeks had been beset with factions and troubles; so Solon took council from the priests of the city of Sais.
>
> "An old priest told him, oh Solon, Solon, you Greeks are never anything but children. There is no old opinion handed down among you, nor any science that is white with age. The old priest then preceded to tell him the story of the lost *city* of Atlantis."[28]

Eusebius, the 4th century bishop of Caesarea wrote that Enoch [Cain's son] was Atlas, king of Atlantis;[29] and masonic philosopher, Manly P. Hall, claimed that Atlantis had once been a vast and mighty empire that extended to the entire world.[30]

According to Hall, Atlantis was divided into ten governments with a prince or king having general control over his own kingdom. "The mutual relationship" of these ten kingdoms were "governed by a code engraved" on a gold-like stone column in the temple. "In the midst of the central island of Atlantis was a lofty mountain... whose summit touched the sphere of aether. This was supposed to be the axis mountain of the world, sacred among many races and symbolic of the human head." Upon this summit "stood the temple of the gods." "Its capital city was known as the city of the *Golden Gates*."[31]

---

[27] Genesis 6:5.

[28] Christian J. Pinto, *Secret Mysteries of America's Beginnings*, Antiquities Research Films. Transcribed.

[29] Praep. Ev. Ix, 17.

[30] Pinto.

[31] Manly P. Hall, *The Secret Teachings of All Ages*, pp. 16-17

In *Timaeus*, Plato tells of Atlantis' destruction: "But afterwards there occurred violent earthquakes and floods; and in a single day and night of rain all [its] warlike men in a body sank into the earth, and the island of Atlantis in like manner disappeared, and sank beneath the sea."[32]

—Rebuilding Atlantis

Manley Hall claimed Atlantis was a philosophic commonwealth of nations that one day is destined to be rebuilt.[33] His opinion expresses the collective hidden wisdom of all ages.

> "Manley P. Hall was probably the most highly esteemed occultist and Freemason of the 20th Century. He understood the secrets of the ages long before he joined the Masons. He was really the foremost authority on the occultist side of Freemasonry, the deep, dark side of Freemasonry—the one that most Masons never ascend to."
>
> "Hall authored over 200 books and is said to have given some 8000 lectures on ancient philosophy."
>
> "When he died in 1990, the *Scottish Rite Journal*, a Masonic publication, noted that he was often called 'Masonry's greatest philosopher.'"
>
> "Among his teachings was that contained in Masonry (and all secret orders), was the ancient wisdom of lost Atlantis. Hall wrote that for more than 3000 years; secret societies had been laboring to create a background of knowledge necessary to the establishment of an enlightened democracy among the nations of the world."
>
> "He claimed that these societies could be traced back to ancient Egypt—and have for centuries known of a secret place, hidden from the eyes of common men—a place that would one-day be revealed."
>
> "In the seventeenth century, as settlers were colonizing the new world, Sir Francis Bacon—the leader of secret societies in England, set down his classic work, *The New Atlantis*. While archaeologists and treasure hunters were searching the globe looking for the lost continent of Atlantis, 400 years ago, Bacon, like many of his contemporaries, believed that Atlantis was America itself."
>
> "While the Atlantis of Plato was a mighty empire, known for the philosophy of its kings, Bacon would write of a nation governed by *scientific* achievement, filled with marvels and wonders never before seen."
>
> "While many of the early settlers came to work the land for the cause of religious freedom, there were with them, secret societies who came to the new world with another agenda.
>
> "Tradition often claims that America was founded as a Christian nation only; but if this is the case, why are its symbols... [those hidden in plain sight all around our capital and our greatest cities] those of the pagan religions, rather than the images of Christ, the apostles, and stories from

---

32 Ibid., Quoted.

33 Pinto.

the Bible?"[34]

It's a simple fact of history, stonemasons have been the primary builders of the great cities of our nation—even as they have been for centuries in all the major cities around the world. And stonemasons trace the secrets of their craft back to the Babel-Builders. They are the guardians of their craft, and the guardians of the secret wisdom of the ages.

In his lifetime, Sir Francis Bacon referred to himself as the *herald of a new age*. He promoted a new universal order for the whole world.

—The Secret Seal

Occult philosopher, Manley P. Hall, in the early part of the twentieth century, wrote that,

> "On the reverse of our nation's *Great Seal* is an unfinished pyramid to represent human society itself, imperfect and incomplete. Above floats the symbol of the esoteric orders, the radiant triangle with its all-seeing eye... There is only one possible origin for these symbols, and that is the secret societies which came to this country 150 years before the Revolutionary War... There can be no question that the *Great Seal* was directly inspired by these orders... and that it set forth the purpose for this nation..."[35]

Dr. Obadiah Harris, president of the *Philosophical Research Society* says Hall...

> "saw the secret destiny of America as the beginning for a world democracy, and that this was a kind of experiment in democracy that had been envisioned for thousands of years before. So he saw this much like Francis Bacon envisioned what he called the new Atlantis."[36]

In 1926, Manley Hall published a newspaper called *The All-Seeing Eye*, dedicated to his occult views of philosophy. It was during Hall's era that the all-seeing eye would be taken out of obscurity and placed on the back of the dollar bill, by President Franklin D. Roosevelt in 1935.

FDR was familiar with Manley Hall's teaching on the occult, and the arcane literature of Hall's so-called *Wisdom Library*. The library is a collection of over fifty thousand occult books that Hall had gathered from all over the world.[37] Dr. Obadiah Harris—now president of Hall's *Philosophical Research Society*—says that "Mr. Roosevelt himself... back in 1942, after the Pearl Harbor invasion, sent some of his people to

[34] Ibid.
[35] Manly P. Hall, *The Secret Destiny of America*, pp. 174, 181.
[36] Pinto.
[37] Ibid.

microfiche the works in Hall's *wisdom library* because he looked upon it as a national treasure and wanted to preserve it."[38]

According to the *United Nations* website, it was also in 1942, that Franklin Roosevelt coined the name "*United Nations* when during the Second World War, representatives of 26 nations pledged their governments to continue fighting against the Axis Powers."

FDR's Secretary of Agriculture, Henry Wallace, was well known in political circles for his occult connections—something that eventually cost him his political career. The story of Wallace's role with FDR is told by the State Department in an official history: *The Eagle and the Shield, a History of the Great Seal of the United States*.[39]

One day, Henry Wallace, while sitting in the State Department, found a booklet on the *Great Seal of the United States*. Wallace recollects that day in letters he wrote in 1951, and in 1955. He says, "Turning to page 53, I noted the colored reproduction of the reverse side of the *Seal*. The Latin phrase, *Novus Ordo Seclorum* impressed me as meaning the *New Deal* of the Ages."

—The Great Architect

Initially, Wallace envisioned the Great Seal appearing on a coin. He took the idea to President Roosevelt. Wallace wrote that, "Roosevelt, as he looked at the colored reproduction of the *Seal*, was first struck with... the All-Seeing Eye... a masonic representation of the *Great Architect of the Universe*." "Next, he was impressed with the idea that the foundation for that *new order of the ages* had been laid in 1776, but that it would only be competed under the eye of the *Great Architect*."

He wrote that, "Roosevelt, like myself, was a 32-degree Mason." Roosevelt "suggested that the *Seal* be put on the dollar bill rather than a coin, and took the matter up with the Secretary of the Treasury."

Masons worship a god they call the "Great Architect of the Universe." The symbol they have chosen to represent their god, is the All-Seeing Eye—which the Egyptians used to represent their pagan god, Osiris. Masons know the pagan connection.[40]

Roosevelt talked to Henry Morgenthau—then Secretary of the Treasury—and convinced him to put this esoteric emblem on the back of the

---

[38] Ibid. *Published by the Office of the Historian, Bureau of Public Affairs, Department of State, Publication 8900, released 1978.*

[39] Richard Sharpe Patterson, *The Eagle and the Shield, a History of the Great Seal of the United States*,1908-1976. Washington: Office of the Historian, Bureau of Public Affairs, Dept. of State: for sale by the Supt. of Docs., Govt. Print. Off. 637 pages.

[40] See *The Master Mason*, pp. 2-4; *The Indiana Monitor and Freemason's Guide*, pp. 27-39, 172; *Kentucky Monitor*, p 116; *Coil's Masonic Encyclopedia*, pp. 444-445; *The Builders*, pp. 57-59; *The Mysteries of Magic*, p 428.

dollar bill. Morgenthau wrote extensively about this point; and he said there's some strange cabal, some mystical order behind the scenes, calling shots on the artwork that appears now on our dollar bills.[41]

—World Leaders Speak

World leaders show a patient underlying tenor to regather the nations of Babel. In 1991, then President George Bush (senior), tried to step up the pace. He announced the following to the world in a joint session of Congress:

> "Some may ask: Why act now? Why not wait? The answer is clear: the world can wait no longer. This is a historic moment. We have in this past year made great progress in ending the long era of conflict and cold war. We have before us the opportunity to forge for ourselves and our future generations, a *new world order*, a world where the rule of law, not the law of the jungle, governs the conduct of nations. When we are successful, and we will be, we have a real chance at this *new world order*—an order in which a credible United Nations can use its peace-keeping role to fulfill the promise and vision of the U.N. founders."[42]

His son also became president. On January 20, 2005 (during his second inaugural address), George Bush (junior) said, "When our founders declared a *new order of the ages*, they were acting on an *ancient hope* that is meant to be fulfilled."

In 2007, Gordon Brown announced his bid to be prime minister of the United Kingdom. He said, "a new world order has been created... an era that history will record as the beginning of a *new Golden Age*."[43]

Winston Churchill once said, "The creation of an authoritative world order is the ultimate aim toward which we must strive."[44]

Notice what Jim Garrison, president of the *Gorbachev Foundation*, says, "We are going to end up with world government. It's inevitable... There's going to be conflict, coercion, and consensus. That's all part of what is required as we give birth to the *first global civilization*."[45]

---

[41] Pinto.

[42] George Bush, January 16, 1991,The History Place, Great Speeches Collection, President George Bush Announcing War in Iraq, (http://www.historyplace.com/speeches/bush-war.htm). Accessed 3/6/2019.

[43] Wikipedia, *Premiership of Gordon Brown*, updated November 15, 2018. (http:/en.wikipedia.org/wiki/Premiership_of_Gordon_Brown). Accessed 3/6/2019.

[44] Quoted, George W. Blount, *Peace Through World Government* (Durham, North Carolina: Moore Publishing Company, 1974): p. 30.

[45] Jim Garrison, as quoted in Dennis Laurence Cuddy, *Ruling Elite Working Toward World Govt.*, The Daily Record (October 17, 1995): p. 4.

Robert Muller, a former assistant secretary general of the *United Nations*, says, "We must move as quickly as possible to a one-world government; a one-world religion; under a one-world leader."[46]

Evidently this has always been the aim of the *United Nations*. Here's what the first president of the UN General Assembly—Paul-Henri Spaak—said:

> "What we want is a man, of sufficient stature to hold the allegiance of all the people and to lift us out of the economic morass into which we are sinking. Send us such a man, and whether he be God, or devil, we will receive him."[47]

—Seething Energy

This should be no surprise to students of Bible prophecy. The book of Revelation portrays just such an end-of-the-world scenario with global alliances and forced worship; and it's the dragon who is pulling all the strings. This is really the problem, isn't it? The god of these mystery religions, and secret societies—the *Great Architect* in masonry, and the new age *Universal Christ*—is really Lucifer.

In his new-age book, *Reflections on the Christ*, David Spangler admits that Lucifer is the one whom the *initiates* really serve:

> "Lucifer comes to give us the final... Luciferic initiation... that many people now and in the days ahead, will be facing—for it is an initiation into the New Age... No one will enter the New World Order unless he or she will make a pledge to worship Lucifer. No one will enter the New Age unless he will take a Luciferian Initiation."[48]

Manley P. Hall concurs. In his book, *The Lost Keys of Freemasonry*, he says, "When the Mason learns... the mystery of his Craft... the seething energies of Lucifer are in his hands, and before he may step onward and upward, he must prove his ability to properly apply energy."[49]

We need to make this point. The reason so much is said here about this whole unseemly topic is because it's something important that the last generation needs to understand. The *Spirit of Prophecy* concurs:

> "As we near the close of time, there will be greater and still greater external parade of heathen power; heathen deities will manifest their signal power, and will exhibit themselves *before the cities of the world*, and this delineation has already begun to be fulfilled. By a variety of images

[46] Dwight L. Kinman, *The World's Last Dictator* (Woodburn, Oregon: Solid Rock Book, Inc. 1995, p. 81.

[47] Leo Giampietro, *Final War*, p. 55, Author House.

[48] David Spangler Director of Planetary Initiative, United Nations, *Reflections on the Christ* [Book: 1978], quoted in 'Unicorn in the Sanctuary', by Randy England, 1978.

[49] Manly P. Hall, *The Lost Keys of Freemasonry*, p. 48.

> the Lord Jesus represented to John the wicked character and seductive influence of those who have been distinguished for their persecution of God's people. All need wisdom *carefully to search out* the mystery of iniquity that figures so largely in the winding up of this earth's history. God's presentation of the detestable works of the inhabitants of the ruling powers of the world who bind themselves into *secret societies and confederacies*, not honoring the law of God, should enable the people who have the light of truth to keep clear of all these evils. More and more will all false religionists of the world manifest their evil doings; for there are but two parties, those who keep the commandments of God and those who war against God's holy law."[50]

And here again we come to the city-component. "Heathen deities... exhibit themselves before the *cities* of the world.

—Hidden in Plain Sight

Books can be burned. People can be scattered, language can be confounded. The Babel-Builders figured out long ago that information could be encoded into shapes and symbols, and formed into various mystical buildings and constructions, and they stand for centuries. All over the world, they hide their secrets in plain sight.

In their book, *Talisman, Sacred Cities, Secret Faith*, Graham Hancock and Robert Bauval soundly document that the architecture of great cities such as Paris and Washington DC have been used by hermeticists, masons, and alchemists to preserve and transmit a hidden knowledge from antiquity.

When the Babel-Builders said, "let us make us a city." They envisioned a city that would become the metropolis of a universal empire. Ancient Babylon was a mighty global empire—and the city-Babylon was emblematic of all that the empire was. When modern Babel-Builders decipher all the symbols hidden in plain-sight around the world, they see an emerging global empire rising out of the earth—out of America—the New Atlantis.

—Emblematic City

But is there an emblematic city for New Atlantis? Is it Atlantic City? or Atlanta?—they have its name. Is it Washington DC?—it was masonically designed; and it has all the symbolism carved into its buildings. Does such a city exist in America?—one that is a microcosm of all that Atlantis, and Babel, and Babylon stood for? Is there a city with a three-

---

[50] Ellen G. White, *Manuscript 139*, 1903, (October 23, 1903). Emphasis added.

protocol connection?—that prides herself on her *educational, ministerial,* and *medical* superiority? At least one modern occultist thinks so. He says that there is a city in America that—if "understood in its spiritual sense," "may be the ultimate... city [of light]."[51] His name is William Henry; and he tells how he discovered the importance of this city in his book, *City of Peace.*

—Apex of Meru

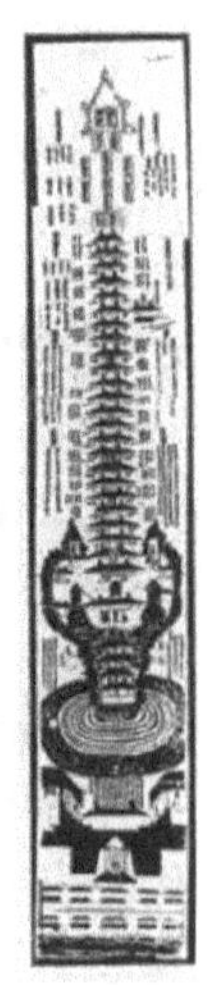

It happened like this: he was researching FDR's 1934 quest for the secrets of the *Apex of Meru*, in Mongolia. Henry Wallace, (you remember him—he was FDR's occultist Secretary of Agriculture), was his partner in this quest.

Modern occultists know Mount Meru as the cosmic pillar or axis point of the world. Sound familiar? To modern Babel-Builders, it is what the site of E-temen-an-ki was to the ancient world, and the lofty mountain of the Golden-City was to the antediluvians. A second-century drawing shows Enki's mystical Meru-rod, supposedly a kind of antenna to transmit a *healing universal life force.* Its triangular apex symbolizes the dwelling of the gods. The Meru-rod is the Buddhist and Hindu version of the unfinished pyramid and triangular all-seeing eye.

> "One well-known scholar of Buddhism says that Meru is 'the seat of cosmic powers, the axis which connects the earth with the universe, the super-antenna for the inflow and outflow of the spiritual energies of the planet.'"[52]

According to legend, Budda ascended Mount Meru—and when he died, the Rod of Enki disintegrated.[53] William Henry admits that it's all difficult stuff to prove, since the old temple can only be discovered in ancient Chinese manuscripts and may be nothing more than fantasy. "Mount Meru is in Mongolia, but that exists on the edge of history and myth, you can't actually go there today. It's gone."[54]

---

[51] William Henry, *The City of Secrets Nashville's Temple Code Unveiled.* December 5, 2008, (http://www.william-henry.net/2008/12/the-city-of-secrets-nashvilles-code-unveiled/). Accessed 3/6/2019.

[52] William Henry, Jesus, FDR, and the Meru Super-Antenna, February 11, 2008, (http://www.williamhenry.net/2008/02/jesus-fdr-and-the-meru-super-antenna/). Accessed 3/6/2019.

[53] *Hermetic Secrets in Architecture: Nashville, Tennessee.* July 4, 2013, (http://hiddenarchaeology.com/hermetic-secrets-in-architecture-nashville-tennessee/). Accessed 3/6/2019.

[54] Heather Johnson, *Meru-sic City USA*, May 10, 2001, (https://www.nashvillescene.com/news/article/13005719/merusic-city-usa). Accessed 3/6/2019.

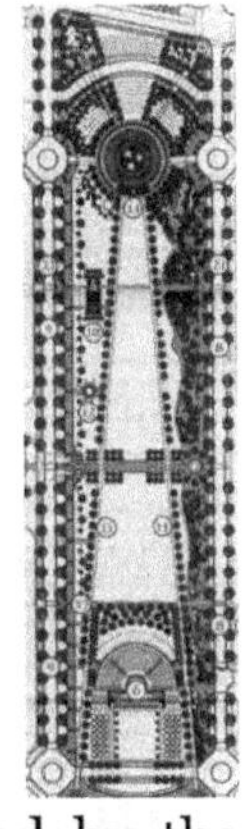

Anyway, William Henry was following a clue in a letter sent by Henry Wallace, (FDR's Secretary of Agriculture), to a famed Russian guru in 1934, while the three of them (Wallace, FDR, and the guru—Nicholas Roerich) were searching for the secret of the Apex of Meru. The clue led William Henry to a U. S. city where he discovered that the 55 million-dollar, 19-acre mall (a park) at the base of the Tennessee State Capitol mound, is elaborately patterned like the Mount Meru Rod—the axis at the center of the world. He shows the uncanny similarities of its design to the second century drawing of Enki's mystical Meru rod. The Capital building itself, is of *Greek Revival* 'temple of democracy" architecture, designed by the famed Philadelphia architect, William Strickland in 1845.[55]

—Temple at Edfu

The *Downtown Presbyterian Church* (also constructed by William Strictland, in 1848) is built in *Egyptian Revival* style. The sanctuary resembles the interior of an Egyptian pyramid; and an obelisk stands in front of the grand entrance.[56] The church's façade duplicates Horu's temple at Edfu.[57]

—Parthenon

A few short miles from the Capital building and Bicentennial mall, is the city's Centennial Park. In this space we can find sculptor Alan LeQuire's almost 42-foot tall masterpiece statue of the lost Athena-Parthenos. It is displayed inside a full-sized replica of the Parthenon. Built in 1897 to celebrate Tennessee's centennial, and rebuilt in the 1920's, the Parthenon, together with the Capital Mall and the Presbyterian Church, makes Nashville, home of three epic temples from the ancient world.

55 William Henry, *The City of Secrets Nashville's Temple Code Unveiled.* December 5, 2008, (http://www.william-henry.net/2008/12/the-city-of-secrets-nashvilles-code-unveiled/). Accessed 3/6/2019.

56 *Hermetic Secrets in Architecture: Nashville, Tennessee.* July 4, 2013, (http://hiddenarchaeology.com/hermetic-secrets-in-architecture-nashville-tennessee/). Accessed 3/6/2019.

57 William Henry, *The City of Secrets Nashville's Temple Code Unveiled.* December 5, 2008, (http://www.william-henry.net/2008/12/the-city-of-secrets-nashvilles-code-unveiled/). Accessed 3/6/2019.

The statue of Athena (inside the Parthenon) is the tallest indoor sculpture in the Western world. She is clothed with 24-karat[58] gold leaf; and she is bedazzling when the 8-ton bronze doors let the sunshine in. Athena is said to be the Serpent's Eve, reborn and exalted after the deluge sinking of Atlantis. She stands with her *"holy rod of power"* and spear in her hand. A giant serpent rises at her feet—the protector of the secrets at Athens.

The East Frieze of the original Parthenon is said to have contained all the elements of Plato's Atlantis text.[59] In Greek myth, Enki, the god of smithcraft and alchemy, is the one who crafted this rod for Athena.

—Ultimate City of Light

To William Henry, the fact that Nashville is home to these three "epic temples from the ancient world" means that in a spiritual sense, Nashville is the ultimate mystical city of light. Of interest to us, is that the symbolism all ties into the New Atlantis, the pyramid topped with a radiant triangle and all-seeing eye; and the tower of Babel, and Babylon.

Even more important is the *three-protocol connection*. In mythology, Athena is the Greek goddess of reason, wisdom, intelligent activity, arts, and literature. The *Parthenon* in Centennial Park is an esoteric monument to human *education*.

In mythology, Horus is the child-god of Osiris and ISIS. He is the incarnation god with a falcon's head on a human body. His Mesopotamian counterpart is Dagon. The *First Presbyterian Church building* in Nashville is an esoteric monument to human *worship*.

In mythology, Enki's mystical Meru rod is an antenna for transmitting healing force. It's similar to the snake-wound rod of Aesculapius—the modern symbol for medicine. *The State Capital Mall in Nashville* is an esoteric monument to *human healing*.

So in ancient-mysteries architecture and symbols, Nashville is unrivaled as a microcosm of what Atlantis, Babel, and Babylon stood for. And symbolically, Nashville is unrivaled in its *three-protocol connection*—a monument to counterfeit the educational, ministerial, and medical protocols.

But is that enough? Hidden, secret, esoteric symbolism? Do these things really define a culture or make a city what it is? Probably not. But

---

[58] Well, almost 24 karat gold—23.75.

[59] Ibid.

since the hidden mysteries point to Nashville, perhaps we should look for a better measure of her cultural priorities.

—Athens of the South

"When in the 1820's, the first president of the University of Nashville Philip Lindsley... declared Nashville to be the 'Athens of the West,' he was not describing the frontier town of only 4,000 people, he was describing his aspirations for his city."[60]

> "By the 1850s, Nashville had already earned the nickname of the 'Athens of the South' by having established numerous higher education institutions; it was the first American southern city to establish a public-school system. By the end of the century, Nashville would see Fisk University, St. Cecilia Academy, Montgomery Bell Academy, Meharry Medical College, Belmont University, and Vanderbilt University all open their doors.
>
> "At the time, Nashville was known to be one of the most refined and educated cities of the south, filled with wealth and culture. Nashville had several theaters, as well as plenty of elegant accommodations, and it was a vibrant, expanding town. Nashville's state capital building was completed in 1859.[61]

Home of 24 post-secondary educational institutions, Nashville has long been compared to Athens, the ancient city of learning and the site of Plato's Academy. *Education is a cultural priority for Nashville.*

—Protestant Vatican

Nashville has more per capita churches than anywhere else in the USA,[62] produces America's largest volume of religious tracts, has several seminaries, and several Christian music companies. It is the headquarters for the publishing arms of the Southern Baptists and the United Methodists; the seat of the National Baptist Convention and the National Association of Free Will Baptists, the Gideons International, the Gospel Music Association, and Thomas Nelson—the world's largest producer of Bibles.[63]

---

60 Savanhah Marquardt, *Collective Memory: A Tennessee monument that ties the Confederacy to the glory of the classical ere*, March 31, 2018. (http://www.olywip.org/collective-memory-tennessee-monument-ties-confederacy-glory-classical-era/). Accessed 3/7/2019.

61 Jan Duke, *The History of Nashville: Athens of the South*, Updated 12/12/2018, (https://www.tripsavvy.com/athens-of-the-south-2476869). Accessed 3/7/2019.

62 Tim, *Protestant pope, Protestant Vatican, evangelical pope*, Dictionary of Christianese, June 18, 2013, Accessed 11/8/2019 at https://www.dictionaryofchristianese.com/protestant-pope-protestant-vatican-evangelical-pope/.

63 About Nashville, Accessed 11/8/2019 at https://bestthingstodoinnashville.com/about-nashville/.

Nashville is known as the *Protestant Vatican*, the *Buckle of the Bible Belt*,[64] and Music City, U.S.A. So we see *worship is also one of Nashville's cultural priorities.*

—Healthcare Capital, U.S.A.

In Wikipedia, there is an interesting statement: "Although Nashville is renowned as a music recording center and tourist destination, its largest industry is health care."[65]

The *Nashville Health Care Council* claims that *economic-impact studies* show Nashville's health care industry has a far global reach—generating 500,000 jobs and more than $84 billion in revenue worldwide. Joey Jacobs, current chairman of the Council... says that 'with finding of this magnitude, it is easy to understand why Nashville is often referred to as the health care capital of the U.S.'[66] *Healing is a cultural priority for Nashville too.*

—Ground-Zero

So, is there a city in America with a *three-protocol connection?*—one that prides herself on her *educational*, *ministerial*, and *medical* superiority? As we near the end of earth's history, and approach that time when the judgments of God against the cities of our country are about to fall, significant prophecies emerge from the *Ellen G. White Estate.* They tell of a fireball soon to fall from heaven to hit Nashville.[67] The visions seems to identify the place of impact to be the Parthenon.[68]

At first, this begs the question: "Why Nashville?" Why would God choose Nashville, Tennessee as ground-zero—the inaugural spot for end-time judgment on the cities of America? Maybe now we know.

In light of Ancient Babylon, and the Worthies' three-protocol testimony... In light of Pagan Rome, and Jesus' three-protocol testimony... In light of the Three Angels' Messages, with their three-protocol everlasting gospel—and their emphasis on judgment, the wrath of God, and standing against the wine of spiritual Babylon... In light of historic Adventism, and the three-protocol emphasis that God has meticulously

---

64 Sid Griffin, *Heart and Soul: The Buckle of the Bible Belt*, November 2, 2019, BBC Media Centre, Accessed at https://www.bbc.co.uk/mediacentre/proginfo/2014/44/buckle-bible-belt.

65 Wikipedia, *Nashville, Tennessee*, (https://en.wikipedia.org/wiki/Nashville,_Tennessee). Accessed 3/7/2019.

66 Healthcare Finance, *Health Care Industry Contributes $30 Billion Annually to Nashville Economy*, July 8, 2010, (https://www.healthcarefinancenews.com/press-release/health-care-industry-contributes-30-billion-annually-nashville-economy). Accessed 3/7/2019.

67 See Ellen G. White, *Manuscript 188*, 1905 (first released in 2015).

68 See Ellen G. White, *A Place Called Oakwood*, p. 138

built into our mission... In light of our self-supporting work, and its role in preserving the three-protocols in a modern, secular, liberal age... In light of all these things, we should ask one more question: Why did God choose Nashville for the home of the Madison[69] school—the birthplace and epicenter of the Seventh-day Adventist self-supporting work?

The answer seems too obvious to require elaboration.

—No Kingdom Yet

Will there ever be this final philosophical commonwealth of nations such as the secret initiates of all ages have been seeking? Well, yes, and no. The Lord introduces a composite beast representation to John in Revelation 13. It comes from the sea, so we know it comes out of the many languages, peoples, and nations scattered at Babel.[70] It looks like a leopard with bear's feet and a lion's mouth. It has seven heads and ten, crowned horns. It gets its power and authority from Satan.[71]

An angel explains in chapter 17 that the ten heads are ten kings. In John's day—five of them had already fallen, one was, and the seventh had not yet come.[72] This seven-headed composition will be a final global power containing the fully ripened philosophical essence of all the world powers since Babel: Egypt, Assyria, Babylon, Medio-Persia, Greece, Pagan, and Papal Rome.[73]

The ten horns (ten crowns) "are ten kings, which have received no kingdom yet; but receive power as kings one hour with the beast. These have one mind, and shall give their power and strength unto the beast."[74]

It's just a matter of putting the pieces together. We understand the lamb-like beast in chapter 13 to be the United States.[75] This nation will empower the seven-headed beast to rule a world again divided into *ten regions,*[76] as the antediluvian Atlantis—a "king" for each region.[77]

---

[69] Realizing the collage in Battle Creek was going to favor classical education, Sutherland and Megan followed Sister White's counsel to go south and start a school there—one that would follower the SOP blueprint. A sight near Nashville was chosen and Sister White encouraged them to keep it independent. See the timeline in chapter two.

[70] See Revelation 17:15.

[71] See Revelation 13:1-2, and Daniel 7.

[72] Revelation 17:7-10.

[73] See Ranko Stefanovic, *Revelation of Jesus Christ*, p. 521. 2009, Andrews University Press, Berrien Springs, Michigan.

[74] Revelation 17:12-13.

[75] See Ellen G. White, *The Great Controversy*, pp. 439-440.

[76] It's interesting to note that in 1942, the UN was already mapping the "new world order" into 10 regions. See https://bigthink.com/strange-maps/286-the-new-world-order-1942. In 1973, the Club of Rome's "think tank," issued a report that was published by the UN. It divided the world into 10 political/economic regions. See http://www.enter-through-the-narrow-gate.com/Studies/The_Revelation/z10_regional_kingdoms.pdf.

[77] Their power is assigned, notice that "they receive power."

So the answer to the question is yes—kind of. A final global commonwealth of nations will be the philosophical culmination of the *mysteries of the ages*. But it will not be the panacea the world hopes for. Their mighty tower will quickly topple. The ten kings will soon turn against the "great city, which reigneth over the kings of the earth."[78]

We don't know exactly when these ten kings will receive their kingdoms; but we know that the Nashville fireball will happen sooner than we think it will.[79]

> "O that God's people had a sense of the impending destruction of thousands of cities, now almost given to idolatry."[80] "When God shall bid His angels loose the winds, there will be a scene of strife as no pen can picture... A moment of respite has been graciously given us. Every power lent us from heaven is to be used in doing the work assigned us by the Lord for those who are perishing in ignorance... God's people should make a mighty intercession to Him for help now. And they must put their whole energies into the effort to proclaim the truth during the respite that has been granted."[81]

Nashville is the perfect context for the *Galilee Protocol...* because sometimes it takes a storm!

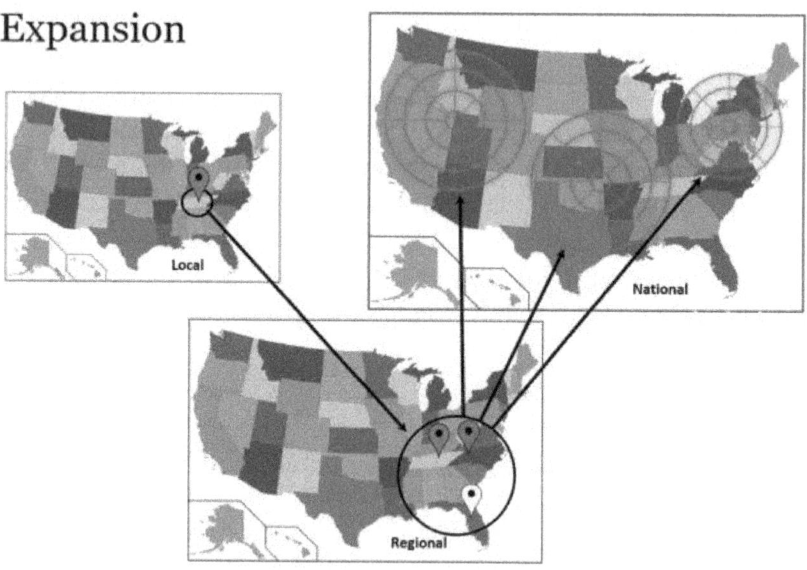

[78] See Revelation 17:12-18.

[79] See Ellen G. White, *Letter 217*, 1904. Mrs. White describes how some *knew*, but didn't know it would be so *soon*. Since the vision was not available to the public until 2015, the idea of "knowing" and "soon" should be understood in relation to that time.

[80] Ellen G. White, *Evangelism*, p. 29.

[81] Ellen G. White, *The Review and Herald*, November 23, 1905.

CHAPTER TWENTY-THREE

The Hand of the Man from Galilee

In Elisha's day, Ben-hadad, the king of Syria, defeated the armies of Israel. This resulted in continual skirmishes on the border between the two nations. Naaman was the captain of the Syrian army. Though mighty in battle—he was a leper.

In one raid, Naaman captured a little girl—who he took home to be a servant to his wife. One day, *Little Maid* suggested that he seek healing from Israel's prophet. She "knew that the power of heaven was with Elisha, and she believed that by this power Naaman could be healed."[1]

Elisha told Naaman to wash seven times in the Jordan River. God healed him; and Naaman gratefully returned to Elisha saying, "Behold, now I know that there is no God in all the earth, but in Israel."[2]

God is the healer of body and soul. He links physical healing to the gospel. Jesus said, "That you may know that the Son of man hath power on earth to forgive sins, (then saith He to the sick of the palsy,) Arise, take up thy bed, and go to thine house."[3] "Medical missionary work is as

[1] Ellen G. White, *Prophets and Kings*, p. 245.
[2] 2 Kings 5:15.
[3] Matthew 9:6.

the right arm of the third angel's message which must be proclaimed to a fallen world."[4]

—The Base Alloy of Worldly Wealth

Consistent with the custom of the times—this captain of the Syrian army asked Elisha to accept a costly present. "But the prophet refused. It was not for him to take payment for a blessing that God had in mercy bestowed."[5] Naaman *urged* him to take it; but Elisha refused. His servant felt differently about the matter:

> "Elisha's servant had opportunity during the years to develop the spirit of self-denial characteristic of his master's lifework. It had been his privilege to become a noble standard-bearer in the army of the Lord. The best gifts of heaven had long been within his reach; yet, turning from these, he had coveted instead the *base alloy of worldly wealth*. And now the hidden longings of his avaricious spirit led him to yield to an overmastering temptation."[6]

The *Galilee Protocol*'s approach to financial matters is of paramount importance. Living like the world short-circuits our mission in several ways. Many think the lifestyle of a missionary is impractical and unnecessary in these modern times: but it is self-sacrificing service that opens the ears of the world.

> "Many... have neither faith in God nor confidence in man. As they see one with no inducement of earthly praise or compensation come into their wretched homes, ministering to the sick, feeding the hungry, clothing the naked, and tenderly pointing all to Him whose love and pity the human worker is but the messenger—as they see this, their hearts are touched. Gratitude springs up. Faith is kindled. They see that God cares for them, and they are prepared to listen as His Word is opened."[7]

Self-sacrificing service is also necessary for character transformation.

> "The work for these last days is in a special sense a missionary work. The presentation of present truth, from the first letter of its alphabet to the last, means missionary effort. The work calls for sacrifice at every advance step. From this unselfish service the workers will come forth purified and refined as gold tried in the fire."[8]

Christ came to this world poor. It was no random circumstance that placed Him in humble surroundings. He *chose* the life of a servant so He

---

[4] Ellen G. White, Counsels on Health, p. 331.
[5] Ellen G. White, Prophets and Kings, p. 250.
[6] Ibid. Emphasis added.
[7] Ellen G. White, *Evangelism*, p. 517. Emphasis added.
[8] Ellen G. White, Counsels on Health, p. 216. Emphasis added.

could show the heart of God. Carefully consider the following statements. They are vital to our mission.

> "The *purest unselfishness* is to be shown by our workers as, with knowledge and experience gained by practical work, they go out to give treatments to the sick. As they go from house to house, they will find access to many hearts. Many will be reached who otherwise would never have heard the gospel message."[9]
>
> "In no way would the Lord be better glorified and the truth more highly honored than for unbelievers to see that the truth has wrought a great and good work upon the lives of naturally covetous and penurious men. If it could be seen that the faith of such had an influence to mold the characters, *to change them from close, selfish, overreaching, money-loving men* to men who love to do good, who seek opportunity to use their means to bless those who need to be blessed, who visit the widow and the fatherless in their affliction, and who keep themselves unspotted from the world, it would be evidence that their religion is genuine."[10]
>
> "All heaven is looking on with intense interest to see what character medical missionary work will assume under supervision of human beings. *Will men make merchandise* of God's ordained plan for reaching the dark parts of the earth with a manifestation of His benevolence? Will they cover mercy with selfishness, and then call it medical missionary work?"[11]

—The Cost of Discipleship

The *Galilee Protocol's* missionarial directive distinguishes it from *worldly enterprise* and protects it from becoming *merchandise*. In our comfortable age and affluent society, contemporary lifestyle norms make it necessary for most of us to rediscover the foundations of Christian discipleship. Jesus said that whosoever does not forsake all, cannot be His disciple.[12] He said it—*and* He lived it. "The foxes have holes, and the birds of the air have nests; but the Son of man hath not where to lay his head."[13]

The old hymn says, "I'm a pilgrim, and I'm a stranger; I can tarry, I can tarry but a night."[14] Our pilgriming is no aimless wandering, though. Christ had a mission—a vital job to do. And so do His disciples—all of us. He had a mission; we have a mission—hence the term applies: *missionaries*. "Go ye therefore, and teach all nations, baptizing them in the name of the Father, and of the Son, and of the Holy Ghost: teaching

---

[9] Ellen G. White, *Welfare Ministry*, p. 74. Emphasis added.

[10] Ellen G. White, Testimonies for the Church, vol. 2, p. 239. Emphasis added.

[11] Ellen G. White, *Letters to Physicians and Ministers*, p. 19. Emphasis added.

[12] Luke 14:33.

[13] Matthew 8:20.

[14] Mary S. B. Dana, *I'm a Pilgrim*, 1841, from the Seventh-day Adventist Hymnal, p. 444, Review and Herald Publishing Association, 1985.

them to observe all things whatsoever I have commanded you."[15] "Ye shall be witnesses unto me, both in Jerusalem, and in all Judaea, and in Samaria, and unto the uttermost part of the earth."[16] "Seventh-day Adventists have been set in the world as watchmen and light-bearers. To them have been entrusted the last warning for a perishing world... They are to allow nothing else to absorb their attention."[17]

—A Road Less Traveled

Missionarial has intrinsic ties to the three protocols. Not only does it favorably present the gospel as selfless, loving service: it is *salvific to the core:* It fosters the transformation of human nature—and this restoration of the physical, mental, and spiritual is what the *Galilee Protocol* is about. *Sacrificing* to save others, saves us. Self-sacrifice teaches us to lean on Jesus; and prepares us for the latter rain.

> "Christ crucified for our sins; Christ risen from the dead; Christ ascended on high as our intercessor—this is the *science of salvation* that we need to learn and to teach. This is the burden of our work."[18]
>
> "When in our daily experience we learn His meekness and lowliness, we find rest. There is then no necessity to search for some mysterious science to soothe the sick. We already have the science which gives them real rest—the science of salvation, the science of restoration, the science of a living faith in a living Savior."[19]

Salvation is a science. Restoration is a science. "The Bible is God's great lesson book, His great educator," for teaching salvation science. He teaches with parables and symbols. He illustrates with stories of patriarchs, and prophets, and kings. The earthly sanctuary is an illustration—a shadow,[20] a figure,[21] a pattern,[22] "to teach us that perfect system of redemption... devised in the councils of heaven and wrought by 'the only Begotten of the Father.'"[23] Says the Psalmist, "Thy way O God is in the sanctuary."[24]

The path we are to follow is inscribed in the sanctuary; and our Redeemer illustrated it in His own footsteps. He saw *John the Baptist*

---

[15] Matthew 28:19-20.
[16] Acts 1:8.
[17] Ellen G. White, *Evangelism*, p. 119.
[18] Ellen G. White, *Counsels to Parents, Teachers, and Students*, p. 22.
[19] Ellen G. White, *Medical Ministry*, p. 117.
[20] Hebrews 10:1.
[21] Hebrews 9:24.
[22] Hebrews 9:23.
[23] Ellen G. White, *The Sanctuary*, p. 16.
[24] Psalms 77:13.

preaching by the Jordan River, saying, "Repent ye: for the kingdom of heaven is at hand."[25] So to "fulfil all righteousness,"[26] He went to John "to be baptized of him."[27] "And immediately the Spirit driveth Him into the Wilderness."[28]

The first step on the path has to do with repentance, confession, turning away from sin, and putting faith in the Redeemer. This was the essence of John's preaching. This is the essence of *altar-of-burnt-offering* symbolism.

The second step has to do with the *great sea*—the laver. Paul describes how ancient Israel "were all baptized unto Moses in the cloud and in the sea."[29] Crossing the Red Sea illustrated their separation from Egypt—the pattern[30] of this world. Coming up out of the sea they separated from the "peoples and multitudes and nations and tongues"[31] of the world (plural): to join the chosen generation, the royal priesthood, an holy nation, a peculiar people (singular). Paul likens baptism to being buried in death (the old life) and rising in "newness of life."[32] For the "old man is crucified with [Christ]...and raised by the glory of the Father."[33] This was the essence of John's baptizing.

The children of Israel corporately took these two steps at the start of the Exodus. First, they observed the Passover: an *altar-of-burnt-offering* event. Second, they 'passed through the sea."[34] This was a *laver* event. Being separated from the inhabited world—they found themselves in the wilderness. "It is characteristic of God in scripture to lead chosen people into the isolation and barrenness of the wilderness or desert."[35] God led Abraham into the wilderness. Revelation describes the church as a woman "given two wings of a great eagle that she might fly into the wilderness, into her place, where she is nourished for a time, and times, and a half a time, [away] from the face of the serpent."[36]

---

[25] Matthew 3:2.
[26] Matthew 3:15.
[27] Matthew 3:13.
[28] Mark 1:12.
[29] 1 Corinthians 10:2.
[30] Romans 12:2. "Do not conform to the pattern of this world, but be transformed by the renewing of your mind." NIV.
[31] Revelation 17:15.
[32] Romans 6:4.
[33] Romans 6:6, 4.
[34] 1 Corinthians 10:1.
[35] Juliana Weber, *The Meaning of the Wilderness*, May 31, 2015 Homiletic & Pastoral Review, https://www.hprweb.com/2015/05/the-meaning-of-the-wilderness/ Accessed 5/13/2019.
[36] Revelation 12:14.

—Wilderness Refuge

A wilderness is a barren place—yet God makes it a place of nourishing. It seems the only time we rely fully on God is when we have no other resources. In the desert we have to rely on Him for refuge and nurturing; and in the wilderness we are away from contaminating influences and worldly philosophy. In the wilderness God *can* nourish the church—physically, mentally, spiritually.

John the Baptist was familiar with the wilderness—it was the place of his education. Moses was familiar with the wilderness—it was the place of his re-education. Israel was familiar with the wilderness—for after telling about their baptism through the sea, Paul says, "And did all drink the same spiritual drink: for they drank of that spiritual Rock that followed them: and that Rock was Christ."[37]

> "Therefore, behold, I will allure her, and bring her into the wilderness, and speak comfortably unto her. And I will give her her vineyards from thence, and the valley of Achor for a door of hope: and she shall sing there, as in the days of her youth, and as in the day when she came up out of the land of Egypt."[38]
>
> "I will open rivers in high places, and fountains in the midst of the valleys: I will make the wilderness a pool of water, and the dry land springs of water. I will plant in the wilderness the cedar, the [acacia] tree, and the myrtle, and the oil tree; I will set in the desert the fir tree, *and* the pine, and the box tree together: That they may see, and know, and consider, and understand together, that the hand of the LORD hath done this, and the Holy One of Israel hath created it."[39]

Crossing the Red Sea, the children of Israel "went out into the wilderness of Shur; and they went three days in the wilderness, and found no water."[40] They came to Marah and found bitter water. So the Lord gave them sweet water to drink. The biblical account links this sweet water to God's statutes and ordinances[41] and with His commandments.[42] It also links this sweet water to God's healthcare: "I will put none of these diseases upon thee, which I have brought upon the Egyptians: for I am the LORD that healeth thee."[43]

---

[37] 1 Corinthians 10:2-5

[38] Hosea 2:14-15.

[39] Isaiah 41:18-20.

[40] Exodus 15:22.

[41] Exodus 15:25.

[42] Exodus 15:26.

[43] Ibid.

In the wilderness, God provided twelve wells of water. In the wilderness, He gave them seventy palm trees. In the wilderness, God fed them the heavenly manna. In the wilderness—when the feeble lagged, and were weary and faint,[44] with Amalek picking off the stragglers from behind—God gave Israel strength to prevail against them. So long as Moses stood on the hill, holding up the Rod of God (and so long as the leaders held up the hand of Moses): Israel prevailed against Amalek.[45]

—Wilderness Testing

The wilderness is also a place of *testing*. Before God made the waters of Marah sweet, they were bitter. The Bible says that the LORD *proved* them there;"[46] and that "the people murmured against Moses, saying, what shall we drink?"[47]

This wilderness testing also appears in Revelation. When the angel tells John to eat the little book, it is sweet in his mouth, but bitter in his belly.[48] This passage helped the disappointed Millerites realize that *bitter testing* is part of the science of salvation—and it happens in the wilderness.

Sanctuary symbolism reveals seven steps in the path of salvation. We won't deep dive into all of them here; but the courtyard (altar and sea) is where Christ *physically* prepares His people for the *mental* reformation characteristic of the holy place. The holy place (wilderness) is the school of Christ that *mentally* prepares His people for the *spiritual* reformation characteristic of the most holy. The sanctuary was built on three planes: the *courtyard* being low and the *most holy* being high. These correspond to the spaces identified at creation—the sea, the dry land, and the heavens. The church is associated with heaven and described as a city on a hill. The people of God inhabit it; and the temple is there.

Moving along the path of transformation, we go from the courtyard, through the holy place, on to the most holy. God is leading us by the hand through the holy place wilderness; but His holy law is actually inscribed on our hearts and minds in the most holy.[49] The church of the most holy is the *new covenant* church. She is the New Jerusalem—a

---

[44] Deuteronomy 25:17-19.
[45] Exodus 17:8-16.
[46] Exodus 15:23, 25.
[47] Exodus 15:24.
[48] Revelation 10:9-11.
[49] See Jeremiah 31:31; Hebrews 10:16.

"glorious church" without "spot or wrinkle or any such thing," "holy and without blemish."[50] When the church reaches this stage, she is the pure, white bride of Christ. Paul calls her "the Jerusalem which is above."[51]

The Bible teaches that, "In the days of His flesh" Jesus "learned" "obedience by the things which He suffered."[52] As "the author of eternal salvation,"[53] He too progressed through the steps of Salvation. So He was baptized; and the Holy Spirit immediately drove Him into the wilderness. Christ was tested when the wilderness was *barren;* and He was tested again after it had become a well-planted garden—Gethsemane.

The nature of the test at the beginning was physical; and for His defense He deferred to Scripture. The nature of the test at the end was an intellectual struggle; and Christ was prepared for it by His wilderness training in the things of God. The Word was written into His experience.

Knowing the consequences of His decision in Gethsemane, Christ went on to the final test—the *spiritual* test of the most holy place.[54] His wilderness experiences (the seen) built the platform of faith He would rely on through the overwhelming darkness at Calvary (the unseen.[55]).

—Wilderness Separation

The first three steps (especially the third) set the stage for understanding discipleship, Christian lifestyle, and the financial orientation of the *Galilee Protocol*. What happened to Christ at the wilderness temptation helps us understand the *wilderness needed in our experience*. The early wilderness *testing* proves our commitment to separating from the world. Israel was weak here—they always wanted to return to Egypt. Then wilderness *nurturing* develops our growing dependence on God. And the wilderness *testing* at the end, proves our *full* dependence on *Him*. This sounds easy enough—but try it sometime.

We could call the *Galilee Protocol* the *Wilderness Protocol*.[56] It's about trusting God's methods and depending on His plan. It's about *Christ's Method Alone!* Knowing what we do about the *Galilee Protocol*, it's no

---

50 Ephesians 5: 27.

51 Galatians 4:26.

52 Hebrews 5:7-8.

53 Hebrews 5:9.

54 Genesis 15:12; Ellen G. White, *The Great Controversy*, p. 18.

55 See Ellen G. White, *The Desire of Ages*, p. 756.

56 The three spaces of creation are the sea, the dry land that is planted (wilderness), and the heavens (often represented as mountains or clouds in Bible symbolism). This is why the temple was built on three plains with the courtyard low, and the most holy high. Jerusalem was God's city built on the top of the mountain. Christ was working from top to bottom when He started His ministry in Judea (Jerusalem-church), followed by Galilee (wilderness-nation), and concluding in the regions beyond the Jordon (sea-whole world).

surprise that the devil approached Christ with three temptations—one for each of man's three natures. Remember that Satan's whole career is about making merchandise of the physical, mental, and spiritual glory of God—and trafficking in that merchandise. He showed up in the wilderness as a skilled salesman—arrogantly trying to sell Christ a counterfeit of His own glory! Christ refused to buy Satan's basket of goods; but, mostly, we do.

> "The Son of God in His humanity wrestled with the very same fierce, apparently overwhelming temptations that assail men—temptations to indulgence of appetite, to presumptuous venturing where God has not led them, and to the worship of the god of this world, to sacrifice an eternity of bliss for the fascinating pleasures of this life."[57]

John says, "the desires of the flesh [physical], the desires of the eyes [spiritual] and the pride of life [intellectual] come not from the Father, but from the world."[58] Notice especially the last one: human wisdom—the pride of human wisdom presumptuously leads away from the will of God—we presumptuously venture where God has not led us. It's the one that names the tree in Eden—the tree of the *knowledge* of good and evil.[59] It enticingly tells us, "ye shall be as gods, *knowing* good and evil."[60]

Human wisdom has such a strangle-hold on the masses of this world, that we must separate from the world before we can really enroll in the school of Christ. So the descendants of Seth did not live in the cities of Cain;[61] and the sons of God were not to mix with the daughters of men.[62] So Enoch only visited the cities to preach the gospel there.[63] So Abraham had to leave Ur; and Lot did not fare so well in Sodom. Jacob separated from his family; Joseph from his people. So Moses had to go to the land of Midian—away from the wisdom and lifestyle of Egypt:

> "He had yet to learn the same lesson of faith that Abraham and Jacob had been taught—not to rely upon human strength or wisdom, but upon the power of God for the fulfilment of His promises. And there were other lessons that, amid the solitude of the mountains, Moses was to receive. In the school of self-denial and hardship he was to learn patience, to temper his passions. Before he could govern wisely, he must be trained to obey. His own heart must be fully in harmony with God before he could teach the knowledge of His will to Israel. By his own

---

[57] Ellen G. White, *Selected Messages*, book 1, p. 95

[58] 1 John 2:16.

[59] Genesis 2:17.

[60] Genesis 3:5.

[61] Genesis 4:16-24.

[62] Genesis 6:1-5.

[63] Ellen G. White, *The Review and Herald*, September 27, 1906.

> experience he must be prepared to exercise a fatherly care over all who needed his help"[64]

The need for separation required the removal of the Canaanites from the promised land: partially so their human policy would not contaminate Israel, and partly so that Israel (lacking worldly alliances) would have to depend fully on God.

> "Be ye not unequally yoked together with unbelievers: for what fellowship hath righteousness with unrighteousness? and what communion hath light with darkness? And what concord hath Christ with Belial? or what part hath he that believeth with an infidel? And what agreement hath the temple of God with idols? for ye are the temple of the living God; as God hath said, I will dwell in them, and walk in *them*; and I will be their God, and they shall be my people. Wherefore come out from among them, and be ye separate, saith the Lord, and touch not the unclean *thing*; and I will receive you, And I will be a Father unto you, and ye shall be my sons and daughters, saith the Lord Almighty."[65]

Earth's last days revives the call for separation: God's people are to separate from the cities; and the cry of the fourth angel to the faithful in Babylon is: "Come out of her, my people, that ye be not partakers in her sins, and that ye receive not of her plagues."[66]

—Wilderness Dependence

Christ's three wilderness temptations correlate with the three areas of temptation in Eden. The forbidden tree offered something for each of the three natures. It was good for food (physical); it was pleasant to the eyes (spiritual); and it was a tree to be desired to make one wise (mental).[67] But God had not left it to Adam and Eve to provide for themselves. This is the capital point of the story.

Unlike the barren desert we start with today—Eden was a flourishing garden. God Himself filled it with all manner of trees good for food[68]—and He specifically identified them as such. He made ample provision for their education too: "The holy pair were not only children under the fatherly care of God but *students receiving instruction* from the all-wise Creator. They were visited by angels, and were granted communion with

---

[64] Ellen G. White, *Patriarchs and Prophets*, p. 247.
[65] 2 Corinthians 6:14-17.
[66] Revelation 18:4.
[67] Genesis 3:6.
[68] Genesis 2:9.

their Maker, with no obscuring veil between... They held converse with leaf and flower and tree, gathering from each the secrets of its life."[69]

The Sabbath was their spiritual benefit. Man "needed the Sabbath to remind him more vividly of God and to awaken gratitude because all that he enjoyed and possessed came from the beneficent hand of the Creator."[70]

The world bases human enterprise on its own wisdom—which is works oriented. It's man powered. It started with Cain offering the fruit of his labor, then the city he built; Jabal's cattle and housing industry; Jubal's music services; and Tubalcain's school of metallurgy. Humanity's solution for physical, spiritual, and educational security has always tried to break dependence upon God—and teach us to be responsible for ourselves. It's against this the Sabbath stands: "For he that is entered into his rest, he also *has ceased from his own works*, as God did from His."[71]

Deliberately learning *not* to rely upon human strength and wisdom; and intentionally favoring circumstances of self-denial and hardship, goes against everything human wisdom teaches. Just the mention of it elicits protests about loafing and low achievement. But before going too far down that line of thinking, re-read Hebrews eleven. The difference between the faithful and the vagrant has to do with accepting the authority of God in the life. It was Jesus who gave us this hard saying:

> "Therefore I say unto you, Take no thought for your life, what ye shall eat, or what ye shall drink; nor yet for your body, what ye shall put on. Is not the life more than meat, and the body than raiment? Behold the fowls of the air: for they sow not, neither do they reap, nor gather into barns; yet your heavenly Father feedeth them. Are ye not much better than they? Which of you by taking thought can add one cubit unto his stature? And why take ye thought for raiment? Consider the lilies of the field, how they grow; they toil not, neither do they spin: And yet I say unto you, That even Solomon in all his glory was not arrayed like one of these. Wherefore, if God so clothe the grass of the field, which today is, and tomorrow is cast into the oven, *shall He* not much more *clothe* you, O ye of little faith? Therefore take no thought, saying, What shall we eat? or, What shall we drink? or, Wherewithal shall we be clothed? (For after all these things do the Gentiles seek:) for your heavenly Father knoweth that ye have need of all these things. But seek ye first the kingdom of God, and his righteousness; and all these things shall be added unto you.

[69] Ellen G. White, *Patriarchs and Prophets*, pp. 50-51.

[70] Ibid., p. 48.

[71] Hebrews 4:10. Emphasis added.

> "Take therefore no thought for the morrow: for the morrow shall take thought for the things of itself. Sufficient unto the day *is* the evil thereof."[72]

But... But... But...

Maybe we're thinking Jesus doesn't mean this the way it sounds. Or maybe we're not really getting what happened to Him in the wilderness. Common sense would have sent you and me to the nearest *Olive Garden®* before the end of the very first day. Forty days? Come on now! Consider Abraham with Isaac. Maybe we're not getting what happened there either. What about Daniel and the Lion's den?—Why not pray in the closet for a few days?

Couldn't Jesus have backed off on *healing during the Sabbath* hours? Wasn't the whole "*eat my flesh and drink my blood*" speech a bit over the top?—most of His disciples left after that one. Telling the rich young ruler to sell all his stuff and give the money away seems counterintuitive—and maybe even irresponsible.

Jesus, by His teaching, preaching, and healing, caused an educational crisis, a ministerial crisis, and a healthcare crisis in the church, in the nation, and in the world. His peculiar approach to ministry, education, and healthcare *was* counterintuitive. It challenged the norms of society. His own humanity felt the tension. He was not immune to these crises—He faced them Himself in the wilderness.

He followed the same path we have to follow. Understanding the significance of "the voice crying in the *wilderness*"[73] (John's preaching), Jesus—through baptism—committed to "not relying on human strength or wisdom, but upon the power of God for the fulfilment of His promises."[74] He committed "to learn patience, to temper His passions" "in the school of self-denial and hardship." He chose to have His humanity "trained to obey," and to "be fully in harmony with God."[75] "Though He were a Son, yet learned He obedience by the things which He suffered."[76]

How many meals missed and supplied? involvement in how many healings? how many urgent, midnight prayers were needed to prepare Christ's humanity for the trial that loomed before Him? Can we ever hope to prevail unless we actually train under the tutelage of the Master Teacher? He knows what's coming. He knows our individual need.

---

[72] Matthew 6:25-34.

[73] Mark 1:3.

[74] Ellen G. White, *Patriarchs and Prophets*, p. 247.

[75] Ibid.

[76] Hebrews 5:8.

Just to be sure that it is said (for those who need to hear it said): The *Galilee Protocol* does not promote a life of inactivity or irresponsibility. God put Adam and Eve in the garden "to dress it and to keep it."[77] Paul told the Thessalonian Christians that "if any would not work, neither should he eat."[78] Jesus worked longer hours than we do. It's not about work or no work—it's about "working the works of Christ."[79] The issue boils down to this: "Obedience to God is your first duty. You are to leave all the consequences in His hands."[80]

To the same crowd it should also be said: Before any real transformation of character takes place—we have to pass the first tests in the wilderness. We have to put our physical, mental, and spiritual security fully into the hand of the man from Galilee. Satan will surely do everything he can to prevent this.[81] He will cause this test to be no small trial. Many people claim to be Christians who never really get past these early tests. Nominal Christians spend most of their time in town.

—Hint Missionaries?

Andrew grew up in Holland when it was under occupation during World War II. The Nazi's used the local school building as their headquarters; so Andrew's education came to a halt. He eventually became a Christian; and at the promptings of an evangelist he found himself committed to becoming a missionary.

The *Dutch Reform Church* operated many overseas missions. He contacted them to see what the qualification were for serving. All the missions said that ordination was the first step. He wrote to the *Dutch Reformed Seminary* and "discovered that making up the schooling [he] had missed during the war and then studying theology would take twelve years."[82] He was already twenty-four; and he had no money. Twelve years of school seemed impractical.

One day he was "grumbling about the delays and formalities of education"[83] to a friend, Sidney Wilson. Mr. Wilson laughed—saying that Andrew talked like the people at WEC. The *Worldwide Evangelism*

---

[77] Genesis 2:15.

[78] 2 Thessalonians 3:10.

[79] Ellen G. White, *Counsels to Parents, Teachers, and Students*, p. 399, "when the life is devoted to working the works of Christ, the fruit of the higher education is seen."

[80] Ellen G, White, *Evangelism* p.243.

[81] Ellen G. White, *The Desire of Ages*, P. 116.

[82] Brother Andrew with John and Elizabeth Sherrill, *God's Smuggler*, p. 47, 1967, Guideposts Associates, INC. Carmel, New York.

[83] Ibid.

Crusade was an English group that trained missionaries to go out to parts of the world where the churches have no programs. "They feel like you about waiting."

> "Church missions, he explained, were run on budgets. A mission board waited until it had the money, or at least knew where it was coming from, before they sent a man out. Not WEC. If they thought God wanted a man in a certain place, they sent him there and trusted God to worry about the details.
>
> "'Same with the men they send.' Mr. Wilson went on. 'If they think a man has a genuine call and a deep enough commitment, they don't care if he hasn't a degree to his name. They train him at their own school... and then send him out.'"[84]

The part about the training appealed to Andrew. Besides studying systematic theology, homiletics, world religions, linguistics—normal courses for any seminary—they worked on practical skills in the afternoon: bricklaying, plumbing, carpentry, first aid, tropical hygiene, motor repair. But Andrew wasn't so sure about the financing part. He knew several people who "trusted in God" for their needs, and most of them were really beggars. They rarely came right out and ask for money—they hinted at it. They were known around those parts as the "*hint missionaries*." People said they didn't live by *faith*, but by *feelers*. Andrew wasn't impressed. It seemed grubby and undignified. "If Christ were a king, and these were His ambassadors, it surely did not speak well of the state of His [royal treasury]."[85]

—Learning to Trust

Eventually Brother Andrews got to London to enroll at WEC. He sat down with the director—Mr. Dinnen:

> "'The real purpose of this training... is to teach our students that they can trust God to do what He has said He would do. We don't go from here into the traditional missionary fields, but into new territory. Our graduates are on their own. They cannot be effective if they are afraid, or if they doubt that God really means what He says in His Word. So here we teach not so much ideas as trusting.'
>
> "'As for finances—you know of course, Andy, that we charge no tuition. That's because we have no paid staff. The teachers, the London people, myself—none of us receives a salary. Room and board and other physical costs for the year come to... a little over ninety pounds. It's as low as this because the students do the cooking, cleaning, everything, themselves. But we do request the ninety pounds in advance. Now I

[84] Ibid., p. 48.

[85] Ibid.

understand you will not be able to do this.'

"'No sir.'

"'Well, it's also possible to pay in installments, thirty pounds at the start of each session. But for your sake and for ours we like to insist that the installments be paid on time.'"[86]

Andrew agreed. This was going to be his first experiment in trusting God for the material things of life. He had the thirty pounds for the first session's fee. After that, he was looking forward to seeing how God would supply the money.

—Not About Money

Right from the start, something kept happening that bothered Brother Andrew. The students often talked at mealtime about inadequate funds.

"Sometimes after a whole night of prayer for a certain need, half of the request would be granted, or three-quarters. If an old-people's home... needed ten blankets, the students would perhaps receive enough to buy six. The Bible said that we were workers in God's vineyard. Was this the way the Lord of the vineyard paid His hired men?"[87]

Observing how drunks in the slums at the bottom of the hill begged for money to buy their drinks, it occurred to Andrew that they received a better income than the missionaries-in-training did.

"I could not understand why this bothered me so. Was I greedy? I didn't think so. We had always been poor, and I had never worried about it. What was it then?... The answer was not about money at all. What I was worried about was a relationship."[88]

When Andrew had worked at a factory, he trusted the manager to pay in full and on time. If an ordinary factory worker could be financially secure, so could one of God's workers. He didn't need the security of a certain amount of money. He needed the security of a relationship.

"If I was going to give my life as a servant of the King, I had to know that King. What was He like? In what way could I trust Him? In the same way I trusted a set of impersonal laws? Or could I trust Him as a living leader, as a very present commander in battle? The question was central. Because if He were a King in name only, I would rather go back to the... factory. I would remain a Christian, but I would know that my religion was only a set of principles, excellent and to be followed, but hardly demanding devotion.

"Suppose on the other hand that I were to discover God to be a Person,

---

[86] Ibid., p. 59.
[87] Ibid., p. 60.
[88] Ibid.

> in the sense that He communicated and cared and loved and led. That was something quite different. That was the kind of King I would follow into any battle."[89]

Andrew realized that his probing into God's nature that day would begin with the issue of money. He knelt in front of the window and made a covenant with God. "Lord," he said, "I need to know I can trust You in practical things. I thank you for letting me earn the fees for the first semester. I ask You to supply the rest of them. If I have to be so much as a day late in paying, I shall know that I am supposed to go back to the... factory."

He admits it was a childish prayer—"petulant and demanding;" but then he was still a child in the Christian life. The remarkable thing is that God honored his prayer—but not without testing him in some remarkable ways.

—The Royal Way

When it came time for the first training trip, Mr. Dinnen told Andrew that it would be an exercise in trust. The rules were simple. Each student on the team would be given a one-pound banknote. With it he was expected to pay his own transportation, lodging, food, advertising, renting of halls, refreshments, and so on. Also, they were each expected to pay it back when they returned to the school. There was another catch. They were not supposed to mention money at any of their meetings—all their needs had to be provided with no manipulation on their part—or the experiment would be a failure.

> "I was a member of a team of five boys. Later when I tried to reconstruct where our funds came from during those four weeks, it was hard to. It seemed that what we needed was always just there. Sometimes a letter would arrive from one of the boys' parents with a little money. Sometimes we would get a check in the mail from a church we had visited days or weeks earlier. The notes that came with the gifts were always interesting. 'I know you don't need money, or you would have mentioned it,' someone would write. 'But God just wouldn't let me get to sleep tonight until I had put this in an envelope for you.'"
>
> "But money or produce, we stuck fast to two rules: we never mentioned a need aloud, and we gave tithe of whatever came to us as soon as we got it—within twenty-four hours if possible.
>
> "Another team that set out from school at the same time we did, was not so strict about tithing. They set aside their ten percent all right, but they didn't give it away immediately, 'in case we ran into an emergency.'

---

[89] Ibid., p. 61.

Of course they had emergencies! So did we, every day. But they ended their month owing money to hotels, lecture halls, and markets all over Scotland, while we came back to school almost ten pounds ahead. Fast as we could give money away, God was always swifter, and we ended with money to send to the WEC work overseas."

Brother Andrew tells a story that bolsters our faith in the *Royal Way*. That's what Andrew called what was happening—*the game of the Royal Way*. He had "discovered that when God supplied money, He did it in a Kingly manner, not in a groveling way."[90]

One weekend they were holding meetings in Edinburgh. They had attracted a large group of young people for the first day but were not sure what to do to get them all to come back the next. One of the team members blurted out an unplanned announcement offering to serve everyone tea before the meeting the next evening. Four o'clock. The team was horrified as a couple dozen hands went up. They were committed; but they had no tea, no cake, no bread, no butter, and exactly five cups. They had no money either. They had used it all to rent the hall.

The young people themselves came forward, saying they would like to help. One offered milk, another the tea, another sugar, another the dishes. The tea was taking shape, but they were still missing the cake. Andrew tells the story like this:

> "Without cake, these Scottish boys and girls wouldn't consider tea tea. That night in our evening prayer time, we put the matter before God. 'Lord, we've got ourselves into a spot. From somewhere we've got to get a cake. Will You help us?'
>
> "So that night as we rolled up in our blankets on the floor of the hall, we played guessing games: How was God going to give us that cake? Among the five of us, we guessed everything imaginable—or so we thought.
>
> "Morning arrived. We half expected a heavenly messenger to come to our door bearing a cake. But no one came. The morning mail arrived. We ripped open the two letters, hoping for money. There was none. A woman from a nearby church came by to see if she could help. 'Cake' was on the tip of all our tongues, but we swallowed the word and shook our heads.
>
> "'Everything,' we assured her, 'is in God's hands.'
>
> "The tea had been announced for four o'clock in the afternoon. At three the tables were set, but still no cake. Three-thirty came. We put on the water to boil. Three forty-five.
>
> "And then the doorbell rang.
>
> "All of us together ran to the big front entrance, and there was the postman. In his hand was a large box.

[90] Ibid., p. 66.

"'Hello, lads,' said the postman. 'Got something for you that feels like a food package.' He handed the box to one of the boys. 'The delivery day is over, actually,' he said, 'but I hate to leave a perishable package overnight.'

"We thanked him profusely, and the minute he closed the door the boy solemnly handed me the box. 'It's for you Andrew. From a Mrs. William Hopkins in London.'

"I took the package and carefully unwrapped it. Off came the twine. Off came the brown outside paper. Inside there was no note—only a large white box. Deep in my soul I knew that I could afford the drama of lifting the lid slowly. As I did, there, in perfect condition, to be admired by five sets of wondering eyes, was an enormous, glistening, moist, chocolate cake."[91]

—Historagorical Principles

All these stories touch on important principles concerning money and mission work.

1. We saw from Elisha and Elisha's servant that missionaries are not merchants. The grace God imparts through us has to be freely accessible to all who seek Him. Even the skeptic has to be able to discern it as grace and not vocation—that we follow God, not a career path. The world needs to know we walk after the Spirit not after the flesh. It may be appropriate for fees to help defray the costs of providing services—but those fees need to benefit the mission rather than personal pecuniary interests.
2. The *great commission* applies to all who follow Christ. We're pilgrims and strangers here. Regardless of our station, we are *missionaries*—and we need to live as missionaries. It is our high privilege to stay focused on our mission by not being drawn into worldly comforts and worldly lifestyles.
3. From all the wilderness stories, we see that the role of self-sacrificing service and full dependence upon the providences and provisions of God, are *absolutely necessary* for the development of character. More than this, it provides a powerful witness to those we reach. The wilderness validates ministry—"One crying in the wilderness, Prepare ye the way of the Lord."[92] Even when God blesses us financially—we are to choose simple, self-sacrificing

[91] Ibid., pp. 63-64.
[92] Mark 1:3.

lives. It's no coincidence that John wore *plain dress,*[93] and the Waldensian missionaries passed through the great cities with naked feet and *course garments.*[94] God blesses us so we can be a blessing to others. Enoch was a missionary to the cities;[95] Abraham to the nations;[96] Joseph to Egypt;[97] Daniel to the courts of Babylon;[98] Elijah and *John the Baptist* to Israel. Paul was a missionary to the Gentiles. Peter, James and John were missionaries to the Jews in Jerusalem.[99] While we are all supposed to reach out to our families, coworkers, neighborhoods and foreign lands: *American Seventh-day Adventists* have a specific missionary responsibility to the large cities of this nation.[100] This is our essential work for this time.[101]

4. God's servants are to live by faith—*not by feelers*. We are not to behave as though we are grubby and undignified. We are ambassadors of a King who has a royal treasury. So long as we work as He instructs us to work and go where He leads us to go: He will care for us according to His plan for our lives. "Keep your lives free from the love of money and be content with what you have, for God has said: 'Never will I leave you, never will I forsake you.'"[102]
5. Trust is not about money. Brother Andrew shows us how it is about a relationship. God is a Person. He communicates. He cares. He loves; and He leads. He is the King we can follow into any battle!
6. God plays *The Game of the Royal Way*. When He supplies money, He does it in a Kingly manner, not grovelingly.

—The King's Way

Wilderness dwellers find that learning to trust God for the material things of life can be a difficult proposition. Abraham kept trying to work

[93] Ellen G. White, *The Desire of Ages*, p. 100.
[94] Ellen G. White. *The Spirit of Prophecy*, vol. 1, p. 76.
[95] Ellen G. White, *The Review and Herald*, September 27, 1906.
[96] Ellen G. White, *The Desire of Ages,* p. 27.
[97] Ibid.
[98] Ibid.
[99] Ellen G. White, The Acts of the Apostles. p. 165.
[100] Ellen G. White, Medical Ministry, p. 304. "The work in the cities is the essential work for this time. When the cities are worked as God would have them, the result will set into operation a mighty movement such as we have not yet witnessed."
[101] Ellen G. White, Medical Ministry, p. 304.
[102] Hebrews 13:5.

things out himself. The Children of Israel constantly murmured and complained even though they could see a pillar of cloud leading them by day, and a pillar of fire by night.[103] The inaugural wilderness challenge for Christ brought Him very near starvation.

In his first experiment in trusting God for the material things of life, Brother Andrew was tested too. He never mentioned school fees to anyone. Gifts always came such that he could pay them in full and on time—always from some different place, and never more than the school costs. His other needs seemed to operate under a different plan. Real needs were always suppled; but Andrew had to be creative and thrifty concerning things like laundry soap, toothpaste, and razor blades.

Foreigners in Britain needed to renew their visas periodically. Andrew's was due for December 31, 1954, or He would have to leave the country.[104] He needed a shilling (twelve cents) to send the forms to London by registered mail; but he didn't even have one penny. Three times he was nearly lured from the *Royal Way* in this matter.

First, on December twenty-eight, he realized he was in charge of the student tract fund that year. He could borrow just one shilling from the fund. He put the idea behind him. On the twenty-ninth, he thought maybe he could find those pennies lying on the ground. He put on his coat and started for the street—before realizing that was no *Royal Way*.

On December thirty he had a visitor. It was Richard—a drunk he had befriended in the nearby slums. "Andrew," he said, "would you be having a little extra cash? I'm hungry." Andrew laughed as he told Richard about the laundry soup and the toothpaste. Out of the corner of his eye he saw a shilling laying among the pebbles. The sun caught it just so. Andrew could see it but Richard could not. He instinctively put his foot over it. Still talking to Richard, he reached down and pick up a hand full of pebbles and aimlessly tossed them down one by one until he only had the shilling in his hand. He dropped it in his pocket and the battle began.

> "The coin meant I could stay in school. I wouldn't be doing Richard any favor by giving it to him: he'd spend it on drink and be thirsty as ever in an hour.
>
> "While I was still thinking up excellent arguments, I knew it was no good. How could I judge Richard when Christ told me so clearly that I

---

[103] Exodus 13:21.

[104] Brother Andrew with John and Elizabeth Sherrill, *God's Smuggler*, p. 47, 1967, Guideposts Associates, INC. Carmel, New York.

> must not? Furthermore, this was not the Royal Way! What right had an ambassador to hold on to money when another of the King's children stood in front of him saying he was hungry? I shoved my hand back into my pocket and drew out the silver coin.
> "'Look, Richard,' I said, 'I do have this. Would it help any?'

Before Andrew reached the door to go back inside, the postman turned down his walk. There was a letter for him—from a prayer group back home. They sent along a pound and a half—*thirty* shillings. It was more than enough to mail the forms to London, buy a large box of laundry soap, Gillette Supers instead of Blues, and to buy his favorite toothpaste. *The King had done it His way!*

—Hand of the Man from Galilee

Jesus attacked the temple's denominated business model both at the start and the end of His public ministry. There is a song about it that was popular in the 70s—

> "Every time I look into the Holy Book I want to tremble, when I read about the part where a carpenter cleared the temple. For the buyers and the sellers were no different fellas than what we profess to be; and it causes me shame to know we're not the people we should be."[105]

Chances are there are things in our experience that God asks us to give to Him. Are we working some things out ourselves? Are we doing things the way the world says they must be done? Are we afraid God will not do what He says? Do we have the faith to put ourselves completely into His care—into His work? Do we really depend fully on Him?

Has the Lord put something on your heart today? What is He asking you to do? The details will be different for each one of us. But one thing is sure: He calls us all into the wilderness!

Will you give Him full control of your physical, mental, and spiritual matters? What about money? How much of your life (your time, your spending) is dictated by financial insecurities? Are there shackles that keep you from progressing along the path God has for you?

> "Put your hand in the hand of the Man who stilled the waters. Put your hand in the hand of the man who calmed the sea. Take a look at yourself and you can look at others differently, by putting your hand in the hand of the man from Galilee."[106]

---

[105] Gene Maclellan, *Put Your Hand in the Hand*, the song was composed by Gene Maclellan and first recorded by Anne Murray. There are a number of versions of the song, and the wording of the verses tend to vary quite a bit.
[106] Ibid.

> "The mighty shaking has commenced and will go on, and all will be shaken out who are not willing to take a bold and unyielding stand for the truth and to sacrifice for God and His cause. The angel said, 'think ye that any will be compelled to sacrifice? No, no. It must be a freewill offering. It will take all to buy the field.'... Then I saw that the judgments of the Almighty were speedily coming, and I begged the angel to speak in his language to the people. Said he, 'all the thunders and lightenings of Mount Sinai would not move those who will not be moved by the plain truths of the Word of God, neither would an angel's message awake them.'"[107]

"There are those, even among Seventh-day Adventists, who are under the reproof of the word of God, because of the way they acquired their property and use it, acting as if they owned it, and created it, without an eye to the glory of God, and without earnest prayer to direct them in acquiring or using it. They are grasping at a serpent, which will sting them as an adder. Of God's people He says, 'Her merchandise and her hire shall be holiness to the Lord: it shall not be treasured nor laid up.' But many who profess to believe the truth do not want God in their thoughts, any more than did the antediluvians or Sodomites. One sensible thought of God, awakened by the Holy Spirit, would spoil all their schemes. Self, self, self, has been their God, their alpha and their omega."

— Counsels on Stewardship, p. 141.

[107] Ellen G. White, *Early Writings*, pp. 50-51.

CHAPTER TWENTY-FOUR

Navigating the Twilight Zone

Christ asked the question: "When the Son of man cometh, shall He find faith in the earth?"[1] He seemed to imply that faith would be a rarity. As the True Witness to Laodicea, He further detailed how things would be with Christians in our time.[2] He described our church as though she where living in some kind of self-perception *twilight zone*—all warm and fuzzy about her miserable condition.

This is the context we need to consider when we tackle the confusing and controversial subject of the medical side of missionary work. As Laodiceans, we should be leery of trusting our warm and fuzzy attitude about Adventist Healthcare.

Let's begin where we all agree. We all agree medical work is the *right arm of the gospel*.[3] But which medical work? To some, the right arm of the gospel is healthcare the way we do it now, and to others, it is not.

---

[1] Luke 18:8.

[2] Revelation 3:14-22.

[3] Ellen G. White, *Manuscript Releases*, vol. 13, p. 203.

—Right-Arm Wrestling

There are many reasons this is not an easy topic. We should address it, anyway. To calibrate the healing-side of the *Galilee Protocol* properly, we need to know the role drug medications play in medical missionary work. The anti-drug statements by Sister White seem inconsistent with the normal medical practice we use and promote in the church today. This causes tension. In 1863, Sister White received the famous health vision. Instruction to begin a health institute followed a couple years later. These visions placed the health work solidly on our denominational mission platform. The visions kept coming; and buried deep in all that counsel are some hard-hitting references bewailing the harmful effects of drug medication, and urgent calls to keep them from—and remove them from—our work.

Buried deep is more of a euphemism for our present tendency to avoid and ignore. Actually, the references are abundant and easy to find. To narrow the discussion, we'll assume that both sides accept the inspiration of Sister White; and that the issue is not whether she is right or wrong, but more a matter of perspective.

Society's view of modern medicine is that it is a great blessing. So, when Ellen White says: "We must leave drugs entirely alone,"[4] "drugs never cure disease,"[5] "drug medication should never have been introduced into our institutions,"[6] and "those who make a practice of taking drugs sin against their intelligence and endanger their whole afterlife,"[7] it is natural to think she must be talking about something different. Regardless of how it might seem, she can't really be talking about the miracle of modern medicine. Right?

But when we take her statements in their full context, there is an eerie overall sense that her statements against drugs cut closer to modern practice than what we are comfortable with. So we avoid and ignore—it's a hard thing to explain away the statements of a prophet without sounding like we question the gift.

---

[4] Ellen G. White, *Letter* 67, 1899.

[5] Ellen G. White, *Spiritual Gifts*, vol. 4a, p. 135.

[6] Ellen G. White, *Manuscript 105*, 1898.

[7] Ellen G. White, *Selected Messages*, book 2, p. 290.

—A Pill Hard to Swallow

In her landmark work on health—*The Ministry of Healing*—we find a plain statement concerning the great healing work of a notable *Galilean* Physician:

> "Christ made use of the simple agencies of nature. While He did not give countenance to the use of drug medication, He sanctioned the use of simple and natural remedies."[8]

Read it again; and pay close attention to the contrast. Two approaches are contrasted here. We can't honestly say that statins (for cholesterol), coumadin (for blood thinning), and morphine (for pain), are "*simple and natural remedies*,"—the "*simple agencies of nature*." But if we also exclude them from being "*drug medication*," then where do they fit in? Suggesting that Sister White left such a big hole in the healthcare discussion is a pill hard to swallow.

—What Is a Drug?

The clarity of this statement—and so many others like it—becomes muddled unless we can accurately define what she means when she says "*drug medications*." We know what *we* mean today; and some people conclude that Ellen meant that too. But others say it is more complicated than that.

There was a time when some popular medicines contained mercury, arsenic, or strychnine—things that today we all agree are *poisons*. Since it was not unusual for Sister White to call drug medications poison; some find logic in limiting her statements to only apply to those outdated formulas that contained those specific ingredients.[9] We know better than to use them now. But it is more complicated than that too.

> "In William Shakespeare's time, 400 years ago, poisonous extracts were combined into cough medicine. Well into the 20th century, mercury was an ingredient in popular remedies, from purgatives to infants' teething powder.
>
> "But modern scientific techniques have allowed researchers to better understand, and then take advantage of, the underlying mechanisms by which plant toxins and animal venoms attack normal metabolic processes. For example, some neurotoxins block the release of chemical messengers called neurotransmitters; some stop neurotransmitter messages from being received; some send false signals; and still others

---

[8] Ellen G. White, *The Ministry of Healing*, p. 223.

[9] See Mervyn G. Hardinge, *A Physician Explains Ellen White's Counsel on Drugs, Herbs, & Natural Remedies*, pg. 69-75, 2001, Review and Herald Publishing Association.

> disrupt nerve cell activity by opening channels in cell walls. If muscles in the heart or lungs fail to get the proper signal to function, the results are fatal. But applying the same effect in nonlethal doses can stem tremors or the registering of pain.
>
> "'What is a poison?' asks Mark Siddall, curator in the Division of Invertebrate Zoology who is also curator of the special exhibition *The Power of Poison*... 'It's a substance that interferes with normal physiological processes, that alters or stops them, or makes things happen. That is essentially what medicines are, too.'"[10]

Many see it the same way that Mark does; and they argue that *all* drugs are poison; but coumadin (warfarin), methotrexate (chemo), and mercury (vaccines) are poisons for sure. These are not the only ones either. Four medications are made from the very poisonous belladonna plant—one berry of which can kill instantly! Foxgloves flowers (digitalis purpurea) are deadly poisons. From them heart medications are made.[11] We could go on and on; but it's not necessary.

The fact is that the argument about Sister White only referring to outdated medicines containing such things as mercury and arsenic only works with the uninformed or misinformed (and with Adventists who want to throw Ellen White off the modern medicine trail). We still use mercury in medicine today, only now we usually inject it. We use[12] arsenic, too. Now we administer it intravenously.[13]

Dr. Barry M. Charles, MD, has studied findings from over 10,000 articles, reports, and scientific research published in the medical literature; and he claims that modern medicine has abandoned its prime purpose and is contravening the basic prescription of Hippocrates' oath: "first, do no harm."[14] He claims that "medical care is often based on much less scientific evidence than assumed and undergoes radical reversals." He continues, "The editor of the *British Medical Journal* revealed that only 15 percent of all medical therapies have a scientific basis or have been demonstrated to be effective."[15]

"Every medication, including those that are sold over the counter without a prescription, has an associated side effect. Commonly used drugs

---

[10] American Museum of Natural History, *The Power of Poison: Poison as Medicine*, November 13, 2013, (http://www.amnh.org/explore/news-blogs/on-exhibit-posts/the-power-of-poison-poison-as-medicine), accessed 3/1/2019.

[11] Linda Cramption, *Floxgloves: Beautiful Flowers and Digitalis Health Effects*, October 16, 2017. (https://owlcation.com/stem/Foxgloves-Beautiful-Flowers-Digitalis-and-Health-Effects), accessed 3/1/2019.

[12] U.S. Food & Drug Administration, *Thimerosol and Vaccines*, updated 2/2/2018, (https://www.fda.gov/BiologicsBloodVaccines/SafetyAvailability/VaccineSafety/UCM096228), accessed 3/1/2019.

[13] WebMD, *Arsenic*, (https://www.webmd.com/vitamins/ai/ingredientmono-1226/arsenic), accessed 3/1-2019.

[14] Sepp Hasslberger, *Modern Medicine Pushing Poisonous Drugs – Says Doctor*, July 30, 2004, (http://www.newmediaexplorer.org/sepp/2004/07/30/ modern_medicine_pushing_poisonous_drugs_says_doctor.htm.) accessed 3-1-2019.

[15] British Medical Journal. 1991; 303: 798-799.

have been found to affect every system. Frequent reactions include skin rashes, nausea, headaches, dizziness, lethargy, diarrhea, and gastric bleeding in a significant number of people. More severe reactions that can be fatal or severely debilitating include deafness, depression, abnormal heart rhythms, angina, bronchospasm, electrolyte disturbances, immune system dysfunction, serious blood disorders such as aplastic anemia, liver or kidney toxicity, Stevens-Johnson syndrome, or anaphylactic shock. These occur in a statistically significant proportion of the population. Despite what is known about adverse drug effects, Dr. David Kessler, Chief of the U.S. Food and Drug Administration, believes that 'only one percent of all serious drug reactions are reported.'[16]"[17]

—Louder Than Words

In practical terms, arguably the most convincing mitigating factor is the *perceived* success of modern drugs. People simply believe in them. There are risks; we all know and except that. Still the combined weight of society's faith in modern medications is hard to oppose. When dealing with the ethical, emotional, and rational issues involving life and death—the contemporary pressures in their favor speaks louder to the modern mind than anything a little old lady in the late 1800s could muster. But again, shouldn't we proceed cautiously here? Remember, we are pitting the senses of Laodiceans (living in a self-perception twilight zone) against the acuity of inspired vision.

The evidence does not support the idea that Sister White's counsels against using drug medication are limited to the course elixirs of yesteryear. This is not to grind an axe against the pharmacist, the doctor or even against modern medicine itself. What it is, is failing to do well the work of *avoiding and ignoring*. And it's recognizing that there are reasons drugs are supposed to be left out of church work. *Medical ministry* played no small role in the *Galilee Protocol* of Christ's day; and it will play no small role in the *Galilee Protocol* of ours. The entire conceptual model of modern medicine is diametrically opposite to Christ's methods. This may not be self-evident to everyone, so we'll explore it here in more detail.

[16] US News and World Report. January 9, 1995: 49-54.

[17] Barry M. Charles, MD, *Hazards of Modern Medicine*, (http://www.newmediaexplorer.org/sepp/2004/07/30/ modern_medicine_pushing_poisonous_drugs_says_doctor.htm.) accessed 3-1-2019.

—A Better Approach

Inspiration doesn't give us a definitive list of good drugs and bad drugs. The counsels are not product-specific regarding the negative side of the question. Instead, it takes a better approach. It's like the Bible's approach to Sabbath vs Sunday. Sure, the Bible talks about both the seal-of-God and the mark-of-the beast; but you have to make the case *for* the Sabbath before you can unravel the case *against* Sunday. Bible students have to apply some simple deductive reasoning.

Brand names and product formularies come and go, but God's methods are stable and timeless. So Ellen White *was direct* concerning this positive side of the question. We have ample information available to make a definitive list of those things that Heaven approves. Just as Scripture is very clear about the Sabbath, so the Spirit of Prophecy is very clear about God's remedies.

> "There are many ways of practicing the healing art, but there is only one way that Heaven approves. God's remedies are the simple agencies of nature, that will not tax or debilitate the system through their powerful properties. Pure air and water, cleanliness, a proper diet, purity of life, and a firm trust in God, are remedies for the want of which thousands are dying, yet these remedies are going out of date because their skillful use requires work that the people do not appreciate. Fresh air, exercise, pure water, and clean, sweet premises, are within the reach of all with but little expense; but drugs are expensive, both in the outlay of means and the effect produced upon the system."[18]

We can expand the list: pure air,[18] fresh air,[18] deep breathing,[19] pure water,[18] cleanliness,[18] clean sweet premises,[18] proper diet,[18] abstemiousness,[20] fasting,[21] avoiding meat,[22] purity of life,[18] clear conscience,[23] firm trust in God,[18] prayer,[24] gratitude,[25] praise,[25] singing,[25] exercise,[18] walking,[26] visiting nature,[27] simple herbs,[28] catnip tea,[29] pulverized charcoal,[28] charcoal/smartweed,[28] water treatments,[30] hydrotherapy,[27] sunlight,[20] rest,[29]

[18] Ellen G. White, *Counsels on Health*, p. 323.
[19] Ibid., p. 59.
[20] Ellen G. White, *The Ministry of Healing*, p. 127.
[21] Ellen G. White, *Counsels on Health*, p. 148.
[22] Ibid., p. 70.
[23] Ibid., p. 261.
[24] Ellen G. White, *The Ministry of Healing*, p. 223.
[25] Ibid., pp. 252-256.
[26] Ellen G. White, *Counsels on Health*, p. 200.
[27] Ellen G. White, *The Ministry of Healing*, p. 237.
[28] Ellen G. White, *Manuscript Releases*, vol. 21, pp. 289-290.
[29] Ellen G. White, *Loma Linda Messages*, p. 335.
[30] Ellen G. White, *The Ministry of Healing*, p. 236-237.

and helping others.[25]

Now let's add in some descriptive phrases: simple agencies of nature,[18] not taxing to the system,[18] not debilitating to the system,[18] requires skillful work,[18] little expense,[18] hygienic method,[28] leaves no baleful effects,[28] cleanses the system,[31] old fashioned,[28] simple home treatments,[30] no deadly aftereffects,[29] and harmless.[31]

By way of contrast, she describes drugs: powerful properties,[18] not natural,[32] taxing,[18] debilitating,[18] a lazy method,[33] expensive in means,[18] expensive in effect,[18] weakens and clogs,[31] leaves a baleful influence,[28] intricate names,[28] deadly aftereffects,[29] never heals disease,[34] faithless,[35] foreign substances of a poisonous nature,[35] vegetable & mineral poisons,[36] poisonous productions planted by Satan,[37] paralyze nature's efforts to heal,[33] require no personal religion,[38] non-hygienic agencies,[39] unfavorable to natural laws,[33] interferes with laws of nature,[40] weaken directly and through inheritance,[41] increases the depreciation of the race,[42] and an offense to God.[43]

—A Blindsided Prophet?

In the many descriptions of what God approves, never do we find anything that resembles modern medication. This is a concern, really. While in Basel, Switzerland, and in Christiana, Norway, Ellen White saw printing presses in operation, that she had seen in vision ten years earlier.[44] Once, when some men secretly moved a meeting from its scheduled location in Boston, to a place in Randolph, thirteen miles south of Boston (just to be sure she wouldn't attend), she was told of the new location in vision.[45] While in vision that same day—at the Randolph location—she held a large family Bible over her head turning the pages and quoting the passages she was pointing at—but unable to see.[46] Before

31 Ellen G. White, *Selected Messages*, book 2, pp. 289-290.
32 Ellen G. White, *Healthy Living*, pp. 247-248.
33 Ellen G. White, *Medical Ministry*, pp. 221-224.
34 Ellen G. White, *Selected Messages*, book 2, p. 451.
35 Ellen G. White, *Spiritual Gifts*, vol. 4, p. 133-134.
36 Ibid., p. 140.
37 Ellen G. White, *Letter to S. N. Haskell*, 1898.
38 Ellen G. White, *Medical Ministry*, pp. 234-235.
39 Ibid., pp. 259-260.
40 Ellen G. White, *Manuscript 22*, 1889.
41 Ellen G. White, *Healthy Living*, p.53.
42 Ellen G. White, *Disease and Its Causes*, pp. 53-54.
43 Ellen G. White, *Medical Ministry*, p. 229.
44 Arthur L. White, *Ellen G. White, A Brief Biography*, p. 15. (https://m.egwwritings.org/en/book/781.51#51) Accessed 3/5/2019.
45 Arthur L. White, *Ellen G. White, The Early Years: 1827-1862*, vol. 1, p. 103.
46 Ibid., p. 104.

the *Review and Herold* office burned down, she saw a sword of fire hanging over it.[47] Before the great San Francisco earthquake occurred, the Lord made it known to her.[48] She saw events that happened before the world was created.[49] She was shown event to take place to the close of time—and even beyond.[50]

Still somehow we're to believe that the Lord had her to condemn categorically the use of drug medications in the strongest of terms, without letting her in on the little secret that within a couple years, He would take over the whole drug business and turn it into the greatest blessing the world has ever seen—and that then, drugs would play a prominent role in spreading the final warning message to a world that is already using them without us! What was it we said about the *twilight zone?*

—A Divine Protocol

Modern healthcare cannot share the same footing with medical missionary work. Even just the medical element of medical missionary work is part of a divine protocol. Let's look at the role that natural remedies play in medical missionary work. For context we turn to Ellen White's description of the beginning days of Adventist medical work:

> "The treatment we gave when the sanitarium was first established required earnest labor to combat disease. We did not use drug concoctions; we followed hygienic methods. This work was blessed by God. It was a work in which the human instrumentality could cooperate with God in saving life. There should be nothing put into the human system that would leave its baleful influence behind. And to carry out the light on this subject, to practice hygienic treatment, and to educate on altogether different lines of treating the sick, was the reason given me why we should have sanitariums established in various localities."[51]

Can you hear the gospel tones in this description? No wonder medical work is the right-arm of the gospel—it is the moral gospel for our physical bodies! Natural remedies help to bring our activity into harmony with God's physical laws by supporting the body's divinely established tendency to maintain and restore health. Notice these facts from the Spirit of Prophecy:

---

47 Ellen G. White, *Manuscript Releases*, vol. 4, p. 367.

48 Ellen G. White, *Manuscript 114*, 1902.

49 See Ellen G. White, *Patriarchs and Prophets*, chapter one.

50 See Ellen G. White, *The Great Controversy*, chapters 38 to the end of the book.

51 Ellen G. White, *Manuscript Releases*, vol. 21, 289.

"Disease is an effort of nature to free the system from conditions that result from a violation of the laws of health."[52] "Christ's remedies cleanse the system."[53] "We cannot be too often reminded that health does not depend upon chance. It is a result of obedience to law."[54] "The laws governing the physical nature are as truly divine in their origin and character as the law of the Ten Commandments."[22]

"To make plain natural law, and urge the obedience of it, is the work that accompanies the third angel's message to prepare a people for the coming of the Lord."[55] "The Lord has made it part of His plan that man's reaping shall be according to his sowing."[56]

Inspiration clarifies that all healing comes from God.

"God has pledged Himself to keep the living machinery in healthful action, if the human agent will obey His laws and cooperate with God."[57]

"It is God who has made the provision that nature shall work to restore the exhausted powers. The work is of God. He is the great Healer."[58]

"The same power that upholds nature is working also in man. The same great laws that guide alike the star and the atom control human life. The laws that govern the heart's action, regulating the flow of the current of life in the body, are the laws of the mighty Intelligence that has the jurisdiction of the soul. From Him all life proceeds. Only in harmony with Him can be found its true sphere of action. For all the objects of His creation, the condition is the same,—a life sustained by receiving the life of God, a life exercised in harmony with the Creator's will. To transgress His law, physical, mental, or moral, is to place one's life out of harmony with the universe, to introduce discord, anarchy, and ruin."[59]

The foregoing references illustrate how—in the *Galilee Protocol*—healing functions in a specific context, with certain program absolutes.

1. *True healing glorifies God (His love)*. This is to say that His character is exonerated. The law is a transcript of God's character[60]—and His law is a law of love[61]—the perfect law of liberty.[62] From this it must follow that healing must show God's love and gracein a way that preserves the integrity of His physical and moral laws. Every disciple's work as a medical missionary must show God's true character of love—we demonstrate

52 Ellen G. White, *The Ministry of Healing*, p. 127.
53 Ellen G. White, *Selected Messages*, book 2, p. 289.
54 Ellen G. White, *The Ministry of Healing*, p. 128.
55 Ellen G. White, *Manuscript Releases*, vol. 16, p. 60.
56 Ellen G. White, *Healthful Living*, p. 25.
57 Ellen G. White, *Counsels on Diets and Foods*, p. 69
58 Ellen G. White, *Medical Ministry*, p. 11.
59 Ibid., p. 10.
60 Ellen G. White, *Christ's Object Lessons*, p. 305, 315.
61 Mark 12:30-31.
62 James 1.25.

that "Christ is the same compassionate physician now that He was during His earthly ministry."[63]

2. *True healing glorifies God (His justice).* As we just said, God's character of love has to embody full reverence to His law. "[Health] is a result of obedience to law."[64] "The Lord has made it part of His plan that man's reaping shall be according to his sowing."[65]

3. *True healing presents the gospel.* We cannot heal ourselves.[66] Only God can heal.[67] "Those who come to the great Healer must be willing to do His will, to humble their souls, and confess their sins."[68] "Christ came to this world and lived the law of God, that man might have perfect mastery over the natural inclinations which corrupt the soul. The physician of soul and body, He gives victory over warring lusts. He has provided every facility, that man may possess completeness of character."[69]

4. *True healing is the work of faith.* "We cannot heal. We cannot change the diseased condition of the body. But it is our part, as medical missionaries, as workers together with God, to use the means He has provided. Then we should pray that God will bless these agencies. We do believe in God; we believe in a God who hears and answers prayer."[70]

5. *The object of true healing is cleansing.* It's not just relief from symptoms. "Christ's remedies cleanse the system."[71] "Let it ever be kept before the mind that the great object of hygienic reform is to secure the highest possible development of the mind and soul and body."[72]

6. *True healing shows authority.* "Following Christ's example is our medical missionary work, we shall reveal to the world that our credentials are from above... United with Christ in God, we shall reveal to the world that as God chose His Son to be His representative on the earth, even so has Christ chosen us to represent His character."[73]

7. *True healing exerts a powerful influence.* "A time will come when medical missionaries of other denominations will become jealous and

---

[63] Ellen G. White, *The Ministry of Healing*, p. 223.
[64] Ibid., p. 128.
[65] Ellen G. White, *Healthful Living*, p. 25.
[66] Ellen G. White, *Medical Ministry*, p. 13.
[67] Ibid., p. 11.
[68] Ibid., p. 40.
[69] Ellen G. White, *Medical Ministry*, p. 130.
[70] Ibid., p. 13.
[71] Ellen G. White, *Selected Messages*, book 2, p. 289.
[72] Ellen G. White, *Counsels on Health*, p. 386.
[73] Ellen G. White, *Medical Ministry*, p. 23.

envious of the influence exerted by Seventh-day Adventists in these lines."[74]

8. *True healing is a test.* "All heaven is looking on with intense interest to see what character medical missionary work will assume under the supervision of human beings. Will men make merchandise of God's ordained plan for reaching the dark parts of the earth with a manifestation of His benevolence? Will they cover mercy with selfishness, and then call it medical missionary work?"[75] "This test will come to the churches in connection with the true medical missionary work, a work that has the Great Physician to dictate and preside in all it comprehends."[76]

—A Curious Statement

While in Australia, Ellen White wrote to Dr. Kellogg. In that letter she referred to a manuscript of one of her books soon to be published. Her son Willie had sent her a draft copy for approval. Dr. Kellogg had written the preface.

She said she saw nothing that she objected to except the subject of *drug medication*. Then she makes a curious statement:

> "I will not educate or sustain the use of drugs. *I try not to speak of these things*, but if the book is already out, I shall have to insert something that I may place the truth of the matter before the people. After seeing so much harm done by administering drugs, I cannot use them, and cannot testify in their favor. I must be true to the light given me by the Lord."[77]

She makes a couple curious statements in the letter. She also said,

> "Dr. Kellogg, many things have been opened before me *that no one but myself is any the wiser for* in regard to the management of sickness and disease—the effect of the use of drug medication, the thousands in our work who might have lived if they had not sent for a physician and had let nature work the recovery herself. But the simplest remedies may assist nature, and leave no baleful effects after their use."[78]

One could wonder just what mysteries the Lord showed Sister White about drugs that no one knows about—and *why* she tried not to speak of those things?

---

[74] Ellen G. White, *Loma Linda Messages*, p. 545.
[75] Ellen G. White, *Series B*, No. 1, p. 19.
[76] Ellen G. White, *1888 Materials*, p. 1710.
[77] Ellen G. White, *Manuscript Releases*, vol. 21, p. 290. Emphasis added.
[78] Ibid. Emphasis added.

—The Back Track

Actually, the march wasn't going well. The church was not keeping her focus on God's plan. She had ideas of her own that suited her better. It was clear as early as 1881. Sister White wrote, "My heart aches day after day and night after night for our churches. Many are progressing, but in the back track." What did she mean by back track? In chapter two[79] we saw how this would play out over time. We refused to march under the banner of God's authority. We retreated toward Egypt.[80]

"The sin of ancient Israel was in disregarding the expressed will of God and following their own way according to the leadings of unsanctified hearts. Modern Israel are fast following in their footsteps and the displeasure of the Lord is as surely resting upon them."[81] God had provided a detailed plan—the *Galilee Protocol*—for the church to prepare the world for the final events. But the church didn't like the plan.

> "The same disobedience and failure which were seen in the Jewish church have characterized *in a greater degree* the people who have had this great light from heaven in the last messages of warning."[82]

The apostle Paul warned us about this.

> "Moreover, brethren, I would not that ye should be ignorant, how that all our fathers were under the cloud, and all passed through the sea; And were all baptized unto Moses in the cloud and in the sea; And did all eat the same spiritual meat; And did all drink the same spiritual drink: for they drank of that spiritual Rock that followed them: and that Rock was Christ. But with many of them God was not well pleased: for they were overthrown in the wilderness.
>
> "Now these things were our examples, to the intent we should not lust after evil things, as they also lusted. Neither be ye idolaters, as were some of them; as it is written, the people sat down to eat and drink, and rose up to play. Neither let us commit fornication, as some of them committed, and fell in one day three and twenty thousand. Neither let us tempt Christ, as some of them also tempted, and were destroyed of serpents. Neither murmur ye, as some of them also murmured, and were destroyed of the destroyer. Now all these things happened unto them for ensamples: and they are written for our admonition, upon whom the ends of the world are come. Wherefore let him that thinketh he standeth take heed lest he fall."[83]

---

[79] Chapter Two, *By Whose Authority*.

[80] Ellen G. White, *The Great Controversy*, pp. 457-458.

[81] Ellen G. White, *Testimonies for the Church*, vol. 5, p. 94.

[82] Ibid., p. 456. Emphasis added.

[83] 1 Corinthians 10:1-12.

—Navigating the Twilight Zone

Living as we do in this Laodicean self-deception *twilight zone*, how should *the trusting ones* navigate through medical waters in this time?—when even the church plants it's banner on the side of poison? This is a real question—and fair to ask—because *twilight-zoning* tends to self-perpetuate. This is especially true in terms of healthcare.

Christ clearly stipulates that His healing is proportional to faith—that of the recipient and that of the instrument. To the degree that God's people put their faith in worldly medicine—that which God specifically "did not give countenance to"[84]—He is necessarily limited in His ability to heal us (and heal through us). And to the extent that His healing work is limited, our faith-building experience with His healing languishes. In those cases where individual faith is strong, it can seem like there is still a weakening corporate component.

So in a real pinch, we go for the slow-dosing poisons for their somewhat predictable short-term effect. This exacerbates the characteristic haziness of the *twilight zone*. No faith, no healing. No healing, no faith. So how do we break out of this ever-rolling, ever-growing snowball? The Psalmist offers his counsel. We move from strength to strength:

> "Blessed *is* the man whose strength *is* in thee; in whose heart *are* the ways *of them. Who* passing through the valley of Baca make it a well; the rain also filleth the pools. *They go from strength to strength*, every one of them in Zion appeareth before God."[85]

Here are some suggestions:

1. Commit to full-fledged wilderness faith-building. God's promise to the children of Israel to spare them from the diseases of Egypt was given at the beginning of their wilderness journey.[86]
2. Walk consistent with your faith and do the best you can. Willie White once wrote a letter where he refers to a question that a brother who lost his son to malaria asked Sister White. "Would I have sinned to give the boy quinine when I knew no other way to check malaria?" She replied, "No, we are expected to do the best we can." Willie explained that "the 'testimonies' strongly condemn the use of quinine and everyone knows that it is bad for the constitution, but there are at the present time only a few persons who

[84] Ellen G. White, *The Ministry of Healing*, p. 233. "Christ did not give countenance to drug medication, He sanctioned the use of simple and natural remedies."

[85] Psalms 84:5-7. Emphasis added.

[86] See Exodus 15:26 and the surrounding context.

have been able to check malarial fever without quinine." He also wrote:

> "In His revelations to His people in these last days regarding health and disease, God has set before us the highest standards, and it is His wish that we strive to attain to them. He also understands our weakness and all the difficulties with which we are surrounded.
>
> "God wishes us to be examples to the world, and also that we shall minister to the world, He wishes that we educate, educate, educate. He knows our weaknesses and pities our helplessness, and pardons our transgressions. He holds out His hand all day to a faithless and rebellious people."[87]

3. Learn to do better. Here's another account from that letter from Willie. Sister White was often very busy with her public work and "never found time to become an expert cook. She employed many cooks, and each one was instructed to study diligently how to follow the instructions that God had given us regarding healthful food." She "always instructed them to follow the most hygienic and health-giving method and sometimes a new cook would say, 'You advise the non-use of soda and baking powder. I do not know how to cook without some baking powder. What shall I do?'... 'Do the best you can. If you feel that you must have some baking powder, get the best and use little and then study how to cook without it.'"
4. Go from strength to strength. Often the causes of disease work for years before they break down health. Rebuilding health is also often gradual—as building faith can be. The goal is for both; and the method requires diligent effort. Keep in mind that when a hygienic course requires more time than the body can endure—premature death is *not* a healthy choice. But as a primary approach to healthcare, neither are drugs. They may have some desirable short-term effects—but they are still poisons. Grow your faith in God, and obey all His commandments. This approach can even raise the dead.
5. Prayerfully and seriously consider God's will. Ease, speed, and comfort are often *not* adequate justifications for choosing poisonous treatment; but health related trials *are* often some of the most effective tools the Lord has to teach us to depend on Him and improve character.

---

[87] W. C. White, Letter to a Sister in Memphis Tennessee, September 10, 1935.

"For which cause we faint not; but though our outward man perish, yet the inward *man* is renewed day by day. For our light affliction, which is but for a moment, worketh for us a far more exceeding *and* eternal weight of glory."[88]

6. Do not use drug-based medicine as ministry. This is important. Do absolutely nothing to confuse the two. Leave the world's method's to the world. We are to be medical missionaries; and there is only one way of practicing the healing art that heaven approves.[89]
7. Be leery of *products*. Marketing adds a lot of hype; and commercials make many claims. But our bodies get what they need for good health from God's eight remedies. Use quality, nutritious, whole-foods for nutrition—not all the fancy derivatives thereof.
8. Realize God will eventually take the matter into His own hands. Practice now for a time when drugs will lose their glitter, or won't be an option at all.

—Medical Quantitative Easing

We are familiar with the concept of probation. We can think of it in terms of a moral/legal safety zone that temporarily shields the sinner from some of the psychological effects of transgression. The grace of God offers and maintains this *safety zone*, so man's guilt doesn't spiritually paralyze his ability to repent and accept the great offer of salvation. But sin is physically destructive too. Probation has to also provide physical shielding. Could it be that the Spirit of God who strives with man, also holds off some of the physical consequences of sin?

So what if there is more to this drug toxicity than meets the eye? What if all those side effects do really add up over time? What if drugs really are "laying the foundation of a vast amount of disease and of even more serious evils."[90] What if the Lord has been intervening by mitigating the full extent of the hereditary degeneration of the race, caused by three or four generations of cell damaging medication and food reengineering? If it's true, what happens when He withdraws His spirit from the land?

Remember how the Lord protected apostate Israel from the snakes during their forty years of wilderness wandering—that there was not a feeble person among them. You might also recall how He withdrew that protection just before their final marches to the promise land. He

[88] 2 Corinthians 4:16-17.
[89] Ellen G. White, *Counsels* on Health, p. 323.
[90] Ellen G. White, *The Ministry of Healing*, p. 126.

allowed them a taste of reality. Isn't non-probationary reality what the time-of-trouble is all about?—a taste of fallen-reality at and around probation's close? In Israel's time-of-trouble with the fiery serpents they quickly learned that healing *only* comes from cooperating with Jesus.

If drugging is a kind of medical quantitative-easing, then what happens to the race's genetic-economy when the bubble breaks? What will humans do when drugs lose their efficacy? Ask yourself these questions in light of the following prophetic insights:

> "We must have medical instructors who will teach the science of healing without the use of drugs... We are to prepare a company of workers who will follow Christ's methods."[91]

> "A time will come when medical missionaries of other denominations will become jealous and envious of the influence exerted by Seventh-day Adventists who are working in these lines."[92]

> "As religious aggression subverts the liberties of our nation, those who stand for freedom of conscience will be placed in unfavorable positions. For their own sake, they should, while they have opportunity become intelligent in regard to disease, its causes, prevention, and cure. And those who do this will find a field of labor anywhere. There will be suffering ones, *plenty of them*, who will need help, not only among those of our own faith, but largely among those who know not the truth."[93]

> "I wish to tell you that soon there will be no work done in ministerial lines but medical missionary work."[94]

---

[91] Ellen G. White, *Medical Ministry*, p. 7.

[92] Ellen G. White, *Loma Linda Messages*, p. 54.

[93] Ellen G. White, *Counsels on Health*, p. 506. Emphasis Added.

[94] Ibid., p. 533.

CHAPTER TWENTY-FIVE

Sabbath—The Three-Dimensional Test

During the week before Calvary, Jesus said some disturbing things about the future of Jerusalem and the temple there. On Wednesday, He was alone with some disciples on the Mount of Olives. From that vantage-point they could see across the Valley of Jehoshaphat to Mount Zion. They could see Jerusalem—and had a great view of the magnificent temple.

Peter, James, John and Andrew came to Jesus and asked Him when those disturbing things would happen. "What are the signs of Your coming—and the end of the world?"

Jesus' answer both *revealed* the future and *veiled* the future. "His words were not then fully understood; but their meaning was to be unfolded as His people should need the instruction therein given."

"The prophecy which He uttered was twofold in its meaning; while foreshadowing the destruction of Jerusalem, it prefigured also the terrors of the last great day."[1] "Between these two events, there lay open to Christ's view long centuries of darkness, centuries for His church marked with blood and tears and agony. Upon these scenes His disciples

---

[1] Ellen G. White, *The Great Controversy*, p. 25.

could not then endure to look, and Jesus passed them by with a brief mention."[2]

Christ spoke a three-dimensional prophecy: one applied to the destruction of Jerusalem; one applied to the last days; and one applied to the long ages in between. Central to the Olivet prophecy is the mysterious *abomination of desolation*. Consistent with the three-dimensional structure of Christ's prophecy, it too has three distinct applications: one for Jerusalem, one for the end of time, and one for the dark ages.

—The Abomination of Desolation

The end-time application has to do with future United States legislation; and when God's people will flee from the cities.

> "'When ye therefore shall see the abomination of desolation, spoken of by Daniel the prophet, stand in the holy place, (whoso readeth, let him understand:) then let them which be in Judea flee into the mountains.'[3] The time is not far distant when, like the early disciples, we shall be forced to seek a refuge in desolate and solitary places. As the siege of Jerusalem by the Roman armies was the signal for flight to the Judean Christians, so the assumption of power on the part of our nation in the decree enforcing the papal sabbath will be a warning to us. It will be time to leave the large cities, preparatory to leaving the smaller ones for retired homes in secluded places among the mountains."[4]

This future legislation is tied to the decree of Revelation 13 and its *mark of the beast.*

> "The light we have received upon the third angel's message is the true light. The mark of the beast is exactly what it has been proclaimed to be. Not all in regards to this matter is yet understood, nor will it be until the unrolling of the scroll; but a most solemn work is to be accomplished in our world."[5]

Here are some reasonable deductions. First, the *most solemn work* mentioned in this quote must have some time-relation to the *mark of the beast* and the *abomination of desolation*. Second, it is reasonable to conclude that we play a central role in this *most solemn work*. And finally, a better understanding of all this should come about the time we need it.

---

[2] Ellen G. White, *The Desire of Ages*, pp. 630-631.
[3] Matthew 24:15.
[4] Ellen G. White, *Maranatha*, p. 180.
[5] Ellen G. White, *Testimonies for the Church*, vol. 6, p. 17.

—Covenant Blessings and Curses

The idea of an *abomination of desolation* goes back to when Israel first entered the promised land. It's about Mount Ebel and Mount Gerizim—the covenant blessings and curses.

God promised great blessings to Israel, so long as they acknowledged Him as their Lord. They were to keep His Sabbaths, reverence His sanctuary, walk in His statues, and obey His commandments.[6] In return, God promised to do good things for them—prosper them and protect them. He would establish His covenant with them.[7] He would set His tabernacle among them.[8] He would walk with them. He would be their God; and they would be His people. Especially notice that last part. He says, "*And I will walk among you, and will be your God, and ye shall be my people.*"[9] This is covenant language; and it shows up frequently in scripture.

Their blessed status would change if they broke the covenant.[10] God had specific legal remedies—the covenant curses. These were progressive punishments, that if unheeded, would ultimately result in God dismantling their covenant status and His hedge of protection.

Leviticus 26 and Deuteronomy 28 discuss these punishments in some detail. They correspond to God's "four sore judgments"[11] in Ezekiel, and His "four kinds of destroyers"[12] in Jeremiah.

> "The covenant curses were, in the initial phase, preliminary judgments from God on His people. They were intended to wake them from their apostate condition, lead them to repentance, and move them toward a positive relationship with God. What seems clear in the Old Testament is that, in implementing those curses, God used enemy nations, such as Assyria and Babylon. These nations were often used as instruments of God's judgment on His own people."[13]

Because they were corrective in nature, the curses would increase in severity as needed to keep Israel's attention. Here is the order presented in Leviticus 26:

---

[6] Leviticus 26:2-3.
[7] Leviticus 26:9.
[8] Leviticus 26:11.
[9] Leviticus 26:12. Emphasis Added.
[10] Leviticus 26:14.
[11] Ezekiel 14:21.
[12] Jeremiah 15:2-3. Berean Study Bible.
[13] Ranko Stefanovic, *Revelation of Jesus Christ, Commentary on the Book of Revelation*, p. 220. Second Edition, (Berrien Springs, Michigan: Andrews University Press, 2009).

PESTILENCE: After the Exodus, God promised (on condition of obedience) to bring upon the Israelites, none of the diseases of the Egyptians. In the first punishment, that protection is reversed. "He *will* bring upon thee *all* the diseases of Egypt:"[14] consumption, burning ague, fever, inflammation, extreme burning, the botch of Egypt, emerods, scabs, itch, every sickness and every plague.[15]

> "If... you fail to obey Me and to carry out all these commandments, and if you reject My statutes, despise My ordinances, and neglect to carry out all My commandments, and so break My covenant, then this is what I will do to you: I will bring upon you sudden terror, wasting disease, and fever that will destroy your sight and drain your life. You will sow your seed in vain, because your enemies will eat it. And I will set My face against you, so that you will be defeated by your enemies. Those who hate you will rule over you, and you will flee when no one pursues you. [16]

FAMINE: "The sky is as iron, and the earth is as brass."[17] "The rain is as powder and dust."[18] The land yields no increase. The trees give no fruit. Locust eat the seed. Worms eat the vintage. The olive trees cast their fruit. Israel was an agrarian people—so this punishment is equivalent to economic hardship.

> "And if after all this you will not obey Me, I will proceed to punish you sevenfold for your sins. I will break down your stubborn pride and make your sky like iron and your land like bronze, and your strength will be spent in vain. For your land will not yield its produce, and the trees of the land will not bear their fruit."[19]

CAPTIVITY: The land is oppressed and spoiled by attackers. They will take your wives, your houses, your crops, your cattle, and your children.[20] A foreign nation shall take the fruit of the land and the fruit of your labors; and they shall make you few in number.[21]

> "If you walk in hostility toward Me and refuse to obey Me, I will multiply your plagues seven times, according to your sins. I will send wild animals against you to rob you of your children, destroy your livestock, and reduce your numbers, until your roads lie desolate."[22]

---

[14] Deuteronomy 28:60. Emphasis added.

[15] Leviticus 26:16, Deuteronomy 28:22, 26, 27, 61.

[16] Leviticus 26:14-17. Berean Study Bible

[17] Leviticus 26:19.

[18] Deuteronomy 28:24.

[19] Leviticus 26:18-20. Berean Study Bible.

[20] Deuteronomy 28:30.

[21] Deuteronomy 28:33, 41.

[22] Leviticus 26:21-22. Berean Study Bible.

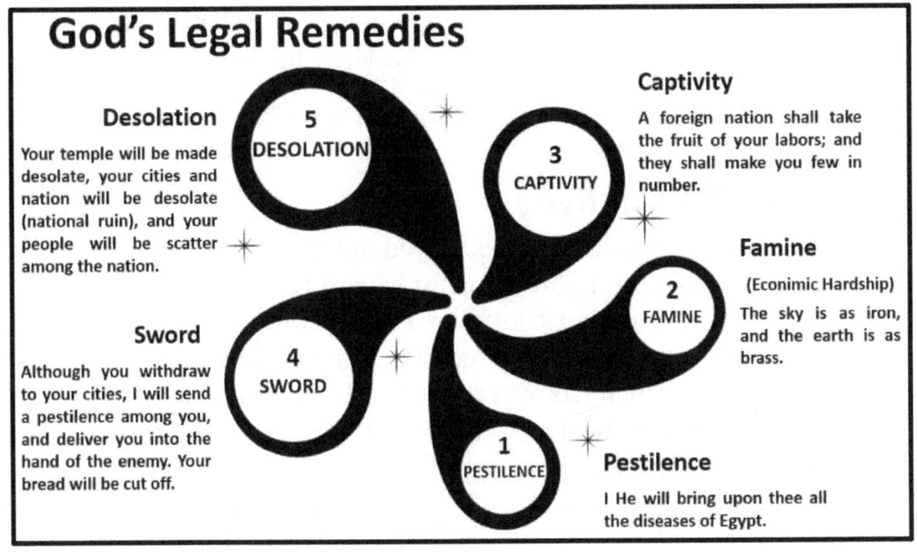

God's Legal Remedies
Desolation
Your temple will be made desolate, your cities and nation will be desolate (national ruin), and your people will be scatter among the nation.
5
DESOLATION
3
CAPTIVITY
Captivity
A foreign nation shall take the fruit of your labors; and they shall make you few in number.
Famine
(Econimic Hardship)
The sky is as iron, and the earth is as brass.
2
FAMINE
Sword
Although you withdraw to your cities, I will send a pestilence among you, and deliver you into the hand of the enemy. Your bread will be cut off.
4
SWORD
1
PESTILENCE
Pestilence
I He will bring upon thee all the diseases of Egypt.

SWORD: The cities are besieged. They are attacked by enemies, and by pestilence, and by famine.

> "And if in spite of these things you do not accept My discipline, but continue to walk in hostility toward Me, then I will act with hostility toward you and strike you sevenfold for your sins. And I will bring a sword against you to execute the vengeance of the covenant. Though you withdraw into your cities, I will send a pestilence among you, and you will be delivered into the hand of the enemy. When I cut off your supply of bread, ten women will bake your bread in a single oven and dole out your bread by weight, so that you will eat but not be satisfied."[23]

DESOLATION: If these corrective measures do not produce acceptable results, complete desolation follows. The cities will be destroyed. Starving parents will eat their children;[24] and children will have no regard for their parents. Those who survive will be scattered from one end of the earth to the other.[25]

> "But if in spite of all this you do not obey Me, but continue to walk in hostility toward Me, I will act with furious rage against you, and I Myself will punish you sevenfold for your sins. You will eat the flesh of your sons and the flesh of your daughters. I will destroy your high places, cut down your incense altars, and heap your dead bodies on the remains of your idols; and My soul will despise you. "I will reduce your cities to rubble and

---

[23] Leviticus 26:23-26. Berean Study Bible.

[24] Deuteronomy 28:53.

[25] Deuteronomy 28:64.

> lay waste to your sanctuaries, and I will refuse to smell the pleasing aroma of your sacrifices. And I will lay waste to the land, so that your enemies who dwell in it will be appalled. But I will scatter you among the nations and will draw out a sword after you as your land becomes desolate and your cities are laid waste."[26]

—Babylonian Captivity

This sequence of covenant curses played out more than once is Israel's history. Their persistent failure to comply with the covenant conditions resulted in the Babylonian captivity. Daniel prayed that God would cause His face to shine upon His sanctuary that was desolate, and incline His ear to hear, and open His eyes to see the desolation of His city.[27] Even before he finished praying, Gabriel came with an amazing prophecy. He told Daniel that Israel would get another chance. They would have four hundred and ninety more years to accomplish God's purpose for them—the same purpose identified in the original covenant blessings.

—The New Covenant

Don't let Jeremiah's calling it a new covenant confuse you. It was new in relation to the covenant made at Sinai, but the same covenant of grace made with Adam, Noah, and Abraham.[28] It is the same covenant associated with the blessings and curses. Jeremiah describes it this way: "I will put my laws in their inward parts, and write it in their hearts; and will be their God, and they shall be My people."[29] This is the new covenant also articulated in the new testament by Paul.[30]

The Sabbath is this same covenant. This is the promised rest that Israel failed to enter fully. The temple is this same covenant. "What agreement hath the temple of God with idols? for ye are the temple of the living God; as God hath said, I will dwell in them, and walk in them; and I will be their God, and they shall be My people."[31] This is covenant language; so the temple-covenant connection is clear.

Gabriel told Daniel that Israel had four hundred and ninety more years to make good on the covenant. They had four hundred and ninety more years to enter the promised Sabbath rest. They had four hundred and

---

[26] Leviticus 26:27-33. Berean Study Bible.

[27] Daniel 9:17-18.

[28] See Ellen G. White, *Patriarchs and Prophets*, pp. 370-373. "To all men this covenant offered pardon and the assisting grace of God for future obedience through faith in Christ. It also promised eternal life on condition of fidelity to God's law."

[29] Jeremiah 31:33

[30] Hebrews 8:10. Hebrews 10:16.

[31] 2 Corinthians 6:16.

ninety more years to complete the spiritual tabernacle. He said: "Seventy weeks are determined upon thy people and upon thy holy city, to finish the [rebellion], and to [put a stop to sin], and to [blot out] iniquity, and to bring in everlasting righteousness, and to seal up the vision and prophecy, and to anoint the most holy place."[32]

Gabriel's prophecy pinpointed the timing of the Messiah—His work would start seven years before Israel's probation would end. But Daniel's prophecy also had a dark side to it. It foretold Israel's rejection of the Messiah and their final rejection of His covenant. "He shall confirm the covenant with many for one week: and in the midst of the week he shall cause the sacrifice and oblation to cease, and,"[33] "on the temple shall be the *abomination of desolations*."[34]

Not just the temple, the city too—for Gabriel said if Israel did not fulfill the terms of the covenant in the allotted time, the Messiah would be cut off; and a prince would come and destroy the city and make it desolate.

—Dismantling the Covenant Again

It was Sunday, March 30, AD 31. Jesus triumphantly entered Jerusalem. It was spectacular. He was riding on a donkey—like the kings of Israel used to do. The whole multitude of excited believers paved the road before him with coats and palm branches. They sang and praised God with loud voices: "Blessed be the King that cometh in the name of the Lord: peace in heaven, and glory in the highest."[35]

The Pharisees wanted it to stop. They were so desperate that they asked Jesus to rebuke the multitude. But He replied: "I tell you that, if these should hold their peace, the *stones* would immediately cry out."[36]

Approaching the city, He wept.

> "If you, even you, had only known on this day what would bring you peace—but now it is hidden from your eyes. The days will come upon you when your enemies will build an embankment against you and encircle you and hem you in on every side. They will dash you to the ground, you and the children within your walls. They will not leave one stone on another, because you did not recognize the time of God's coming to you."[37]

---

[32] Daniel 9:24. See Holman's Christian Standard Bible for the alternate wording.
[33] Daniel 9:27.
[34] Daniel 9:27 (from the LXX). Emphasis added.
[35] Luke 19:38.
[36] Luke 19:40.
[37] Luke 19:42.

For Israel, the course of covenant curses was nearing its end.

Later, Jesus and His disciples spent the night in Bethany. Monday morning they passed a fig tree on the way back into the capital city. Its pretentious foliage promised an abundance of good fruit: but it had no fruit. "Christ uttered against it a withering curse. 'No man eat fruit of thee hereafter forever,' He said."[38]

Making His way to the temple, Jesus entered there and began driving out those who were selling. "It is written," he said, "My house will be a house of prayer;" but you have made it "a den of robbers."[39]

There were children there—and those who were blind and lame. These did not leave when the business folk were hastily making their exit. Instead, they gathered around Jesus. He healed those who needed healing. The children began to sing His praises: "Hosanna to the Son of David."[40]

The children knew and understood. Jesus said, "Have you never read: 'From the mouth of children and infants You have ordained praise'?"[41]

Monday night, Jesus and company returned to Bethany.

Tuesday morning, they came again to Jerusalem. Again they passed the fig tree—now a withered wreck. Its condition surprised the disciples; but Jesus said: "Verily I say unto you, If you have faith, and doubt not, ye shall not only do this which is done to the fig tree, but also, if ye shall say unto this mountain, Be thou removed, and be thou cast into the sea; it shall be done."[42]

"Jerusalem is a 'mountain city enthroned on a mountain fastness.' It stands on the edge of one of the highest tablelands in Israel, and is surrounded on the southeastern, the southern, and the western sides by deep and precipitous valleys."[43] Looking down the corridors of time, Jesus knew that it would not be long before Jerusalem would be sacked—and that those who survived would be scattered among the peoples, and multitudes, and nations, and tongues.[44] That *mountain* would, indeed, be cast into the *sea*.

Again, Jesus and the disciples make their way to the temple. The leaders challenge Christ's authority. He tells them the parable of the wicked husbandmen; who, when the lord of the vineyard sent servants to

---

[38] Mark 11:14.

[39] Luke 19:46.

[40] Matthew 21:15.

[41] Matthew 21:16. Berean Study Bible.

[42] Matthew 21:22.

[43] ChristianAnswers.Net, *What is... Jerusalem*, Updated September 10, 2019, Accessed on 12/12/19 at (http://www.christiananswers.net/dictionary/jerusalem.html).

[44] See Revelation 17:15.

receive of its fruit, they beat them and sent them away empty. So he sent his own son—one whose authority they could not mistake. But they took him and killed him.

Then Jesus says, "Have ye not read this Scripture; the *stone* which the builders rejected is become the head of the corner: this was the Lord's doing, and it is marvelous in our eyes?"[45] And then He pronounces the woes against the scribes and the Pharisees, concluding with these words:

> "Fill ye up then the measure of your fathers... Upon you [will] come all the righteous blood shed upon the earth, from the blood of righteous Abel unto the blood of Zacharias son of Barachias, whom ye slew between the porch and the altar. Verily I say into you, All these things shall come upon this generation."[46]

He then says:

> "O Jerusalem, Jerusalem, thou that killest the prophets, and stonest them which are sent unto thee, how often would I have gathered thy children together, even as a hen gathereth her chickens under her wings, and ye would not! *Behold your house is left unto you desolate."*[47]

As He leaves the temple for the last time, He knows the separation is complete. The leaders of God's own people will never accept Him as the Messiah. But in the outer court, certain Greeks—men from the West are there to see the Savior. Jesus goes to them.

While He talks to them, the Father's voice is heard from a cloud, saying the same thing that was heard at Christ's baptism. Most of the people don't understand what they hear, but the Greeks do. They see the cloud. They hear the voice. They comprehend its meaning. They discern that Christ is the *Sent of God.*

Again, Jesus and His disciples, cross the valley of Jehoshaphat. They make their way to spend the night in Bethany.

—Not One Stone...

In the morning—it's Wednesday now—they gather at a place on the Mount of Olives where they can see the temple edifice across the valley. What Jesus has lately been saying about the temple has shocked the disciples. From their vantage point the temple looks magnificent. The buildings are beautiful and wonderful to behold.

---

[45] Mark 12:10-11. Emphasis added.

[46] Matthew 23:32-36.

[47] Matthew 23:37-39. Emphasis added.

Hoping to point this out to the Savior, the disciples speak of its splendor—how it is adorned with goodly stones and gifts.[48]

But Jesus says to them: "See ye not all these things? verily I say unto you, there shall not be left here one *stone* upon another, that shall not be thrown down."[49] And then Jesus charts out the great Olivet prophecy and the mysterious abomination of desolation.

Stones. Have you been noticing all the big to-do about stones?

Jesus said that unless the multitude sang His praises, the stones would cry out. When Jesus wept over Jerusalem, He told how enemies would come, and how they would not leave one stone on another. He spoke of Himself as the stone that the builders rejected.

On Olivet, the disciples point out the magnificent stones of the temple: but Jesus tells them that not one of those stones will be left upon another, but that they all will be thrown down.

And have you been hearing the contrast that Jesus is making between two temples?—one is growing desolate, and another is growing with the glory of God.

When Jesus wept over Jerusalem, He saw a temple of lifeless, fruitless stones that soon the armies of Rome would destroy. But along the road to that spot, He saw living stones, loving stones, stones ringing with praises to God, and shining with the glory of heaven. These are the stones that make up His temple on earth.

While at the tabernacle, He saw a merchandising temple. He saw buying and selling. He saw a commercial enterprise. He saw those engrossed in worldly riches and earthy comforts. But He also saw those who were blind—but now see because they looked to Jesus. He saw the lame—who now walk because they came to Jesus. And He saw the children—and from them He heard perfect praise. These are the lively stones that Peter talks about: who are being built up as a spiritual house into a holy priesthood; and offering spiritual sacrifices acceptable to God through Jesus Christ—who, he says, "should shew forth the *praises* of Him who called them out of darkness into His marvelous light."[50]

When on Tuesday, the Jewish leaders confronted Jesus and questioned His authority, He made it clear that the temple's demise was

---

48 Luke 21:5.

49 Matthew 24:2. Emphasis added.

50 1 Peter 2:5; 2:9. Emphasis added.

because of them. Woe to the scribes and Pharisees. The greatest light men ever knew was entrusted to them; but they filled up the measure of their fathers—and crucified the Son of God.

When the *Sent of Heaven* finally walked away from their temple of wood and stone, God's glory forever departed with Him. But as Jesus left the temple, He found other stones in the courtyard. Those stones were not even Jewish stones; but they accepted the authority of Heaven's most precious Gift. Their ears could hear, and their eyes could see; so they too became living stones in the temple of our God.

—The Three Abominations of Desolations

Yes, the abomination of desolation is about geopolitical stuff. It's about the breaking of a national covenant between the United States and God. It's about withdrawing divine protection against diseases. It's about financial ruin. It's about being oppressed and spoiled by terrorists. It's about U.S. cities being attacked and knowing the horrors of famine and sword. It's about war and national ruin. But it's even more. The back story has to do with the remnant church, a living temple, the Sabbath rest, the new covenant, and the *Galilee Protocol.*

The *armies of Rome in AD 70 did not cause the abomination* that destroyed the Jewish temple and the Jewish people. Neither did King Herod. It was the leaders of the Jewish church of AD 31 that were to blame. It was the Jewish people of AD 34 (who stoned Steven)—they too were to blame. It was their children (who for some thirty-five years persisted in their parents' rebellion), who were responsible. Rome decimated a temple and a people who had destroyed themselves.

We've identified three distinct abominations of desolation: one that destroyed Jerusalem, one that disqualified the church of the dark ages, and a coming abomination concerning disloyalty to God's law and Sabbath. Each was significant for the people in its time—and time determining the nature of the test.

The first (*Old Testament*) was physical, the second (*New Testament*) was intellectual, and the third (*Day of Atonement*) will be spiritual. Correspondingly, the restoration of man (the human temple—if you will) is a progressive process divided into these three, specific dispensations—one for each of the three natures.

Sin has defiled this human temple—this sanctuary. Notice how Ezekiel handles this subject in regards to the fall of Lucifer:

> "Thou hast defiled thy *sanctuaries* by the multitude of thine iniquities, by the iniquity of thy *traffick*; therefore will I bring forth a fire from the midst of thee, it shall devour thee..." "Thou art the annointed cherub that covereth; and I have set thee so: thou wast on upon the *mountain* of God; thou hast walked up and down in the midst of the *stones* of fire."[51]

Do you hear the same language we've been seeing?—sanctuaries, mountain, traffic (buying/selling), stones? The work of redemption is all about rebuilding "the old wastes," raising "up the former desolations," and repairing "the waste cities, the desolations of many generations."[52] Its about restoring the tabernacle, reestablishing the priests of the Lord,[53] and reviving the Sabbath.[54]

> "To restore in man the image of his Maker, to bring him back to the perfection in which he was created, to promote the development of body, mind, and soul, that the divine purpose in his creation might be realized—this was to be the work of redemption."[55]

—Three Phases of Rebuilding

Phase One of this restoration is Old-Testament. God's redemptive work for man centered on *physical activity*. The sinner literally, physically took a physical, living, breathing lamb across camp to the literal, physical altar. He confessed his sin and cut the throat of the innocent victim. The priest carried the real blood into the physical tabernacle structure where God's actual glory dwelt.

This process was highly symbolic. While sinners were saved through grace and faith—God required their specific, physical obedience. It was not optional. During this dispensation, those who were God's chosen people accessed salvation through specific physical activity.

Be careful not to devalue the importance of the physical nature—of physical obedience and physical activity. It was Christ who gave this system to the Jews; it was Christ who physically lived a life of perfect activity; and it was Christ who physically bore our sins—as He physically died on our behalf. As author and finisher of our salvation, Jesus demonstrated the path we must follow for physical restoration. The sanctuary courtyard is associated with the physical. The altar and the laver are centers of physical activity. The *medical protocol* is

[51] Ezekiel 28:18, 14. Emphasis added.

[52] Isaiah 61:4.

[53] Isaiah 61:6.

[54] Isaiah 58:13.

[55] Ellen G. White, *Education*, pp. 15-16.

physical, and obedience to the laws of health and God's methods is not optional.

Phase Two of this restoration is New-Testament. During the early new-testament era, God's redemptive work for man centered on mental activity—the intellectual understanding of the symbols introduced under a more physical dispensation.

For those who would now take part in salvation, *belief* is the new essential. Paul and Silas told the Roman jailer: "Believe on the Lord Jesus Christ, and thou shalt be saved, and thy house."[56]

The new dispensation did not undo the progress made under the old. Intellectual obedience expresses itself through physical activity. There was still something for the jailer to do. The Bible says, "he took them the same hour of the night, and washed their stripes; and was baptized."[57]

The sanctuary holy place is associated with mental activity. The table of shewbread is about the Word. The altar of incense is about prayer. The candlesticks are about the light of truth fed to the church by the oil of the Holy Spirit. The *educational protocol* is mental, and believing requires enrolling in the wilderness *school-of-Christ.*

Phase Three of this restoration is *time-of-the-end* stuff. 1844 marks the beginning of the third era. During this final era, God's redemptive work for man centers on spiritual activity—the spiritual application of all the symbols, and understanding the previous two dispensations.

This is when the tabernacle is fully restored. This is when we fully enter the Sabbath rest. The ark of the covenant contains tables of *stone* upon which the law is being written by the finger of God. "I will put my law in their inward parts, and write it in their hearts."

—An Abomination for Each Era

In each era there is an *abomination of desolation.* At each stage, the established church must either accept or reject God's authority over His tabernacle. And in each dispensation, the specific issue around which this acceptance or rejection centers has to do with the nature of that dispensation.

In AD 31, the established Jews *physically* rejected the Messiah. They *physically* put Him to death because He did not bring the worldly kingdom they wanted.

---

[56] Acts 16: 31.

[57] Acts 16:34.

During the middle ages, the papal church *intellectually* rejected Christ by putting *their* priesthood in place of His—because His was not compatible with the worldly kingdom they were building.

Prophecy tells us that at the *end-of-time*, the professed followers of Christ will *spiritually* accept an antichrist who's spurious sabbath is the kingpin of his global kingdom.

—The Importance of the Law

Remember how Adam and Eve were created in the image of God; and how redemption was about restoring that image.

> "Love, is the basis of creation and of redemption. This is made plain in the law that God has given as the guide of life. The first and great commandment is, 'Thou shalt love the Lord thy God with all thy heart, and with all thy soul, and with all thy strength, and with all thy mind.'[58] To love Him, the infinite, the omniscient One, with the whole strength, and mind, and heart, means the highest development of every power. It means that in the whole being—the body, the mind, as well as the soul —the image of God is to be restored.
>
> "Like the first is the second commandment—'Thou shalt love thy neighbor as thyself.'[59] The law of love calls for the devotion of body, mind, and soul to the service of God and our fellow men. And this service, while making us a blessing to others, brings the greatest blessing to ourselves. Unselfishness underlies all true development. Through unselfish service we receive the highest culture of every faculty. More and more fully do we become partakers of the divine nature. We are fitted for heaven, for we receive heaven into our hearts."[60]

The Sabbath has everything to do with what these references are talking about. It is the seal of God and the very heart of the law. Love is the basis of creation and redemption as made plain in the law that God has given. Love causes our loyalty to God and our obedience to His Sabbath commandment. Love drives the *Galilee Protocol* as we heal, and teach, and preach—selflessly serving in His name—according to His authority and power.

Remember how we earlier noted that not all is yet understood in the matter of the mark of beast—and that we wouldn't understand it all until the unrolling of the scroll? We also noticed—connected to that understanding—"a most solemn work is to be accomplished in our world." Earlier we didn't finish the thought. Here is the rest of it—

---

58 Luke 10:27.

59 Matthew 22:39.

60 Ellen G. White, *Education*, p. 16.

> "...a most solemn work is to be accomplished in our world. The Lord's command to His servants is, 'Cry aloud, spare not, lift up thy voice like a trumpet, and show my people their transgression, and the house of Jacob their sins.'"[61]

That's Isaiah 58! That's Sabbath reform! That's the *Sabbath Protocol for Service!* The solemn work that is to be accomplished in our world—in connection with the mark of the beast—is the *Galilee Protocol.*

—The Three-Dimensional Sabbath

The Sabbath test at the end will come in three dimensions—for there will still be those three theaters of operation. All will have to choose but the people in each theater will be at a different level of progress in the process of salvation.

For the pagan *world* the choice will be theologically simple. Not being familiar with the Bible, they won't understand all *intellectual* and *spiritual* nuances of the Sabbath. But the final battle will be enough to show the stark physical contrast between good and evil; and on that basis they will choose their loyalty to either Christ or Satan. These are the "*Greeks*"—the people of the courtyard. The Sabbath choice for them will be a *physical act of obedience*; and God will honor them.

For the protestant *nation*, the test will come sooner. They too, may not understand all the deep *spiritual* nuances of the Sabbath. But they do claim to accept the authority of Scripture and will understand the Bible-basis for the Sabbath. The national battle will be enough to intellectually support the Sabbath truth. The fundamental principles of the Sabbath will be so plain that they will be left without excuse. These are those in "*Galilee*"—the people in the holy place, still in the *school-of-Christ*. The Sabbath choice for them will be a *physical and mental* act of obedience. They will obey because they believe the truth. And God will honor them.

For Adventism, the test will come even sooner—even before the national Sunday law. If you're waiting for legislation to wake you up, you're playing a deadly game. God has blessed us with a knowledge of truth that boggles the mind. We're not responsible for what we know; we're responsible for what God has given us to know. We are from "*Judea*"—the people of the most holy. To us the test is how we *spiritually apply* the *truth of the Sabbath* to our lives. Are *we* lively stones? Are we the temple of the living God? Have we ceased from our own works? Is the law and the Sabbath so written in our lives that we—compelled by a force

[61] Ellen G. White, *Counsels on Health*, p. 520.

of love stronger than all the powers of hell—are working the *Galilee Protocol*?

Soon the Seventh-day Adventist Church will be in its final week of probation. *In the coming days we will see a desperate struggle* between the man-made structure and the living stones. This shaking will be a terrible ordeal. Is there still hope for the bricks and mortar?—for the establishment leaders? Many are terribly invested in worldly policy. But we hope and pray it is not too late!

Not all is doom and gloom, though. We can have great confidence in the little flock—the *trusting ones*[62] who have felt the healing touch of the Master's hand—and the children; we can have confidence in the children: *for out of the mouth of babes...*

We can have confidence in those who *sigh and cry for the abominations done in the land*. We can have confidence because the Savior has promised to take the work into His own hand. He *will* send His servants into the highways and byways to invite whosoever will...

Take comfort because God is calling on people—like you, like me, to join Him in *a most solemn work to do in our world*. How is it with you, brother? How is it with you, Sister? Is God calling you? Are you ready now to take inventory of your life?—ready to reorder your priorities? Are you willing to sell all to buy the field? Make your commitment today to *reactivate* the *Galilee Protocol!*

"When the hand of the Lord was upon Ezekiel in the vision of the valley of dry bones, he was commanded to prophecy to the wind; and in answer to his word, life was restored to the slain, and they stood up before him, an exceeding great army. This figure was presented before the prophet to show him that no work of restoration can be too hard for God to do, and none who trust in Him need ever say, as Israel had said, 'Our hope is lost.'"

— The Signs of the Times, July 26, 1883.

62 See the preface: *To the Trusting Ones...*

CHAPTER TWENTY-SIX

When Both Ears Tingle

Israel went to battle against the Philistines. Their forces were routed; and the enemy captured the *ark of the covenant*. Israel suffered defeat; but the ark did not. It went on the offensive through the cities of Philistia. We join the story already in progress.

As the ark moved through several of the cities of the Philistines, God's judgements fell. Think of the ark (with its law-of-God, most-holy-place, hour-of-judgment associations) as carrying a warning message—a judgment message—to those cities. Our end-time savvy might suggest this is the *three angel's messages*[1]—the "hour of judgment"[2] messages of Revelation 14. Picture the ark as faithful souls[3]—radiant with the glory of God—and bearing the final warning message.

As already noted,[4] the message of the first angel refers to the three protocols. Educational: "The *fear of God* is the beginning of knowledge."[5] Medical: *"Glorify God* in your body."[6] "Whether therefore ye eat, or

---

[1] Revelation 14:6-12.

[2] Revelation 14:7, first part.

[3] See Ellen G. White, *The Acts of the Apostles*, p. 11.

[4] See Chapter 8, *A Mission with Protocols.*

[5] Psalms 1:7. Emphasis added.

[6] 1 Corinthians 6:19-20. Emphasis added.

drink, or whatsoever ye do, do all for the *glory of God.*"[7] And Ministerial: "In six days the Lord made heaven and earth, the sea, and all that in them is, and rested the seventh day: wherefore the Lord blessed the seventh day, and hallowed it."[8]

The second angel boldly declares: "*Babylon is fallen, is fallen*;"[9] and the third angel warns of the coming judgment upon those who receive the *mark of the beast* in the *forehead* or the *hand*.[10]

—Pagan Protocol Cities

"Now the hand of the LORD was heavy on the people"[1] of the cities where the ark was—"ravaging them and afflicting them with tumors."[2]

The ark goes to three specific cities. The number three should automatically pique your curiosity by now. So what do we know about Ashdod, Gath, and Ekron?

Ashdod is known for Dagon—the national god of the Philistines.[3] He was top-of-the-totem-pole among their pagan deities; and his temple was at Ashdod. Dagon worship was complex, with a sophisticated *ministerial* program. They put the captured ark next to the idol of Dagon—but the idol fell over two nights in a row. This was an affront to their religion, so they moved the ark to Gath.

Gath was a massive mountain fortress city. Recent digs have uncovered layers at Gath corresponding to this biblical era. "This was the largest Philistine city and probably one of the largest in the Iron Age Levant," says Aren Maeir, a professor of archaeology at Bar-Ilan University. He led the expedition in Gath. "Larger cities were only found outside the Levant, such as in Egypt and the Mesopotamia."[4] Gath covered about 125 acres; and had an estimated population close to ten thousand. In some areas the walls were thirteen feet thick. Goliath and his brothers were from Gath—where the inhabitants were formidable giant-like warriors. Gath's mighty walls and elite fighting force were the *physical* strength and the security of the philistines.

---

[7] 1 Corinthians 10:31. Emphasis added.

[8] Compare Exodus 20:11 last part of Revelation 14:7 -"And worship him that made heaven, and earth, and the sea, and the fountains of waters."

[9] Revelation 14:8. Emphasis added.

[10] Revelation 14:9-11. Emphasis added.

[1] 1 Samuel 5:6. Berean Study Bible.

[2] Ibid.

[3] Wikipedia, *Ashdod*, updated October 18, 2019. (https://en.wikipedia.org/wiki/Ashdod), accessed 11/11/2018.

[4] Ariel David, *Goliath's True Hometown Found? Lost 3,000-year-old Philistine City Emerges Beneath Gath*, July 24, 2019, accessed at https://www.haaretz.com/archaeology/.premium.MAGAZINE-goliath-s-true-hometown-found-lost-3-000-year-old-philistine-city-of-gath-emerges-i-1.7569569, on 11/11/2019.

Idols that tip over are one thing. As dire as the Philistinian *ministerial crisis* was—it paled alongside the *medical crisis* caused by the ark. The destruction[5] and the tumors terrified the people and threatened the *physical security* of the nation. This showdown between God's protocol's and Satan's merchandise exposes the Philistines' *spiritual and physical* arsenals as powerless against the ark.

Next, they take it to Ekron. The *god of Ekron*—so often referenced by Sister White concerning the contamination of our own *educational* work—was also known as Baalzebub.[6] He "was supposed to give *information*, through the medium of its priests."[7] The idol at Ekron was given "such general credence," that people came a considerable distance *to inquire of the god of Ekron*. "The information given proceeded directly from the prince of darkness."[8]

This *god of knowledge* was also unable to protect the Philistines from the judgments that attended the ark. "Those who did not die were afflicted with tumors, and the outcry of the city went up to heaven."[9]

—Dagon is Fallen, is Fallen

These three specific pagan cities exemplify the worldly counterfeits to the three authentic protocols integral to the first angel's message. The Bible says little of what happened in Gath or Ekron; but what it says about Ashdod bear some remarkable similarities to the second and third angels' messages.

The Philistines interpreted their victory to mean their god was superior to Israel's God. They took the ark to Dagon's temple in Ashdod.[10] Dagonism relates to us today by its connection to *ancient Babylon* and today's *spiritual Babylon*. The nominally converted Constantine sought to unite the world by bringing the "doctrines, ceremonies, and superstitions" of paganism into the worship of the professed followers of Christ.[11] No other pagan religion contributed more to the papacy than Dagonism.

---

[5] 1 Samuel 5:6.

[6] See 2 Kings 1:2, 16; Ellen G. White, *Prophets and Kings*, p. 207; *Review and Herald*, September 7, 1911.

[7] Ellen G. White, *Testimonies for the Church*, vol. 5, p. 192. Emphasis added.

[8] Ibid.

[9] 1 Samuel 5:10-12. Berean Study Bible.

[10] 1 Samuel 5:1-2.

[11] Ellen G. White, *The Great Controversy*, p. 50.

"The most prominent form of worship in Babylon was dedicated to Dagon, later known as Ichthys, or the fish. In Chaldean times, the head of the church was the representative of Dagon, he was considered to be infallible, and was addressed as 'Your Holiness'. Nations subdued by Babylon had to kiss the ring and slipper of the Babylonian god-king. The same powers and the same titles are claimed to this day by... the Pope. Moreover, the vestments of paganism, the fish mitre and robes of the priests of Dagon are worn by the Catholic bishops, cardinals and popes."[12]

"The papacy claims... that it's system of worship has been handed down through tradition, yet the traditions are the traditions of Babylon... Roman Catholic doctrines such as infant baptism, sprinkling of babies during baptism, teachings on death and immortality, prayers to the dead and to relics, repetitive prayers by the use of beads, doctrines on forgiveness of sins, teachings on hell, the mass, and Sunday worship are doctrines derived directly from ancient Babylon."[13]

This is what happened while the ark was in the temple at Ashdod:

"After the Philistines had captured the ark of God, they took it from Ebenezer to Ashdod, carried it into the temple of Dagon, and set it beside his statue. When the people of Ashdod got up early the next morning, there was Dagon, fallen on his face before the ark of the LORD. So they took Dagon and returned him to his place. But when they got up early the next morning, there was Dagon, fallen on his face before the ark of the LORD, with his head and his hands broken off and lying on the threshold. Only the torso remained."[14]

It's fascinating symbolism: Dagon *falls* twice—as does Babylon in the second angel's message. The second time he falls, his head and hands break off—the same two locations associated with the mark of the beast[15] in the third angel's warning.

—Leaving the Cities

"Fearing longer to retain the ark among the homes of men, the people next placed it in the open field. There followed a plague of mice, which infested the land, destroying the products of the soil, both in the storehouse and in the field. Utter destruction, by disease or famine, now threatened the nation."[16]

---

[12] Phil Harris, *The Mitre and the Catholic/Babylonian Connection*, accessed at https://www.theeternalcircle.net/the-mitre-and-the-catholic-babylonian-connection/, on 11/11/2019.

[13] Walter J. Veith, *Truth Matters, Escaping the Labyrinth of Error*, p. 217. Amazing Discoveries, 2017.

[14] 1 Samuel 5:1-4. Berean Study Bible.

[15] Revelation 13:16.

[16] Ellen G. White, *Patriarchs and Prophets*, p. 586.

In applying the symbols to our day, we might hesitate to compare our cities to the pagan cities of the Philistines; but consider this:

> "In this age of boasted enlightenment, the Christian church is confronted with a world lying in midnight and darkness, almost wholly given over to idolatry. A well-nigh universal disregard of the law of Jehovah is rapidly making the world like the cities of Sodom and Gomorrah. As in the days before the Flood, violence is filling the land. Gambling and robbery are coming to be common evils. The use of intoxicating liquors is on the increase. Many who have followed their own unsanctified will seek to end their unprofitable lives by suicide. Iniquity and crime of every order are found in the high places of the earth, and those who assent to these wrongs are seeking to shield the guilty ones from punishment. Not one hundredth part of the corruptions that exist is being made plain to the world. Little of the cruelty that is carried on is known. The wickedness of men has almost reached its limit."[17]
>
> "Though in a different form, idolatry exists in the Christian world today as verily as it existed among ancient Israel in the days of Elijah. The God of many professedly wise men, of philosophers, poets, politicians, journalists—the God of polished fashionable circles, of many colleges and universities, even of some theological institutions—is little better than Baal, the sun-god of Phoenicia."[18]
>
> "O that God's people had a sense of the impending destruction of thousands of cities, now almost given to idolatry!"[19]

Inspiration tells of a time when God's workers—like the early disciples at the siege of Jerusalem—will need to leave the cities for homes in secluded places.[20] "Erelong there will be such strife and confusion in the cities, that those who wish to leave them will not be able."[21]

> "I saw the saints leaving the cities and villages, and associating together in companies, and living in the most solitary places. Angels provided them food and water, while the wicked were suffering from hunger and thirst."[22]

Inspiration tells of when the law of God will "be made void in our land; and national apostacy will be followed by *national ruin*."[23] It tells of "famine, pestilence, and sword, nation... against nation, and the whole world in confusion."[24] It tells of the "impending conflict" where Satan will appear "to the children of men as a great physician who can heal all their

---

[17] Ellen G. White, *Testimonies to Ministers and Gospel Workers, p. 457.*

[18] Ellen G. White, *The Great Controversy*, p. 583.

[19] Ellen G. White, *The Review and Herald*, September 10, 1903.

[20] Ellen G. White, *Country Living*, p. 32.

[21] Ellen G. White, *Maranatha*, p.180.

[22] Ellen G. White, *Early Writings*, p. 282.

[23] Ellen G. White, *Maranatha*, p. 193. Emphasis added.

[24] Ellen G. White, *The Seventh-day Adventist Bible Commentary*, vol. 7, p. 968.

maladies," while bringing "disease and disaster, until populous cities are reduced to ruin and desolation."

> "In accidents and calamities by sea and by land, in great conflagrations, in fierce tornadoes and terrific hailstorms, in tempests, floods, cyclones, tidal waves, and earthquakes, in every place and in a thousand forms, Satan is exercising his power. He sweeps away the ripening harvest, and famine and distress follow. He imparts to the air a deadly taint, and thousands perish by the pestilence. These visitations are to become more and more frequent and disastrous. Destruction will be upon both man and beast."[25]

Of all this, Jerusalem's "terrible desolation was but a faint shadow."[26]

> "All the horrors of starvation were experienced. A measure of wheat was sold for a talent. So fierce were the pangs of hunger that men would gnaw the leather of their belts and sandals and the covering of their shields. Great numbers of the people would steal out at night to gather wild plants growing outside the city walls, though many were seized and put to death with cruel torture, and often those who returned in safety were robbed of what they had gleaned at so great peril."[27]

—Returning to Israel

On its return to Israel, the ark did not go back to Ebenezer where it was captured, nor to the capital, nor to the tabernacle. It was *harvest time*[28] and "the people of Beth-shemesh were harvesting wheat in the valley when they looked up and saw the ark, they were overjoyed at the sight."[29] A team of heaven-driven cows[30] pulled it on a cart "to the field of Joshua of Beth-shemesh and stopped near a large rock. The people chopped up the cart for firewood and offered the cows as a burnt offering to the LORD."[31] The Levites took the ark and placed it on a large rock;[32] and the people worshiped the Lord there.[33]

Some of the people had little respect for the ark. "They began to conjecture wherein lay its peculiar power," and "overcome by curiosity, they removed the covering and ventured to open it."[34] Immediately, seventy

---

[25] Ellen G. White, *The Great Controversy*, p. 589.

[26] Ibid., p. 36.

[27] Ibid., p. 31.

[28] Harvest symbolism: Matthew 9:37-38; 13:30; Mark 4:49; 12:1-9; John 4:35-36; 1 Corinthians 9:10-11; Revelation 14:15-16.

[29] 1 Samuel 6:13. Berean Study Bible.

[30] 1 Samuel 6:7-12.

[31] 1 Samuel 6::14. Berean Study Bible.

[32] The Bible refers to Christ (and His kingdom) as a rock, and His church as lively stones. See Psalms 118:22; Matthew 21:42-44; 1 Peter 2:4-10; Acts 4:11; Isaiah 8:14; Romans 9:33; Daniel 2:34-35, 45; 1 Corinthians 10:4

[33] Ibid., verse 15.

[34] 34 Ellen G. White, *Patriarchs and Prophets*, p. 589.

men were smitten with sudden death. The people of Beth-shemesh sent messengers to Kiriath-jearim, saying, "The Philistines have returned the ark of the LORD. Come down and take it up with you."[35]

> "Then the men of Kiriath-jearim came for the ark of the LORD and took it into Abinadab's house on the hill. And they consecrated his son Eleazar to guard the ark of the LORD. And from that day a long time passed, twenty years in all, as the ark remained at Kiriath-jearim. And all the house of Israel mourned and sought after the LORD. Then Samuel said to all the house of Israel, 'If you are returning to the LORD with all your hearts, then rid yourselves of the foreign gods and Ashtoreths among you, prepare your hearts for the LORD, and serve Him only. And He will deliver you from the hand of the Philistines.' So the Israelites put away the Baals and Ashtoreths and served only the LORD."[36]

The ark stayed at Abinadab's home-church until the establishment of David's throne in Israel. One of the first things David did was to move the capital from Hebron to a place once known as Salem. "Eight hundred years before the coronation of David it had been the home of Melchizedek, the priest of the most high God." More recently it had been under the control of the Jebusites who called the city Jebus. In David's time, Joab conquered it for the Hebrews. David brought the ark to the capital after he was coronated as the *new* King—and after the establishment of the *new* Salem—*Jerusalem*.[37]

—When Both Ears Tingle

We dove right into the middle of this story. Let's go back to its beginning. The reason the ark was in Philistine territory in the first place, was because they captured it during the battle that was to *make both ears tingle* of everyone who heard of it. Actually, it wasn't so much what the Philistines did—that tingles the ears—as what God did.

Here's the setting. The boy Samuel went to bed one night when he heard the voice of God calling. Maybe it was Eli. So Samuel goes to see if something was the matter.

> "Now in those days the word of the LORD was rare and visions were scarce. And at that time Eli, whose eyesight had grown so dim that he could not see, was lying in his room."[38]

---

[35] 1 Samuel 6:21.

[36] 1 Samuel 7:1-4.

[37] *New Jerusalem*, see Revelation 3:12 and 21:2, and Hebrews 12:18-29.

[38] 1 Samuel 3:1-3. Berean Study Bible.

Hearing God's voice was new to Samuel; and it seems God wasn't talking to Eli anymore. It took several tries before Samuel and Eli figured things out. God had an important message for Samuel to relay to Eli:

> "Behold, I will do a thing in Israel, at which both the ears of everyone that heareth it shall tingle. In that day I will perform against Eli all things which I have spoken concerning his house: when I begin, I will also make an end. For I have told him that I will judge his house for ever for the iniquity which he knoweth; because his sons made themselves vile, and he restrained them not. And therefore I have sworn unto the house of Eli, that the iniquity of Eli's house shall not be purged with sacrifice nor offering forever."[39]

Eli's son's were the ministers at the door of the tabernacle. They officiated in the slaying of sacrifices at the altar. They were selfish, covetous, gluttonous, and shamelessly immoral."[40]

The warning was to Eli and his house that the hour of judgment was coming. God had warned them before. He sent an earlier messenger[41] in an attempt to clean up the temple; but that warning was disregarded. Now—before judgment hour closes—God tries again. He sends Samuel to make it known that God will *cleanse and purify His temple in His displeasure*.[42]

God delayed bringing judgments on Eli's house. He delayed after the first warning; and He delayed even after this final warning. Although the warnings were directed at the leaders—they concerned the wellbeing of the whole nation. "Year after year the Lord delayed His threatened judgments. *Much might have been done* in those years to redeem the failures of the past."[43] But the leaders "took no effective measures to correct the evils that were... leading thousands in Israel to ruins."[44]

Hoping to mitigate some of *his* wrong, Eli made the warning and reproof to his house known to the whole nation. "But the warnings were disregarded by the people, as they had been by the priests. The people of the surrounding nations also, who were not ignorant of the iniquities openly practiced in Israel, became still bolder in their idolatry and crime. They felt no sense of guilt for their sins, as they would have felt had the Israelites preserved their integrity. But a day of retribution was

---

[39] 1 Samuel 3:11-14.

[40] Ellen G. White, *Spiritual Gifts*, vol. 4a, p. 103.

[41] 1 Samuel 2:27-36.

[42] This phase is borrowed from Ellen G. White, *Manuscript Releases*, vol. 4, p. 367. She is talking about the fires at the Battle Creek Sanitarium and the Review and Herald Publishing Association.

[43] Ellen G. White, *Patriarchs and Prophets*, p. 582.

[44] Ibid.

approaching. God's authority had been set aside, and His worship neglected and despised, and it became necessary for Him to interpose, that the honor of His name might be maintained."[45] Does this sound familiar?

Samuel's message assured Eli that the storm would come—it was coming for Israel; and it *is* coming for Laodicea.

—Whetting His Sword

As when Israel wandered in the wilderness forty years, the issues for us today are twofold. First, Israel was unwilling to follow the authority of God's leadership—they refused to take Canaan. In chapter two,[46] we looked at the 1902 fires at the Review, and Battle Creek; and we saw in them *judgment* because leading "men had been departing from the right principles" for which those "institutions were established." Specifically, they "failed of doing the very work that God ordained should be done... medical missionary work."[47] The fires were the *first* warning; and as dire as it was—the second warning will be worse:

> "I want to tell you that if after the warnings given in these burnings, the leaders of our people go right on, just as they have done in the past, exalting themselves, God will take the bodies next. Just as surely as He lives, He will speak to them in a language that they cannot fail to understand."[48]

Second, Israel was unwilling to separate from the world—they wanted to return to Egypt. Besides refusing to do medical missionary work—but related to it—is our fascination with everything *worldly*. We're impressed with our post-modern materialism. We're caught-up in the world's sophistication and their trinkets and gadgets, and baubles. We like the busy, comfortable, worldly lifestyles; its learning and sciences; and modern worship and entertainment.[49] This is every bit as ruinous to the church, the nation, and the world as the sins of Eli's house.

The warning is sure. God will yet cleanse and purify *Laodicea*—He will speak to *us* in a language we cannot fail to understand.

> "Young and old, God is now testing you. You are deciding your own eternal destiny. Your pride, your love to follow the fashions of the world, your vain and empty conversation, your selfishness, are all put in the scale, and the weight of evil is fearfully against you. You are poor, and

[45] Ibid., pp. 582-583.
[46] Chapter Two, *By Whose Authority*.
[47] Ellen G. White, *Testimonies for the Church*, vol. 8, p. 218.
[48] Ellen G. White, *Manuscript Releases*, vol. 4, p. 367.
[49] See chapter one, *A Tale of Three Mountains*.

> miserable, and blind, and naked. While evil is increasing and taking deep root, it is choking the good seed which has been sown in the heart; and soon the word that was given concerning Eli's house will be spoken to the angels of God concerning you: Your sins 'shall not be purged with sacrifice nor offering forever.' Many, I saw, were flattering themselves that they were good Christians, who have not a single ray of light from Jesus. They know not what it is to be renewed by the grace of God. They have no living experience for themselves in the things of God. And I saw that the Lord was whetting His sword in heaven to cut them down. Oh, that every lukewarm professor could realize the clean work that God is about to make among His professed people! Dear friends, do not deceive yourselves concerning your condition. You cannot deceive God. Says the True Witness: 'I know thy works.' The third angel is leading up a people, step by step, higher and higher. At every step they will be tested."[50]

The *True Witness* warns of a coming situation worse than *being* Laodicean. It warns of a time worse than wandering in the wilderness. During Israel's forty-years, the tabernacle services continued, the manna still fell, the water ever flowed from the rock. But Eli's house was cut down by the sword of heaven; and they were *cut off completely*. For a time—Israel was cut off from the benefits of atonement. They experienced something akin to a punitively preemptive closing of probation—the loss of the Ark of the Covenant, and the suspension in the mediatory services and covenant privileges. In Laodicean terms—God had indeed spit them out of His mouth.[51]

—Ichabod

The long-deferred day arrived—the battle of Aphek. The philistines utterly defeated the forces of Israel. They killed the priests in battle; and Eli fell out of his chair and died of a broken neck. The enemy captured the Ark of the Covenant;[52] and every man fled to his tent. The wife of a priest went into labor when she heard about the Ark.[53] She gave birth to her son and died. Before dying, "she named the boy Ichabod, saying, 'The glory has departed from Israel.'"[54] "The glory has departed from Israel,' she said, 'for the ark of God has been captured.'"[55]

---

[50] Ellen G. White, Testimonies for the Church, vol. 1, p. 189.

[51] Revelation 3:16. "So because you are lukewarm—neither hot nor cold—I am about to vomit you out of my mouth!" Berean Study Bible.

[52] 1 Samuel 4:10, 18.

[53] In prophecy Israel and the church is often portrayed as a woman. The church is also portrayed at the wife of Christ—our priest. See Jeremiah 6:2; Ezekiel 16:2, 15; 2 Corinthians 11:2; Ephesians 5:23; Revelation 12:1; 19:7; Hebrews 7:14-16.

[54] 1 Samuel 4:20-21. Berean Study Bible.

[55] Ibid., 4:22.

No priests, no sacrifices, to mediation, no services, no Ark of the Covenant—God's glory gone. This was the long-deferred storm that God sent to punish Eli's house—the church and the nation. He sends such storms to His people—to individuals, to churches, to nations, and to the world. During such storms, God *turns His face away*—His presence hidden by terrible and menacing clouds. There is a plethora of biblical examples of these menacing storms.

—A Bible Plethora

The Anguish of Abraham—

God called Abraham from his country and kin to a chapter twenty-three[56] wilderness experience. He needed to learn the "lessons of faith"—"not to rely upon human *strength* or *wisdom,* but on the power of God for the fulfilment of His promises."[57] This *"strength"* is about the *physical nature*. This *"wisdom"* is about the *mental* nature.

Abraham was called into the *school of Christ,*[58] a "school of self-denial and hardship" "to learn patience, to temper... passions."[59] He needed these things. Famine prompted him to turn aside to Egypt, where, by "concealing the fact that Sarah was his wife, he betrayed a distrust of the *divine care*."[60] Later, failing to trust *divine wisdom,* he reasoned Sarah was too old to bear a child, and heeded her suggestion to marry Hagar. But Abraham *was* in the wilderness—learning in the school of Christ:

> "In the obedience of faith, Abraham had forsaken his native country—had turned away from the graves of his fathers and the home of his kindred. He had wandered as a stranger in the land of his inheritance. He had waited long for the birth of the promised heir. At the command of God he had sent away his son Ishmael. And now, when the child so long desired was entering upon manhood, and the patriarch seemed able to discern the fruition of his hopes, a trial greater than all others was before him. The command was expressed in words that must have wrung with anguish that father's heart: 'Take now thy son, thine only son Isaac, whom thou lovest... and offer him there for a burnt offering.'[61]"[62]

[56] Chapter Twenty-Three, *The Hand of the Man from Galilee*.

[57] Ellen G. White, *From Eternity Past*, p. 171.

[58] Ellen G. White, *The Desire of Ages*, p. 330. "We are to enter the school of Christ, to learn from Him meekness and lowliness. Redemption is that process by which the soul is trained for heaven. This training means a knowledge of Christ. It means emancipation from ideas, habits, and practices that have been gained in the school of the prince of darkness. The soul must be delivered from all that is opposed to loyalty to God."

[59] Ellen G. White, *From Eternity Past*, p. 171.

[60] Ellen G. White, *Patriarchs and Prophets*, p. 130.

[61] Genesis 22:2.

[62] Ellen G. White, *Patriarchs and Prophets*, p. 148.

It is this final test that adds this story to the *Biblical Plethora*. Abraham was old—even in his generation. When younger, he was strong to face danger and hardship; but now his feet were faltering toward the grave. *Physically*, he longed for rest from anxiety and toil.

This final test was also *mentally* taxing. "Satan was at hand to suggest that he must be deceived, for the divine law commands, 'Thou shalt not kill,' and God would not require what He had once forbidden."[63]

> "Going outside his tent, Abraham looked up to the calm brightness of the unclouded heavens, and recalled the promise made nearly fifty years before, that his seed should be innumerable as the stars. If this promise was to be fulfilled through Isaac, how could he be put to death? Abraham was tempted to believe he might be under a delusion."[64]

In *spiritual* anguish "he bowed upon the earth, and prayed as never before, for some confirmation of the command if he must perform this terrible duty." He went to where he met with angels about the destruction of Sodom—those same angels who also repeated promises of this same son Isaac. He hoped to meet them there again, but no one came to his relief. "Darkness seemed to shut him in."[65] Only the sound of the command ringing in his ears—"Take now thy son, thine only son Isaac, whom thou lovest."[66] This separation from God—this darkness at His absence—is that which makes both ears of everyone who hears it tingle.

Falling in the Garden—

Everything the Creator made was *very good*. He made Adam and Eve a beautiful garden home, and amply supplied all their wants. He gave every tree—except one—to provision their *physical* needs. Angels taught them the history of Satan's fall,[67] the plan of salvation,[68] and about their employment[69]—daily lessons for their *mental* development. The Sabbath was a day of special *spiritual* communion with the Creator Himself. They were blessed beyond imagination.

Then that fateful day beside the *tree of knowledge of good and evil*—our parents substituted *human provisions* in place of the divine gifts. And so humans felt (for the first time) separated from God—that darkness at His absence that makes both ears of everyone who hears it tingle.

---

[63] Ibid.

[64] Ibid.

[65] Ibid.

[66] Genesis 22:2.

[67] Ellen G. White, *Patriarchs and Prophets*, pp. 52-53.

[68] Ellen G. White, *The Story of Redemption*, pp. 46-47.

[69] Ellen G. White, *Early Writings*, p. 147.

The Passion of Christ—

The Son of Man "has traveled the path He asks His followers to travel"[70]—yea, "a more thorny path than any of his followers."[71] He too, learned the lessons of the wilderness protocol—and "by methods peculiarly His own, Christ helped all who were in sorrow and affliction."[72] The devil temped Him (concerning those protocols) at the start of His ministry; and in Gethsemane at the end.

The final test at Calvary was the storm that makes both ears of everyone who hears it tingle. *Physically* lacerated with stripes; feet "spiked to the tree, that royal head pierced with the crown of thorns,"—and "lips shaped to the cry of woe."[73] Still He refused vinegar or gall to quiet the pain—"for His faith must keep fast hold upon God."[74]

In *mental* anguish He hears Satan and his angels in human form:[75] "If thou be the Son of God, come down from the cross."[76] "Let Him save Himself, if He be the Christ, the chosen of God."[77] Religious leaders uniting with Satan do his bidding: "He saved others; Himself He cannot save. Let Christ the King of Israel descend now from the cross, that we may see and believe."[78]

And Jesus' *spiritual* agony was so great that He hardly felt His physical pain.[79]

> "The guilt of every descendant of Adam was pressing upon His heart. The wrath of God against sin, the terrible manifestation of His displeasure because of iniquity, filled the soul of His Son with consternation. All His life Christ had been publishing to a fallen world the good news of the Father's mercy and pardoning love. Salvation for the chief of sinners was His theme. But now with the terrible weight of guilt He bears, He cannot see the Father's reconciling face. The withdrawal of the divine countenance from the Savior in this hour of supreme anguish pierced His heart with a sorrow that can never be fully understood by man.
>
> "Satan with his fierce temptations wrung the heart of Jesus. The Savior could not see through the portals of the tomb. Hope did not present to Him His coming forth from the grave a conqueror, or tell Him of the Father's acceptance of the sacrifice. He feared that sin was so offensive to

---

[70] Ellen G. White, *Adventist Home*, p. 381.
[71] Ellen G. White, *The Signs of the Times*, June 21, 1883.
[72] Ellen G. White, *The Ministry of Healing*, p. 23.
[73] Ellen G. White, *The Desire of Ages*, p. 755.
[74] Ibid., p. 746.
[75] Ibid.
[76] Matthew 27:40.
[77] Luke 23:35.
[78] Matthew 27:40.
[79] Ellen G. White, *The Desire of Ages*, p. 753.

God that Their separation was to be eternal. Christ felt the anguish which the sinner will feel when mercy shall no longer plead for the guilty race. It was the sense of sin, bringing the Father's wrath upon Him as man's substitute, that made the cup He drank so bitter, and broke the heart of the Son of God."[80]

"Amid the awful darkness, apparently forsaken of God, Christ had drained the last dregs in the cup of human woe. In those dreadful hours He had relied upon the evidence of His Father's acceptance heretofore given Him. He was acquainted with the character of His Father; He understood His justice, His mercy, and His great love. By faith He rested in Him whom it had ever been His joy to obey. And as in submission He committed Himself to God, the sense of the loss of His Father's favor was withdrawn. By faith, Christ was victor."[81]

The Flight of Elijah—

Elijah's soul was "wrung with anguish" as he petitioned the Lord "to save His people if it must be by judgments. He plead with God to withhold from his ungrateful people dew and rain... that they might look in vain to their idols... to water the earth."[82]

Now, public enemy number-one for three-and-a-half-years, Elijah relied upon the Lord for his *physical* survival—food in drought, and protection from Ahab's minions. The Lord was his counsel. Elijah was *mentally* resolute against peer pressure, the syncretistic ideology of his day, and called for all Israel to choose intelligently between a living God and a lifeless imposter. *Spiritually*—he was jealous for the glory of God.[83]

Jezebel was queen of Israel at the time; and is a prophetic symbol showing up in the church of Thyatira[84]—personifying Christianity mixed with paganism. After the signal victory on Carmel, Elijah, spooked by Jezebel, flees a day's journey into the wilderness to sit under a tree and ask the Lord to take his life.

Instead, the Lord sends an angel with food and water. Obediently, Elijah eats for *physical* strength to flee to the mountains. He travels forty days and nights to Horeb—the mountain of God—where he holds up in a cave. Notice the similarity to the end-time sequence: he flees from the city to the country, and then from the country to the mountains. Also notice how God fed Elijah while he was in the country to strengthen him for his journey to the mountains—when food would be scarce.

---

[80] Ibid.

[81] Ibid., p. 756.

[82] Ellen G. White, *The Review and Herald*, September 16, 1873.

[83] Ibid.

[84] Revelation 2:18-29.

"What doest thou here, Elijah?" Having *physically* stabilized Elijah, God now seeks to address his *mental* malaise.

"I have been very jealous for the Lord God of hosts," Elijah cries, "and I, even I only, am left."

The Lord informs him that He has "yet... seven thousand in Israel, all the knees which have not bowed unto Baal, and every mouth which hath not kissed him."[85]

To align Elijah *spiritually*, God asks him to stand before Him on the mount. As the Lord passes by, a great and strong wind tears apart the mountains and brakes up the rocks. After the wind—an earthquake; and after the earthquake—a fire; but God was not in the wind or earthquake or fire. And then—there is a still small voice.

The Lord then sends Elijah on missions to anoint a new king in Syria (the world), a new king in Israel (the nation), and a new prophet—Elisha (the church)—a boy still living at home with his parents.

Ezekiel Prophecies—

The old-testament prophecies against apostate Israel warned of progressive judgments, captivity, and a scattering of the people. Then God "turns the captivity"[86] of Israel, the covenant is realized, and the Holy Spirit fills them—falling like *latter rain*.

God had Ezekiel shave his head, and[87] weigh and divide the hair into three parts. He was to burn one third (pestilence and famine),[88] chop one-third with a knife (sword), and scatter one-third in the wind. "This is Jerusalem."[89] "Therefore thus saith the Lord God; Behold, I, even I, am against thee, and will execute judgments in the midst of thee in the sight of the nations."[90] Israel is separated from God—and the darkness at His absence is enough to make both ears of everyone who hears it tingle. Then He "turns the captivity" of Israel, and it goes like this:

> "Therefore declare that this is what the Lord God says: 'I will gather you from the peoples and assemble you from the countries to which you have been scattered, and I will give back to you the land of Israel.'
>
> "When they return to it... I will give them singleness of heart and put a new spirit within them; I will remove their heart of stone and give them a heart of flesh, so that they may follow My statutes, keep My

---

[85] 1 Kings 19:9, 10, 18.

[86] See Deuteronomy 30:3; Jeremiah 29:14; Zechariah 1; Joel 2.

[87] Ezekiel 5.

[88] Ezekiel 5:12 interprets fire, knife, and wind. See verse 4.

[89] Ezekiel 5:5.

[90] Ezekiel 5:8.

ordinances, and practice them. Then they will be My people, and I will be their God."[91]

Ezekiel vividly describes the work of judgment as a slaughter that begins with "the ancient men which were before the house"[92] of God—and the corresponding sealing of those in the city "that sigh and that cry for all the abominations that be done in the midst thereof."[93]

At one point, the Lord lifts Ezekiel by a lock of hair, and carries him to Jerusalem, to the gate of the inner court of Solomon's temple. The wilderness tabernacle comprised a two-apartment tent in a single courtyard; but Solomon's temple had an *additional* courtyard called the outer court. The original courtyard was then called the inner court.

Ezekiel noticed an idol "standing by the north gateway" that separated the outer court from the inner court. Israel frequently dabbled with idolatry—and it was not uncommon for them to set up asherim[94] in the courtyard. These cult objects related to the worship of the fertility goddess Asherah[95]—known to the Canaanites as the sensual goddess Astarte.[96] He noticed there were women sitting at the north gate—weeping for Tammuz—"another pagan practice, a very sexual one involving ritual prostitution."[97]

We've earlier associated the courtyard with the *physical* protocol, the holy place with the *mental* protocol, and the most holy with the *spiritual* protocol. But in this vision all three counterfeit protocols are in the courtyard areas. *Sensual idolatry* in the outer court takes the place of *physical* faithfulness to God and *physical* restoration.

Ezekiel discovers from the inner court that it's surrounded by a number of secret rooms.[98] He sees a small hole in the wall, and digs until he finds a door going into hidden chambers. Paintings and carvings and murals of creepy things and idols cover the walls. Seventy of the elders of Israel are there with censers in their hand—a thick cloud of smoke ascending. The "elders were all acting as priests and were offering their

[91] Ezekiel 11:17-20. See also Ezekiel 39:23-29.

[92] Ezekiel 9:6.

[93] Ezekiel 9:4.

[94] Ashirm are mentioned about 40 times in the Bible.

[95] A. H. Sayce, *Asherah*, International Standard Bible Encyclopedia, 1915.

[96] M. G. Easton M.A., D. D., *Illustrated Bible Dictionary*, Third Edition. 1897.

[97] Charles Whitaker, *Ezekiel 8:14-17*, Forerunners Commentary, accessed 11/22/2019 at https://www.bibletools.org/index.cfm/fuseaction/Topical.show/RTD/cgg/ID/13229/Weeping-for-Tammuz.htm.

[98] Ezekiel 8:7. Jack J. Blanko, *The Clear Word*, Review and Herald Publishing Association, 1994.

pictured idols the incense that none but the sons of Aaron had a right to use and which was to be offered only to Jehovah."[99]

"Ezekiel puts the philosophy of the group into the form of a popular saying,"[100] "The Lord does not see us; the Lord has forsaken the land."[101] These counterfeit *holy places* take the place of *mental* faithfulness to God and *mental* restoration.

"There between the alter of sacrifice and the entrance of the Holy Place" "twenty-five priests; that is, the high priest and the heads of all twenty-four sets of priests,"[102] have their backs towards the Holy Place and are facing the east—worshipping the sun. Sun worship takes the place of *spiritual* faithfulness to God and *spiritual* restoration.

Idolatry at Sinai—

While Moses was on Mount Sinai receiving the tables of the law, the people were below frolicking before a golden calf. *Physically*, they feasted and danced and indulged in immoral heathen practices remembered from Egypt. *Mentally*, they reasoned that "these be thy gods, O Israel, which brought thee up out of the land of Egypt."[103] *Spiritually*, they sang and worshipped an idol.

God's judgments immediately followed; and lots of people died.[104] There were plagues.[105] God required the tabernacle to be moved "afar off from the camp."[106] "For the LORD had said to Moses, 'Tell the Israelites, "You are a stiff-necked people. If I should go with you for a single moment, I would destroy you."'"[107] "When the people heard these bad tidings, they went into mourning, and... So the Israelites stripped themselves of their jewelry from mount Horeb onward."[108] Again, separated from God—that darkness at His absence that makes both ears of everyone who hears it tingle.

Joshua ("*a young man*"), stayed always in the tabernacle while[109] the congregation worshiped from afar with their faces toward the tent.

---

[99] Commentary on Ezekiel 8:11, *The seventh-day Adventist Bible Commentary*. Review and Herald Publishing Association, 1955.

[100] Ibid., on verse 12.

[101] Ezekiel 8:12.

[102] *Ezekiel 8:16. Jack J. Blanko, The Clear Word, Review and Herald Publishing Association, 1994.*

[103] *Exodus 32:4.*

[104] Exodus 32:27-28.

[105] Exodus 32:35.

[106] Exodus 33:7.

[107] Exodus 33:3,5. Berean Study Bible.

[108] Exodus 33:4, 6. Berean Study Bible.

[109] Exodus 33:11.

Moses pleaded with God that the nation would still be His chosen people. The Lord promised him He would go with *him* and give *him* rest. This wasn't enough for Moses. He asked the Lord to go with *them*. Moses found grace in God's sight—and the Lord eventually agreed.[110]

The Lord told Moses to hew blank tables of stone and to take them with him up into the mountain—that He could write upon them like He did the first.[111] But the first tables had not been supplied by Moses. The original "tables were the work of God, and the writing was the writing of God, graven upon the tables."[112] These originals were broken for the sins of the people,[113] and aptly present the humanity of Christ—where the divine law was written in stone.[114]

The tables hewn by Moses, taken up into the mount were also written upon by God's finger,[115] and aptly present humanity of God's people in whom His character is perfectly reproduced.[116] So it is that Moses' face shown when he came out of the mount[117]—just as Steven's did, and like the faces of the servants of God during the latter rain when they "hasten from place to place to proclaim the message from heaven."[118]

Isaiah 66—

The final prophecy of Isaiah promises a new heaven and a new earth that shall remain forever; where, "from one New Moon to another and from one Sabbath to another, all mankind will come to worship before Me," says the LORD."[119] This is a happy ending for a prophecy that starts out in crisis. Frustrated with Israel, the Lord said:

> "The heaven is my throne and the earth is my footstool: where is the house that ye build for me? And *where is the place of my rest?*"[120]

Zion is the mountain of God—standing *between* heaven and earth. Jerusalem the city of God[121]—she *should* be like a bride adorned for her

[110] Exodus 33:12-17.

[111] Exodus 34:1-2.

[112] Exodus 32:16.

[113] Exodus 32: 19; see 1 Corinthians 11:24.

[114] Consider Ezekiel 11:19, 36:36; Jeremiah 31:33; Hebrews 8:10. Also, Ellen G. White, *The Great Controversy*, p. 434, "The law of God, being a revelation of His will, a transcript of His character, must forever endure."

[115] Exodus 34:1

[116] See Ellen G. White, Christ's Object Lessons, p. 69.

[117] Exodus 34:29-35.

[118] Ellen G. White, *The Great Controversy*, p. 612.

[119] Isaiah 66:22-23.

[120] Isaiah 66:1. Emphasis added.

[121] Hebrews 12:22.

husband.[122] She's on Mount Zion; and she too, is called Zion. The temple is on Zion—it's the house of God. It *should* be a spiritual house made of lively stones, and Christ its foundation. He's the chief cornerstone. This whole arraignment is supposed to be the chapter-one *light on a hill.*[123]

Except (because this temple lighthouse still hasn't been finished) God (His Spirit, His glory) cannot *rest*[124] there! But God knows where to look for those who *will* build His house: "To him that is poor (*physical*) and of a contrite spirit (*spiritual*) and trembleth at my word (*mental*)."[125]

The rest of Israel are those who "have chosen *their own ways* and delighted in their abominations."[126] God is not happy with them—judgment is coming:

> "I will choose their punishment, and will bring terror upon them... Hear the uproar from the city, listen to the voice from the temple, it is the voice of the Lord, repaying His enemies what they deserve!"[127]

In the commotion of judgment, and shaking, and sealing: *Zion travails—she brings forth her children.*

> "Before she travailed, she brought forth; before her pain came, she delivered a man child. Who hath heard of such a thing? Who hath seen such a thing? Shall the earth be made to bring forth in one day? Or shall a nation be born at once? For as soon as Zion travailed, she brought forth her children."[128]

Night Wrestling—

Jacob "knew that his long exile was the direct result of" "his sin in the deception of his father."[129] As he retraced the road from Canaan to Padan-aram that, as a fugitive, he trod twenty years before, the reproaches of a guilty conscience made his journey very sad. But he had repented of his sin;[130] and "the Lord granted Jacob a token of the divine care. "Two hosts of heavenly angels seemed to encompass him behind and before, advancing with his company, as if for their protection."[131]

Along the way, he recited God's promises to him: "The Lord... saith unto me, Return unto they country, and to thy kindred, and I will deal

---

[122] Revelation 21:2.
[123] Chapter One, *A Tale of Three Mountains*.
[124] See Hebrews 3 & 4; 2 Chronicles 7:1.
[125] Isaiah 66:2. Parentheses added.
[126] Isaiah 66:3. Berean Study Bible. Emphasis added.
[127] Isaiah 66:4, 6. Berean Study Bible.
[128] Isaiah 66:7-8.
[129] Ellen G. White, *Patriarch's and Prophets*, p. 195.
[130] Ibid., p. 202.
[131] Ibid., p. 195.

well with thee... Surely I will do thee good, and make thy seed as the sands of the sea, which cannot be numbered for multitude."[132]

Near the river Jabbok, Jacob "decided to spend the night in prayer, and he desired to be alone with God."[133] Suddenly a strong hand was laid upon him. Thinking it was an enemy, he struggled with all his strength to free himself. While fighting "for his life, the sense of his guilt pressed upon his soul, his sins rose up before him, to shut him out from God. But in his terrible extremity he remembered God's promises, and his whole heart went out in entreaty for His mercy."[134] Feeing separated from God, Jacob knew that darkness at His absence; and both ears tingle.

The struggle continued to near daybreak. The stranger touched Jacob's thigh with his finger—instantly crippling him. By this he knew that his antagonist was a heavenly messenger.

> "The patriarch was now disabled and suffering the keenest pain, but he would not loosen his hold. All penitent and broken, he clung to the Angel; 'he wept, and made supplication,'[135] pleading for a blessing. He must have assurance that his sin was pardoned."[136]

Jacob "had power over the Angel, and prevailed."[137] Had he not forsaken his sins and earnestly sought God's blessing (*physical*); had he not laid hold of the promises of God (*mental*); and not been earnest and persevering in prayer (*spiritual*): this sinful, erring mortal would not have prevailed with God.[138] "Jacob would have been instantly destroyed."[139]

The Whirlwind and Job—

Pestilence, sword, and boils *physically* devastated him. The endless conjecture of his three friends and the ungodly counsel of his wife—tormented Job *mentally*. *Spiritually* he cried:

> "My soul is weary of my life... I will speak of it in the bitterness of my soul. I will say unto God, Do not condemn me; shew me wherefore thou contendest with me. Is it good unto thee that thou shouldest oppress, that thou shouldest despise the work of thine hands, and shine upon the counsel of the wicked?"[140]

---

[132] Genesis 32:9, 12.
[133] Ellen G. White, *Patriarch's and Prophets*, p. 196.
[134] Ibid., p. 197.
[135] Hosea 12:4.
[136] Ellen G. White, *Patriarch's and Prophets*, p. 197.
[137] Hosea 12:4.
[138] Compare Ellen G. White, *Patriarch's and Prophets*, p. 203 (last paragraph) and p. 197.
[139] Ellen G. White, *Patriarch's and Prophets*, p. 197.
[140] Job 10:1-3.

Still, in the ear-tingling darkness of his separation from God—the darkness at His absence—Job concludes: "Though He slay me, yet will I trust in Him... He also shall be my salvation."[141] The Lord "turned the captivity of Job when he prayed for his friends."[142] "So the Lord blessed the latter end of Job more than his beginning."[143]

The Day of the Lord—

Joel's prophesy is for spiritual Israel during the *day of the Lord.*[144] He tells of extreme drought brought by a plague of locusts—and describes it in richly symbolic language. "The corn is wasted: the new wine is dried up, the oil languisheth."[145] John uses similar figures in Revelation's third seal: wheat, barley, oil, and wine.[146]

The grains are for *physical* sustenance.

The wine refers to the teachings of Christ—for *mental* development.

> "If through the grace of Christ His people will become new bottles, He will fill them with new wine."[147]

The oil is *spiritual.*

> "The golden oil represents the Holy Spirit;"[148]
>
> "[And those who] cultivate the spirit and habit of prayer... receive the golden oil of goodness, patience, long-suffering, gentleness, love [the fruit of the Spirit[149]]."[150]

The famous outcome of Joel's prophecy is the *latter rain* refreshing:

> "I will pour out My Spirit on all flesh; and your sons and your daughters shall prophecy, your old men shall dream dreams, your young men see visions: and also upon the servants and handmaids in those days will I pour out My Spirit."[151]

The disturbing context of Joel's prophecy is that his people's ears are already tingling. God has *already* judged them—they are desperately trying to undue the verdict—the darkness of His absence:

---

[141] Job 13:15-16.
[142] Job 42:10.
[143] Job 42:12.
[144] Joel 1:15; 2:1
[145] Joel 1:10.
[146] Revelation 6:5-6.
[147] Ellen G. White, *The Desire of Ages*, p. 279.
[148] Ellen G. White, *Testimonies to Ministers*, p. 188.
[149] Galatians 5:2.
[150] Ellen G. White, *Testimonies to Ministers*, p. 511.
[151] Joel 2:28-29. Berean Study Bible.

"'Yet even now,' declares the LORD, 'return to Me with all your heart, with fasting, weeping, and mourning.' So rend your hearts and not your garments, and return to the LORD your God. For He is gracious and compassionate, slow to anger, abounding in loving devotion. And He relents from sending disaster. Who knows? *He may turn and relent* and leave a blessing behind Him—grain and drink offerings for the LORD your God.

"Blow the trumpet[152] in Zion, consecrate a fast, proclaim a sacred assembly. Gather the people, sanctify the congregation, assemble the aged, gather the children, even those nursing at the breast. Let the bridegroom leave his room, and the bride her chamber. Let the priests who minister before the LORD weep between the porch and the altar, saying, 'Spare Your people, O LORD, and do not make Your heritage a reproach, an object of scorn among the nations. Why should they say among the peoples, "Where is their God?"'"

But the hope of Joel's prophecy is how it shows God sparing His people. He *does return;*[153] and causes the rain to fall, "the former rain, and the latter rain."[154]

"Behold, I will send you grain, new wine, and oil, and by them you will be satisfied. I will never again make you a reproach among the nations."[155]

Joseph's Mighty Stand—

When Potiphar's wife "cast her eyes upon Joseph,"[156] he *physically* denied the promptings of the flesh. Potiphar owed his great prosperity to Joseph, and committed all he had to his hand.[157] But Joseph *mentally* rejected any rationalization that he deserved access to Potiphar's promiscuous wife. *Spiritually*, he recoiled from thoughts of doing "this great wickedness;" and *sinning against God.*[158]

He too, seemed forsaken. Prison was his darkness at God's absence—that makes both ears of everyone who hears it tingle. Says the Psalmist,

"He sent a man before them—Joseph, sold as a slave. They bruised his feet with shackles and placed his neck in irons, until his prediction came true and the word of the LORD proved him right."[159]

---

152 KJV, The Berean Study Bible uses "rams horn."

153 See Joel 2:14.

154 Joel 2:23.

155 Joel 2:19. Berean Study Bible.

156 Genesis 39:7.

157 Genesis 39:8.

158 Genesis 39:9.

159 Psalms 105:17-19. Berean Study Bible.

After being called from the dungeon to explain Pharaoh's dream, this "young man—a Hebrew"[160] was promoted to be savior of Egypt—elevated to the highest throne—save that of Pharaoh himself.[161]

The Terror of Judas—

Judas "witnessed the Savior's mighty works in healing the sick, casting out devils, and raising the dead. He felt in his own person the evidence of Christ's power (*physical*). He recognized the teachings of Christ as superior to all that he had ever heard (*mental*). He loved the Great Teacher, and desired to be with Him (*spiritual*)."[162]

But while Christ tried to help Him see and correct his defects of character, he indulged his covetous disposition—even often stealing from the treasury (*physical*).

> "His heart was open to unbelief (*mental*), and the enemy supplied thoughts of questioning and rebellion."[163]
>
> "He might have comprehended *the methods of Christ.* But he was blinded by his own selfish desires."[164]

After realizing that Christ was offering spiritual rather than worldly good," "he determined not to unite himself so closely to Christ but that he could draw away."[165] He sold his Lord for thirty pieces of silver—the price of a common slave.

Watching the trial, a "terrible fear" came over Judas. As it ended, he "could endure the torture of his guilty conscience no longer." "Jesus spoke no word of condemnation, but Judas, kneeling now before him, felt "an awful sense of condemnation and a looking for of judgment." Running from the scene, he exclaimed, "It is too late!" "and in despair he went out and hanged himself."[166]

The Shipwreck of Paul—

The book of *Acts* tells this story so full of symbolism. A nor'easter made the sea rough and stormy. The shipmen tossed cargo and tackling overboard to lighten the ship. Seeing neither sun nor stars many days, they lost hope of being saved[167]—until Paul stood up bearing an angel's

---

160 Genesis 41:12.
161 Genesis 41:40-44.
162 Ellen G. White, *The Desire of Ages*, p. 717. Parentheses added.
163 Ibid., p. 718. Parentheses added.
164 Ibid. Emphasis added.
165 Ibid., p. 719.
166 Ibid., p.721-722.
167 Acts 27:13-20.

message promising safety so long as they stayed with the ship.[168] He then bade them eat their fill and cast the remaining food overboard.

The ship did eventually break-up—when it ran aground on the island Melita. The soldiers wanted to kill the prisoners, but the centurion—wanting to save Paul—kept them from their purpose. Swimming and floating on the ship's debris, they all made it safely to shore.

The barbarous island people showed them kindness. They kindled a fire because of the *present rain* and the cold. As Paul was adding fuel to the fire—a viper arose from the heat and bit his hand. He shook it off into the fire; but the people expected him to die. When he didn't, they believed he was a god. There was sickness and disease with the island people; and they came to Paul. He prayed and laid hands on them, and healed them.

The Despair of Saul—

King Saul had a lot of potential; but he didn't take God's counsel seriously. Instead, he developed his *physical* nature after the pattern of the world. God told Saul to destroy utterly the Amalekites and not take their spoils. But he disobeyed. He took the best of their possessions; and he kept Agag alive.

In his *mental* depravity, Saul consulted the witch of Endor concerning the outcome of an upcoming battle; and *spiritually* he presumed to act as a priest when he was too impatient to wait for Samuel.

Saul "rejected the counsel of Samuel the prophet; he had exiled David, the chosen of God; he had slain the priests of the Lord."[169] Now he was going into battle with the Philistines and longed for help and guidance.

> "But it was in vain that he sought counsel from God... By his own stubbornness and rebellion he had cut himself off from God. There could be no return but by the way of penitence and contrition; but the proud monarch, in his anguish and despair, determined to seek help from another source."[170]

His life was lost in battle; and his kingdom was given to David—who, *as a boy* was anointed by Samuel.

---

[168] See Ellen G. White, Selected Messages, book 2, p. 390. It says, "Let us have faith that God is going to carry the noble ship which bears the people of God safely to port."

[169] Ellen G. White, *Patriarch's and Prophets*, p. 676.

[170] Ibid.

Clearing the Temple—

Jesus had been "about all Galilee, teaching in their synagogues (*mental*), and preaching the gospel of the kingdom (*spiritual*), and healing all manner of sickness and all manner of disease among the people (*physical*)."[171] Now it's just days before Calvary.

On Monday, He cleared the temple of the buyers and the sellers; but He healed the blind and the lame. The leaders were displeased when they saw "the wonderful things He did"[172]—and when they heard the *children* offering their *perfect* praise.

On Tuesday, the *fruitless* fig tree was withered away. A couple days before, Jesus tearfully announced that Jerusalem would be destroyed.[173] Now, as Jesus teaches in the temple—the leaders challenge His authority. He pronounces woes upon the scribes and pharisees; and He says, "Behold, your house is left unto you desolate."[174] He is separating from His people. And a horrible, ear-tingling darkness is coming.

—Confused Laodicea

With such a plethora of witnesses we can tell something of the tingling darkness of *Ichabod*—the storm that sin brings against the soul when *"the glory has departed."* We can see how it leverages our *physical, mental,* and *spiritual* natures against us to *"be tormented day and night forever and ever."*[175] This is the reality of *Ichabod!* So when God destroys the wicked—it's really an act of mercy.

We also see how it is that God gets the righteous through the storm. In the wilderness (the school of Christ), He uses the wilderness protocols (the *Galilee Protocol)* to so fully align our *physical, mental,* and *spiritual* natures with the divine nature that even *Ichabod* is powerless "to separate us from the love of God that is in Christ Jesus our Lord".[176]

We see how Satan deceives to keep people from making real preparation for the storm. In the *protocol cities* (the school of the prince of darkness), he gets us to buy, sell, and drink the wine of the wrath of Babylon's fornication with the kings and merchants of the earth to align our *physical, mental,* and *spiritual* natures into a counterfeit glory after the model of the world—*a pyre of flame.*

---

[171] Matthew 4:23. Parenthesis added.
[172] Matthew 21:15.
[173] Luke 19:41-44.
[174] Matthew 23.38.
[175] Revelation 20:10.
[176] Romans 8:38-39.

But Laodiceans are confused. We have so mixed the *Galilee Protocol* with Satan's *merchandise* that we cannot tell the difference. The mixture is impotent, lukewarm, confusing, and deceptive—and to the True Witness—it is nauseating. The mixture produces "a form of godliness" that denies "the power thereof."[177]

Laodicea's ever-rolling, ever-growing, snowball requires an eventual corporate-level storm. Such a storm will clarify the issues and weed out all those who refuse to abandon the *twilight-zone*. Of course, we've known this for years.

> "I asked the meaning of the shaking I had seen, and was shown that it would be caused by the straight testimony called forth by the counsel of the True Witness to the Laodiceans. This will have its effect upon the heart of the receiver, and will lead him to exalt the standard and pour forth the straight truth. Some will not bear this straight testimony. They will rise up against it, and it will cause a shaking among God's people."[178]

The counsel of the True Witness is for us to *buy from Him*—white raiment, gold tried in the fire, and eye salve. These are the true *physical*, *mental*, and *spiritual* remedies.

It is conceivable that when we realize the *True Witness* is actually calling for Seventh-day Adventists to abandon the counterfeit principles upon which we are conducting our *educational*, *ministerial*, and *medical* work—it will indeed *shake* up the church. So long as there is an ark—faithful souls, radiating with God's glory—bearing the final warning message from city to city, fully implementing the Galilee Protocol, it is conceivable that the storm will spread across the nation. And given our country's position in the world: the national storm is likely to go global.

—White Raiment

White raiment is the righteousness of Christ imparted to the sinner for a life of willing obedience.[179] It's "perfect obedience to the law of Jehovah."[180] White raiment is Christ's *physical* remedy for His people. The *medical* protocol—properly conducted will bear this out.

> "By works of their own," sinners "try to cover their sins, and make themselves acceptable to God." "No fig-leaf garment, no worldly citizen dress, can be worn by those who sit down with Christ and angels at the marriage supper of the Lamb." "Only the covering which Christ Himself has

[177] 2 Timothy 3:5.

[178] Ellen G. White, *Early Writings*, p. 270. 1857.

[179] Ellen G. White, Testimonies for the Church, vol. 4, p. 88.

[180] Ellen G. White, *Christ's Object Lessons*, p. 311.

provided can make us meet to appear in God's presence. This covering, the robe of His own righteousness, Christ will put upon every repenting, believing soul. 'I counsel thee,' He says, 'to buy of Me... white raiment, that thou mayest be clothed, and that the shame of thy nakedness do not appear.[181]'" "By His perfect obedience He has made it possible for every human being to obey God's commandments."[182] "Christ came to this world and lived the law of God, that man might have perfect mastery over the natural inclinations which corrupt the soul. The Physician of soul and body, He gives victory over warring lusts. He has provided every facility, that man may possess completeness of character.[183]

—Gold, Tried in the Fire

The gold is Christ's *mental* remedy for His people. The *educational* protocol—properly conducted will bear this out.

"The gold tried in the fire is faith that works by love,"[184] woven into our life and character of students who are in the school of Christ—where they are purged until they are pure.[185]

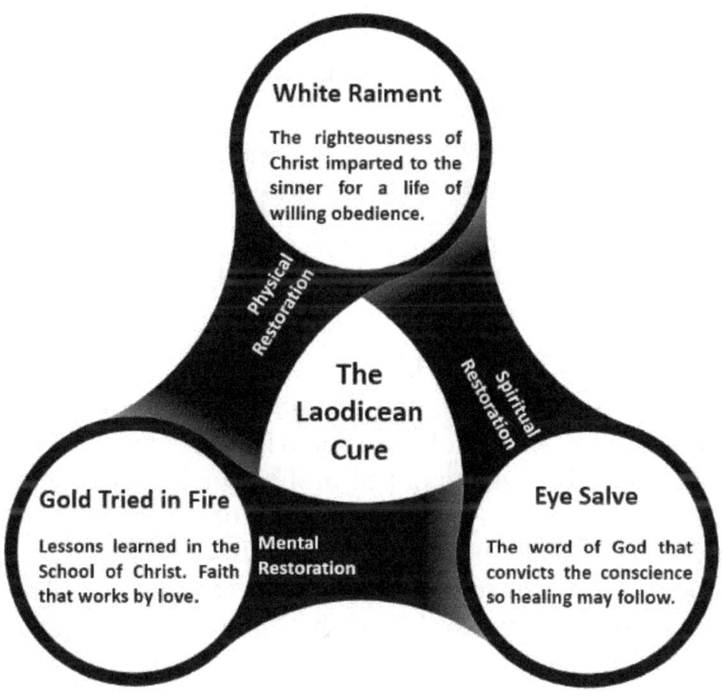

[181] Revelation 3:18.
[182] Ellen G. White, Christ's Object Lessons, p. 311.
[183] Ellen G. White, The Ministry of Healing, p. 130.
[184] Ellen G. White, *Christ's Object Lessons*, p. 158.
[185] Ellen G. White, *Testimonies for the Church*, vol. 4, p. 88.

"We are to enter the school of Christ." Redemption trains the soul for heaven. This training means a knowledge of Christ. It means emancipation from ideas, habits, and practices that we've gained in the school of the prince of darkness.[186] Peter noted how we are "put to grief by various trials, so that the proven genuineness of [our] faith, more precious than gold... being refined by fire, may be discovered to... [reveal the glory] of Jesus Christ."[187]

> "The gold here recommended is faith and love, which we must have interwoven into our life and character. But if the world has a controlling power upon life and character, they are losing the precious lessons of Christ... If we can put these things away, and come right into the school of Christ, and learn of Him the precious lessons He has for us, then we shall grow in grace and in the knowledge of our Lord and Savior Jesus Christ... He will impart to us of His divine nature, and we may bring our godliness into our everyday life, and imitate the great Teacher in seeking to win souls. We must not seek our own will, but seek to serve God with the whole heart. "[188]

—Eye Salve

Eye-salve is His *spiritual* remedy. The *ministerial* protocol—properly conducted will bear this out.

> "The eye is the sensitive conscience, the inner light of the mind. Upon its correct view of things the spiritual healthfulness of the whole soul and being depends. The 'eye-salve,' the Word of God, makes the conscience smart under its application, for it convicts of sin. But the smarting is necessary that the healing may follow, and the eye be single to the glory of God."[189]

—Redeeming the Wrong

Jonah and Nineveh are two of the most amazing turnarounds in the Bible. While Jonah's change of heart could have been more sympathetic towards the Ninevites; they jumped on-board with both feet. In both cases, God's love and mercy are the real stars of the show.

This gives us hope—as does the fact that Eli, the priests, and the nation *could have* taken "effective measures to correct the evils that were polluting the sanctuary of the Lord," and that "much might have been done in *those years* to redeem the failures of the past."[190]

---

[186] Ellen G. White, *The Desire of Ages*, p. 330.

[187] 1 Peter 1:6-7, Berean Study Bible.

[188] Ellen G. White, *The Review and Herald*, May 10, 1887.

[189] Ellen G. White, *Our High Calling*, p. 350.

[190] Ellen G. White, *Patriarchs and Prophets*, p. 582. Emphasis added.

Will it prevent the storm if we heed the counsel of the *True Witness to Laodicea?* Not entirely, our insubordination has damaged our message, church, country, and the world. But God is merciful. He loves us with an everlasting love.[191] We're the apple of His eye.[192] Heeding His counsel—even at this late date—might just mitigate the worst of the damage. It's not too late to reactivate the *Galilee Protocol* right now!

> **"Those who follow their own mind and walk in their own way will form crooked characters. Vain doctrines and subtle sentiments will be introduced with plausible presentations, to deceive, if possible, the very elect. Are church members building upon the Rock? *The storm is coming, the storm that will try every man's faith, of what sort it is.* Believers must now be firmly rooted in Christ, or else they will be led astray by some phase of error. Let your faith be substantiated by the Word of God"**
>
> **—The Review and Herald, August 31, 1905. Emphasis added.**

[191] Jeremiah 31:3.
[192] Zechariah 2:8.

	Physical	**Mental**	**Spiritual**	**Child**	**Rejection**	**Return**
Abraham	Old and tired	Satan suggested he was deceived	"Take your son, your only son whom you love..."	The Promised Son	Silence from God Darkness seems to shut him in.	Covenant Renewed with an oath
Adam & Eve	Every Other Tree "good for food" Naked, Pain, Toil	Taught of Angels ""to make wise" Knowing Evil	Real Sab. Rest "Eye Pleasing" Fear	The Promised Seed	Fall Expulsion No Robe of Light	Promises Sacrifices Probation
Christ	Physical Pain Vinegar and Gall	"If Thou be the Son of God..."	"My God, My God, why hast Thou forsaken Me?"	The Promised Seed -the Child of the Woman	""He lost the presence of His Father"	"It is Finished" Resurrection Ascension
Ear Tingle	Gath	Ekron	Ashdod	Ichabod (mother dies)	Ark Taken	Ark at Abinadab's Home
Elijah Flight	Wanted to Die Had Angel Food & Water	"What doest thou here Elijah?"	Still Small Voice	Young Elisha Double Spirit	Dark Struggle Wind Earthquake Fire	Anointing: King Syria King Israel Prophet Elisha Elijah Ascends
Ezekiel Prophecies	Sensual Idolatry	70 Elders' Philosophies	25 Priests Sun Worship		Sealing Slaughter	Gathering New Spirit New Covenant
Golden Calf	Feasting Dancing	"These be thy gods"	Idolatry Music	"Young man" Joshua always at the temple	Tabernacle moved outside the camp	Moses' Face Law Written in Earthly Stones
Isaiah 66	"Earth is My Footstool"	"Heaven is My Throne"	"Where is the House"? For "My Rest"	"Man Child" Zion Travailed Brought forth her Children	"A Voice of Noise from the Temple"	"He shall appear to your joy"
Jacob	Forsook Sin Earnest Sought the Blessing	Laid Hold of God's Promises	Persevered in Prayer		Sense of Guilt Shut Out God	Prevailed With God
Job	Financial Loss Loss of Family Boils	Arguments of Three Friends	"Though He slay me, yet will I trust Him"		"Is it good that Thou should despise the works of Thine hand?"	"The Lord blessed the latter end of Job more than his beginning"
Joel	"The Corn is wasted"	The new wine is dried up"	"The Oil Languisheth"	"Your sons and daughters will prophesy"	"Who knows if He will return and repent?	Latter Rain Deliverance in Jerusalem and Mount Zion
Joseph	No Promiscuity	No Rationalizing	No Sin Against God	Joseph "young man"	Prison	Throne
Judas	Thief	Thought He Knew Better	Betrayed with a Kiss		Hopeless Despair	
Laodicea	White Raiment Obedience to Law—Healing	Tried Gold Experience in the School of Christ	Eye Salve Spiritual Discernment from the Word		Spewed Out Rebuke Chasten	If you Open the Door I Will Come In
Paul	Ate some food and threw the rest overboard	Headed counsel to stay with the ship	Saved the Prisoners		Fiery Viper Bite	Paul Healed the Sick
Saul	Kept Spoils Amalekites	Consulted Witch of Endor	Acted as Priest	Boy David Anointed	Hopeless Saul's Dearth	
Temple Second Cleansing	Healing	Teaching	Preaching	Children Offering Perfect Praise in the Temple	"Your house is left unto you desolate"	Pentecost Early Rain

"God is presenting to the minds of men divinely appointed precious gems of truth, appropriate for our time. God has rescued these truths from the companionship of error, and has placed them in their proper framework. When these truths are given their rightful position in God's great plan, when they are presented intelligently and earnestly, and with reverential awe, by the Lord's servants, many will conscientiously believe because of the weight of evidence, without waiting for every supposed difficulty which may suggest itself to their minds, to be removed."

Ellen G. White

Evangelism p. 122

APPENDIX

APPENDIX A

The Infinite Glory Barrier

The great controversy between Christ and Satan concerns issues of liberty and security within God's universe. It involves issues of individuality, community, and diversity. It's about justice and mercy. The great controversy is about government, authority and law. It is about perceptions. It probes into righteousness and love. It asks hard questions about God's motives and the viability of His kingdom.

The great controversy attempts to peer into the unsearchable domain of divinity. It places deity on trial—with finite creatures attempting to judge the infinite Creator. The great controversy is about divinity. It concerns the attributes of *inclusivity* and *exclusivity* within the government of God and within the Godhead itself. This is an important topic for our time, since there are those who espouse the notion that there was a time before Christ was God, and that the Holy Spirit is not an actual person in the Godhead.

—An Inclusivity in Government

Lucifer occupied a place of high honor in the government of God—but he was not God. The Ezekiel 28 description of Lucifer establishes that God incorporated an amazing *inclusivity* in bringing a created being into so high a rank in the government. Lucifer dwelt in the very presence of the Almighty. He was "upon the holy mountain of God"—at the very place of God's throne—and he "walked up and down in the midst of the stones of fire."[1]

Notwithstanding this inclusivity, there were limits. There *are* limits. Integral to the order and harmony of the created universe are laws—imposed limits on activity and established consequences associated with behavior. Life is a dynamic gift flowing from God to his creatures and it is contingent upon continual obedience to the laws of His government. Inclusive: the word is, "Obey and live..."[2] but exclusive: adding "but cursed be he that confirmeth not the words of this law to do them."[3]

> "The law of love being the foundation of the government of God, the happiness of all intelligent beings depended upon their perfect accord with its great principles of righteousness. God desires from all His creatures the service of love—service that springs from an appreciation of His character. He takes no pleasure in a forced obedience; and to all He grants freedom of will, that they may render Him voluntary service."[4]

When there is individuality, diversity, and liberty it is necessary for there to be also an arrangement for order and harmony. Every municipality recognizes the hazards of unmanaged traffic. So it is with the government of God. There is order and rank; there are laws and consequences.

Lucifer held a high position in the authority of heaven.[5] He was educated and disciplined in the heavenly courts.[6] He was from the highest order of angels[7] and first among all the angelic host.[8] The other angels[9] honored him and delighted to execute his commands.

> "So long as all created beings acknowledged the allegiance of love, there was perfect harmony throughout the universe of God. It was the joy of the heavenly host to fulfill the purpose of their Creator. They delighted in reflecting His glory and showing forth His praise. And while love to God was supreme, love for one another was confiding and unselfish. There was no note of discord to mar the celestial harmonies."[10]

---

1 Ezekiel 28:14.

2 Deuteronomy 4:1.

3 Deuteronomy 27:26; See Ellen G. White, *Patriarchs and Prophets*, p. 372.

4 Ellen G. White, *Patriarchs and Prophets*, p. 34.

5 Ellen G. White, *The Story of Redemption*, p. 29.

6 Ellen G. White, *Testimonies for the Church, vol. 5* p. 306.

7 Ellen G. White, *Spiritual Gifts*, book 3, p. 36.

8 Ellen G. White, *Selected Messages, book 1,* p. 341.

9 Ellen G. White, *The Story of Redemption*, p. 14.

10 Ellen G. White, *Patriarchs and Prophets*, p. 35.

Lucifer was the one who would give the first note of praise when the heavenly choir poured forth their songs of love and worship to God.[11]

—An Exclusivity in Divinity

Eventually, Lucifer perverted the freedom that God granted.[12] Though he was highest in power and glory among the created inhabitants of heaven—the "son of the morning"—and first of the covering cherubs, holy and undefiled: gradually he came to indulge self, and aspired to power that was the prerogative of God alone.[12] He said, "I will exalt my throne above the stars of God... I will be like the Most High."[13]

By elevating Lucifer to a position of so great honor and authority that he stood at the throne and in the very presence of the Almighty—God showed His generous *inclusivity* in government. But concerning the Godhead and the prerogatives of divinity there must be *exclusivity*.

> "The LORD, He is God; there is none else beside Him."[14]

It has to do with divine attributes that just simply *are* or *are not*—attributes that cannot be assigned or transferred. It is a matter of definition—not of words merely, nor of conferring of title or authority—but of the actual nature and quality of real persons with real substance. God *is* God, and there *is* no other. God *is* God—not by election or title, not by assignment, nor gift, not creation, nor evolution. He *is*. Period.

One does not *become* God. It is not possible for any finite created being to be (or to become) equal to the infinite Creator. In the arena of time alone, this limitation is clear. Finite beings (those with a definite starting point) can never be infinite in relation to time.

—Aspiring to be God

Near the beginning of the great conflict,

> "Lucifer began to insinuate doubts concerning the law that governed heavenly beings, intimating that though law might be necessary for the inhabitants of the worlds, angels, being more exalted, needed no such restraint, for their own wisdom was a sufficient guide. They were not beings that could bring dishonor to God; all their thoughts were holy; it was no more possible for them than for God to err."[15]

---

[11] Ellen G. White, *The Story of Redemption*, p. 25.

[12] Ellen G. White, *Patriarchs and Prophets*, p. 35.

[13] Isaiah 14:13-14.

[14] Deuteronomy 4:35.

[15] Ellen G. White, *Patriarchs and Prophets*, p. 37.

Satan began to blur the distinction between Creator and creature. "He gloried in his brightness and exaltation and aspired to be equal with God."[16] But he was *not* equal to God. Nor *could* he be. Oh, he was glorious to be sure—and exalted—but the glory, wisdom, and great honor attributed to him were not his own. "All his glory was from God, [but] this mighty angel came to regard it as pertaining to himself."[17]

This is the fundamental issue: Righteousness, wisdom, glory, power, honor, and life *belong* to God alone. He alone possesses them natively. Some other did not supply these to Him. He does not contrive them or assemble them from outside parts, processes, or energies. In Him they originate. He does not borrow them. They are not derived from other sources. It is impossible that any creature could be equal to God in this respect—nor even the entire collective universe.

The Great Creator assigns attributes to His creatures as it suits Him—because all that they are has to come from Him. He is the source. The infinite *quality* and *quantity* of life, wisdom, and righteousness, the eternal nature going infinitely forward and backward, cannot be transferred to a finite creature. At a point in time, the created is defined and assembled at the will of, through the activity of, and from the stuff of the Almighty. Life, righteousness, and wisdom cannot be *native* to the creature since Someone else created him or her—they come from a singular external source. Life, righteousness, and wisdom are but gifts from God.

Ellen White refers to the creature as a reflector of God's glory. This understanding better tells the truth of the matter with Lucifer. He was the covering cherub who dwelt in the throne-room of the Almighty. God designed him for greater efficiency in reflecting His glory; and standing as he did continually in the presence of limitless glory, his ability to reflect that glory would naturally exceed that of other angels. Like a solar battery ever positioned to capture the direct rays of sunlight, his charge would always be strong.

But Lucifer supposed that glory and righteousness were his own. Such thinking corrupted his wisdom. He passed this supposition on to his angel peers; and then to Eve in the garden. It is upon this fundamental issue that the great controversy hangs; and it is on this issue the final battle will be waged.

---

[16] Ibid.

[17] Ellen G. White, *Patriarchs and Prophets*, p. 35.

Can the creature become God? Can life exist in isolation or independent of obedience to the Life-Giver? If the *created* choose another god, will the *Creator* abandon His sovereign claim and abdicate His throne? If "the spirits of devils" coming from the mouths of the dragon, the beast, and the false prophet, use miracle-working power to rally the "kings of the earth and of the whole world"[18] in league to battle against the great day of God Almighty, will God really execute the sentence against the violators of His law?[19]

—In the God Class

While we have been sleeping, the world has been preparing for just such a proposition. World religions and governments are planning the philosophical mold for a united world movement, embracing the deification of humanity and a world kingdom capable of operating entirely under the authority of the will of man—and contrary to the laws of God.

Pentecostal televangelist, Kenneth Copeland has done his part to herald in such an idea by saying,

> "Man was created in the God class... We are a class of gods... God Himself spawned us from His innermost being... When I read in the Bible where He says, 'I am,' I just smile and say, 'I am too.'"[20]

The *Catholic Catechism* does its part too:

> "The Son of God became man so that we might become God. The only begotten Son of God, wanting to make us sharers in His divinity... assumed our nature, so that He might make men gods."[21]

Author and researcher, Caryl Matrisciana, warns us that,

> "the whole point of unifying spiritually is to globalize a sort of world religion, to have the idea that through a united mind—through a like-minded mind-consciousness—man can evolve to god-consciousness."[22]

—Analyzing the First Battle

Let's take a careful look at the opening battle of the great controversy so we might adequately understand the closing battle. If God's people are to play a role in the final scenes, Satan will determine to cloud our understanding of the issues and block our access to the Source of

---

[18] Revelation 16:14.

[19] See *Appendix B* for a detailed treatment of the issue of God destroying the wicket.

[20] Christian J. Pinto, *Megiddo II, The New Age*, (Adullam Films, 2005), film clip.

[21] *St. Athanasius & St. Thomas Aquinas*, par. 460, p. 116, (The Wanderer Press, 1994).

[22] Christian J. Pinto, *Megiddo II, The New Age*, (Adullam Films, 2005), video Interview with Caryl Matrisciana, author of *Gods of the New Age*.

strength. Vital to our success will be our careful attention to the issues concerning the *inclusivity* and *exclusivity* of the Godhead.

We need to understand the issues in the opposing claims of God and Satan about the validity of including Christ as divine but excluding Lucifer. These issues will help us interpret the language and symbolism of God's answers. God's entire presentation about Himself to His creatures speaks to the lie that Satan introduced about the exclusivity and inclusivity of *being* God.

We start at the rebellion in heaven that occurred just before the creation of earth. God has revealed fascinating details concerning that war and the arrangement of things back then. Let's rebuild the story from ages past.

Angels are the inhabitants of heaven. They exist because of the creative acts of God. God also lives there. Order and rank illustrates harmony among the angels. Lucifer is highest in rank. Ezekiel describes Lucifer as sealing "up the sum, full of wisdom, and perfect in beauty."[23] Every precious stone was his covering; and the workmanship of his tabrets and pipes were prepared in him by the Creator.

Lucifer "was upon the holy mountain of God"[24] and walked "up and down in the midst of the stones of fire."[25] It was God who put Lucifer there. He was the covering cherub. And he "was perfect in all [his] ways from the day that [he was] created, till iniquity was found in [him]."[26]

God's throne is high and lifted up; and Lucifer stood before this throne—in the presence of Almighty God, and before these burning coals of fire—or in the midst of the stones of fire. When holy angels came before the throne of God, they covered their faces[27] and looked down.[28] They did not directly gaze into God's glory. Besides looking down and using their wings to shield themselves from the brightness of God, Lucifer shielded them—as the "anointed cherub that covereth"[29] With wings outstretched, He stood between them and the Almighty.

[23] Ezekiel 28:13.

[24] Ezekiel 28:14.

[25] Ezekiel 28:14.

[26] Ezekiel 28:15.

[27] Ellen G. White, *Patriarchs and Prophets*, p. 252.

[28] Ibid., pp. 348-349.

[29] Ezekiel 28:14.

—The Standard of Deity

What we see here are issues of identity. This arraignment speaks to individuality and community. The glory that God manifests at the place of His throne displays the fullness of His identity—the realities of infinite energy on three scales.

We've noticed them before[30]—*physical* energy (the unlimited brightness and power of His omnipotence); *intellectual* energy (the all-knowingness of His omniscience); and *spiritual* energy (the unswerving justice and great mercy of His righteousness).[31] In the throne room, the glory of Almighty God is on display to the universe. He dwells there, the *standard of deity* at full scale—infinite power, infinite knowledge, and inimitable righteousness. That standard *is* God—a living, personal, physical Being—and He presents it there at the place of His thrown without attenuation. He is the unmeasurable expression of divinity.

The universe depends upon God's infinite three-fold energy as a source for existence (He is the source of life itself)—but it also depends upon it for security. Community depends upon God's identity. The power of the Almighty must be on full display. Even though finite beings cannot absorb or measure the fullness of infinite glory (they cannot even bear to look directly into it)—still, the display of it imposes a quality of physical, intellectual and spiritual authority they cannot ignore. The perpetual manifestation of the identity of the Creator secures the liberty, individuality, and community of His creatures.

The throne-room presents a dichotomy. It provides a perpetual manifestation to creation while simultaneously shielding creatures from it. When God said, "let them make me a sanctuary, that I may dwell among them,"[32] He instructed Moses to have that earthly sanctuary built according to the pattern in heaven.[33] The tabernacle served as a mechanism to bring God's physical presence into the camp of Israel. But because His presence is a consuming fire,[34] He kept His glory behind the veil. The same principle is at work in the throne-room of heaven—only on a different scale. Holy angels can tolerate far more of God's glory than we humans damaged by sin, but still they use an arrangement of covered faces and covering cherubs to veil *them-finite* from infinite glory.

---

[30] See Chapter One, *A Tale of Three Mountains.*

[31] See Exodus 34:6-7 concerning God's justice and mercy.

[32] Exodus 25:8.

[33] Hebrews 8:5.

[34] Deuteronomy 4:24, Hebrews 12:29.

—Michael the Archangel

Let's get back to rebuilding the story from ages past. Yes, God created Lucifer perfect in all his ways. Yes, Lucifer—with his tabrets and his pipes—led the angel choir. Yes, Lucifer was the highest in rank and authority of all the angelic host. And yes, Lucifer was the angel that stood in the presence of God providing shade to visitors there. Yet there was another who stood in the presence of God.

Michael stood at God's right hand. Apparently, His identity was not altogether clear to the angels. They knew Him as the Archangel who seemed to be like Lucifer in rank and function—at least until that day when God and Michael met in private counsel together. This counsel concerned the creation of a new world and of man. Michael was there, but Lucifer was not.

From a fallen-human point-of-view it seems natural for this to have presented a problem to Lucifer; but from the vantage point of perfection the only problem was in Lucifer's reaction. It was *not* natural. It was *possible*, but not natural. God had imprinted the stamp of His own character—the imprint of His holy law—upon the hearts and minds of all His creatures. The very wiring of the soul predetermined that the synaptic path-of-least-resistance would put God first, and esteem others to be of equal value to one's self. Selfish reactions were contrary to inclination and reason.

—Indulging a Strange Infatuation

Self never sought the first place. Selfishness was incompatible with the impulse of the soul. Rank and authority existed as roles of service for the good of others—wholly devoid of selfish motivation. Violating this natural and impulsive moral code could only occur by the persistent indulgence of an uncomfortable and strange infatuation. Lucifer indulged that strange infatuation; and because he did, he shattered Paradise. Knowing of Lucifer's struggle—and what was about to happen—God called an assembly of the whole heavenly host.

—The Heavenly Assembly

It was time for God to take the next step in revealing the Godhead:

> "The King of the universe summoned the heavenly host before Him, that in their presence He might set forth the true position of His Son and show the relation He sustained to all created beings. *The Son of God shared the Father's throne, and the glory of the eternal, self-existent One*

> *encircled them both.* About the throne gathered the holy angels, a vast unnumbered throng—'ten thousand times ten thousand, and thousands of thousands',[35] the most exalted angels, as ministers and subjects, rejoicing *in the light that fell upon* them from the presence of Deity. Before the assembled inhabitants of heaven the King declared that none but Christ, the only begotten of God, could fully enter into His purposes, and to Him it was committed to execute the mighty counsels of His will. The Son of God had wrought the Father's will in the creation of all the hosts of heaven; and to Him, as well as to God, their homage and allegiance were due. Christ was still to exercise divine power, in the creation of the earth and its inhabitants. But in all this He would not seek power or exaltation for Himself contrary to God's plan, but would exalt the Father's glory and execute His purposes of beneficence and love.
>
> "The angels joyfully acknowledged the supremacy of Christ, and prostrating themselves before Him, poured out their love and adoration."[36]

Let's first notice the natural reaction of the holy angels. The news was joyful to them. Second, let's notice that the revelation concerning Christ's true position was *light* for them—"they rejoiced in the *light* that fell upon them from the presence of Deity." Third, notice that while the *light* was a new revelation, Christ's *position* was not new—He had shared the throne of God even before the creation of angels. "There had been no change in the position or authority of Christ."[37]

Let's look closely at one sentence in the quotation above—"The Son of God shared the Father's throne, and the glory of the eternal, self-existent One encircled them both." This single sentence expresses six concepts:

- The Father's throne is a shared throne.
- Those who share the throne have a Father-Son relationship.
- Their glory is shared ("the *glory...* encircled them both").
- Their eternality is shared ("the glory of the *eternal...* encircled them both").
- Their self-existence is shared ("the glory... of the *self-existent* One encircled them both").
- Although they are two, they are called the "*self-existent One.*"

—The Relationship & The Throne

Some people read this sentence differently than we present it here. They say that it refers to the throne as belonging to the Father alone—that the Father grants the Son's presence there. They also say that the

---

[35] (Revelation 5:11).

[36] Ellen G. White, *Patriarchs and Prophets*, p. 36, emphasis added

[37] Ibid., p. 38.

glory is the Father's—it is only because the Father *grants* it to the Son, that it encircles them both. To clarify these points, we will examine this throne and this relationship. Consider the words of the Psalmist,

> "Thy throne, O God *(Elohim)*, is forever and ever: the scepter of thy kingdom is a right scepter. Thou lovest righteousness, and hatest wickedness: therefore God *(Elohim)*, thy God *(Elohim)*, hath anointed Thee with the oil of gladness above thy fellows."[38]

The writer of the book of Hebrews refers to this verse in his first chapter. He clarifies who is talking to whom,

> "But unto the Son He saith, Thy throne, O God, is forever and ever... therefore God, even Thy God, hath anointed Thee with the oil of gladness above thy fellows."[39]

Here the Father is talking to the Son and saying to Him, "Thy throne O God, is forever and ever." In the original Hebrew language we find that the "forever and ever" comes from two words, *olam* and *ad*. "Olam" means *long duration in antiquity and in the future*.[40] "Ad" means continually, eternal, perpetual; in both past and future.[41]

Since human language began in Eden, it is no surprise that early language incorporates rich meanings and nuances into words—meanings that embrace the eternality of God. The Hebrew language is like that. When the Bible speaks of God in terms of forever and ever, the Hebrew understanding explicitly emphasizes existence extending perpetually in both directions of time.

Also notice the two-way reference to God—the Father calls the Son "God"; and though it is the Father speaking, He tells how the Son also considers Him to be "God." In this verse, the Father refers to the throne as belonging to the Son. This does not imply it does not also belong the Father—but it certainly identifies positive ownership by the Son—an ownership that the verse explicitly states extends perpetually in both directions of time. To the Son, the Father says, 'Thy throne, O God, is from everlasting to everlasting.'

---

[38] Psalms 45:6-7.

[39] Hebrews 1:9.

[40] Strongs Concordance, *Hebrew #5769*; (http://biblehub.com/hebrew/5769.htm). Accessed 3/10/2019.

[41] Strongs Concordance, *Hebrew #5703*; (http://biblehub.com/hebrew/5703.htm). Accessed 3/10/2019.

—The Ineffable Name

When talking to the Jews, "Jesus said unto them, Verily, verily, I say unto you, Before Abraham was, I am."[42] The Hebrew proper name for God is YHWH (there are no vowels in the Hebrew alphabet). Scholars widely propose that the name YHWH is a verb form derived from the biblical Hebrew triconsonantal root (3 consonants) h-y-h "to be", which has h-w-h as a variant form. With the third-person masculine prefix y- it is written as a proper name YHWH meaning "I am that I am."[43]

Jesus was calling Himself the I Am; and claiming to be the God of the Old Testament. But consistent with the meaning of His Old Testament name we can see that He was also claiming to be the *self-existent One*—for YHWH is the source of all *being*, having *being* inherent in Himself. YHWH is known to the Hebrews as the *ineffable name* or *unutterable name*—"being utter transcendence beyond all predication or even the attributes of language. The *I Am* is beyond all definite description."[44]

> "The name of God, given to Moses to express the idea of the eternal presence, had been claimed as His own by this Galilean Rabbi. He had announced Himself to be the self-existent One, He who had been promised to Israel, 'whose goings forth have been from old, from the days of eternity.' Micah 5:2. margin."[45]

According to Scripture, both the Father and the Son confirm the throne has ever belonged to the Son—the eternal, self-existent One.

—The Relationship

The apostle John speaks of the relationship within the deity. He says, "For there are three that bear record in heaven, the Father, the Word, and the Holy Ghost: *These three are one.*"[46] Just before His ascension, Christ instructed the disciples to baptize "in the name of the Father, and of the Son, and of the Holy Ghost."[47] When Jesus was telling the disciples about the many mansions for them in His Father's house—and how He would go to prepare a place for them, He said that He was "the way, the truth and the life: no man cometh unto the Father, but by [Him]."[48]

---

[42] John 5:58.
[43] See Exodus 3:14.
[44] http://www.hebrew4christians.com/Names_of_G-d/YHVH/yhvh.html.
[45] Ellen G. White, *The Desire of Ages*, pp. 569-570.
[46] 1 John 5:7.
[47] Matthew 28:19.
[48] John 14:6.

Philip asked Jesus to show them the Father. Jesus said if they had seen Him, they had seen the Father.[49] Jesus then said He would "pray the Father, and He shall give [them] another Comforter, that He may abide with [them] forever; even the Spirit of truth."[50] It is clear enough from these verses that there are *three* in heaven who exist in close relationship to each other—and who are God.

Scripture refers to each One as God:
• The Father—"God our Father"[51]
• The Son—"The Word was God"[52]
• The Holy Spirit—"[you have] lied to the Holy Ghost... [not] unto men, but unto God"[53]

Scripture also states that each is eternal:
• The Father—"From everlasting to everlasting , thou art God."[54]
• The Son—"Whose goings forth have been from old, from everlasting"[55]
• The Holy Spirit—"Eternal Spirit."[56]

The Bible says that each One is all-knowing:
• The Father—"God... knoweth all things"[57]
• The Son—"Lord, thou knowest all things"[58]
• The Holy Spirit—"The Spirit searcheth all things, even the deep things of God."[59]

And each One gives life:
• The Father—"Raiseth up the dead and quickeneth them"[60]
• The Son—"Even so the Son quickeneth whom He will"[61]
• The Holy Spirit—"The Spirit giveth life."[62]

---

[49] John 14:9.
[50] John 14:16-17.
[51] Philippians 1:2.
[52] John 1:1.
[53] Acts 5:3-4.
[54] Psalms 90:2.
[55] Micah 5:2.
[56] Hebrews 9:14.
[57] 1 John 3:20.
[58] John 21:17.
[59] 1 Corinthians 2:10.
[60] 1 John 5:21.
[61] 2 John 5:21.
[62] 2 Corinthians 3:6; see 3:3, 3:8, 3:18.

The New Testament says of Christ, "In Him dwelleth all the fullness of the Godhead bodily."[63] We also know that "In Christ is life, original, unborrowed, and underived."[64] We know that "The Lord Jesus Christ, the divine Son of God, existed from eternity, a distinct person, yet one with the Father."[65] "He assures us that there never was a time when He was not in close fellowship with the eternal God."[66] "From all eternity Christ was united with the Father."[67] "Christ was God essentially, and in the highest sense. He was with God from all eternity, God over all, blessed forevermore."[68]

"The Comforter that Christ promised to send after He ascended to heaven, is the Spirit in all the fullness of the Godhead."[69] "The Holy Spirit has a personality, else He could not bear witness to our spirits and with our spirits that we are the children of God. He must also be a divine person, else He could not search out the secrets which lie hidden in the mind of God."[70] "Sin could be resisted and overcome only through the mighty agency of the Third Person of the Godhead, who would come with no modified energy, but in the fullness of divine power."[71]

—Godhead Fullness

We refer to these Three collectively as the Godhead. "The Godhead was stirred with pity for the race, and the Father, the Son, and the Holy Spirit gave themselves to the working out of the plan of redemption."[72]

> "The Father is all the fullness of the Godhead bodily, and is invisible to mortal sight. The Son is all the fullness of the Godhead manifested. The Word of God declares Him to be 'the express image of His person.' ...Here is shown the personality of the Father. The Comforter that Christ promised to send after He ascended to heaven, is the Spirit in all the fullness of the Godhead, making manifest the power of divine grace to all who receive and believe in Christ as a personal Savior. There are three living persons of the heavenly trio; in the name of these three great powers—the Father, the Son, and the Holy Spirit—those who receive Christ by living faith are baptized, and these powers will co-operate with the

[63] Colossians 2:9.
[64] Ellen G. White, *The Desire of Ages*, p. 530.
[65] Ellen G. White, *The Review and Herald*, April 5, 1906.
[66] Ellen G. White, The Signs of the Times, August 29, 1900.
[67] Ellen G. White, *Selected Messages*, book 1, p. 228.
[68] Ellen G. White, *The Review and Herald*, April 5, 1906.
[69] Ellen G. White, *Evangelism*, p. 615.
[70] Ibid., pp. 616-617.
[71] Ellen G. White, *The Desire of Ages*, p. 671.
[72] Ellen G. White, *Christ's Object Lessons*, p. 222.

> obedient subjects of heaven in their efforts to live the new life in Christ."[73]

We see from all this that there are three. When John said that there were three in heaven, he also said they were one. The Old Testament Scripture says there is only one God.[74]

—Three or One?

So which is it? Are there three? Or is there one? The Bible answers this question precisely:

> "Hear, O Israel: The LORD our God is one LORD."[75]

Well—it answers it precisely in the *Hebrew* language; unfortunately the English does not adequately convey the full message. The English uses the word "LORD" (all caps in the King James version) for the Hebrew word YHWH. YHWH (we say Yahweh or Jehovah) is the singular masculine proper name—identifying God as the self-existent Source of all being—the One having *being* inherent in Himself. There is another word used in this verse to refer to Deity. The English uses the word "God" for the Hebrew word Elohim. Elohim is the plural form of the noun El or Eloah used to designate *sovereign authority*, *creatorship over all creation*, *supreme deity*, and *Godhood*.

The verse declares that "Yahweh our Elohim is one Yahweh." The English uses the word "one" for the Hebrew word *echad*. Echad comes from the verb meaning to unify; it means "as one", "alike", "altogether". Do not confuse this with *yahad* used to indicate one in a singular sense referring to a single individual or a certain person.

So in Hebrew the meaning is clear. It says, "Yahweh our Gods is as one Yahweh." It is an unusual blending of singular and plural denoting the inclusivity and exclusivity of the Godhead. It gives His proper name, (YHWH) by a word that is singular; but then describes Him as the sovereign and supreme deity (Elohim) by a word that is plural. And then it explains: Jehovah (YHWH) is singular-plural because He is *echad*—united as one and together in thought and purpose.

Another verse in Deuteronomy further emphasizes the exclusivity of their singularity in saying:

---

73 Ellen G. White, *Special Testimonies, Series B*, no. 7, 62-63.

74 Deuteronomy 4:35.

75 Deuteronomy 6:4.

> "YHWH (singular), He (singular) is Elohim (plural); there is none else beside Him (singular)."[76]

This naming construct is in perfect harmony with John's declaration: God is inclusive of the "three that bear record in heaven, the Father, the Word, and the Holy Ghost," but exclusive in that God is one God—there being no others. To illustrate how the Old-Testament Bible uses these words, let's compare some verses. Jeremiah says,

> "Behold the days come, saith the LORD (YHWH), that I will raise unto David a righteous Branch, and a King shall reign and prosper, and shall execute judgment and justice in the earth. In his days Judah shall be saved, and Israel shall dwell safely; and this is his name whereby he shall be called, THE LORD (YHWH) OUR RIGHTEOUSNESS."[77]

Here Jeremiah refers to both He who will raise unto David a righteous Branch (first person) and He who He raises as that Branch (second person). He calls them both the same proper name—YHWH. This is like the verse we looked at in Hebrews 1 (quoted from Psalms 45), where the First Person is calling the Second Person Elohim, and then saying that to the Second Person, He, (the First Person) is also Elohim.

—Us

The Old-Testament often uses Yahweh (or Jehovah) in connection with Elohim. In English this appears as "the LORD God" or "the LORD our God." As we have said, Yahweh is the proper name (singular) and Elohim is a plural form of the generic noun for deity. The early chapters of Genesis sometimes use Elohim by itself as a proper name. But even then, it uses Elohim instead of the singular forms El or Eloah; and in Genesis, Elohim speaks of Himself as "Us" and "Our."

In Genesis, Elohim says,

> "Let us make man in our image, after our likeness."[78]
> "Behold, the man has become like one of us..."[79]

Later, at the story of the tower of Babel, Yahweh (YHWH) is the proper name for God. Here we see the same thing even though the name is now in singular form—still the word "*us*" is used.

> "And (YHWH) came down to see the city and the tower... And (YHWH) said, Behold the people are one... Go to, let us go down, and there

[76] Deuteronomy 4:35.
[77] Jeremiah 23:5-6.
[78] Genesis 1:26.
[79] Genesis 3:22.

> confound their language, that they may not understand one another's speech. So (YHWH) scattered them abroad from thence upon the face of the earth; and they left off to build the city."[80]

—One

We have already noted that in the Hebrew language there are two words that show up in English as meaning "one": yahad and echad. Yahad is from the verb meaning "to be" and is used to refer to a single individual—a certain person, whosoever, or one. Echad (on the other hand) is from the verb meaning "to unify" and is used to refer to more than one acting together in unison as though they were one person. Sometimes it is used to refer to a single unit—but as one of several or as one of many.

Again, at the scene of Babel, Yahweh said, "Behold, the people are *echad*..."[81] Notice that God interferes with their *united* purpose to build the city and tower by confounding their language to bring *disunity* and division.

After Israel heard the law declared from Sinai, the Bible says,

> "All the people answered with *echad* voice, and said, All the words which [YHWH) hath said, we will do."[82]

At the first marriage, Elohim said,

> "Therefore shall a man leave his father and mother, and shall cleave unto his wife, and they shall be *echad* flesh."[83]

So we see that the Scriptures are careful to treat God as being more than one person, but also careful to limit divinity to only those specific divine persons who are (and always have been) *Echad*.

—Grasping the Inconceivable?

To our limited minds, the concept of being singular and plural at the same time is difficult to grasp. Because our own experiences are so limited, it is even more difficult for us to grasp the nature of the divine relationships within the Godhead. It is not possible for the finite to define the infinite—so how can we understand or explain it?

God does not keep us completely in the dark about this, though. In order for us to have some ability to relate to Him, He gives us certain

---

[80] Genesis 11:5-8.

[81] Genesis 11:6.

[82] Exodus 24:3. The Hebrew word "echad" is written here in place of the English word "one" for clarity. Emphasis added.

[83] Genesis 2:24. The Hebrew word "echad" is written here in place of the English word "one" for clarity. Emphasis added.

illustrations useful to our understanding—but we accept that even these illustrations and types are shadowy and limited. They help us *relate* to God; but they are incapable of *defining* God. Remember how the Hebrews considered God's name to be *unutterable* because He *is* beyond the attributes of language. So He also transcends the types and symbols.

—One Flesh

The pre-fall marriage relationship gives us a profound glimpse of how two can be *echad* flesh. As profound as it is, it only suggests the nature of God's unity. Notice three significant elements:

1. The Bible says—

> "God created man in his own image, in the image of God created He him; male and female created he them."[84]

This verse doesn't suggest that there are gender distinctions within the Godhead—there is no support for such a conclusion in Scripture or Spirit of Prophecy. But the human marriage relationship speaks to the divine—even though it cannot fully or perfectly define it.

Marriage illustrates a quality and intensity of *echad* that exceeds every other human relationship. Don't confuse or entangle the physical mechanisms of divine creativity with the physical mechanisms of human procreativity, but both suggest an intimate relationship—an intense knowing of each other—that expresses itself in shared acts of creation. In this way marriage speaks to the inclusivity within the Godhead.

2. The Bible says—

> "Therefore shall a man leave his father and mother, and shall cleave unto his wife: and they shall be [echad] flesh."[85]

Here we see marriage also speaks to the exclusivity of the Godhead. Their relationship is unique and isolated. Marriage is a relationship that distinguishes itself from all other relationships—even the relationships formed between parent and child. Just as the relationship between a pro-creative couple operates on a different plane than the relationships between parents and their children, so the relationship within the creative Godhead operates on a different plane than do the relationships

---

[84] Genesis 1:27.

[85] Genesis 2:24, emphasis added.

between the Creator and the creature. In the context of the great controversy this is an important distinction—one that Lucifer refuses to accept.

3. The Bible says—

> "And the LORD God caused a deep sleep to fall upon Adam, and he slept: and he took one of his ribs, and closed up the flesh instead thereof; and the rib, which the LORD God had taken from man, made he a woman, and brought her unto the man. And Adam said, This is now bone of my bone, and flesh of my flesh: she shall be called woman, because she was taken out of man."[86]

This suggests another important consideration in the context of the great controversy. There is more to the basis for inclusivity within the Godhead than the external relationships between them. There is an organic basis. God could have created Adam and Eve the same way He created the other animals—spoken into existence in swarms (as with the fishes) or in pairs (as with the birds and beasts). Since Adam and Eve would have been male and female—the only two of their kind—they would have formed a close and intimate relationship with each other. But here we see God deliberately forming Eve from Adam's rib. Organically they are even *closer* than kind. They are actually and literally echad flesh *and* yahad flesh. Here things get interesting.

Eve was formed from Adams rib—just his rib. It obvious enough, that she was not an exact copy of Adam—physically, mentally or spiritually. Nor was she related to Adam—say, a cousin, or sister, or even as a daughter. She was to be a helper *corresponding* to him[87]—

> "one who was fitted to be his companion, and who could be one with him in love and sympathy. Eve was created from a rib taken from the side of Adam, signifying that she was not to control him as the head, nor be trampled under his feet, as his inferior, but to stand by his side as an equal, to be loved and protected by him."[88]

This picture illustrates the Godhead as having an interrelated cohesiveness among different parts. We see individuality, personality and uniqueness blended together in *organic* oneness incorporating God's *physical, mental,* and *spiritual* attributes. We see distinct persons with distinct personalities, who are the express image of each other—existing in such harmony that they must be seen and described as being *One*.

---

[86] Genesis 2:21-23.

[87] Genesis 2:18.

[88] Ellen G. White, *Patriarchs and Prophets*, p. 46.

They share a uniqueness that separates them from all other entities. Their relationship is more than shared experience with each other—for in each of them is the *fullness* of the Godhead; in each is *eternity* stretching without end backwards and forwards; in each is *life*—original, unborrowed, and underived. Each is the *self-existent Source* of all being—each having *being* inherent in Himself. In each is infinite *power*—physical, intellectual, and spiritual. These are unique characteristics they share with none but themselves—and contribute to define them individually and collectively.

Such are the qualities and quantities of infinity, that they *must* overlap the others—not in part only—but in the whole. Each is God organically. Organically, each is the *fullness* of God. They are organically One. Yet they are Three—Each possessing individual being and personality.

Our understanding of God is a picture built from language, illustrations, experiences, and types that fall very short of depicting the divine reality. Still it is fascinating to see how the types and shadows convey much more than they are themselves.

Adam and Eve and marriage portray a brilliance of color and hue in the portrait of God that is clearer and brighter and loftier than what Adam and Eve and marriage say about themselves. The Godhead is that great and original relationship of which marriage (even in its prelapsarian state) is a dim reflection. Let's not get the cart before horse—God defines marriage, marriage does not define God.

—An Only Son

When God created marriage, He gave us a shadowy illustration to help us see God. Another shadowy type is that of father and son. Again we find a human relationship helping us to relate to a divine relationship; and again that human relationship is only a shadowy illustration we cannot use to limit or completely define the full nature of divinity.

Like marriage, heredity speaks to a relationship that is both inclusive and exclusive. It points to an *inclusive* connection that is organic and also built upon shared experiences. It tells of shared attributes—physical, mental, and spiritual—written at the DNA level. It illustrates an *exclusive* relationship as well—one defined by boundaries that are nonnegotiable: a DNA-level relationship that one either has the DNA to belong to, or does not.

At Christ's baptism, there was a voice from heaven not heard on earth since the fall.[89] It was the voice of the Father declaring of Jesus: "This is my beloved Son, in whom I am well pleased."[90]

Hebrews 1 emphasizes the Father/Son relationship in some detail, but for now we will look at one verse in particular—

> "For unto which of the angels saith he at any time, Thou art my Son, this day have I begotten thee? And again, I will be to him a Father, and He shall be to me a Son."[91]

Jesus said, "For God so loved the world that he gave his only begotten Son."[92] It seems clear enough that Scripture portrays the relationship between the First and Second persons of the Godhead in terms of father and son. What are we to make of this Scriptural portrayal of the relationship between the First and Second persons of the Godhead? Any understanding will need to take into consideration two important things:

1. The human understanding and experience of fathers and sons (finite) cannot fully or even accurately define the divine (infinite). From the human perspective it has to be a symbolic conceptual device. It helps us relate in certain aspects and to certain degrees—but is incapable of completely defining the fullness of the divine relationship.

2. Clear and certain revelation must inform us about the Father/Son typology. When the earthly example is inconsistent with specific attributes of the heavenly Trio as defined by revelation, we have to acknowledge that the earthly example has limits. This is the case when revelation tells us that:

—"Christ [is] God essentially, and in the highest sense,"
—Christ is the great "I Am,"
—Christ is the "self-existent One";
—Christ was "with God from all eternity,"
—Christ's "goings forth have been from old, from everlasting";
—in Christ is "life, original, unborrowed, and underived";
—"the Lord Jesus Christ, the divine Son of God, existed from eternity, a distinct person, yet one with the Father."

These are direct statements from revelation that have to place limitations upon the father/son typology relating to the Godhead. These

[89] Ellen G. White, *The Desire of Ages*, p. 116.
[90] Matthew 3:17.
[91] Hebrews 1:5.
[92] John 3:16.

statements clarify that the father/son designation (when applied to God) is not intended to convey a limit to Christ's authority, eternality, and originality. Scripture *directly declares* that in these attributes, the details of God the Father and God the Son are incongruous with certain *assumptions* analogous to human fathers and sons—where the authority, eternality, and originality of earthly sons are always limited. So it is that the type must bend in favor of direct revelation because we already know that any type is incapable of painting the perfect picture of God.

—Relating the First Battle

The context of God's first use of the type was in a presentation to created angel-beings at the early stages of Lucifer's rebellion. In that context the purpose of the father/son designation was to establish the fact of Christ's *inclusivity* in Godhead authority, eternality, and originality.

By clarifying the identity of Christ, the Father established the boundaries of *inclusivity* and *exclusivity*. This He did to secure the angels (as much as possible) from being damaged by the ensuing rebellion. The Father called together the assembly of angels so He could "set forth the true position of His Son and show the relation He sustained to all created beings."

> "He who would have the will of all His creatures free, left none unguarded to the bewildering sophistry by which rebellion would seek to justify itself. Before the great contest should open, all were to have a clear presentation of His will, whose wisdom and goodness were the spring of all their joy."[93]

This light presented to the angels concerned the *inclusivity* and *exclusivity* of the Godhead. The ensuing controversy between the *condescending* Michael and *ambitious* Lucifer—when "the morning stars sang together, and all the sons of God shouted for joy."[94]—made it necessary for the definitive *Standard of Divinity* to differentiate between the *Bright Morning Star*[95] and the "Shining One, Son of the Dawn."[96]

The Father drew a distinguishing line between creature (the many sons of God) and the Creator (the only begotten Son of God). The

---

[93] Ellen G. White, *Patriarchs and Prophets*, p. 36.

[94] Job 38:7.

[95] Revelation 22:16.

[96] Isaiah 14:12, literal.

occasion identified who was *organically* included, and who were *organically* excluded from the ranks of divinity.

—Of the Son and of Sons

It is along this order of understanding that we see a line of distinction drawn in Scripture concerning Christ and His people. John declares that "as many as receive [Christ], to them gives He the power to become the sons of God."[97] But John is also very clear to distinguish them from Christ Himself who is the "Word [that] was made flesh, and dwelt among us... the only begotten of the Father."[98] It is the "only begotten" alone—that John declares tó be the Word that was with God, the Word that [is] God.[99]

This is how we should understand Paul back in the first chapter of Hebrews. He tells us that God speaks to us in these last days by His Son, (saying specifically) He—

> "whom He hath appointed heir of all things, by whom also He made the worlds; who being the brightness of His glory, and the express image of His person, and upholding all things by the word of His power, when He had by Himself purged our sins, sat down on the right hand of the Majesty on high."[100]

So, Paul is using the father/son designation to show that the divine inclusivity embraces Christ as organically God—a designation from which Paul deliberately excludes the angels.101 At the same time he establishes that this father/son designation is not to confuse the eternality of Christ's throne or to diminish the infinite quality of His divinity.

—So Why Father and Son?

People sometimes get hung up on this father/son thing as it relates to God. So this question: if the father/son designation (when applied to God) is not intended to convey a limit to Christ's authority, eternality, and originality, then what does it convey? What is it all about?

Let's refer to its first occurrence. Since the Father's announcement to the angelic assembly conveyed new light "setting forth the true position"

---

[97] John 1:12

[98] John 1:14.

[99] John 1:1.

[100] Hebrews 1:2-3.

[101] See Hebrews 1:4-5. Emphasis added.

of Michael's relationship to Him and to the eternal throne—and showing the Son's relation to "to all created beings" (He's their Creator); it follows this was the first time the father/son designation was asserted. God made this presentation to address something about God and His government at the start of rebellion. It was to establish and clarify the boundaries of divinity—boundaries that before rebellion had never needed asserting.

The father/son motif must portray something about the identity and character of Divinity that is vital to the freedom and security of the universe—a move to inoculate two-thirds of the angels from rebellion. This initial portrayal of a two-part demonstration of God—with an uncompromising display of *Standard-of-Divinity power* (justice), coupled with the less-imposing manifestation of *incarnation approachability* (mercy)—would eventually provide two parts of the three-part complete answer about the personality of Godhood, and the viability of His law and government.

It would also play a role in understanding the third part—explaining the fallacy of Lucifer's claim that angels are organically righteous and need no law.[102] The presentation of the Heavenly Trio--Father, Son, and Holy Ghost not only explains, but demonstrates, that created beings only *partake*[103] of the divine nature. It is not organic within them. Satan passed this deceptive claim on to Eve: "You shall not surely die... ye shall be as gods knowing good and evil."[104]

Lucifer twisted the reality of things to tarnish the character of God. Lucifer—

> "sought to falsify the word of God and... misrepresented His plan of government, claiming that God was not just in imposing laws upon the angels; that in requiring submission and obedience from His creatures, He was seeking merely the exaltation of Himself."[105]

How can finite creatures measure the motives of the Infinite? In taking the form of a servant, the *Second Person* of the Godhead placed Himself in a position where we *could* more easily see the motives of God—not a servant merely, but a Son who, being the express image of the Father, showed the Father's personality too.

Recall our earlier discussion about the throne room and the

102 Ellen G. White, *Patriarchs and Prophets*, p. 37.
103 2 Peter 1:4.
104 Genesis 3:4-5.
105 Ellen G. White, *Patriarchs and Prophets*, p. 42.

dichotomy it presents. The throne presents a perpetual manifestation that imposes a quality of physical, intellectual and spiritual authority that we cannot ignore—displaying the *Standard of Divinity* at full scale—infinite power, infinite knowledge, and inimitable righteousness—all is too much to absorb. What it displays is beyond finite comprehension.

Sister White says, "The Father is all the fullness of the Godhead bodily, and is invisible to mortal sight." The unmuted form of God is imposing and incomprehensible. But a muted form—making God more tangible to finite beings—diminishes the apparent fullness of divinity.

We need both visions of God. The Father shows the unmuted form. Christ is this muted form—not essentially diminished; not less divine—but *muted in presentation*. In terms of His human incarnation He is still fully God—but being also fully man—He shrouds His divinity with His humanity. Again we defer to Sister White, "The Son is all the fullness of the Godhead *manifested* (He is not invisible). The Word of God declares Him to be 'the express image of His person'... Here is shown the personality of the Father."

—Stepping Down

Since Christ is God eternally (forward and backward). So it must follow that when the *First Person* of the Godhead—at some point in time—said to the *Second Person*, "Thou art my Son, this day I have begotten Thee, I shall be to You a Father, and You shall be to Me a Son," He did not create Him, or birth Him, or cause Him to come forth out of Himself—for "the Lord Jesus Christ, the divine Son of God, existed from eternity, a distinct person, yet one with the Father."

So it must be He refers to the *point in time* ("this day") that inaugurated Christ's muted presentation of His own divinity. That change was about the *arrangement of condescension* where the *Second Person* of the Godhead ("being in the form of God, [and thinking it not robbery] to be equal with God,") would "[make] Himself of no reputation, [taking on a form of a servant.]"[106] "Christ, was one with the Father, yet... He was willing to *step down* from the exaltation of One who was equal with God."[107]

Michael—the archangel—was one with the Father, and yet stepped

[106] Philippians 2:7, the last part is literal from the Greek.
[107] Ellen G. White, The Faith I Live By, p. 48, emphasis added.

down from the exaltation of One who was equal with God to take on the form of an angel. He stepped down even further to take on the form of man—even the form of fallen humanity—to draw us to Himself and to bring to us the power to become adopted sons of God.

> "[Christ] was equal with God, infinite and omnipotent. He was above all finite requirements. He was Himself the law in character. Of the highest angels it could not be said that they had never borne a yoke. The angels all bear the yoke of dependence, the yoke of obedience... Not one of the angels could become a substitute and surety for the human race, for their life is God's; they could not surrender it. On Christ alone the human family depended for their existence. He is the eternal, self-existent Son, on whom no yoke had come... He could say that which not the highest angel could say—'I have power over My own life. I have power to lay it down, and I have power to take it again."[108]

The very words the Father proclaimed show a change in roles: the time of His speaking ("this day have I begotten Thee") was present-tense, and in saying, "I shall be to You a Father, and You shall be to Me a Son," He declared what was beginning "*today*"—something new.

—What About the Spirit?

So far, we've but briefly mentioned the Holy Spirit. Revelation is clear on two things: First, He is one of three equal, eternal, personal beings composing the Godhead. And second, the specifics of His nature are a mystery to us because God has not revealed them. It is not essential for us to define just what the Holy Spirit is.[109]

But there is plenty about Him that is revealed to us; and so we add what we know to our present discussion. We have seen that the great controversy is very much about the vindication of the character of God, the perfection of His law and the viability of His government. We have also seen that the Father's role in the Godhead nails down the uncompromising *Standard of Divinity*; Christ's role is to make something known about God, that the Father's imposing glory overwhelms. The Spirit's role also answers important questions about God that helps to secure the universe.

The records we have say little about the Holy Spirit in the early times. We have enough to know He is fully God, and that He is (and was) eternal; but His apparent absence in the early drama causes some people concern. We know, however, there are limits to our finite

---

[108] Ellen G. White, Manuscript Releases, vol. 12, p. 395.
[109] Ellen G. White, *The Acts of the Apostles*, pp. 51-52.

comprehension—so God does not reveal everything to us. Our knowledge grows because of our experiences over time—so God reveals things to His people gradually. There has been a gradual presentation about Himself (singular-plural) to created beings. From the first the Father was apparent; and then He introduced the Son. We do not know exactly when He made the Holy Spirit's identity known to the angels. But as we already mentioned, we know that one of Lucifer's arguments concerned the law as it related to angels. He said the law was unnecessary for the angels because "their own wisdom was a sufficient guide,"—that "all their thoughts were holy," and that it was no more possible for them than for God to err."

The universe had yet to experience their first taste of sin; they had no working knowledge of good and evil. Surely, they knew that all good things come from God—but no one had tested the "theory." Now we know the *Third Person* of the Godhead links the Creator's nature to the created. The Holy Spirit settles the third part of the three-part answer about God. He proves the bounties of divinity. Yes, the angels were holy—but only because of the Spirit's ongoing work in their lives. Because of Him they were partakers of the divine nature.[110]

Notice the following statements. They speak of fallen men (not unfallen angels) but the principles are adaptable—

> "The Comforter... is the Spirit in all the fullness of the Godhead, making manifest the power of divine grace to all who believe in Christ as a personal Savior."[111]
>
> "The Holy Spirit... [executes] the divine purpose of bringing to fallen man the power from above, that he may be an overcomer."[112]
>
> "Sin could be resisted and overcome only by the power of the third person of the Godhead, who would come with no modified energy, but in the fullness of divine power. It is the Spirit that makes effectual what has been wrought out by the world's Redeemer."[113]
>
> "Christ our Mediator, and the Holy Spirit are constantly interceding in man's behalf, but the Spirit pleads not for us as does Christ, who presents His blood, shed from the foundation of the world; the Spirit works upon the hearts, drawing out our prayers and penitence, praise, and thanksgiving."[114]
>
> "The Holy Spirit, which proceeds from the only begotten Son of God, binds the human agent, body, mind, and spirit, to the perfect, divine-

[110] See 2 Peter 1:4.

[111] Ellen G. White, *Evangelism*, p. 615.

[112] Ellen G. White, *Manuscript 57*, 1907.

[113] Ellen G. White, Seventh-day Adventist Bible Commentary, vol. 7, p. 992.

[114] Ellen G. White, *Selected Messages*, book 1, p. 344.

> human nature of Christ."[115]

We see that it is the agency of the Spirit that applies the glory of God into the hearts and minds of His creatures. He is their spiritual life. He maintains the wiring of the soul that imprints the law upon the character. When disobedience places *self* upon the throne of the heart, the Spirit moves out. This settles the issue of independence. The angels do not possess native goodness. They are not independently, spontaneously righteous within their own being. None of God's creatures can claim organic holiness. When the Holy Spirit fully withdraws from wicked people at the final battle, the universe will witness the extent of this awful truth about naked humanity.

—Relating to the Final Battle

Some Seventh-day Adventists seem fixated with issues concerning the Godhead. They believe that the Father pre-dates the Son and brought Him into being—that He passed on or conferred to Him the attributes of divinity. They also do not believe that the Holy Spirit is a distinct divine person possessing all the attributes of full-Godhood. In consulting several sources that articulate these positions, a troubling line of logic emerges to address the *Desire of Ages* quote that says, "In Christ is life, original, unborrowed, and underived. 'He that hath the Son hath life.' 1 John 5:12."[116] This same thought shows up in multiple places in Ellen White's works. They attempt to explain one found in *Signs of the Times*:

> "In Him was life, original, unborrowed, underived. This life is not inherent in man. He can possess it only through Christ. He cannot earn it; it is given him as a free gift if he will believe in Christ as his personal Savior."[117]

Then they attach a note like this:

> "Please note that we also will possess original, unborrowed, underived life... Original, unborrowed, underived life was given him by his father. And we also can possess, unborrowed, underived life through Christ."[118]

This is twisted logic. Proponents of such state that the phrase "He [man] can possess it only through Christ," means that man can have life original, unborrowed, and underived. They state that life original, unborrowed, underived can be transferred or given from one being to

---

[115] Ellen G. White, *Selected Messages*, book 1, p. 251.

[116] Ellen G. White, *The Desire of Ages*, p. 530.

[117] Ellen G. White, *The Signs of the Times*, April 8, 1897; also in *Selected Messages*, book 1, pp. 296-297.

[118] Asf Aslan, *Unborrowed, Underived Life*, (http://antiochbeliever.blogspot.com/2011/04/unborrowed-underived-life.html). Accessed 3/11/2019

another. First off, this is a fantastic abrogation of language. Secondly, it is a form of the original lie.

An Abrogation of Language. Words have meaning. Original, unborrowed, underived are words of clear meaning; and that have to apply either to life as an entity of its own, or to life as an integral attribute of Christ. One has to choose between life being an independent force that can be possessed and passed around imparting special privileges to whoever hold her in their hand, or life being an attribute unique to the person of God and ever under His control—original with Him, by Him unborrowed from anyone or anywhere else, that which He does not derive from any source outside of Himself, and which—though for a time (and in some form) He can share with others—inherently belongs to and returns to Him.

Which of these two meaning did Sister White intend?

> "'In Him was life; and the life was the light of men.' It is not physical life that is here specified, but [immortality], the life which is *exclusively the property of God*. The Word, who was with God, and who was God, had this life. Physical life is something which each individual receives. It is not eternal or immortal; for God, the life-giver takes it again... But the life of Christ was unborrowed. No one can take this life from Him. 'I lay it down of Myself,' He said. In Him was life, original, unborrowed, underived. This life is not inherent in man. He can possess it only through Christ."[119]
>
> "A human being lives, but his is a given life, a life that will be quenched. 'What is your life? It is even vapor, that appeareth for a little time, and then vanisheth away.' But Christ's life is not a vapor; it is never-ending, a life existing before the worlds were made."[120]

So we see that Ellen White make a distinction between the life of Christ (intrinsically immortal), and the physical life we receive from Christ (not intrinsically immortal). She also makes it clear that immortality is the exclusive property of God—inherent in the Word, who was with God, and who was God. As the exclusive property of the Godhead, life is not independent of God.

A form of the original lie. The original lie goes to a single concept even though it expresses itself in several ways. It is that "we are (or can become) God (or gods) and thus we shall not surely die." The lie strikes at the very heart of the *inclusivity* and *exclusivity* in the Godhead, and this issue of original, unborrowed, underived life.

---

119 Ellen G. White, *Seventh-day Adventist Bible Commentary*, vol. 5, p. 1130, emphasis added.

120 Ellen G. White, *The Signs of the Times*, June 17, 1897.

These questions illustrate the seriousness of the issue—

•Which is supreme, God or Life?
•Is God supreme because of who He is, or because He possesses and controls Life?
•Is Christ God because of who He is, or because of what He has been given—what He has come to possess?
•Is Christ a divine principle that others can possess?
•Is Godhood transferable? Is it possessable?
•Is God an inanimate force, or is He an animate Being with personality (and rules)?
•Does the collective essence of everything come together to form an all-encompassing immanent God—everything is God (pantheism)?
•Is God in everything (panentheism)?
•Is there just one God or can there be many (polytheism)?
•Is God a transcendent reality embracing all gods, creeds, cults, and religions?
•Is God a life-principle identified with nature, and unifying us all as we progress toward Godhood?

This question of the *inclusivity* and *exclusivity* of divinity, and of life—original, unborrowed, and underived, strikes at the very core of all theology. The *Pulpit Commentary* has this to say about Deuteronomy 6:4—

> "Not only to polytheism, but to pantheism, and to the conception of a localized or national deity, is this declaration of the unity of Jehovah opposed."[121]

—Only Übermensch

Earth is careening toward Armageddon. A planet in rebellion is laying plans to repel the Almighty when He returns in clouds of glory. Just as in the early days of the great controversy—when Lucifer asserted that "if the angels would stand firmly with him... they would yet gain all that they desired"—"the king of the universe would yet agree to his terms,"[122]—so it is now on earth. The so-called prince of this world asserts that if humanity will unite in one voice under his banner—then the

[121] Pulpit Commentary, *Deuteronomy 6:4*, (https://biblehub.com/deuteronomy/6-4.htm). Accessed 3/11/2019.
[122] Ellen G. White, *Patriarchs and Prophets*, p. 39.

onlooking universe will decree that earth should be allowed to serve the god of her choice.

The modern comic book writer, Grant Morrison, admits that he works under occult influences. Becoming very ill with the boils and sicknesses commonly associated with occult worship, Morrison asked Satan to let him live. He claims that Satan granted this permission if through his work he would promote a new kind of gnostic light. His comic book writing has become an "ongoing series of the Bible," but from an occult point of view.

> "Possibly his biggest contribution is in taking characters like Batman and Superman—characters already imbued with occult and biblical meaning and retelling events surrounding Armageddon, or in biblical terms—the Second Coming of Christ."[123]
>
> "The big climax to Grant's run near the end of the nineties, was *World War III*, which climaxed with every man, woman, and child on earth temporarily inheriting superpowers so that they could team up with the Justice League (a fictional superhero team featuring Superman, Batman, Wonder Woman, Flash, Aquaman, etc.) to fight off Armageddon from above."[124]

The comic Batman, with Hotel Bethlehem burning behind him, ends in a similar manor—with Batman stopping the Apocalypse. End-of-the-world scenarios are frequent storylines among comic heroes.

Little Light Studios features a documentary on these stories found in comic books and films. They ask this question: "Are these mythological stories preparing the world to fight against the second coming of Jesus Christ." They believe that is exactly what these stories are doing.

A television drama called Smallville, "is a modern retelling of the classic Superman saga. It follows young Clark Kent as he grows up in obscurity in Smallville, Kansas—until one day he becomes Superman."[125]

The series openly espouses the philosophical notions of Frederick Nietzsche. Nietzsche claimed that the real heroes are those who embrace the life that they have been given and who make it better. He called such a person: *Übermensch* (above-human, or superman); and he believed that we all can be Superman.[126]

The Smallville series tells the story of Superman modeled after a modern-day Jesus Christ. But in its version of the crucifixion (Clark is hung

123 *The Replacement Gods*, (Little Light Studios, 2007). A video documentary.

124 Ibid.

125 Ibid.

126 Wikipedia, *Übermensch*, (https://en.wikipedia.org/wiki/Übermensch). Accessed 3/11/2019.

on a cross on the outskirts of Smallville), Clark Kent doesn't die—or even stay on the cross. In the Biblical account of Jesus, the priests and rulers mocked Jesus, telling Him to come down from the cross if He was really God. Clark comes down from the cross—he's the Christ that the pharisees were looking for, a superhero, a political hero, a temporal hero, a strong-man to overthrow the political powers that oppress us.

On Krypton (Superman's home planet) they worship the sun-god Roa (like the Egyptian RA), and Superman's religion is based on the Kryptonian Bible—the Book of Roa. In it are prophesies of a sort of second coming of Roa to earth, to "bring forth from her ashes a new paradise."

In Smallville the *Apocalypses* turns out to be a planet that descends to earth much like the Bible describes the New Jerusalem's decent from heaven. But in Smallville, an evil overlord named *Darkside rules this New Jerusalem.* The series reverses the Biblical characters and makes it appear that it is Lucifer or Satan that will return at the Second Coming instead of Jesus.

The reversal is alarming. Darkside's prophets prepare the hearts of the people around the world offering them eternal life, salvation, and a place in the rapture when he returns. His followers warn the world that the Apocalypse is coming; and those who are ready receive an omega shaped seal on their foreheads instead of the mark of the beast.

When Armageddon comes—Superman flies up and stops the *Second Coming* and removes the seal of God from everyone's foreheads. Everyone cheers. Superman defeats the second coming of a God who offers the world salvation—because Nietzsche said, "We need no God, we only need *Übermensch.*"

APPEDIX B

God's Righteous Cry

Beware of those who espouse the notion that God's reaction to sin is of little consequence, and that divine love is incompatible with retributive justice.

God is love! This is plainly declared in scripture; and scripture powerfully demonstrates that love in Christ Jesus. The apostle Paul says "God commended His love toward us, in that, while we were yet sinners, Christ died for us."[1] So confident was Paul in this love that he was "persuaded, that neither death, nor life, nor angels, nor principalities, nor powers, nor things present, nor things to come, nor height, nor depth, nor any other creature, shall be able to separate us from the love of God, which is in Christ Jesus our Lord."[2]

Christ's own testimony confirmed the love of God, "For God so loved the world, that He gave His only begotten Son, that whosoever believeth in Him should not perish, but have everlasting life. For God sent not His Son into the world to condemn the world; but that the world through Him might be saved."[3]

God's justice is also expressly conveyed in scripture. "The Lord cometh out of His place to punish the inhabitants of the earth for their iniquity:

---

[1] Romans 5:6.

[2] Romans 8:39.

[3] John 3:16-17.

the earth also shall disclose her blood, and shall no more cover her slain."[4]

> "And this shall be the plague wherewith the Lord will smite all the people that have fought against Jerusalem; Their flesh shall consume away while they stand upon their feet, and their eyes shall consume away in their holes, and their tongue shall consume away in their mouth. And it shall come to pass in that day, that a great tumult from the Lord shall be among them; and they shall lay hold everyone on the hand of his neighbor and his hand shall rise up against the hand of his neighbor."[5]
>
> "In the mad strife of their own fierce passions, and by the awful outpouring of God's unmingled wrath, fall the wicked inhabitants of the earth—priests, rulers, and people, rich and poor, high and low. 'And the slain of the Lord shall be at that day from one end of the earth even unto the other end of the earth: they shall not be lamented, neither gathered, nor buried.'[6]"[7]

God's righteous character perfectly combines these two attributes. "Justice and judgment are the habitation of thy throne: mercy and truth shall go before thy face."[8]

Speaking to Moses, the Lord described Himself: "The Lord is longsuffering, and of great mercy, forgiving iniquity and transgression, and by no means clearing the guilty, visiting the iniquity of the fathers upon the children unto the third and fourth generation."[9]

—The Bible Says... God Will Punish

The Biblical notion of God's justice embraces the concept that God will punish those who persist in unrighteousness. Ever since the death of Abel,[10] the cost of rebellion has been paid for by the blood of the righteous. In Revelation's fifth seal,[11] the blood of these martyrs, cry out from the ground for judgment and justice, even as Abel's blood cried out because of Cain.[12]

The rebellious not only destroy righteous people; their selfish activity proves destructive to everything in its path. Under Revelation's *sixth trumpet* we read, "Thy wrath is come, and the time of the dead, that they should be judged, and that thou shouldest give reward unto thy servants

---

4 Isaiah 26:21.
5 Zechariah 14:12, 13.
6 Jeremiah 25:33.
7 Ellen G. White, *The Great Controversy*, p. 656.
8 Psalms 89:14.
9 Numbers 14:18.
10 Genesis. 4:1-8.
11 Revelation. 6:9-11.
12 Genesis 4:10.

the prophets, and to the saints, and them that fear thy name, small and great; and shouldest destroy them which *destroy the earth.*"[13]

It is apparent that we are standing near the end of time. It is especially important for *us* to notice how scripture is not subtle or shy about the soon coming wrath against sin and against unrepentant sinners. It is equally important for us to be serious about how the love of God compels Him (and us) to warn the world of the coming conflagration. In light of today's urgent situation, mercy's most precious and delicate gesture comes in the form of a startling warning—and in opportunities of grace to change before it is forever too late.

The Bible leaves no room for doubt. The day is soon coming when justice shall demand that mercy no longer delay God's long-deferred wrath. The third angel's message contains "the most fearful threatening ever addressed to morals."[14] It is the express mission of our church to warn the world of this fact—not to confuse its certainty.

The love of God does not exist in a vacuum. Mercy enables unimaginable terror if it is uncoupled from justice. For the Almighty to allow murder, hate, and torture to expand with impunity would be neither loving nor responsible.

We cannot see the enormity of sin; God's mind is infinite, while ours are not. Our brains are so limited in their capacities to simultaneously focus on multiple data streams that we can never begin to grasp the full weight of sin. Any single mental snapshot can capture but the smallest fragment of the full picture. We cannot accurately measure the impact of even our own indiscretions of a single day or hour. What is the individual moral impact of a lifetime of unrighteousness? What is the social cost of your life or mine?

God knows. He weighs the combined horrors of sin; and the injustice it brings is simply intolerable. Could our vision be as His—we'd rather wonder how it is that God is so long-suffering. In spite of the horrors of sin, God's attitude toward the sinner is that of mercy. But when sin turns into persistent and hardened rebellion, mercy turns to wrath.

> "The wrath of God is not declared against unrepentant sinners merely because of the sins they have committed, but because, when called to repent, they choose to continue in resistance, repeating the sins of the past in defiance of the light given them."[15]

---

[13] Revelation 11:18. Emphasis added.

[14] Ellen G. White, *The Great Controversy*, p. 449.

[15] Ellen G. White, *The Acts of the Apostles*, p. 62.

—The First War

This is demonstrated in the case of Satan.

> "Lucifer in heaven had sinned in the light of God's glory. To him as to no other created being was given a revelation of God's love. Understanding the character of God, knowing His goodness, Satan chose to follow his own selfish independent will. This choice was final. There was no more that God could do to save him."[16]
>
> "In great mercy, according to His divine character, God bore long with Lucifer... Such efforts as infinite love and wisdom only could devise, were made to convince him of his error. His disaffection was proved to be without cause, and he was made to see what would be the result of persisting in revolt. *Lucifer was convinced that he was in the wrong...* that the divine statues were just, and that he ought to acknowledge them as such before all heaven."[17]

But this he wouldn't do.

> "Pride forbade him. It was too great a sacrifice for one who had been so highly honored to confess that he had been in error, that his imaginings were false, and to yield to the authority which he had been working to prove unjust."[18]

Notice the issue in heaven was concerning the nature of God's justice—and that Lucifer eventually realized it was indeed just and merciful. It was his own *pride* that kept him tied to his unjust war against the character of his Creator.

According to Christ, the fires of God's wrath were prepared for Satan and his angels.[19] But Peter makes sure we realize our own risk. He says, "God spared not the angels that sinned... but [reserves them] unto judgment." God "spared not the old world... bringing in the flood upon the ungodly; and turning the cities of Sodom and Gomorrah into ashes." These things are made "an [example] unto those that after should live ungodly,"[20]—because those fires that are reserved for the devil and his angels are also reserved unto the "perdition of ungodly men."[21]

—The Limit of Mercy's Reach

Mercy's reach has its limits. Once the limits are passed there is no saving the sinner. When we fill up our cup of iniquity there is nothing left "but

---

[16] Ellen G. White, *The Desire of Ages*, p.761-762. Emphasis added.

[17] Ellen G. White, *Patriarchs and Prophets*, p. 39.

[18] Ibid.

[19] Matthew 25:41.

[20] 2 Peter 2:4-7.

[21] 2 Peter 3:7.

a certain fearful looking for of judgment and fiery indignation."[22] Satan and his angels passed their limit. The antediluvian world passed their limit. Sodom and Gomorrah passed their limit. Judas passed his limit—and the third angel is shouting that earth is about to pass its limit![23]

> "The love of a holy God is an amazing principle, which can stir the universe in our behalf during the hours of our probation and trial. But after the season of our probation, if we are found transgressors of God's law, the God of love will be found a minister of vengeance. God makes no compromise with sin. The disobedient will be punished. The wrath of God fell upon His beloved Son as Christ hung upon the cross of Calvary in the transgressors place. The love of God now reaches out to embrace the lowest, vilest sinner that will come to Christ with contrition. It reaches out to transform the sinner into an obedient, faithful child of God; but not a soul can be saved if he continues in sin."[24]

God's righteousness is written in His whole being. Like man, God's personhood is comprised of three natures, the physical, the mental, and the spiritual.[25] In the physical realm, His righteousness is manifest in intense glory—a glory that is like a consuming fire to the sinner.[26] In the intellectual realm, His righteousness is manifest in His word—it is "quick, and powerful, and sharper than any two-edged sword, piercing even to the dividing asunder of soul and spirit, and of the joints and marrow, and is the discerner of the thoughts and intents of the heart."[27]

The spiritual realm—at least so far as man is concerned—is a complex combination of chemical and electrical impulses that are somehow guided by a general subconscious "awareness" of our experiences. Our spirit is our emotional being—the medium through which heaven communicates with man and affects and adjust the innermost life.

God also has a spiritual nature; and in the spiritual realm, God's love and justice are manifested through His emotional expression of *His* experiences—and His experience is vast and complete. It is infinite. His emotional Being *must* include His experience with all the horrors of the injustices of sin. God's anger and furry against sin is His righteous emotional reaction to an evil whose darkness is beyond our ability to

---

[22] Hebrews 10:27.
[23] Revelation 14:9-11.
[24] Ellen G. White, *Selected Messages*, book 1, p. 313.
[25] See Ellen G. White, *Education*, p. 15.
[26] Hebrews 12:29.
[27] Hebrews 4:12.

comprehend. *His wrath is His emotional cry against the atrocities of sin*; and that cry is every bit as rational and appropriate as His emotional response to righteousness.

When the sinner passes the limits of his guilt, Christ stops pleading in his behalf. Without a mediator, grace no longer shields the sinner from the consuming fire of God's glory, and from the condemnation of His word, and from God's intense displeasure with sin. The sinner has chosen to fully associate himself with sin—and divine justice requires that the sinner finally and fully face God's expression of justice against evil.

Because the sinner has moved himself to a place where he can no longer sense God's love—he can find within himself no reason for hope. He knows he is utterly hopeless. He is left alone and hopeless to experience God's wrath without the benefits of an abiding sense of divine love and mercy. Physically, intellectually, and spiritually—the sinner is consumed by the manifest power of divine righteousness. In righteousness God has turned His wrath toward the guilty, and the sinner, having separated himself from Christ, is consumed.

> "It was the expression of justice against sin that crushed out the life of the Son of God. It was the weight of sin that in the garden of Gethsemane caused Him to sweat as it were great drops of blood, and that led Him upon the cross to cry, 'My God, My God, why hast Thou forsaken Me?' The sins of the transgressor were placed to Christ's account; but in His justice the love of God was manifested toward every human being.
>
> "In dying upon the cross, Christ did not lessen in the slightest particular the vital claims of the law of Jehovah. He endured punishment in the sinner's stead, that those who believe in Him might become the sons and daughters of God. But in His death Christ gave evidence to the heavenly universe that God will punish for the sins of a guilty world. The cross of Christ testifies that the law is not changed to meet the sinner in his sins, but that through Christ's sacrifice the sinner has opportunity to repent."[28]

Here we see again, that love and justice are inseparable.

> "The power that inflicted retributive justice upon man's substitute and surety, was the power that sustained and upheld the suffering One under the tremendous weight of wrath that would have fallen upon a sinful world. Christ was suffering the death that was pronounced upon the transgressors of God's law.
>
> "It is a fearful thing for the unrepenting sinner to fall into the hands of the living God. This is proved by the history of the destruction of the old world by a flood, by the record of the fire which fell from heaven and

[28] Ellen G. White, *Bible Echo,* May 30, 1898.

destroyed the inhabitants of Sodom. But never was this proved to so great an extent as in the agony of Christ, the Son of the infinite God, when He bore the wrath of God for a sinful world."[29]

But even in bearing the guilt of the world, Christ did not put himself in a position where He was fully cut off from hope. Through faith, He was still able to trust in God. Herein lies the difference between the faithful and the faithless.

"Amid the awful darkness, apparently forsaken of God, Christ had drained the last dregs in the cup of human woe. In those dreadful hours He had relied upon the evidence of His Father's acceptance heretofore given Him. He was acquainted with the character of His Father; He understood His justice, His mercy, and His great love. By faith He rested in Him whom it had ever been His joy to obey. And as in submission He committed Himself to God, the sense of the loss of His Fathers' favor was withdrawn. By faith, Christ was victor."[30]

—The God's Character Movement

There are some professors and leaders in the church who oppose the clear teaching of the Bible and the Spirit of Prophecy concerning God's wrath and the nature of His justice. This movement is especially strong on the west coast, and in our schools there. I will refer to this movement by a name some of them use to identify themselves. They call it the "God's Character Movement" (GCM).

Frankly, their position advances Satan's argument as amended after Calvary—that God's love manifested on the cross destroyed His justice. We have been warned that this is the very issue that will compel "the last conflict of the great controversy between Christ and Satan."[31]

Those in GCM are using their positions of learning and influence, to perfect among us the very arguments that will be turned against us in the final struggle. GCM is a movement within Adventism that denies the biblical teaching of retributive punishment; and they promote the following six errors:

1. GCM damages the integrity of language. They are experts at redefining the meaning of words found in verses or quotations they do not agree with. Since their understanding is inconsistent with the Bible and the

[29] Ellen G. White, *Manuscript 35*, 1895.
[30] Ellen G. White, *The Desire of Ages*, p.756.
[31] Ellen G. White, *The Desire of Ages*, pp. 762-763.

Spirit of Prophecy, they continually redefine words and concepts. To facilitate this opportunity, they distribute their own commentary on the Adult Sabbath School lesson, so each week they can redefine the vocabulary of the lesson.

Here is an example: What the Bible calls "God's anger" they redefine to mean a process by which sinners choose to separate themselves from the source of life.[32]

2. GCM does damage to the concept of inspiration and the impact of God's Holy Word. Here is a statement from their beliefs. Notice how it uses careful wording to suggests that words chosen by Bible writers may be suspect in some ways. They say,

> "The Bible is written by inspired yet fallible individuals. The actual words were not dictated by God, rather the writers expressed the reality of heaven in human language. The Bible primarily tells the story of God and how He has dealt with the rebellion that began in heaven and spilled over to Earth. The Bible is meant to bring us to Jesus as the full and complete revelation of God's character."[33]

Adventist already have a statement of belief on the inspiration of the Bible. Notice the differences, and how clarity is lost in the GCM revision:

> "The Holy Scriptures, Old and New Testaments, are the written Word of God, given by divine inspiration through holy men of God who spoke and wrote as thy were moved by the Holy Spirit. In this Word, God has committed to man the knowledge necessary for salvation. The Holy Scriptures are the infallible revelation of His will. They are the standard of character, the test of experience, the authoritative revealer of doctrines, and the trustworthy record of God's acts in history. (Ps. 119:105; Prov. 30:5, 6; Isa. 8:20; John 17:17; 1 Thess. 2:13; 2 Tim. 3:16, 17; Heb. 4:12; 2 Peter 1:20, 21.)."[34]

This change in understanding inspiration allows then to maneuver around the fact that the Bible and the Spirit of Prophecy *do* use certain words that if taken at face value, disprove their basic position and teachings. Here they reiterate their concern:

> "God uses imperfect people to convey His perfect truth. In the same way, the writers of the Bible as well as modern prophets today have conveyed the perfect truth of God in human language which, by its very nature, is imperfect." [35]

---

[32] *About the Final End of Sin and Sinners*, (http://godscharacter.com/about/). Accessed 3/9/2019.

[33] *About the Bible and Inspiration*, (http://godscharacter.com/about/). Accessed 3/9/2019.

[34] *The Holy Scriptures*, (https://www.adventist.org/en/beliefs/god/holy-scriptures/). Accessed 3/9/2017.

[35] *About the God of the Old Testament*, (http://godscharacter.com/about/). Accessed 3/9/2019.

In other words—even though they were inspired—sometimes they just used the wrong words. Fortunately, such errors have been corrected by GCM approved word redefinition.

3. GCM presumes to defend God against His own revelation of Himself. Let's face it, God is big enough to present Himself however He chooses to—and as we have already seen, His own Word presents Him as a loving God, who will nonetheless, judge, punish, and destroy, the wicked. GCM proponents suggest that such actions are contrary to God's character. They say,

> "God's character has been misunderstood and many have believed Him to be harsh and vengeful – a stern judge."[36]

They assert that in the Old Testament,

> "[The] dramatic interventions of God were not for the sake of retributive punishment—rather they were the only methods God was left with to reach His rebellious children."[37]

This is a rather drastic assertion. It is to say that God did not destroy the antediluvians, or Sodom and Gomorrah, to punish them for their crimes against humanity (retributive justice), but rather to teach them a lesson. The distinction is important. To separate the lesson (of destroying the world by flood) from retributive justice, changes it from punishment to *forced sacrifice*. The lesson would come too late to be of any value to antediluvians, so it would have to be for the benefit of others that they died. Since they didn't die for justice (punished for their unrighteousness) they would have died unjustly (slaughtered to scare others into compliance). In this way GCM—while trying to defend God, really turns Him into a tyrant.

We have already seen that the Bible presents the flood as an example. The antediluvians got what they deserved—and from that we learn a lesson: we too will get what we deserve unless we take advantage of God's offer while mercy pleads in our behalf.

4. GCM destroys the fundamental concepts of law and government. They say,

> "The Cross is the strongest argument against legalism – the idea that by keeping a set of rules we can be accepted by God. Christ was killed by

[36] *About the Origin of Sin*. (http://godscharacter.com/about/). Accessed 3/9/2019.

[37] *About the God of the Old Testament*, (http://godscharacter.com/about/). Accessed 3/9/2019.

> perhaps the most careful law-keepers of all time who even petitioned Pilate to break the legs of Jesus to speed His death so that they could make it home to keep the Sabbath. Eternal life is to know God (John 17:3), not to keep the list of rules. The rules were only given as a means to bring us to God, not as an end all."[38]

But what says the servant of the Lord?

> "The trials and sufferings of Christ were to impress man with a sense of his great sin in breaking the law of God, and to bring him to repentance and obedience to that law, and through obedience to acceptance with God. He would impute His righteousness to man and so raise him in moral value with God that his efforts to keep the divine law would be acceptable. Christ's work was to reconcile man to God through His human nature, and God to man through His divine nature."[39]

Notice the two-way nature of Christ's mediation; we'll refer back to that in a minute. God's government demands obedience in every particular.

> "The transgression of God's law in a single instance, in the smallest particular, is sin. And the non-execution of the penalty of that sin would be a crime in the divine administration. God is a judge, the Avenger of justice, which is the habitation and the foundation of His throne. He cannot dispense with His law; He cannot do away with its smallest item in order to meet and pardon sin. The rectitude, justice, and moral excellence of the law must be maintained and vindicated before the heavenly universe and the worlds unfallen."[40]

5. GCM makes a mockery of the sanctuary system. According to their stated beliefs,

> "The intercession of Jesus works in one direction–to bring us to God, not to shield us from God."[41]

Actually (as already noted), the sanctuary system teaches that the intercession of Christ works in two directions. Ellen White writes:

> "Man's substitute and surety must have man's nature, a connection with the human family whom He was to represent, and, as God's ambassador, He must partake of the divine nature, have a connection with the Infinite, in order to manifest God to the world, and be a mediator between God and man.
>
> "These qualifications were found alone in Christ. Clothing His divinity with humanity, He came to earth to be called the Son of man and the Son of God. He was the surety for man, the ambassador for God—the

---

[38] *About Jesus' Death*, (http://godscharacter.com/about/). Accessed 3/9/2019.

[39] Ellen G. White, *Selected Messages*, book 1, 272.

[40] Ellen G. White, *Manuscript 145*, December 30, 1897, Notes of Work.

[41] *About Jesus' Death*, (http://godscharacter.com/about/). Accessed 3/9/2019.

surety for man to satisfy by His righteousness in man's behalf the demands of the law,—and the representative of God to make manifest His character to a fallen race."[42]

"As Jesus moved out of the most holy place, I heard the tinkling of the bells upon His garment; and as He left, a cloud of darkness covered the inhabitants of the earth. There was then no mediator between guilty man and an offended God."[43]

"Oh, how many I saw in the time of trouble without a shelter! They had neglected the needful preparation; therefore they could not receive the refreshing that all must have to fit them to live in the sight of a holy God. Those who... fail to purify their souls in obeying the whole truth... will come up to the time of the falling of the plagues, and then see that they needed to be hewed and squared for the building. But there will be... no Mediator to plead their cause before the Father."[44]

"The religious services, the prayers, the praise, the penitent confession of sin ascend from true believers as incense to the heavenly sanctuary; but passing through the corrupt channels of humanity, they are so defiled that unless purified by blood, they can never be of value with God. They ascend not in spotless purity, and unless the Intercessor who is at God's right hand presents and purifies all by His righteousness, it is not acceptable to God. All incense from earthly tabernacles must be moist with the cleansing drops of the blood of Christ. He holds before the Father the censer of His own merits, in which there is no taint of earthly corruption. He gathers into this censer the prayers, the praise, and the confessions of His people, and with these He puts His own spotless righteousness. Then, perfumed with the merits of Christ's propitiation, the incense comes up before God wholly and entirely acceptable. Then gracious answers are returned.

"As the high priest sprinkled the warm blood upon the mercy-seat while the fragrant cloud of incense ascended before God, so, while we confess our sins and plead the efficacy of Christ's atoning blood, our prayers are to ascend to heaven, fragrant with the merits of our Saviour's character. Notwithstanding our unworthiness, we are to remember that there is One who can take away sin, and who is willing and anxious to save the sinner. With His own blood He paid the penalty for all wrongdoers."[45]

6. GCM discredits the concept of the blood atonement of Jesus Christ. Their concept of the atonement goes like this:

"Sin is rooted in the misunderstanding of God's character which caused men to fear and hate God."[46]

---

[42] Ellen G. White, *Selected Messages*, book 1, p. 257.

[43] Ellen G. White, *Early Writing*, p. 280.

[44] Ibid., p. 41.

[45] Ellen G. White, *The Review and Herald*, September 29, 1896.

[46] *About the Atonement*, (http://godscharacter.com/about/). Accessed 3/9/2019.

They say that the atonement is simply the process of correcting man's misunderstanding of God's character—that the relationship will be restored when we stop running from Him in fear.

But as we saw earlier, sin—in Lucifer's case (and in the cases of all who will suffer divine wrath) is not due to a misunderstanding. Remember:

> "Understanding the character of God, knowing His goodness, Satan chose to follow his own selfish will."[47]

In their explanation of the atonement, they make no mention of the demands of the law, the incompatibility of sin with God's righteousness, the effects of guilt, or the social cost of the atrocities of sin. They completely neglect the concepts of guilt, judgment, punishment, and the wrath of God against sinners. They believe that the blood of Christ represents no more than a demonstration of God's love—that He was willing to die for us (killed only because His murderers were afraid of Him). They say that,

> "the solution to the sin problem does not involve appeasement. Any form of appeasement toward God is inconsistent with His character and is ultimately rooted in a false picture of God. The essence of paganism and idolatry all throughout human history is based on the notion of appeasement of an angry god."[48]

In this statement they depend a great deal upon making an impact by controlling the language. *Appeasement* is a word that has come to have negative connotations, although sharing the same basic meaning as propitiation and reconciliation. Propitiation and reconciliation are both biblical concepts associated with the atonement.

Let's not allow them to control the language though. The actual dictionary definitions of the word *appeasement* include "to bring to a state of peace," "to satisfy,"[49] "to make someone pleased or less angry by giving or saying something desired," and to "make a problem less painful or troubling."[50]

Appeasement is really not the best word to use because it tends to conjure up implications of undue demands, greed for power, and injustice. These are attributes that *we all agree* do not apply to God—nor will they even on that day when He will "do His work, His strange work."[51] His

---

[47] Ellen G. White, *The Desire of Ages*, pp. 761-762.

[48] *About the Origin of Sin*, (http://godscharacter.com/about/). Accessed 3/9/2019.

[49] dictionary.com, *appeasement*, (https://www.dictionary.com/browse/appeasement?s=ts), Accessed 3/9/2019.

[50] Merriam-Webster, *appeasement*, (https://www.merriam-webster.com/dictionary/appeasement), Accessed 3/9/2019.

[51] Isaiah 28:21.

anger on that day is righteous anger against those "who knowing the judgment of God, that they which commit such things are worthy of death, not only do the same, but have pleasure in them that do them."[52]

The Bible teaches that Christ's blood *does* make *reconciliation* for us to God. We read,

> "And the priests killed them [the animal sacrifices—types of Christ], and they made reconciliation with their blood upon the altar, to make an atonement for all Israel."[53]

Ellen White says,

> "That blood alone is efficacious. It alone can make *propitiation* for our sins. It is the blood of the only-begotten Son of God that is of value for us that we may draw nigh unto God, His blood alone taketh "away the sin of the world."[54]
>
> "Christ has made a sacrifice to satisfy the demands of Justice... [the] holy law could not be maintained with any smaller price."[55]

The law and justice are necessary to protect the universe from the ongoing atrocities of sin. God must maintain their exalted authority.

> "God is [the] judge, the Avenger of justice... [who must maintain and vindicate] the rectitude, justice, and moral excellence of the law."[56]

He does this by showing His "expression of justice against sin."[57] It is "the wrath of God against sin—the terrible manifestation of His displeasure because of iniquity."[58] Since Christ was equal in value to the moral law, He could take our iniquity and be counted as a transgressor—bearing for us the expression of His Father's wrath. Christ "tasted the sufferings of death for every man."[59]

> "Christ has made a sacrifice to satisfy the demands of Justice... [the] holy law could not be maintained with any smaller price. [Instead] of the law being abolished to meet sinful man in his fallen condition, it has been maintained in all its sacred dignity."[60]
>
> "Christ alone could... [make] an offering equal to the demands of the divine law."[61]

---

52 Romans 1:32.

53 2 Chronicles 29:24.

54 Ellen G. White, Seventh-day Adventist Bible Commentary, vol. 7, p. 97.

55 Ellen G. White, *Manuscript Releases*, vol. 21, 194.

56 Ellen G. White, *Manuscript 147*, December 30, 1897.

57 Ellen G. White, *Bible Echo*, May 30, 1898.

58 Ellen G. White, *The Desire of Ages*, p. 753.

59 Ibid., p. 694.

60 Ellen G. White, *Manuscript Releases*, vol. 21, 194.

61 Ellen G. White, *The Spirit of Prophecy*, vol. 2, pp. 11-12.

"The church is justified through Him, its representative and head... [The] Father ratifies the contract with His Son, that He will be *reconciled* to repentant and obedient men, and take them into divine favor through the merits of Christ. Christ guarantees that He will make man 'more precious than fine gold, even a man, than the golden wedge of Ophir.'"[62]

—What Wilt Thou?

Marvelous is the provision that infinite love has made for our salvation. Such love would not risk our eternal safety by hiding the startling reality of the horrors of sin and the crisis soon to fall upon the wicked.

> "God does not send messengers to flatter the sinner. He delivers no message of peace to lull the unsanctified into fatal security. He lays heavy burdens upon the conscience of the wrongdoer, and pierces the soul with arrows of conviction. The ministering angels present to him the fearful judgments of God to deepen the sense of need, and prompt the cry, "What must I do to be saved?" Then the hand that has humbled in the dust, lifts up the penitent. The voice that has rebuked sin, and put to shame pride and ambition, inquires with tenderest sympathy, "What wilt thou that I shall do unto thee?"[63]
>
> "The crisis is fast approaching. The rapidly swelling figures show that the time for God's visitation has about come. Although loath to punish, nevertheless, He will punish, and that speedily. Those who walk in the light will see signs of the approaching peril; but they are not to sit in quiet, unconcerned expectancy of the ruin, comforting themselves with the belief that God will shelter His people in the day of visitation. Far from it. They should realize that it is their duty to labor diligently to save others, looking with strong faith to God for help."[64]

—God's Amazing Love...

> "The love of a holy God is an amazing principle, which can stir the universe in our behalf during the hours of our probation and trial. But after the season of our probation, if we are found transgressors of God's law, the God of love will be found a minister of vengeance. God makes no compromise with sin. The disobedient will be punished.
>
> "The wrath of God fell upon His beloved Son as Christ hung upon the cross of Calvary in the transgressors place. The love of God now reaches out to embrace the lowest, vilest sinner that will come to Christ with contrition. It reaches out to transform the sinner into an obedient, faithful child of God; but not a soul can be saved if he continues in sin."[65]

---

[62] Ellen G. White, *The Spirit of Prophecy*, vol. 3, p. 203.

[63] Ellen G. White, *The Desire of Ages*, p. 104.

[64] Ellen G. White, *Testimonies for the Church*, vol. 5, p. 209.

[65] Ellen G. White, *Selected Messages*, book 1, p. 313.

APPEDIX C

Historagorical Financial Methods

Here are some of the ways that God provides for His work and for His workers:

1. Tentmaking. While in Corinth and Ephesus, Paul labored faithfully to proclaim the gospel. He also worked at tentmaking so that he could preach the gospel to them *freely*.[1] This is one reason why our schools are supposed to provide "practical instruction in agriculture and various trades in connection with instruction in book learning."[2] It is interesting to notice how WEC also followed this plan even though they had no connection to *Adventism*.
2. Third-Party Gifts. "Paul was not wholly dependent upon the labor of his hands for support while at Thessalonica. Referring later to his experiences in that city, he wrote to the Philippian believers in acknowledgment of the gifts he had received from them while there, saying, 'Even in Thessalonica ye sent once and again unto my necessity.'[3]"[4]

   "Silas and Timothy joined Paul in Corinth. These brethren brought with them funds from the churches in Macedonia, for the

[1] 2 Corinthians 11:7. See Ellen G. White, *The Acts of the Apostles*, p. 349.
[2] Ellen G. White, *Manuscript* 54, 1903.
[3] Ellen G. White, *The Acts of the Apostles*, p. 348.
[4] Philippians 4:16.

support of the work."[5] After there was a strong church in Corinth, Paul wrote to them and reviewed his manner of life among them. Telling them that he preached the gospel of God to them freely, he adds, "I robbed other churches, taking wages of them, to do you service. And when I was present with you... that which was lacking to me the brethren which came from Macedonia supplied."[6]

Third-party gifts can happen in the form of sponsorships, donations, and offering. Tithes are also third-party gifts that are administered through the organized church. When Paul went to Jerusalem, he had a large sum of money from the Gentile churches to give to those who had charge of the work in Judea.

3. Local Support. The hospitality of local people can sometimes be appropriate. A woman and her husband in Shunem made a room for Elisha to stay whenever he happened to be in the area. They were Israelites and made this arrangement because they perceived that he was "an holy man of God."[7] Elijah was fed by the widow in Zarephath for "many days."[8] She was not an Israelite.

   When Jesus sent out the disciples, He told them not to take food and extra clothing. He told them to stay in somebody's home where they were working.

   Paul established the appropriateness of those proclaiming the gospel to receive their living from the gospel. "So also, the Lord has prescribed to those proclaiming the gospel to live from the gospel."[9] "The one who is taught the word is to share all good things with the one who teaches him."[10] "If we sowed spiritual things in you, is it too much if we reap material things from you?"[11]

   This has to be done carefully as not to commercialize the gospel. Paul was also sensitive to this. "When Paul first visited Corinth, he found himself among a people who were suspicious of the motives of strangers... The Greeks on the seacoast were keen traders... trained in sharp business practices.... They... believed that to make money, whether by fair means or foul, was commendable. Paul was acquainted with their characteristics, and he would give them

---

[5] Ellen G. White, *The Acts of the Apostles*, p. 349.

[6] 2 Corinthians 11:7-10.

[7] 2 Kings 4:9.

[8] 1 Kings 17:15.

[9] 1 Corinthians 9:14. Berean Study Bible.

[10] Galatians 6:6.

[11] 1 Corinthians 9:11. New American Standard Bible.

no occasion for saying that he preached the gospel to enrich himself. He might justly have claimed support from his Corinthian hearers; but this right he was willing to forgo."[12]

4. Volunteerism. Some people are financially stable, not needing additional income while they are doing missionary work. Some retired people fit into this category. Some people do full-time missionary work only now and then when they are able—saving up enough money during the between times.
5. Financierism. God blesses some people with enough resources to finance the mission work of others. These people are missionaries too—so long as they are heeding the Lord's specific will for their life. Let's consider some of the women who followed Jesus in this regard.

"And it came to pass soon afterward that He was traveling throughout the city and village, preaching and proclaiming the good news of the kingdom of God. And the twelve were with him, and certain women who had been cured from evil spirits and infirmities: Mary who is called Magdelene, from whom seven demons had gone out, and Joanna wife of Chuza, a steward of Herod, and Susanna, and many others, who were ministering to them out of their means."[13]

6. Universal Missionarialism. As we have all heard it said, a penny saved is a penny earned. God's servants should be committed to sacrificial giving and sacrificial living. This is universally applicable; and if it were universally practiced then there would be means enough to support far more work. When one area of the work is blessed with more than it needs, the extra should be moved to a more needful area.[14]
7. Divine Providence. Abraham, the Israelites at the Red Sea, Brother Andrew's four-week training trip—sometimes we are called to just step into the water having faith in the providences of God. While God uses all these methods (and more) to provide for His servants—often these are at His disposal, not ours. When He sends, we're to go. Sometimes that means trusting God to worry about the details.

---

[12] Ellen G. White, *The Acts of the Apostles*, p. 349.

[13] Luke 8:1-3. Berean Study Bible

[14] Ellen G. White, *Counsels on Health*, pp. 220, 224, 225, 308-310; Medical Ministry p. 164-1655,

"Christians are safe only in acquiring money as God Directs, and using it in channels which He can bless. God permits us to use His goods with an eye single to His glory, to bless ourselves, that we may bless others. Those who have adopted the world's maxim, and discarded God's specifications, who grasp all they can obtain of wages or goods, are poor, poor indeed, because the frown of God is upon them. They walk in the paths of their own choosing, and do dishonor to God, to truth, to His goodness, to His mercy, His character. "

— Counsels on Stewardship, p. 141.

"Yet some refused to be converted. They were not willing to walk in God's way, and when , in order that the work of God might be advanced, calls were made for freewill offerings, some clung selfishly to their earthly possessions. These covetous ones became separated from the company of believers. "

— 9 Testimonies, p. 126.

BIBLIOGRAPHY

Brother Andrew with John and Elizabeth Sherrill, *God's Smuggler*, Guideposts Associates, INC. Carmel, New York, 1967.

Burrill, Russell C., Dr., *Recovering an Adventist Approach to The Life & Mission of the Local Church*, Fallbrook, California, Hart Books, 1998.

Campbell, T. Colin, PhD and Campbell, Thomas M, MD, *The China Study, Startling Implications for Diet, Weight Loss and Long-term Health,* Dallas, Texas, BenBella Books, Inc., 2006.

Ferrell, Vance, *The Broken Blueprint*, Altamont, Tennessee, Harvestime Books, 2003.

Ferrell, Vance, *The Medical Missionary Manual*, Altamont, Tennessee, Harvestime Books, 2002.

Ferrell, Vance, *Prophet of the End*, Altamont, Tennessee, Harvestime Books, Altamont, Tennessee, 1984.

Fiedler, Dave, *D'Sozo, Reversing the Worst Evil*, Remnant Publications, 2012.

Hardinge, Mervyn G., MD, Dr.PH, PhD, *A Physician Explains Ellen White's Counsel on Drugs, Herbs, & Natural Remedies*, Review and Herald Publishing Association, 2001.

Moore, A. Leroy, Ph.D., *Adventism in Conflict*, Review and Herald Publishing Association, 1995

Nichol, Frances, *The Midnight Cry, A Defense of William Miller and the Millerites*, Takoma Park, Washington, D.C., The Review and Herald Publishing Association, 1944.

Pinto, Christian J., *Megiddo II, The New Age*, (2005), Los Angeles, California, Adullam Films. 2005.

Pinto, Christian J., *Secret Mysteries of America's Beginning, The New Atlantis,* Los Angeles, California, Adullam Films. 2006.

Santee, Willard, *Circle of Apostacy*, an audiotape series, 1981.

Sutherland, Edward A., MD, *Studies in Christian Education*, Leaves of Autumn Books, 1978.

Schwarz, R. W., *Light Bearers to the Remnant*, Mountain View, California, Pacific Press Publishing Association, 1979. Denominational History Text for Seventh-day Adventist College Classes prepared by the Department of Education, General Conference of Seventh-day Adventists.

Taylor, Dr. Arlene R., PhD, and Brewer, W. Eugene, EdD, Your Brain Has a Bent (Not a Dent!), Napa, California, Success Resources International, 2009.

White, Ellen G., multiple books, manuscripts, letters and articles are referenced throughout in the footnotes; and are too numerous to list here. These are from books published by The Review and Herald Publishing Association or The Pacific Press Publishing Association, and/or available at the Ellen G. White Estate website: http://ellenwhite.org/.

Your Story Hour, *Pathway of the Pioneers*, 117 dramatized audio stories that relive the beginnings of the Seventh-day Adventist church. Review and Herald Publishing, 2007. Also available at https://whiteestate.org/resources/pioneers-stories/.